DIVIDED DEMOCRACY

DIVIDED DEMOCRACY

Cooperation and Conflict
Between the
President and Congress

Edited by

James A. Thurber
American University

A Division of Congressional Quarterly Inc.
Washington, D.C.

Copyright © 1991 Congressional Quarterly Inc.
1414 22nd Street, N.W., Washington, D.C. 20037

FEB 2 4 1993

Printed in the United States of America
Second Printing

Cover design: Paula Anderson
Cover photo: Susan Biddle/The White House

Library of Congress Cataloging-in-Publication Data

Divided democracy: cooperation and conflict between the President and Congress/
   edited by James A. Thurber
      p.   cm.
   Includes bibliographical references and index.
   ISBN 0-87187-582-9
   1. Presidents—United States—Powers and duties. 2. Executive power—United
States. 3. United States. Congress—Powers and duties. 4. Legislative power—
United States. 5. United States—Politics and government. 6. Separation of powers—
United States—Politics and government. 6. Separation of powers—United States. 7.
Democracy. I. Thurber, James A., 1943- .
JK585.D53   1990
320.4′ 04′ 0973--dc20   90-42485
                                                               CIP

To Claudia

CONTENTS

TABLES

PREFACE

Divided Democracy: Cooperation and Conflict Between the President and Congress examines the dynamic relationship between the executive and legislative branches of government. Conflict between Congress and the president is natural, indeed essential, under the constitutional system of separation of powers, an arrangement of shared authority. Tension is also inherent in partisan politics. For the political system to function, however, the president and Congress must cooperate. This is what the American people expect. As Sen. David Boren, D-Okla., explained, voters "are tired of the bickering ... they want us to work together." [1]

Divided Democracy presents a balance of views between presidential and congressional scholars. As the only current reader that evaluates the relations between Congress and the presidency, it is useful to students of Congress, the presidency, and American government. The thirteen essays in the volume address the most important questions about cooperation and conflict between presidents and Congress. What are the root causes? Has the current relationship between the president and Congress adversely affected the political system's ability to produce timely and effective public policy? Is the system too representative, fragmented, and inefficient and consequently beyond popular control? Does divided democracy produce only stalemate and poor public policy?

In the past two decades, an era of fiscal austerity, the two institutions found it difficult to cooperate in making the critical choices they faced, no matter what party controlled the White House, the Senate, or the House of Representatives. Some of this dissension can be attributed to the decline of political parties, the increased role of the media, the shortening of presidential coattails, reforms in congressional organization, and ticket splitting in the voting booth. All of these factors ultimately have made it harder for presidents and Congress to translate their electoral support into governing support.

Much of the literature on presidential-congressional relations has a reformist perspective, calling for more or less executive or legislative power. Contemporary Madisonians would like to see a more democratic and powerful Congress that would limit the power of the president, while latter-day Hamiltonians argue that Congress should grant broader discretion to presidents, giving them room to implement policy more efficiently. Presidential scholars often call for less congressional micromanagement, while congressional scholars call for more legislative oversight and control of the executive. These arguments often center on efficiency versus representativeness, leadership versus democracy. This book has no one viewpoint, no one dominant ideology for or against Congress or the presidency. Some of the contributors believe the system is working well, a stable yet responsive pluralist democracy; others believe reform is badly needed. Some argue that institutional gridlock has developed between Congress and the president and that it deepened during the Reagan years. Congress, they assert, has gradually accrued power at the expense of the presidency and has been able to hamstring foreign, defense, and domestic policy through its budget authority. Others believe the value of responsiveness to public demands and democratic representation should override concerns about efficiency, direction, and effectiveness. This debate is at the heart of *Divided Democracy.*

In the first chapter I describe the major sources of conflict and cooperation between the president and Congress. Michael L. Mezey in Chapter 2, "Congress Within the United States Presidential System," explores the connection between political stability and governmental institutions. Mezey's findings have clear contemporary implications for East European nations as they struggle to build new democracies and debate what form of governing system they will adopt. James P. Pfiffner in Chapter 3 examines differing perspectives on the consequences of divided government. He analyzes several approaches to solving what many see as a problem with split-party control of the presidency and Congress. Roger H. Davidson in Chapter 4 describes three eras of the modern Congress: the era of strong committee chairmen (1937-1964), the reform era (1965-1978), and the postreform era (1979-present). His analysis casts doubt on the assumption that unified party control improves legislative productivity and that divided government leads to stalemate. In the fifth chapter Walter J. Oleszek takes a close look at how Congress makes policy in the 1990s, assessing specific effects of contemporary issues, changes in the party system, and divided government on Congress's dealings with the president.

Michael Mezey concludes in Chapter 6 that the current relationship between the president and Congress has hurt the political system's ability to produce good public policy. An earlier version of this award-winning essay appeared in *Congress and the Presidency,* the journal of the Center for Congressional and Presidential Studies. In the next chapter Christopher H. Foreman, Jr., gives an inside view of congressional oversight of the president and executive branch. In Chapter 8, I evaluate the effect of the 1974 budget act and the Gramm-Rudman-Hollings legislation of 1985 and 1987 on presidential-congressional governance.

The next three chapters survey the relationship between the president and Congress with regard to foreign and defense policy. Essays by Louis Fisher and Christopher J. Deering put the current debate over presidential-congressional war powers in constitutional and historical perspective. Writing about Congress and Nicaragua, Philip Brenner and William M. LeoGrande present a thought-provoking case study of presidential-congressional cooperation and conflict.

In Chapter 12, "Congress and the Removal Power," Louis Fisher describes the source of one of Congress's most important powers, the authority to remove a government official. This is another award-winning essay that first appeared in *Congress and the Presidency*. The book concludes with Lawrence C. Dodd's provocative essay, "Congress, the Presidency, and the American Experience." Dodd applies his theory of political transformation to Congress and the president while challenging the assumptions of our major rational and substantive theories of politics. He focuses on the causes of political change in the United States and places congressional-presidential interaction within that context of change.

These contributors have written original and insightful essays, heeded my suggestions, and met the deadlines. My first thanks go to them. Earlier versions of some of the essays were presented on November 8, 1989, at the tenth anniversary conference of the Center for Congressional and Presidential Studies (CCPS) at American University. Samantha Durst at CCPS gave valuable research assistance that greatly helped to improve this book. I would also like to thank Washington State University for selecting me as Centennial Professor and on February 14, 1990, sponsoring my centennial lecture, "Presidential and Congressional Governance: Cooperation, Conflict, and Change," which became the basis of Chapter 1. Special thanks also to the students at American University in my graduate seminar on the legislative process, spring 1990, who read and commented on the chapters in the book.

Thank you to the following colleagues who carefully reviewed the essays and commented on them: Jeff Fishel, Susan Hammond, Thomas Mann, David R. Mayhew, Norman J. Ornstein, Catherine Rudder, Steven S. Smith, Patricia Sykes, and Aaron Wildavsky. I am also grateful to the CCPS board of academic advisers—especially Roger

Davidson, John Kornacki, and Nelson Polsby—for many helpful suggestions. I also wish to thank American University and the School of Public Affairs, especially Dean Neil Kerwin, for their continued support of my scholarship and the activities of CCPS.

The CQ Press editorial staff provided me with exceptional assistance. My thanks to David R. Tarr, director of CQ's book department, and Nancy Lammers, managing editor, for their support and encouragement throughout this project. My principal editor, Ann Davies, is a thoughtful polisher of prose and investigator of facts. She has contributed immeasurably to the quality, accuracy, and readability of this book. I would also like to thank Barbara de Boinville for her special assistance in editing several chapters. Also thanks to the CQ book sales and marketing staff for assistance in the marketing plan for the book.

My greatest thanks go to my wife Claudia, son Mark, and daughter Kathryn for their support of my scholarship and their continuing love. I dedicate this book to them.

James A. Thurber

Note

1. John Felton, "Will Bush-Hill Honeymoon Bring Bipartisanship?" *Congressional Quarterly Weekly Report*, February 18, 1989, 333.

1. INTRODUCTION:
THE ROOTS OF DIVIDED DEMOCRACY

James A. Thurber

Immediately after his inauguration President George Bush, in a gesture of good will, praised Congress: "To the Members of the Congress, to the institution of the House of Representatives and the Senate of the United States, may they flourish and may they prosper." In response to President Bush's efforts to build better relations with Congress, Thomas S. Foley, D-Wash., then House majority leader, said, "That's another example of President Bush reaching out. We're going to respond very positively to that." [1]

Good will, however, does not generally characterize the institutional relationship between Congress and the president. In his first year in office, President Bush fared worse than any other president elected in the postwar era, winning only 63 percent of the roll-call votes on which he took an unambiguous position in 1989. [2] Despite Bush's popularity with the American people (the highest in the polls of any postwar president at the end of his first year) and his sincere efforts to build bridges between the White House and Capitol Hill, executive-legislative relations during his presidency remained deeply rooted in political and institutional divisions.

Through separation of powers and checks and balances, the Constitution structured executive-legislative rivalry into the American system of government. The competing interests of the two political parties have further entrenched this interbranch rivalry over the past thirty years. Since 1980 Democrats have been frustrated by their inability to retake the White House, but in Congress they have learned to push their own agendas and are almost guaranteed reelection. "They have learned how to take advantage of a Republican presidency, in order to ensure their own positions in government, by running against the presidency," according to Republican representative Tom Tauke, R-Iowa. Likening congressional-presidential relations to a "power game," Tauke explained the lack of interest in making George Bush a success: "If Bush is enormously successful, the power of Congress is diminished somewhat. If you work from the assumption that there has been some shift of power to Capitol Hill, Members and especially their staffs are not going to be inclined to let all that power back down Pennsylvania Avenue just because we have a new president." [3]

The Roots of Divided Democracy

In this introduction I will examine six root causes of divided democracy: constitutional ambiguities, different constituencies, varying terms of office, weak political parties, divided government, and fluctuating congressional power.

Constitutional Ambiguities

The Constitution invests Congress with "all legislative Powers," but it also authorizes the president to recommend and to veto legislation. If the president vetoes a bill, "it shall be repassed by two thirds of the Senate and the House of Representatives" (Article I, section 7). Because it is so difficult for Congress to gain a two-thirds vote, presidential vetoes usually are sustained. According to Michael L. Mezey, "What the Founders probably did not anticipate was the dramatic increase in the number of presidential vetoes and the infrequency of congressional overrides." [4] Through 1988 presidents had used the veto 2,469 times; 1,050 of these were "pocket vetoes" not subject to congressional override. [5] Congress overrode presidential vetoes slightly more than 7 percent of the time (103 times) when it had the opportunity to vote on them. [6] Thus, the threat of a veto in the legislative process gives the president an important bargaining tool.

Congress is given a variety of specific powers in Article I, section 8, of the Constitution. [7] The list of powers is broad, but the greatest power of Congress is its authority to pass laws directly binding upon all citizens. Also of great importance is the power of the purse. Congress must authorize and appropriate funds for the president and the executive branch agencies. Presidents may propose budgets for the federal government, but Congress has the final say on spending. Congress also has the power to levy and collect taxes, to borrow and coin money, and to regulate foreign and interstate commerce. The powers to declare war, to provide for a militia, and to adopt laws concerning bankruptcy, naturalization, patents, and copyrights is also bestowed on Congress. Congress has the authority to establish executive branch agencies and departments and to oversee their operations. The Senate must approve cabinet nominees, ambassadors, and Supreme Court and federal judicial appointees before they can take office. A president cannot enter into a binding treaty with a foreign government without a two-thirds vote of the Senate, nor can the president "declare war," a power the Constitution purposely gives to Congress.

A dramatic but rarely employed check on the president is impeachment. Executive branch officials can be impeached (formally accused) by a majority vote in the House and tried in the Senate. If two-thirds of the senators vote to convict, the official is removed from office. Only President Andrew Johnson has been tried on impeachment charges; the vote fell one short of the number required to convict him. The House Judiciary Committee recommended that Richard M. Nixon be impeached for transgressions in connection with the Watergate burglary of the offices of the Democratic National Committee and the ensuing cover-up. Nixon, however, resigned the presidency before a full session of the House could vote on the impeachment issue.

The Framers of the Constitution deliberately fragmented power between the national government and the states and among the executive, legislative, and judicial branches. They also divided legislative powers by creating two coequal houses, a bicameral Congress. Although divided, Congress was designed to be independent and powerful, able to check the power of the executive and directly linked with the people through popular, periodic elections. The Framers wanted an effective and powerful federal government, but they wanted to limit its power in order to protect personal and property rights. Having experienced the abuses of English monarchs and their colonial governors, the men who wrote the Constitution were wary of excessive authority in an executive. They also feared "elective despotism," or excessive legislative power, something the Articles of Confederation had given their own state legislatures.

Therefore, the Framers created three branches of government with none having a monopoly. This separation of powers restricted the power of any one branch, and it required cooperation among the three in order for them to govern effectively. Today, as then, political action requires cooperation between the president and Congress. Yet the Constitution, in the way it divided power between the two branches, created an open invitation for conflict.[8]

Different Constituencies

The U.S. system of government, unlike parliamentary systems throughout the world, elects the executive and members of the legislature independently. The president is elected from vastly broader electoral coalitions than are representatives and senators, who have narrow constituencies in districts or states. Members of Congress, even those who belong to the president's party or hail from his home state, represent specific interests that can conflict with the interests of the president, who represents the nation as a whole. James Madison well understood this dichotomy of interests as an important source of conflict between the president and Congress: "The members of the federal legislature will be likely to attach themselves too much to local objects.... Measures will too often be decided according to their probable effect, not on the national prosperity and happiness, but on the prejudices, interests, and pursuits of the governments and the people of the individual States." [9]

Terms of Office

The interaction of Congress and the president is shaped not only by their different constituencies but also by their different terms of office. House members are elected every two years; senators, every six. Presidents have only four years, possibly eight, in which to establish their programs. They are expected to set the national policy agenda and usually in the first year move rapidly before the traditional decline in their popularity.[10] Congress moves more slowly; it is inefficient primarily because it represents a vast array of local interests. Congress passes new laws slowly and reviews old ones carefully. The decision-making pace of Congress and of the president is not the same because of their different terms of office. The result is often conflict and deadlock.

Political Parties

The federal system of state-based political parties contributes to the independence of members of Congress from the president. The president must work with weak, decentralized political parties that exercise little discipline and even less leverage over members. Senators and representatives usually run their own races with their own financing. The way they respond to local conditions has little to do with national party platforms or presidential politics. Members freely pursue their own interests without fear of discipline from the president.

Independence from political parties and the president allows legislators to seek benefits for their own constituents and to serve specialized interests. Thomas Mann argues further that

> [t]he changes that swept through the political system during the 1960s and 1970s—the increase in split-ticket voting, the growing cost of campaigns and reliance on contributions from special interests, the rise of television, the expansion and growing political sophistication of interest groups in Washington, and the democratization and decentralization of Congress—may well have weakened the classic iron triangles, but they also heightened the sensitivity of politicians to all forms of outside pressure.[11]

Divided Government

Another electorally based impediment to legislative-executive co-operation is divided government. There are two varieties: divided party control of Congress and split control of Congress and the White House. Opposing parties have controlled the presidency and one or both houses of Congress in twenty-six of the past thirty-eight years, with the Republicans mainly controlling the White House and the Democrats controlling Congress. From 1887 to 1954, divided government occurred only eight years (14 percent of the time), but from President Dwight D. Eisenhower's first term (1953) to President Bush's second year in office (1990), it occurred twenty-four years (63 percent of the time). It has occurred more than 80 percent of the time since 1969. (See Chapter 3.)

The trend toward ticket splitting between presidential and con-gressional candidates further exacerbates already strained relations. Election returns for Congress have increasingly diverged from national presidential returns; "the range in the variance, which measures the extent to which changes in local returns differ from the change in national returns, has more than doubled." [12] During the past thirty years, as the power of political parties has declined significantly, there has been a corresponding rise in individualistic candidacies for the presidency, the Senate, and the House. Fewer and fewer members of Congress ride into office on the electoral "coattails" of the president. This has led to the election of presidents who find it difficult to translate electoral support into governing support. The scarcity of presidential coattails by Bush in 1988 prompted Nelson Polsby to conclude that "the emperor has no coat." [13] Bush was the first candidate since John F. Kennedy to win the White House while his party lost seats in the House.

Power in Flux

The balance of power between and within the institutions of Congress and the presidency is in constant flux. This is another root cause of divided democracy. What the public expects from each institution varies over time. [14] For two hundred years Congress has continued to represent local interests and to respond (some think too much) to political preferences and public pressures. [15] Nevertheless, the institution has changed dramatically. The reforms of the past two decades have made Congress even more representative and accountable. They have changed the way it makes laws and passes budgets and have better equipped it to oversee the executive branch.

Pressure to check the power of the president through the War Powers Resolution of 1973 and the Budget and Impoundment Control

Act of 1974 brought changes that helped Congress reclaim some of the power it had lost to the president during the previous decades. The institutional reforms of the 1970s, however, resulted in decentralization, which made Congress more democratic but also less efficient. With the new openness came greater accountability and responsiveness but at the price of efficiency and effectiveness as a lawmaking body. Modern presidents find Congress harder to influence than did their predecessors in the White House. Members of Congress are more independent. And with the weakening of strict seniority rules wielded by strong parties, coordinating the legislative process has become more difficult for congressional party leaders.

Although Congress created new ways of checking presidential power in the 1970s, ultimately legislative-executive relationships are not zero-sum games.[16] If one branch gains power, the other does not necessarily lose it. The expansion of the federal government since World War II has given vast new power to both branches. Events and public policy issues contribute to the policy-making power of both the president and Congress. The war on drugs, environmental concerns, the savings and loan crisis, and continuing budget deficits have led to new powers for both branches. Even these crises, however, are not enough to keep the two institutions from bickering.

Conclusion

Organization theorists suggest that conflict produces incentives for organizations to centralize decision-making power.[17] When an organization is threatened, a premium is placed on efficiency, effectiveness, and cohesiveness in setting strategy. Indeed, faced with a Republican Senate and a Republican president in 1981 to 1987, House Democrats became more cohesive. Throughout the decade the transformation of many issues into budget issues encouraged centralization within Congress and the executive branch.

But conflict is inevitable in an electoral system that produces divided government. Cooperation may be more likely when both the president and Congress are of the same party. Even so, because of the wide range of views within a party, unified government is no safeguard against conflict. Partisanship may also serve to move legislation. The 1986 tax reform law benefited from the battle between the Democrats and Republicans because both sides saw political advantage in moving the bill or disadvantage in being seen as obstructionist. The give-and-take between representativeness and efficiency, openness and accountability, specific interests and the "public good" ensures a certain amount of confrontation between Congress and the president. As we have seen, their relations are shaped by an amalgam of factors:

ambiguities in the Constitution, different constituencies, different terms of office, weak political parties, divided government, and fluctuating congressional power. Although conflict between Congress and the president is inherent in our system of government, presidents must find support in Congress and members must seek assistance from the White House. To succeed in office every president must surmount the constitutional and political obstacles to pass their legislative program and establish a working relationship with Congress.

Separation of powers and the division of political control between Republican presidents and Democratic Congresses do not present an insurmountable barrier to good public policy making. Presidents need to lead both public opinion and a consensus among the policy communities in Congress to solve the problems that are so readily visible. Overcoming divided government, changing public opinion, building consensus, and establishing the nation's policy priorities calls for leadership, accommodation, and compromise by Congress and the president. It does not call for further red-hot rhetoric about how serious our problems are and how the two institutions are deadlocked and cannot function. The authors of each chapter in this book address this conclusion in a variety of ways and advance suggestions about how conflict and cooperation between the president and Congress help and hinder our divided democracy.

Notes

1. Quoted in James A. Barnes, "Political Focus," *National Journal,* February 11, 1989, 377.
2. Janet Hook, "Bush Inspired Frail Support for First-Year President," *Congressional Quarterly Weekly Report,* December 30, 1989, 3540.
3. Quoted in Barnes, "Political Focus," 377.
4. Michael L. Mezey, *Congress, the President, and Public Policy* (Boulder, Colo.: Westview Press, 1989), 61.
5. A pocket veto is the act of the president in withholding his approval of a bill after Congress has adjourned. See Harold W. Stanley and Richard G. Niemi, *Vital Statistics on American Politics,* 2d ed. (Washington, D.C.: CQ Press, 1990), 252.
6. For vetoes and overrides from the 80th to the 100th Congresses (1947-1989), see Norman J. Ornstein, Thomas E. Mann, and Michael J. Malbin, *Vital Statistics on Congress, 1989-1990* (Washington, D.C.: Congressional Quarterly, 1990), 162.
7. See James A. Thurber, "Congress and the Constitution: Two Hundred Years of Stability and Change," in *Reflections on the Constitution,* ed. Richard Maidment (Manchester, England: University of Manchester

Press, 1989), 51-75.

8. See George C. Edwards III, *Presidential Influence in Congress* (San Francisco: Freeman, 1980); and Cecil V. Crabb, Jr., and Pat M. Holt, *Invitation to Struggle: Congress, the President, and Foreign Policy,* 3d ed. (Washington, D.C.: CQ Press, 1989).

9. James Madison, *Federalist* no. 46, in *The Federalist Papers,* ed. Clinton Rossiter (New York: New American Library, 1961), 296.

10. See Stephen Wayne, *The Legislative Presidency* (New York: Harper & Row, 1978).

11. Thomas E. Mann, "Breaking the Political Impasse," in *Setting National Priorities: Policy for the Nineties,* ed. Henry J. Aaron (Washington, D.C.: Brookings Institution, 1990). 302.

12. Ornstein, Mann, and Malbin, *Vital Statistics,* 45.

13. *Congress and the Nation, vol. VII, 1985-1988* (Washington, D.C.: Congressional Quarterly 1990), 21-22.

14. See Stephen J. Wayne, "Great Expectations: What People Want from Presidents," in *Rethinking the Presidency,* ed. Thomas E. Cronin (Boston: Little, Brown, 1982), 185-199; and Glen R. Parker, "Some Themes in Congressional Unpopularity," *American Journal of Political Science* 21 (February 1977): 93-119.

15. See Committee on the Constitutional System, *A Bicentennial Analysis of the American Political Structure* (Washington, D.C.: Committee on the Constitutional System, 1987).

16. On the balance of power between Congress and the president, see Roger H. Davidson and Walter J. Oleszek, *Congress and Its Members,* 3d ed. (Washington, D.C.: CQ Press, 1990), 249-250.

17. See James G. March and Herbert A. Simon, *Organizations* (New York: Wiley, 1958).

2. CONGRESS WITHIN THE U.S. PRESIDENTIAL SYSTEM

Michael L. Mezey

One of the distinctive qualities of the U.S. political system is its remarkable continuity. Although the system has altered in several respects during the two centuries that it has functioned, it has done so gradually and for the most part without formal constitutional changes. Its fundamental governing design remains essentially as it was when the Constitution was created: a federal system of divided power between the states and the national government, and within that national government a system of shared powers among a president, a bicameral Congress, and a Supreme Court, with each institution independent of the other and each possessing its own policy-making prerogatives.

Similar presidential systems, particularly in the Third World, have exhibited relatively high levels of political instability compared with single party or parliamentary systems.[1] Why, then, has the set of institutional arrangements in the United States been so stable? At the national level especially how does one explain the continued coexistence of a Congress that by comparative standards is the strongest legislative institution in the world and a presidency that for two hundred years has, by most estimates, steadily expanded its policy-making prerogatives? And what lessons, if any, does the experience of the U.S. presidential system have for nations in the Second as well as the Third World that are today experimenting with new institutional forms?

My discussion of these questions proceeds in four parts. First, the theoretical link between political stability and political institutions will be reviewed, drawing for the most part on analyses of less developed political systems. Second, the view of the issue reflected in the development literature will be compared with the one held by the Founders of the American political system. The design of the Founders squared admirably with their understanding of the issue, but the system that they produced, from a modern perspective, should not have been capable of establishing and maintaining political order. That it has done so for more than two hundred years is attributable in part to the several noninstitutional factors that will be identified in the third section of this chapter. Finally, the role that the modern Congress plays in maintaining political stability in the United States will be assessed.

Political Institutions and Political Stability

The connection between form of government and political stability has been one of the continuing questions of comparative politics. Using the British political system as a prototype, some argue that the parliamentary model is associated with political stability, particularly when it operates in the context of a strong political party system that can deliver dependable legislative majorities for the government of the day. But in countries with multiple political parties and unstable legislative majorities, the parliamentary system can produce frequent changes in government personnel and policies. The current Italian political system as well as the Third and Fourth Republics in France are often cited as examples of such unstable parliamentary systems.[2] Given the success of the American experience, the remedy sometimes prescribed for parliamentary instability has been presidentialism. The French Fifth Republic, in the view of many, exemplifies a regime that established greater political stability by introducing a strong, independent president beyond the reach of transient legislative majorities.[3]

Although parliamentary models can be unstable when their party systems are weak and fractionalized, as they often are in non-Western political systems, presidential systems usually have been the more unstable of the two constitutional models. Juan Linz has outlined some of the reasons that presidentialism is associated with political instability. In his view presidentialism

> narrows available options, creates zero sum situations, . . . discourages the development of party organization and discipline, risks provoking a stalemate if parliament falls into the hands of an opposing party or parties, and reduces the flexibility of governments to respond to crises with shifts in personnel and policy.[4]

One other possibility is also open: that the structure of a nation's political institutions may have little independent effect on political stability. Political systems, it can be argued, become unstable because of deep societal cleavages—economic, ethnic, regional, and ideological cleavages that are beyond the capacity of mere political institutions to bridge. From that perspective, institutional arrangements of political power may reflect rather than affect these societal cleavages. While certain institutional forms may ameliorate, and others exacerbate, the forces that create instability, in the end institutions cannot bring stability to an essentially unstable society.

Those who have sought to explain the relatively high level of political stability in the United States seem to have adopted this last perspective. Except for references to the Supreme Court's application of old constitutional provisions to new political issues, they seldom have taken into account the contribution of American political institutions to stability. Put differently, the hypothesis that American political institutions are stable because of the manner in which they operate has seldom been addressed, at least in a scholarly manner.[5] Rather, the best scholarship has focused on the character of the American people and on cultural, social, and economic explanations for the continuity of the U.S. constitutional framework and for the absence of internal revolts against the regime.[6] Certainly, any explanation of American political stability that fails to take these factors into account is incomplete. But equally incomplete is an approach that omits the effect of America's institutional arrangements, and particularly the unique combination of a strong Congress and a strong presidency, on the stability of the nation's political system.[7]

While the omission of American political institutions from these accounts is a weakness of the literature on the American experience, one of its strengths is its comparative perspective. Scholars such as Seymour Martin Lipset and Louis Hartz, for example, recognize that one cannot speak of the uniqueness of the American case without comparing it with other nations. But students of American political institutions rarely think comparatively. And it is just such a comparative perspective that can provide a theoretical purchase for addressing the role of American political institutions in achieving political stability.

Stability Defined

The word *stability,* when applied to political systems, indicates "the absence of revolutions, the lack of internal violence factors, the lack of continual constitutional revision, the lack of anti-system protest, and the lack of institutional and governmental instability."[8] From the perspective of systems theory, a stable political system exhibits high levels of "support" for the larger national community, for the community's system of government (the regime), and for those who happen to be in power at the time (the authorities).[9] Thus, a stable polity will be characterized by a shared sense of nationhood, by a continuity of governmental forms, and by a gradual and orderly turnover in governing elites. Although these three levels of political stability are analytically separable, they are related in the sense that instability with regard to one may lead to instability with regard to the others. Secessionist activities by a politically disaffected regional minority, for example, can lead to, or be caused by, a drop in support for the constitutional system or incumbent political leaders.

Stability Explained

Most explanations of political stability begin from the premise that stability is more likely if the political institutions of the regime are able to respond to the demands of its citizens. Such demand responsiveness yields "specific support" for the regime and its incumbents and, in the long term, "diffuse support"—support that is not dependent on demand satisfying outputs—for both the regime and the community. High levels of diffuse support can help maintain stability when a regime is unable to respond to the most immediate demands of its citizens.[10]

Among the most salient demands of citizens are those concerning their economic welfare. As Ted Gurr suggests, "men rebel" because of relative deprivation; that is, unrest is caused when people believe that their economic condition is worse than it should be.[11] In new nations with widespread economic privations and rapidly rising popular expectations, people are more likely to be disappointed by the regime's failure to deliver policies that respond to these needs. When these rising expectations are accompanied by high levels of political participation, instability can result. As Joan Nelson has observed, widespread participation often has provoked instability "by heightening group conflict and by escalating demands, prompting frustration when those demands were not met."[12]

Instability may be further exacerbated by the absence of a political culture that supports obedience as well as participation. Gabriel Almond and Sidney Verba suggest that a "civic culture" is characterized by relatively high levels of stability because the citizen's role as a participant "has been added to the subject and parochial roles. This means that the active citizen has maintained his traditional non-political ties as well as his more passive political role as a subject."[13] When, because of rapid movement from a parochial to a participant culture or from a traditional to a modern society, these nonparticipatory roles or other moral codes of behavior erode or break down entirely, rootlessness, or anomie, can set in. Citizens then can become vulnerable to the appeals of charismatic leaders to join mass movements, which can destabilize the political system.[14]

Social and cultural variables that adversely affect political stability can be mediated by political institutions. If institutions operate effectively to meet the most salient demands of citizens, particularly those demands that arise from severe economic needs, political instability can be averted. The question, however, is whether political institutions have the capacity to respond in such a manner. Samuel Huntington suggests that the threats to political stability engendered by heightened levels of political participation can be handled by strong political institutions. But when political institutions are weak, high levels of participation can be destabilizing. In the Third World, Huntington argues,

> social frustration leads to demands on the government and the expansion of political participation to enforce those demands. The political backwardness of the country in terms of political institutionalization, moreover, makes it difficult if not impossible for the demands upon the government to be expressed through legitimate channels and to be moderated and aggregated within the political system. Hence the sharp increase in political participation gives rise to political instability.[15]

If stability is to be maintained, political participation may have to be restricted until political institutions are strong enough to support higher levels of participation. Another implication of Huntington's argument is that political instability is primarily attributable to the weakness of the state, to its inability to act.[16]

Legislatures and Stability

The role of the legislature in maintaining political stability is complex.[17] Because legislatures are typically selected through elections in which virtually the entire adult population is eligible to participate, their creation and persistence is likely to be accompanied by relatively high levels of political participation and by increased expectations that government will be able to respond to the demands of the electorate. To advance their own careers, political leaders may use their positions in legislatures, or their candidacies for legislative positions, to stir up popular discontent with the regime. If governments are unable to respond to these demands, the result could well be public frustration, heightened unrest, and greater levels of political instability.

Because legislatures by their very nature are slow to act, they may impede the state's response to the demands that their members have been partially responsible for inciting. If the legislatures are independent of the executive (as in presidential systems), institutional conflict and governmental immobilism may characterize the policy-making process, making it difficult for the state to respond to pressing issues confronting the society. While parliamentary systems have the capacity to avoid stalemate, this capacity may not be realized in fractionalized multiparty systems characterized by endemic cabinet instability. From this perspective, strong and effective government may require a reduction in the power of the legislature and the enhancement of executive power.

But legislatures can maintain as well as impede political stability. As legislators link the nation's periphery with its center, they act as conduits for popular demands and grievances, thereby contributing to the responsiveness of the regime. Discontent can be reduced by legislators' efforts to resolve problems that individuals and groups in their constituencies have with the central government. And representation in the legislature will provide regional, ethnic, and partisan minorities with an arena within which to express their concerns. Even if policy is not immediately responsive to their demands, such representation can encourage political minorities to view the regime as legitimate, and it may build diffuse support for the regime, even in the absence of policies that will raise levels of specific support. Finally, legislatures can be instruments for making elites accountable to the populace, which in turn should reduce the likelihood that elites will resort to repressive tactics to deal with mass discontent. The absence of elite accountability and the presence of repression are closely associated with political instability.[18]

Summary

The model connecting political stability and political institutions that emerges from this discussion is fairly straightforward. Political stability is threatened when popular discontent is directed against the nation's political institutions and incumbents. Strong, effective political institutions that are able to govern can deal with discontent before it leads to political instability. Weak political institutions are less capable of dealing with discontent, and the result is instability. Legislatures can intensify demands and therefore intensify conflict, and in the case of independent legislatures operating in presidential systems, legislative obstructionism can lead to stalemate and reduce the likelihood of effective government action. However, legislatures also can contribute to stability by restraining executive elites from pursuing their goals through repressive means. The representational activities of individual legislators can increase the legitimacy of the regime, either by encouraging responsiveness to demands or by giving citizens the impression that their demands are being heard.

The Founders and Political Stability

Political instability was very much on the minds of those who wrote the U.S. Constitution. One of the reasons that the new Constitution was necessary, they said in the document's preamble, was "to ensure domestic tranquility." And James Madison, in the course of justifying the proposed Constitution to the citizens of New York in the *Federalist Papers,* noted that "complaints are heard from our most considerate and virtuous citizens ... that our governments are too unstable." [19] "Stability in government," he would later write, "is essential to national character." [20]

The Founders worried about political instability because of their experiences with the postrevolutionary constitutions of the several states. Most of these documents provided for legislative supremacy and a subservient executive, an understandable reaction to the prerevolutionary abuses that the colonies had experienced at the hands of the king and his royal governors. In the years before independence, it was the colonial assemblies that represented the colonists and articulated their demands; the assemblies, said James Wilson of Pennsylvania, "were the guardians of our rights, the objects of our confidence, and the anchors of our political hopes." [21] It was not surprising, therefore, that power to govern was consigned to those assemblies after the revolution had been won. In contrast, the upper chambers of the state legislatures had little independent power and, with the exception of New York, most states had governors who were almost entirely dependent on the legislature.[22]

These dominant legislatures soon became targets of intense public pressures. Many of the Founders thought that the legislators were too easily intimidated by these pressures and by the threats to public order that sometimes accompanied them. They were appalled by the tendency of the state legislators to knuckle under to popular demands for "the confiscation of property, the paper money schemes, and the various devices suspending the ordinary means for the recovery of debts." [23] The writer Noah Webster lamented the state of affairs: "so many legal infractions of sacred rights, so many public invasions of private property, so many wanton abuses of legislative power." [24]

These experiences led Madison to conclude that in legislatures "passion never fails to wrest the scepter from reason." [25] At the Constitutional Convention, Edmund Randolph decried "the turbulence and follies of democracy," [26] and Benjamin Franklin suggested that while in prerevolutionary times the problem faced by the American people was an excess of power in the hands of the rulers, "our present danger seems to be a defect in the obedience of the subjects." [27] And with popularly elected legislatures virtually in complete control of the governments of most of the states, there was no way to check the imprudent actions of these legislatures. As historian Gordon Wood notes, by the time the Founders arrived in Philadelphia in 1787, the legislature in their view had replaced the executive as "the institution to be most feared." [28]

In the terminology of development literature, the Founders saw themselves confronted first by excess political participation and second by political institutions at the state and national levels that they believed were too weak to cope with the resulting popular pressures. Just as developmental theorists would have advised, the Founders set about strengthening their political institutions and restricting popular participation. Their plan had two components: first, create a strong national government that would control those powers being abused by the state legislatures; second, insulate that government as much as possible from popular pressures, thereby ensuring political stability.

What for many contemporary leaders would be the most obvious strategy for achieving these goals—creating a weak legislature and vesting most governmental power in executive-centered elites—the Founders rejected because of their republican principles and commitment, despite their postrevolutionary experiences, to a strong legislature. In the *Federalist Papers,* Madison tersely acknowledges that in a republic "the legislative authority necessarily predominates," [29] and he states the republican case for a strong legislature:

> The genius of republican liberty seems to demand on one side not only that all powers should be derived from the people but that those entrusted with it should be kept in dependence on the people by a short duration of their appointments; and that even during this short period, the trust should be placed not in a few but a number of hands.[30]

But, he went on, political stability required institutional characteristics not associated with legislatures:

> Stability required that the hands in which power is lodged should continue for a length of time the same. A frequent change of men will result from a frequent return of elections; and a frequent change of measures from a frequent change of men; whilst energy in government requires not only a certain duration of power, but the execution by a single hand.[31]

For the Founders to have resolved the problem of instability by establishing a weak national legislature and a strong presidency would have been to deny their republican principles and, more practically, to have rendered the task of ratifying the new Constitution all but impossible. Instead, they chose to balance the power of the legislature with a strong executive. The new presidency would be electorally independent of the legislature (unlike in the states, where the governors were often chosen by the legislature) and therefore would supply the desired stability in government. An independent executive, said Hamilton, would be characterized by energy, and an energetic executive would be able to "protect the community against foreign attacks," provide "steady administration," and secure "liberty against the enterprises and assaults of ambition, of factions, and of anarchy." [32]

When the Founders spoke about "the legislature," they were almost always referring to the popularly elected House of Representatives. A further remedy for the political instability that they associated with the House was bicameralism. The Founders provided for an indirectly elected Senate that would share equal legislative powers with the directly and more frequently elected House (senators' terms were six years). Such an arrangement, said Madison, would guard against "the mutability of public councils arising from a rapid succession of new members." [33] Gouverneur Morris suggested at the Constitutional Convention that the Senate would "check the precipitation, changeableness, and excesses of the first branch." [34]

In sum, the Founders strengthened their political institutions by creating a strong national government with broad policy-making powers, especially in important areas such as taxation, commerce, military defense, and foreign affairs. To ensure stability and prevent the abuse of these powers, they prohibited the House of Representatives from taking any action without the agreement of the Senate and the president. Finally, they reduced popular pressures on these institutions by arranging a process for selecting senators that removed them by at least one step from the voting public (indirect election by state legislatures), and a process of presidential selection (the electoral college) with which the people would have as little to do as possible.[35]

But the careful design of the Founders had at least one serious flaw. So acute was their fear of legislative abuses of power that they created institutional arrangements that would make power extraordinarily difficult to exercise. The system of shared powers that they established for the new national government would not simply check legislative abuses but would operate reciprocally, to restrict the power of both the president and Congress. In truth, this system of power sharing among a popularly elected House, an indirectly elected Senate, and an independently elected president amounted to a constitution *against* government, a set of institutional arrangements more likely to produce inaction than action.[36]

Whereas modern development theorists argue that a strong state is needed to control political participation and avert political instability, the Founders, convinced that the primary threat to political stability was precipitous government action provoked by popular demands, created a weak state with a questionable capacity to govern. While some of the Founders recognized that such a state might have difficulty governing, its saving grace was that it would not be in a position to govern unwisely or tyrannically. But a weak state of this sort, our contemporary views suggest, should not be particularly effective in maintaining political stability. Why then would political institutions seemingly designed to prevent government action be associated with a political system with a historically high level of stability? The answer, in part, stems from the context in which these institutions developed.

The Context of Political Development

The theory that political instability arises when the government is unable to deal effectively with popular demands presupposes a politically active citizenry making excessive demands upon its political leaders. But this was not the situation when American national political institutions were in their embryonic stage. The volume of demands was relatively low for several reasons.

First, in the United States of the late eighteenth century, the politically active and involved public constituted a small percentage of the total population. In most states the franchise was available only to white male property holders, a relatively homogeneous and elite electorate. While certainly there were political differences among these voters, their demands were fairly moderate. This situation stands in marked contrast to the universal suffrage that characterizes most contemporary new nations. Moreover, the modern institutions of mobilization (such as mass political parties, organized interest groups, and mass communication systems, all of which serve in new nations today to focus and intensify popular demands) would not emerge in the United States for many years.

Second, demands were moderated by the federal structure of the new government. That is, while the national government had significant powers and responsibilities, its scope was still relatively narrow compared with what it is today and, more to the point, what it is today in new nations with relatively new political institutions. According to historian James Sterling Young,

> almost all of the things that republican governments do which affect the everyday lives and fortunes of their citizens, and therefore engage their interest, were, in Jeffersonian times, not done by the national government. The administration of justice, the maintenance of law and order, the arbitration of disputes, the chartering and supervision of business enterprises, road building and the maintenance of transportation systems, the schooling of the young, the care of the indigent, even residual control over the bulk of the military forces—these functions fell principally within the province of state and local governments to the extent that any governmental bodies performed them.[37]

The federal government's role in those early days was restricted to the important but nonetheless narrow areas of public finance, national defense, and delivery of the mail. Thus, if people had problems, their first instincts were to deal with them on their own or to turn to local authorities for help; their last recourse was the national government, except in matters where it had specific responsibilities, such as dealings with Native American or foreign nations.

Public demands today are often provoked by economic privations. While eighteenth and nineteenth century America had serious economic problems, these problems did not always create political difficulties for the new government. The expectation that government at any level should be responsible for the economic welfare of its citizens had not yet emerged, whereas today it is a given in every nation, new and old. Also, the seemingly unlimited availability of land and resources in the West provided the American nation with a safety valve. Those who were suffering economically could pick up and go, and the history of westward expansion in the United States indicates that many took that option. Developing nations with large populations, clearly defined borders, and equally meager opportunities from region to region have no such safety valve; there is simply no place for the discontented to go, except perhaps to the cities, and in the Third World the city has been the primary locus of popular unrest. But the economic wealth of the United States, particularly in terms of land, made its citizens a "people of plenty." [38] American cities did not become magnets for the economically deprived and the politically discontented until a century after the founding of the nation.

Thus in the early years the volume and intensity of the economic and social demands generated in the new nation were quite moderate by contemporary standards. And relatively few of the demands that were generated reached the new political institutions of the nation. As designed, these institutions may have been too weak to resolve the problems that confront a new nation in today's world. When they were created, however, these institutions were not subject to the same popular pressures as they would have been had they been created today. As Young explains, the "modern image of Washington as a vital center and government as a target for citizen demands of every sort ill prepares us for the image of a sequestered and secluded governmental community that emerges from the record of 1800-1828." [39]

Once again, to use the terminology of development theory, political institutionalization in the United States in its early years was aided by relatively weak political participation and by relatively few demands directed at the government. In time, the franchise expanded (and with it the scope of government) and the frontier closed, but not until the political institutions of the new nation had become entrenched. As

Lipset concludes, the "United States gradually acquired legitimacy as a result of being effective," and low participation and manageable demands allowed it to be effective.[40]

The Context of Modern American Politics

There is today significant debate on exactly how effective the American political system really is. The propensity toward stalemate, sewn in the very fabric of the Constitution, continues and in the view of many observers has become more pronounced.[41] Indicators of legislative-executive policy stalemate are abundant. The beginning of the fiscal year, October 1, is the deadline for passage of bills appropriating funds for each federal agency. Between 1976 and 1986, only 31 percent of these bills were passed on time.[42] Budget delays have been accompanied by spiraling budget deficits and by deadlock between the president and Congress about what should be done (beyond easy accounting gimmicks) to deal with this problem. Stalemate is apparent in other policy areas as well. For many years nearly everyone has agreed that the nation's welfare system is inefficient, unfair, and, most important, that it does little to break the cycle of poverty. Yet year after year nothing is done except minor tinkering at the margins of the policy—a formula change here, an experimental program there. Similar statements could be made about agricultural policy, health care, and a legion of other domestic policy areas, to the point where two prominent scholars ask, "Can the government govern?" Their answer, at least with regard to energy, trade, and fiscal policy, is no; "established structures no longer can contain political tensions between Congress, the president, and the bureaucracy, and, riven by conflicts, they often do not permit successful management of the nation's problems." [43]

This marked tendency toward policy stalemate has not led to the political instability that has plagued other nations with presidential systems. The balance of power between the president and Congress has shifted over the years. Despite repeated predictions to the contrary, Congress has not been eclipsed as a policy-making force by the president. Stability has characterized not only America's political institutions but also the larger society. In the two-hundred-year history of the U.S. Constitution, the Civil War era represents the single period in which the survival of the regime was seriously in question. During the 1960s an epidemic of urban riots by the poor and civil disobedience by the young in response to racial discrimination and the Vietnam War caused some to fear an era of political instability in the United States. But in the 1970s and 1980s this political activism was replaced by either satisfaction or apathy, depending upon one's point of view.

There are several contextual reasons for this consistent record of stability. Although many of the conditions that gave rise to minimal demands early in the political history of the United States have changed, others continue to reduce the burden on national political institutions. Most important, the federal system remains. Even though the scope of activities of the national government has expanded, especially during the twentieth century, many public service issues— schools, safety, sanitation, and transportation—remain the primary responsibility of state and local governments. The stalemate of national political institutions would be less tolerable to the American people if it resulted in closed public schools, mass transit strikes, and breakdowns in sanitation services, as it sometimes does in other nations and as it well might in the United States if the national government were responsible for these services.

The United States continues to be a nation of plenty. Economic differences persist and economic misery is far from unknown, but resources are sufficient and sufficiently distributed to have produced a large middle class. Whatever economic discontent this class exhibits is seldom translated into politically destabilizing activity. Nor have the economic privations of the lower classes resulted in political instability, partly because, as Lipset suggests, "adaptive mechanisms" within American political culture "reconcile low status individuals to their position and thus contribute to the stability and legitimacy of the larger system." Among these mechanisms are religious beliefs that poor people will enjoy a higher status in heaven and secular beliefs that social mobility is possible (if not for oneself, then for one's children). Another stabilizing factor is the opportunity for citizens to participate in political movements whose ostensible goals are to raise the status of the needy.[44]

The continued strength of capitalism, both culturally and politically, also reduces economic discontent. Capitalism as a culture serves to convince those with less that those with more deserve what they have and that their own lower status is attributable to personal failings rather than to any failings of the regime. Politically, many economic issues that other countries view as primarily national responsibilities— issues such as economic planning, prices and wages, and the allocation of goods and services—are largely viewed in the United States as matters for individuals and corporations to decide and are therefore not appropriate concerns of political institutions. People's expectation that government will deal with the economic issues closest to their lives is lower in the United States than in many other countries. The volume of demands that reach U.S. political institutions is lower as well.

Citizens' participation in the U.S. political system continues to be low. Even beyond the well-known statistics showing declining percentages of eligible voters going to the polls, Americans seem not to involve themselves very much in, or even to think very much about, politics. Political involvement is a sometimes thing, restricted for the most part to elections, primarily to presidential elections. Other sorts of political activity—joining interest groups, attending political meetings, participating in demonstrations, signing petitions, writing to legislators, performing acts of civil disobedience—are engaged in by minuscule percentages of the population. Politics, in short, is not high on the personal agendas of most Americans.[45]

There are several possible reasons for this apolitical society, both structural and attitudinal. Lack of participation may indicate that people are pleased with the way the political system operates, although public opinion data suggesting high rates of cynicism would tend to discredit such an explanation.[46] Voter turnout may be significantly diminished by institutional barriers to participation, primarily registration laws, and by a lack of political competitiveness.[47] The absence of mass party organizations capable of mounting class-based appeals may be a contributing factor to citizens' weak political participation.[48] Finally, because capitalism removes from the public agenda the issue that is of most concern to most Americans—their economic well-being—Americans may be apathetic and see no reason to participate. Rather, they are distracted by social and cultural issues such as abortion, ethics, patriotism, and the flag, or they distract themselves with the consumer culture, sports, television, and the other diversions that our society provides.

In sum, the continued stability of the U.S. presidential system, despite persistent stalemates on major policy issues, is a product of a political environment characterized, as it was in the period after the Constitution's ratification, by low participation and moderate levels of political demands. After two hundred years the nation's political institutions are stronger, more firmly entrenched, and more legitimate—a status that indicates, and also contributes to, political stability. But it also may be that the stability of the U.S. presidential system is attributable in part to the unique legislature at the heart of the system. Certain specific characteristics of Congress may allow the American political system to avoid the instability that has characterized other presidential systems. In addition, Congress may contribute to political stability by moderating the forces of change, by encouraging political responsiveness, by enforcing executive accountability, and by acting in a symbolically responsive manner.

Congress and Political Stability

The U.S. Congress is different in certain crucial aspects from all other legislative institutions.[49] Unlike other legislatures that for the most part react to, and usually approve, proposals from the executive, Congress is often the source—some scholars claim the dominant source—of major public policy initiatives.[50] Unlike other legislatures that are constitutionally barred from legislating in certain areas of executive prerogative, or whose decisions may be overridden by an executive veto or by a popular vote, Congress has a jurisdiction that is virtually coterminous with that of the national government. Congress, rather than the president or the voters, has the final say on public policy questions.[51] Although policy proposals from the president and executive agencies are accorded serious and often priority consideration by Congress, Congress says no to the president almost as often as it says yes, and even when it supports an executive initiative, such proposals rarely get through the legislative process without significant amendment.[52]

Of the world's legislative bodies, Congress has a support staff that is unmatched in size and professionalism and a committee system that is highly specialized and autonomous.[53] Members of Congress are well educated, and most have had previous political experience at other levels of government. Once elected to Congress, they tend to stay. Salaries are relatively high, fringe benefits generous, and the retirement plan truly excellent. The institutional power of Congress is matched by the power individual legislators can exercise in making policy. Through their committee assignments, members acquire policy expertise and with it the ability to shape public policy in the area of their committee jurisdictions. But the policy-making influence of individual legislators is no longer restricted to those policy areas relevant to their committee assignments. For some time the formal and informal rules of the Senate have supported a great deal of individual autonomy so that senators can make decisions on a wide range of policy issues.[54] And the House may be moving toward more collegial decision-making practices, characterized by "egalitarian norms that encourage and tolerate the full participation of any member seeking to influence policy outcomes." [55]

Much of the policy-making autonomy exhibited by Congress and its members can be traced to the independent political bases of the legislators. National political party organizations in the United States tend to be weaker than they are in many other political systems, which means that representatives and senators must be elected from their local constituencies largely on their own efforts. This arrangement has two important consequences. First, legislators develop strong personal ties to their constituents and to the interest groups that finance their elections. Second, once in office, members have a great deal of autonomy from their party leaders. To remain in office, members see to the most salient needs of their constituencies and of the groups that back their reelection efforts, and they do so even when this may be contrary to the wishes of the president or their party leaders.

The policy-making strength of the U.S. Congress, its decentralized policy-making processes, and the resistance of its individual members to party and executive leadership undoubtedly have contributed to policy conflict and stalemate between the president and Congress.[56] But these same characteristics also may permit the system of presidential-congressional relations to "work" better than one would expect in the presidential system of government. While the lack of party discipline and the strong constituency ties of members of Congress often foster legislative-executive stalemates, these factors also make legislators susceptible to influence by the president.[57]

In presidential systems with stronger political parties and more nationally oriented legislators than in the United States, control of Congress by a party different from the president's would always lead to deadlock because the president would have a great deal of difficulty rounding up a majority of votes in support of executive initiatives. But in the American political system, opposition legislators can be induced to support the president by ideological considerations or through favors from the executive that can benefit their constituents. Although President Ronald Reagan never had a partisan majority in the House of Representatives, he was nonetheless able to persuade numerous congressional Democrats to vote his way in the first two years of his administration. A stronger, more disciplined party system might have prevented such bipartisan coalitions from developing.[58]

The congressional committee system, which has more than occa-sionally frustrated presidents' efforts to implement a broad policy agenda, also has contributed to the stability of the presidential system. First, division of labor has enabled committees to deal with the greatly expanded workload produced by the explosion of federal government activity during the twentieth century. Although the committee system does make the legislative process slow and tedious, without it policy making certainly would come to a halt. In unstable presidential systems, committees typically have little support from staff, little autonomy, and quite broad and amorphously defined jurisdictions.

A second stabilizing feature of the congressional committee system is the close relationship between committees and the bureaucracies over which they have jurisdiction. These "subgovernments," while major obstacles to presidents seeking to lead the bureaucracy, make the ties between bureaucrats and legislators stronger than in most other political systems. Whereas in Third World nations the civilian bureaucracy typically allies itself with the president and the military to threaten parliamentary institutions, in the United States the permanent bureaucracy is often closer to the legislators who serve on the committees that authorize and fund their programs than to the president and his cabinet members—people who could be hostile to the mission of the agency.[59] For this and other reasons, presidents bent on potentially destabilizing policy changes will often be defeated by a coalition of congressional and bureaucratic forces allied in defense of current public policy; such a coalition, of course, would be unlikely to appear in most other political systems.

Mediating the Forces of Change

Instability may result from demands for political participation by previously excluded groups, especially when such demands are resisted by incumbent elites. On the other hand, sudden and dramatic changes in the turnover of political elites also can be destabilizing. This, as noted earlier, was what worried the Founders with regard to the House of Representatives. They feared that a rapid turnover in the membership of the House would lead to destabilizing shifts in public policy from one session of Congress to the next. If such political instability is to be avoided, the trick is to allow for change but to arrange matters so that change will be gradual.

Although the Founders did not anticipate it, Congress became an institution that allowed for exactly this sort of nondestabilizing change in political elites. A careful analysis of biographical data on members of the House finds evidence during the late nineteenth century of "democratization of the congressional elite" and "increasing similarity between characteristics of representatives, on the one hand, and the general population, on the other." But the same analysis uses the adjective "glacial" to describe the pace of this movement toward "increasing openness of the House." [60] Congress thus can be seen as both facilitating and moderating demands for political inclusion. It allows the political system to adapt at a pace rapid enough to avoid rebellion among the excluded, but deliberate enough to prevent destabilizing change.

The pace of change was further slowed, and stability further enhanced, by the emergence of congressional careerism. Low turnover of members was a primary reason for the glacial pace of change. For most of the nineteenth century, membership turnover in the House of Representatives was quite high; Nelson Polsby counted fifteen elections, the last in 1882, that produced turnover rates above 50 percent.[61]

But after that time turnover declined; for most of the twentieth century, gradual rather than rapid change in the membership of the House and Senate has been the rule. The average tenure of House members rose from just over six years at the turn of the century to just over eleven years in the 1980s. Today, no more than 15 percent of House members usually are serving their first term, while a similar number have served for at least twenty years.[62]

Change is also moderated by the kind of people elected to Congress. Contrary to the concerns of the Founders that legislators, particularly members of the House, would be people of relatively low quality and status and therefore overly sympathetic to the potentially destabilizing demands of mass publics, most members are well-educated, middle and upper class citizens. During the twentieth century the electoral role of political parties has declined and the expense of election campaigns has increased. Consequently, legislators are more likely than in the past to be people who are either wealthy themselves or have close connections to groups or individuals with financial resources. The possibility that legislators would undertake radical actions on behalf of mass publics or would attack the fundamental values of the American political economy is, to say the least, extraordinarily unlikely. As Philip Brenner concludes, Congress continues to foster the "capitalist mode of production in the United States, and the social relations that attend this mode of production." [63]

One reason Congress has been able to attract and retain the services of people of quality is the congressional committee system. Its highly refined division of labor enables talented politicians committed to careers in Congress to increase their influence and to make their mark on public policy.[64] The committee system's decentralization of power is another source of congressional resistance to radical changes in policy. Committees and subcommittees tend to be dominated by members and staff who continue in place from one legislative session to the next and who have political and personal stakes in current public policy. This ensures that policy changes will be largely incremental and therefore nondestabilizing. In addition, the decentralized nature of congressional decision making means that passage of most policy initiatives takes a long time and requires the support of a broad coalition of legislators. All of this virtually eliminates the possibility of extreme or radical action in Congress and guarantees that whatever emerges from the legislative process will be a compromise proposal calling for, at most, moderate change.

The slow and deliberate pace of the congressional process also works to moderate the changes presidents can make. The plebiscitary nature of the modern American presidency has caused presidential candidates to promise during their campaigns more than they can fulfill once elected and to inflate the public's expectations of the victorious candidates.[65] As a result, newly elected presidents may come to office promising a "sea change" in public policy; however, they soon confront the rather conservative congressional policy-making process that will always slow the rate of changes they can initiate and usually modify, if not reject, their more radical proposals.

Policy Responsiveness

If political systems are to remain stable, their policy-making institutions must be responsive to public pressures. "Responsive" in this sense does not mean doing whatever the constituents wish. Rather, it means "acting in the interests of the represented" and calculating those interests with some degree of public consultation but also with some degree of discretion and judgment.[66] Members of Congress stay responsive by staying in touch with their constituents. The two-year term for members of the House requires continuous contact if members wish to be reelected. And although senators have a longer term in office, one-third of the Senate's membership is always no more than two years away from the next election day. This electoral connection has sharpened the sensitivity and responsiveness of representatives and senators to constituency concerns. The result is strong personal ties between legislators and their constituencies. In fact, citizens think highly of their legislators even while maintaining a relatively low opinion of Congress as an institution. It seems that citizens evaluate the performance of their legislators primarily in terms of their record of constituency service and their personal characteristics, and they con- clude that their legislators are doing well on these criteria.[67]

This phenomenon has served to insulate Congress from the effects of episodic periods of national political discontent. If voters are unhappy, they take their displeasure out on presidential candidates while reelecting members of Congress whom they tend to evaluate on how they have served the constituency rather than on how they have stood on the salient issues of the day.[68] In 1968, when political unrest in the United States was great, only 13 of the 409 members of the House who sought reelection were defeated. Although the composition of Congress was virtually unaltered by the events of 1968, an incumbent president was driven from office by members of his own party, one candidate to replace him was assassinated, a radical third party candidate garnered more than 13 percent of the popular vote, and the opposition party candidate ultimately captured the presidency.

Today the continuity of congressional membership largely depends on members' ability to serve and benefit their constituents. As the modern administrative state expanded its activities and touched the lives of increasing numbers of citizens, more people came to think of themselves as adversely affected by government or as deserving of government services or funds. Soon they began to expect legislators to resolve their problems and complaints with the administrative apparatus of the modern state. As legislators responded to these expectations, they encouraged a degree of bureaucratic responsiveness that might otherwise have been absent, and to some extent they reduced the incidence and severity of public discontent with government.

Congress also has proven to be responsive to the policy demands of constituents on those occasions when citizens or well-organized interests have made their views clear. One example of the process at work is Congress's decision in 1989 virtually to repeal the catastrophic health care legislation that it had passed with much fanfare the year before. When the members of senior citizens' groups became aware of the law's provisions (particularly the new taxes that many of them would need to pay), they voiced their discontent to their legislators in no uncertain terms. The image of Rep. Dan Rostenkowski, chair of the House Ways and Means Committee, being chased down a Chicago street by enraged senior citizens dramatized for the national media what virtually all members of the House and Senate were experiencing when they went home to their constituencies. After several failed attempts to "educate" their constituents about the catastrophic health care issue, the legislators finally threw in the towel and repealed most of the benefits and most of the taxes associated with the new program. Whether this was wise is not the point here; what repeal of these measures demonstrates is the very real sense in which Congress responds to public pressures, especially pressures generated by an intense minority.

Enforcing Executive Accountability

"To watch and control the Government," John Stuart Mill suggested, is the "proper office" of representative assemblies.[69] Legislatures as open public arenas are admirably suited to perform this oversight function. To the extent that such activities discourage the executive from acting corruptly, arbitrarily, repressively, or unconstitutionally, they enhance the stability of the political system.

Congress, through its committee system, exercises continuous oversight of executive agencies. Although it has been suggested that members' reelection concerns distract them from their oversight responsibilities, these same electoral concerns may well make members more zealous in investigating corrupt or arbitrary bureaucratic action.[70] Hearings during the 101st Congress on the improprieties in the Department of Housing and Urban Development are a case in point.

Legislators who might have seen no reelection payoff in improving the quality of the nation's housing policies likely saw a major payoff in the news coverage usually given to legislators who ferret out incidents of bureaucratic malfeasance. And to the extent that such instances of intense legislative oversight inhibit the bureaucracy from acting in this manner in the future, the legitimacy and therefore the stability of the political system are enhanced.

Similarly, when presidents have acted corruptly or beyond their prerogatives, Congress has often provided a highly visible institutional check. Some of the most vivid and positive images of Congress in action arise from those episodes when an imperial-minded president has been confronted and ultimately censured or deterred by Congress. The congressional hearings on the Vietnam War during the Johnson administration, the Watergate and impeachment hearings during the Nixon administration, and the Iran-contra hearings during the Reagan administration illustrate the capacity of Congress to sanction presidents who have engaged in repressive, illegal, or corrupt activities.

In presidential systems less stable than that of the United States, the legislature has no real capacity to check the actions of presidents or military and civilian bureaucrats. When it tries to do so, it may jeopardize its institutional survival as well as the political and personal security of its members. As a result, power is frequently abused, citizens lose respect for their political institutions, and the likelihood of instability increases.

Symbolic Responsiveness

Finally, Congress and its members play an important symbolic role that both dampens and diverts political discontent. In all political systems the act of voting for legislators as well as for other officeholders gives citizens the impression that they are involved in political decision making even when their ballots may have little real effect on policy decisions. This sense of involvement contributes to the legitimacy of a political system, even in situations where concrete responses to public discontent may not be forthcoming.

In the same manner regional, demographic, economic, and ideological groups with minority status in the nation as a whole can achieve representation in Congress by virtue of their strength in particular legislative districts. Representation may then lead to policy actions that speak to certain of the substantive demands of such groups. But even if responsive public policy is not forthcoming, representation, simply by providing these groups with spokespeople for their point of view, will make them more inclined to accept their political lot.

The public articulation of dissenting views also can function as a safety valve for the political system, releasing potentially explosive political pressures before they can have a destabilizing effect. In authoritarian regimes apparently powerless legislatures are used as a "safety valve" for pent-up frustrations within society.[71] But this function is also performed by legislatures in more open political systems, and Congress is no exception. During the summer of 1989, the public furor over a Supreme Court decision that seemed to condone flag burning was in part defused by congressional debate that gave vent to the anger and frustration felt by many Americans about this issue. The action Congress decided to take was relatively moderate, but it had the effect, at that time, of sidetracking the much more destabilizing response, endorsed by the president, of a constitutional amendment.

Finally, the activities of members of Congress when they are at home in their constituencies have a similar symbolic effect. As members listen to and empathize with the concerns of discontented constituents, they supply them with a safe and relatively inconsequential outlet for their grievances. The appearance of the legislator in the district symbolizes for citizens in a very concrete manner that they are being represented in Washington and that their voices are being heard.

These various symbolic activities make a crucial contribution to political stability. As John Wahlke has observed, such "symbolic satisfaction with the process of government is probably more important than specific, instrumental satisfaction with the policy output of the process." [72] A process of government that is viewed as legitimate has the effect of domesticating conflict by channeling political discontent in relatively benign directions. While such activities by themselves cannot eliminate destabilizing pressures and render legitimate an essentially illegitimate political system, they can, in an essentially stable political system such as the United States, help maintain stability or at least head off incipient discontent.

Conclusion

Legislatures in the Third World are, more often than not, resistant to change. Robert Packenham has offered the even broader generalization that "legislatures tend to represent, all over the world, more conservative and parochial interests than executives, even in democratic polities." [73] While this "conservative legislature" hypothesis might well be exaggerated, it does offer an important corrective to the instinctive view of many democrats that legislatures in general and the U.S. Congress in particular are likely to be progressive, change-oriented institutions. Even if legislatures do function as conservative institutions, however, they will not necessarily contribute to political stability. If legislatures are overly rigid and consistently block necessary changes, instability certainly will result; however, if legislatures provide an institutional setting for moderating or diverting the forces of change, they are likely to contribute to, more than they will detract from, political stability.

The latter possibility is much more descriptive of the role of Congress in the American political system than the former. Members of Congress, some of whom represent those who are politically disaffected, are drawn disproportionately from those strata of society with the fewest grievances against the political system. The representational activities of these legislators often enhance the responsiveness of the political system to those who do have grievances, and they consistently operate at a symbolic level to reduce the potential impact of popular discontent. The operation of the congressional policy-making process ensures that potentially destabilizing policy proposals seldom make it onto the agenda, let alone the statute books. Congress restrains the president from pursuing radical policies while at the same time providing the votes for the president's more moderate policy initiatives. It also checks any propensity that the president or the bureaucracy might have to act arbitrarily or corruptly. In all these senses, then, Congress enhances political stability.

Whether legislatures in other nations, particularly those nations experiencing rapid political change, will perform the same stabilizing function as the U.S. Congress is open to debate. Certainly, as the Marxist systems of Eastern Europe began their transitions toward more open political systems, the previously weak legislatures in those countries came to have an increasingly conspicuous role. In Poland and Czechoslovakia the legislature provided the only institutional setting within which change could take place because it was the only institution that retained some degree of legitimacy among the forces advocating change. Often the first voices of dissent within the Communist parties of these nations came from members of the national legislature. Later, as these parties gave up their monopoly of power, those calling for change from outside the party gained increased representation in the legislature. The legislature became the place for planning and implementing major political change.

Although these legislative bodies have helped to manage the transition from authoritarian to more open political systems, they will not necessarily develop into powerful legislatures similar to the U.S. Congress. That is because these institutions are not likely, in the long term, to produce much more than symbolic policy responses to the economic and ethnic problems at the root of instability in these political systems. In fact, the confrontation and stalemate that characterize decision making in presidential systems will reduce the likelihood of substantive policy responses, the American case to the contrary notwithstanding. Without substantive solutions, higher rather than lower levels of political instability will result.

The modern Congress is able to contribute to political stability because the United States has an essentially stable political system. The political system is stable because of the unique circumstances under which it was permitted to develop and because of the cultural and political norms that have come to characterize the nation. Nations that today seek to foster political stability by emulating the American institutional model are unlikely to succeed because the context in which they try to build new political institutions little resembles the context in which American political institutions developed.

Notes

An earlier version of this chapter was presented at the annual meeting of the American Political Science Association, Atlanta, Ga., September 1989. I am grateful to Rose Spalding for her comments on the earlier version.

1. Fred W. Riggs, "Bureaucratic Links Between Administration and Politics" (Paper presented at the annual meeting of the American Political Science Association, Atlanta, Ga., September 1989), 19-20.
2. See C. F. Strong, *A History of Modern Political Constitutions* (New York: Capricorn Books, 1963), 272-273; and Jean Blondel, *Comparing Political Systems* (New York: Praeger, 1971), 178-182.
3. See Philip M. Williams and Martin Harrison, *Politics and Society in de Gaulle's Republic* (Garden City, N.Y.: Doubleday, 1971), 205. Maurice Duverger categorizes systems such as the French Fifth Republic as "semi-presidential," a form of government "intermediary between presidential and parliamentary systems." See Maurice Duverger, "A New Political System Model: Semi-Presidential Government," *European Journal of Political Research* 8 (June 1980): 165-187.
4. This quote is from Guillermo O'Donnell and Philippe C. Schmitter, *Transitions from Authoritarian Rule: Tentative Conclusions About Uncertain Democracies* (Baltimore: Johns Hopkins University Press, 1986), 60-61. See also Juan Linz, "Stability and Regime Change" (Paper presented to the Committee on Political Sociology, International Political Science Association—International Studies Association, Werner-Reimers Stiftung, Bad Homburg, May 1981). For other critiques of presidentialism, see Arthur Schlesinger, Jr., *The Imperial Presidency* (Boston: Houghton Mifflin, 1973); Theodore Lowi, *The Personal President* (Ithaca, N.Y.: Cornell University Press, 1985); and Harold M. Barger, *The Impossible Presidency: Illusions and Realities of Presidential Government* (Glenview,

Ill.: Scott, Foresman, 1984).

5. One exception is the work on separation of powers. See, for example, James W. Ceaser, "In Defense of Separation of Powers," in *Separation of Powers: Does It Still Work?* ed. Robert A. Goldwin and Art Kaufman (Washington, D.C.: American Enterprise Institute, 1986). Other exceptions are several discussions of the role of the American party system in nurturing consensus. See, for example, Austin Ranney and Willmoore Kendall, *Democracy and the American Party System* (New York: Harcourt, Brace, 1956), chaps. 21 and 22; also see Herbert Agar, *The Price of Union* (Boston: Houghton Mifflin, 1959).

6. See Daniel Boorstin, *The Genius of American Politics* (Chicago: University of Chicago Press, 1953); Louis Hartz, *The Liberal Tradition in America* (New York: Harcourt, Brace, 1955); David Potter, *People of Plenty* (Chicago: University of Chicago Press, 1954); and Seymour Martin Lipset, *The First New Nation: The United States in Historical and Comparative Perspective* (New York: Basic Books, 1963).

7. A notable exception is Fred W. Riggs, "The Survival of Presidentialism in America: Para-Constitutional Practices," *International Political Science Review* 9 (1988): 247-278.

8. Robert J. Jackson and Michael B. Stein, *Issues in Comparative Politics* (New York: St. Martin's Press, 1971), 196.

9. See David Easton, *A Systems Analysis of Political Life* (New York: Wiley, 1965), esp. pt. 3.

10. Ibid., 269-277. On the distinction between specific and diffuse support, see John Wahlke, "Policy Demands and System Support: The Role of the Represented," *British Journal of Political Science* 1 (July 1971): 271-290; and Gerhard Loewenberg, "The Influence of Parliamentary Behavior on Regime Stability: Some Conceptual Clarifications," *Comparative Politics* 3 (January 1971): 177-200.

11. Ted Robert Gurr, *Why Men Rebel* (Princeton, N.J.: Princeton University Press, 1970).

12. Joan M. Nelson, "Political Participation," in *Understanding Political Development: An Analytic Study,* ed. Myron Weiner and Samuel P. Huntington (Boston: Little, Brown, 1987), 114.

13. Gabriel Almond and Sidney Verba, *The Civic Culture* (Boston: Little, Brown, 1963), 339.

14. William Kornhauser, *The Politics of Mass Society* (New York: Free Press, 1959). See also Nelson, "Political Participation," 110.

15. Samuel P. Huntington, *Political Order in Changing Societies* (New Haven, Conn.: Yale University Press, 1968), 55.

16. See Joel S. Migdal, "Strong States, Weak States: Power and Accommodation," in *Understanding Political Development,* ed. Weiner and Huntington.

17. See Michael L. Mezey, *Comparative Legislatures* (Durham, N.C.: Duke University Press, 1979), chap. 12; William Mishler and Anne Hildreth,

"Legislative Correlates of Political Stability: An Exploratory Analysis" (Paper presented at the Conference on Parliaments, Policy, and Regime Support, Durham, N.C., December 1982); and Robert Packenham, "Legislatures and Political Development," in *Legislatures in Developmental Perspective*, ed. Allan Kornberg and Lloyd Musolf (Durham, N.C.: Duke University Press, 1970).

18. See Douglas A. Hibbs, Jr., *Mass Political Violence: A Cross-National Causal Analysis* (New York: Wiley, 1973); and Edward N. Muller, "Income Equality, Regime Repressiveness, and Political Violence," *American Sociological Review* 50 (February 1985): 47-61.

19. James Madison, *Federalist* no. 10, in *The Federalist Papers*, ed. Clinton Rossiter (New York: New American Library, 1961), 77.

20. Ibid., *Federalist* no. 37, 226.

21. Quoted in Charles C. Thach, Jr., *The Creation of the Presidency, 1775-1789* (Baltimore: Johns Hopkins University Press, 1923), 27.

22. See Merrill Jensen, *The Making of the American Constitution* (New York: Van Nostrand Reinhold, 1964), 20. On the New York governorship, see Thach, *Creation of the Presidency,* chap. 2.

23. Gordon Wood, *The Creation of the American Republic, 1776-1787* (Chapel Hill: University of North Carolina Press, 1969), 404.

24. Quoted in Wood, *Creation of the American Republic,* 411.

25. Madison, *Federalist* no. 55, in *Federalist Papers,* 342.

26. Max Farrand, ed., *The Records of the Federal Convention of 1787* (New Haven, Conn.: Yale University Press, 1966), vol. 1, 51.

27. Quoted in Wood, *Creation of the American Republic,* 432.

28. Ibid., 409.

29. Madison, *Federalist* no. 51, in *Federalist Papers,* 323. The parliamentary system as it is understood today had not yet emerged in Great Britain, so this model could not be emulated by the Founders. They believed a system in which the executive was selected by the legislature would result in one of two undesirable situations: either the executive would be manipulated by the legislature, or the executive would attempt to stay in office by corrupting legislators with bribes and other favors. See Michael L. Mezey, *Congress, the President, and Public Policy* (Boulder, Colo.: Westview Press, 1989), 30-34.

30. Madison, *Federalist* no. 37, in *Federalist Papers,* 227.

31. Ibid.

32. Alexander Hamilton, *Federalist* no. 70, in *Federalist Papers,* 423. See also David F. Epstein, *The Political Theory of the Federalist* (Chicago: University of Chicago Press, 1984), 171-172.

33. Madison, *Federalist* no. 62, in *Federalist Papers,* 380.

34. Farrand, *Records of the Federal Convention,* vol. 1, 511-512.

35. On the Founders' fear of popular election of the president, see James W. Ceaser, *Presidential Selection: Theory and Development* (Princeton, N.J.: Princeton University Press, 1979), chap. 1.

36. Mezey, *Congress, the President, and Public Policy,* chap. 2.

37. James Sterling Young, *The Washington Community, 1800-1828* (New York: Columbia University Press, 1966), 31.

38. See Potter, *People of Plenty.*

39. Young, *Washington Community,* 34.

40. Lipset, *First New Nation,* 59.

41. Mezey, *Congress, the President, and Public Policy,* chaps. 5 and 6. See also James Sundquist, *Constitutional Reform and Effective Government* (Washington, D.C.: Brookings Institution, 1986); and John Chubb and Paul E. Peterson, eds., *Can the Government Govern?* (Washington, D.C.: Brookings Institution, 1989).

42. Howard Shuman, "Congress and Budgeting," in *Congress and Public Policy: A Source Book of Documents and Readings,* 2d ed., ed. David C. Kozak and John D. Macartney (Chicago: Dorsey Press, 1987), 446.

43. Chubb and Peterson, *Can the Government Govern?* 5.

44. Lipset, *First New Nation,* 271-272.

45. See Sidney Verba and Norman Nie, *Participation in America: Political Democracy and Social Equality* (New York: Harper & Row, 1972).

46. On political cynicism, see Seymour Martin Lipset and William Schneider, *The Confidence Gap: Business, Labor and Government in the Public Mind* (New York: Free Press, 1983).

47. See Raymond E. Wolfinger and Steven J. Rosenstone, *Who Votes?* (New Haven, Conn.: Yale University Press, 1980); and G. Bingham Powell, "American Voter Turnout in Comparative Perspective," *American Political Science Review* 80 (March 1986): 17-44.

48. Walter Dean Burnham, "The Appearance and Disappearance of the American Voter," in *Electoral Participation: A Comparative Analysis,* ed. Richard Rose (Beverly Hills, Calif.: Sage, 1980).

49. Among the volumes treating the U.S. Congress comparatively are Mezey, *Comparative Legislatures;* Gerhard Loewenberg and Samuel C. Patterson, *Comparing Legislatures* (Boston: Little, Brown, 1979); David Olson, *The Legislative Process: A Comparative Approach* (New York: Harper & Row, 1980); and John E. Schwarz and L. Earl Shaw, *The United States Congress in Comparative Perspective* (Hinsdale, Ill.: Dryden Press, 1976).

50. See Gary Orfield, *Congressional Power: Congress and Social Change* (New York: Harcourt Brace Jovanovich, 1975); Lawrence Chamberlain, *The President, Congress and Legislation* (New York: Columbia University Press, 1946); and Ronald C. Moe and Steven C. Teel, "Congress as Policy-Maker: A Necessary Reappraisal," in *Congress and the President,* ed. Ronald C. Moe (Pacific Palisades, Calif.: Goodyear, 1971).

51. See Jean Blondel, *Comparative Legislatures* (Englewood Cliffs, N.J.: Prentice-Hall, 1973), 35-38. On a few issues, of course, the Supreme Court does have the final say, but the Court does not often declare acts of Congress unconstitutional. See Stephen Wasby, *The Supreme Court in the Federal Judicial System,* 3d ed. (Chicago: Nelson-Hall, 1988), 79.

52. See George C. Edwards III, *Presidential Influence in Congress* (San

Francisco: Freeman, 1980); and Mezey, *Congress, the President, and Public Policy,* chap. 5.

53. See Susan Webb Hammond, "Legislative Staffs," in *Handbook of Legislative Research,* ed. Gerhard Lowenberg, Samuel C. Patterson, and Malcolm E. Jewell (Cambridge, Mass.: Harvard University Press, 1985); and Malcolm Shaw, "Conclusions," in *Committees in Legislatures: A Comparative Analysis,* ed. John D. Lees and Malcolm Shaw (Durham, N.C.: Duke University Press, 1979).

54. See Richard F. Fenno, Jr., *The United States Senate: A Bicameral Perspective* (Washington, D.C.: American Enterprise Institute, 1982).

55. Steven S. Smith, *Call to Order: Floor Politics in the House and Senate* (Washington, D.C.: Brookings Institution, 1989), 4.

56. See Norman J. Ornstein, "The Open Congress Meets the President," in *Both Ends of the Avenue: The Presidency, the Executive Branch, and Congress in the 1980s,* ed. Anthony King (Washington, D.C.: American Enterprise Institute, 1983); James Sundquist, *The Decline and Resurgence of Congress* (Washington, D.C.: Brookings Institution, 1981), esp. chaps. 7, 14, 15, and 16; and Mezey, *Congress, the President, and Public Policy,* chap. 5.

57. See Riggs, "Survival of Presidentialism in America," 260-261.

58. James Sundquist argues that this may be changing and that increasingly rigid partisanship seems to be characterizing the relationship between Congress and the presidency. See James L. Sundquist, "Needed: A New Theory for the New Era of Coalition Government in the United States," *Political Science Quarterly* 103 (Winter 1988-1989): 613-635.

59. See Riggs, "Survival of Presidentialism in America," for a similar discussion.

60. Allan Bogue et al., "Members of the House of Representatives and the Processes of Modernization: 1789-1960," *Journal of American History* 63 (1976): 287-288.

61. Nelson W. Polsby, "The Institutionalization of the U.S. House of Representatives," *American Political Science Review* 62 (March 1968): 146; also see H. Douglas Price, "Congress and the Evolution of Legislative Professionalism," in *Congress in Change: Evolution and Reform,* ed. Norman J. Ornstein (New York: Praeger, 1975).

62. Mezey, *Congress, the President, and Public Policy,* 72.

63. Philip Brenner, *The Limits and Possibilities of Congress* (New York: St. Martin's Press, 1983), 188.

64. Kenneth A. Shepsle, "Representation and Governance: The Great Legislative Tradeoff," *Political Science Quarterly* 103 (Fall 1988): 461-484.

65. See Lowi, *Personal President,* for a discussion of the plebiscitary presidency.

66. The concept of responsiveness is discussed more thoroughly in Hanna Fenichel Pitkin, *The Concept of Representation* (Berkeley: University of California Press, 1967), chap. 10; and Heinz Eulau and Paul Karps, "The Puzzle of Representation: Specifying Components of Responsive-

ness," *Legislative Studies Quarterly* 2 (August 1977): 233-254.
67. Glen Parker and Roger Davidson, "Why Do Americans Love Their Congressmen So Much More Than Their Congress? " *Legislative Studies Quarterly* 4 (February 1979): 53-61.
68. There is, of course, a vast literature on congressional elections. The best summary continues to be Gary C. Jacobson, *The Politics of Congressional Elections,* 2d ed. (Boston: Little, Brown, 1987).
69. John Stuart Mill, *Considerations on Representative Government* (1861; reprint, New York: Liberal Arts Press, 1958), 81.
70. See Lawrence Dodd and Richard Schott, *Congress and the Administrative State* (New York: Wiley, 1979), chaps. 5 and 6; and Sundquist, *Decline and Resurgence of Congress,* 332-340.
71. See Mezey, *Comparative Legislatures,* 266-267; and Packenham, "Legislatures and Political Development."
72. John Wahlke, "Policy Demands and System Support: The Role of the Represented," *British Journal of Political Science* (July 1971): 271-290.
73. See Packenham, "Legislatures and Political Development, 578. Also see Huntington, *Political Order,* 388ff. For a review of research relevant to the conservative legislature hypothesis, see Michael L. Mezey, "The Functions of Legislatures in the Third World," in *Handbook of Legislative Research,* 750-754.

3. DIVIDED GOVERNMENT AND THE PROBLEM OF GOVERNANCE

James P. Pfiffner

Despite the significant increase in their power over the course of the twentieth century, presidents still cannot always prevail in the political system. Part of this "weakness" of the presidency is due to congressional reassertions of power and to the reforms of the 1970s, but a larger cause is the basic nature of the system of separated powers. The tendencies toward conflict and stalemate inherent in the system have been exacerbated in recent decades by the prevalence of divided government. This chapter examines differing perspectives on the consequences of divided government and analyzes different approaches to solving what many see as a constitutional problem. Although there are no simple fixes, some procedural changes could improve relations between the executive and legislative branches.

Presidential Ascendancy and Congressional Reaction

Presidential ascendancy—the increasing control of the government by the president—has developed as an outgrowth of three overlapping and cumulative trends. The first is the institutionalization of the presidency beginning in the early twentieth century. The second is the centralization of control of the executive branch in the White House beginning in earnest in the 1960s. The third is the harnessing of the presidential apparatus to respond to the personal political interests of presidents, sometimes at the expense of the longer term institutional interests of the presidency, a process often referred to as politicization.[1] Presidential ascendancy has generally been aided and abetted by delegations of authority from Congress, though at times Congress has tried to regain some of the power it relinquished to presidents.

These trends were driven by successive developments in American politics and government. The first was the public's heightened expectations of presidents. The Progressive vision of the president as an activist leader of a national constituency and the denigration of Congress as parochial raised public expectations about presidential performance.[2] The ability of presidents to deliver on their campaign promises was undermined, however, by the breakdown of political parties beginning in the 1950s and 1960s. The breakdown included the gradual disintegration of the New Deal coalition and the dealignment of the electorate in which the number of self-identified "independents" increased significantly.

The second development was this breakdown of political parties, which progressed from the 1950s through the 1980s and is still continuing.[3] Presidential hopefuls began to depend less on political parties and more on their own resources and public popularity. As a result, once they were in office they could no longer depend on a governing coalition based on a political party apparatus in the states and within Congress. The increase of ticket splitting further separated the political fates of presidents from their party colleagues in Congress.

The third development, which accelerated the breakdown of political parties, was the proliferation of primaries after 1968 and the rise of the personal candidate in the 1970s and 1980s. With the proliferation of primaries after 1968, presidential candidates no longer were controlled by, nor could they control, their parties. They had to create their own campaign organizations, mount their own campaigns, and design their own convention strategies. They also needed to raise large sums of money to conduct extended preprimary campaigns and pay for expensive media time. This increased the candidates' reliance on political action committees (PACs). Presidential recruitment became a game of independent political entrepreneurs who raised their own money and made personal rather than partisan appeals to the voters.

These three developments undermined the ability of presidents, once elected, to put together a governing coalition within Congress. According to Terry Moe, presidents "readily embrace politicization and centralization because they have no attractive alternatives. The causes are systemic."[4] Even though the presidency has become more institutionalized, centralized, and politicized, presidents are still unable to prevail in the policy process because the rest of the political system has not become more amenable to their control.

While Congress was very assertive in the 1920s and 1930s, especially in foreign affairs, the first three decades after World War II were an "unmatched period of congressional submissiveness."[5] Louis Fisher uses the metaphor of a swinging pendulum to describe the relative power of Congress and the presidency. He argues that the pendulum, especially in foreign policy, got stuck on the president's side during the administration of Franklin D. Roosevelt (see Chapter 10).

While President John Kennedy could not get much of what he wanted out of Congress, his successor, Lyndon Johnson, led the 89th Congress (1965-1967) in one of the most fruitful lawmaking periods in history. Then when public and congressional opinion began to turn against the war in Vietnam, Johnson and Congress clashed.

Richard Nixon's election in 1968 began a period marked by divided government and presidential frustration with congressional constraints on the executive. Nixon faced a Congress controlled by Democrats, many of whom had passed Johnson's domestic agenda and had become, since his presidency, more firmly against the war. Nixon and Congress had a number of confrontations over the war, including the secret bombing of Cambodia, considered by many in Congress to be presidential usurpation.

President Nixon's confrontations with Congress covered a much broader front than the war, however. One of Nixon's key tactics was the impoundment of funds (that is, he refused to release funds that had been provided by Congress for programs that he thought were overfunded or not needed). To justify his unprecedented impoundment of funds, Nixon claimed that the president had the constitutional right to withhold funds at his own discretion.[6] Of the many cases that were brought in federal court, the Nixon administration did not win even one. The assertion of the constitutional power to impound was finally dismissed by the Supreme Court.

Congress perceived in many of the Watergate activities presidential usurpation of powers and prerogatives that undermined the political system and the constitutional balance. It initiated impeachment hearings that eventually led to Nixon's resignation. But the longer range congressional reaction was a reassertion of congressional prerogatives vis-à-vis the presidency. These included the War Powers Resolution, passed over President Nixon's veto in 1973. The 1974 Budget Act, signed by Nixon in July 1974, reformed the congressional budget process and provided for an orderly process for presidentially proposed rescission of funds. Other congressional actions to limit presidential power included the increased use of the legislative veto and the requirement that all executive agreements be reported to Congress.

At the same time, Congress increased its capacity to deal with the executive branch. The Congressional Budget Office provided the legislative branch with the expertise to challenge the economic projections and estimates of the Office of Management and Budget. The Office of Technology Assessment enabled Congress to make independent judgments without relying so heavily on executive branch analyses. Personal and committee staffs of members of Congress were greatly expanded.

While these actions to right the power balance with the executive branch were being taken, Congress reformed its own institutional processes. The seniority system was weakened, and a "subcommittee bill of rights" was enacted. Most committee hearings, and even mark-up sessions, were opened to the public.

These reforms undermined the power of congressional leaders and fragmented power within Congress. They also made it more difficult for presidents to influence Congress. To get legislation enacted, presidents had to court many more members than in the past. Gone were the days when a president could cut a deal with a few "whales" and expect the little fishes to follow. With more power centers in Congress, presidential liaison teams had to work harder to win congressional support.

Presidents Gerald Ford and Jimmy Carter became frustrated in their dealings with the newly reformed Congress. President Ford resorted to active use of the veto power.[7] His fiscally conservative economic policies were rejected by the Democratic Congress. President Carter, despite some significant victories, was not as successful as he had hoped to be with his legislative proposals.[8] With the immediate memory of five presidents who were frustrated in one way or another by Congress, scholars began to write of the "no win presidency."

The first year of Ronald Reagan's presidency, 1981, seemed to promise a reversal of this trend. The administration successfully pushed through Congress virtually all of Reagan's first-year agenda, and it significantly changed the nation's priorities. But the last seven years of the Reagan presidency did not live up to the promise of the first year. His legislative successes declined steadily, his budgets were "dead on arrival" when they were sent to Congress, and his initiatives in Central America were blocked by congressional opposition.[9]

Partisan Conflict Reinforces Institutional Rivalry

Having a majority in each house of Congress never guaranteed a president success, but it made easier the job of seeking congressional support. Presidents could count on support from their own party in Congress, but the level of support was often not enough to guarantee passage of the legislation they favored. Party members in Congress can be counted on to support their presidents only about two-thirds of the time, even on votes that are important to the president.[10]

Despite the uncertainty of congressional support to presidents of the same party, the model of responsible party government has been the dominant prescription for successful national policy making. One of the foremost proponents of this model of governance, James Sundquist, explains:

> For coherent and timely policies to be adopted and carried out—in short, for government to work effectively ... the president, the

Senate, and the House must come into agreement. When the same party controls all three of these power centers, the incentive to reach such an agreement is powerful despite the inevitable institutional rivalries and jealousies. The party *does* serve as a bridge or the web, in the metaphors of political science.[11]

For decades, party-responsibility advocates have sought ways to strengthen the parties, but they have largely been unsuccessful. Presidents have been faced with the difficulty of putting together governing coalitions that would support their agendas and lend coherence to governmental policy.

But the forging of effective governing coalitions, which has been undercut by the disintegration of political parties, has been made even more difficult by the increasing incidence of divided government, when one political party does not control the presidency and both houses of Congress. From 1897 to 1954, divided government occurred only eight years (14 percent of the time), but from 1955 to 1990 it occurred twenty-four years (67 percent of the time), and it has occurred more than 80 percent of the time since 1969.[12] Elections in which the president's party failed to win both houses of Congress occurred only four times in the nineteenth century and never in the twentieth century until 1956. But in the past twenty years it happened six of nine times.

Divided government in the twentieth century has been accompanied by increased ticket splitting by voters. While ticket splitting occurred less than 10 percent of the time in the first two decades of this century, it increased to 43.7 percent in 1984.[13] In the 1988 elections split tickets occurred in 34 percent of the total congressional districts, but the relationship between presidential and congressional votes continued to weaken. In 1988 thirty-four of the split-ticket districts gave George Bush more than 60 percent of the vote, and 80 percent of the House Democrats won by at least 55 percent of the vote.[14] Presidential coattails, which had been decreasing for some time, were low in the 1980s and by 1988 had virtually disappeared.[15]

This historically significant increase in the incidence of divided government has added the element of partisan conflict to institutional rivalry. To make matters worse, the cleavage has stabilized along ideological and partisan lines: conservatives and Republicans have controlled the presidency, and liberals and Democrats have dominated Congress. This has led to more frustration on the part of presidents and more attacks on the legitimacy of Congress as an institution.

When Lyndon Johnson left office in 1969, control of the presidency shifted to the Republicans, and Congress remained the stronghold of the Democrats. With the exception of Jimmy Carter (who was not a traditional liberal), the presidency for the past two decades has been dominated by Republicans, who won five of the past six elections. Congress, with the exception of the Republican Senate from 1980 to 1986, has been controlled by the Democrats. Thus, ideological and partisan cleavages have reinforced the institutional cleavages created by the system of separated powers.

The frustration of Republican presidents led them to use extraordinary institutional measures (such as the impoundment of funds by President Nixon and the record number of vetoes by President Ford). After the first-year victories of the Reagan administration, the conservative agenda was thwarted by Congress, which would not go along with Reagan's extreme budget proposals or his policies on Central America.

This frustration of the conservative agenda led to attacks from the right on the legitimacy of Congress as an institution. Some of these attacks echo those of the Progressives: Congress is dominated by local interests, and only the president truly represents the national interest. Conservatives also argued that low turnover in the House of Representatives meant that the House was not the responsive institution that the Framers intended it to be.

The Consequences of Divided Government

What are the consequences of increased ticket splitting and divided government? Scholars, pundits, and politicians have come to different conclusions, including "it's bad," "it's good," and "it doesn't matter."

It's Bad

The judgment that the system of separated powers impedes coherent government action has a long and venerable history. Woodrow Wilson complained:

> You have an arrested Government. You have a Government that is not responding to the wishes of the people. You have a Government that is not functioning, a Government whose very energies are stayed and postponed. If you want to release the force of the American People, you have got to get possession of the Senate and the Presidency as well as the House.[16]

In the middle of the twentieth century, James MacGregor Burns made a similar complaint: "Our government lacks unity and teamwork.... We oscillate. fecklessly between deadlock and a ruse of action.... We can choose bold and creative national leaders without giving them the means to make their leadership effective." He argued that periods of productive cooperation between the two branches were the exception rather than the rule in U.S. history.[17]

Others have concluded that the American governmental system lacks one of the primary requisites of democracy: the ability to assign responsibility and hold rulers accountable. Douglas Dillon, former secretary of the Treasury, argued that "our governmental problems do not lie with the quality or character of our elected representatives. . . . Rather they lie with a system which promotes divisiveness and makes it difficult, if not impossible, to develop truly national policies." He went on to expound the problem: "The President blames the Congress, the Congress blames the President, and the public remains confused and disgusted with government in Washington." [18] The normally healthy competition between political parties "is translated into an unhealthy, debilitating conflict between the institutions of government themselves," according to James Sundquist.[19]

Even the absence of divided government does not guarantee coherent policy making. Lloyd Cutler, White House counsel to President Carter, wrote an article in which he argued that the constitutional roadblocks to coherent action were too great and that it was time for a series of reforms to move the United States toward a more parliamentary system of government.[20]

Scholar Michael Mezey argues that the system of separated powers cannot deliver coherent, informed, timely, and effective public policy. Much more likely is stalemate, when "neither the executive nor the Congress is capable of acting on its own and each is capable of stopping the other from acting." This situation develops, argues Mezey, because Congress is structurally incapable of producing good public policy. Although the presidency is better able to produce coherent policy, it does not because the executive branch is fragmented and needs to compromise to get any policy through Congress. Consequently, policy stalemate or bad public policy is more likely than good public policy.[21]

Sundquist argues that "when one party controls the executive branch and the opposing party has the majority in one or both houses of Congress, all of the normal difficulties of attaining harmonious and effective working relationships between the branches are multiplied manifold." [22] For example,

> Eisenhower and the Democratic Congress were stalemated on domestic measures throughout his six years of coalition government; the Nixon-Ford period was one of almost unbroken conflict and deadlock on both domestic and foreign issues; and the last seven years of Reagan found the government immobilized on some of the central issues of the day. . . .[23]

The foremost example of policy stalemate in recent years is the inability of the president and Congress to agree on budget priorities. While most politicians in the 1980s denounced the national debt and the record deficits, they could not agree on any combination of spending cuts and tax increases to reduce them significantly.

It's Good

Some claim that the separation of powers in the U.S. system of government is operating as it should and as the Framers intended. The Framers feared precipitous governmental action by a majority that might abuse the rights of a minority. Only an extraordinary consensus would allow the government to make major policy changes. The development of many checkpoints in the national policy process reinforced this natural inability of the system to move quickly. Barber Conable, when he was Republican representative from New York, argued: "The Founding Fathers didn't want efficient, adventurous governments, fearing they would intrude on our individual liberties. I think they were right, and I offer our freedom, stability, and prosperity as evidence." [24] Significant legislation can be passed only with a broad consensus. If legislation were passed without such a consensus, this position holds, it would be difficult to implement anyway.

Even some scholars who think that the ability to act is important for contemporary American government believe that divided government presents opportunities. At times policy proposals are facilitated by the condition of divided government, they claim. Timothy Conlan, Margaret Wrightson, and David Beam argue that the traditional, or "old style," model of policy change in the American system, the responsible-party-government model, does not explain well the important 1986 Tax Reform Act. President Reagan and his administration's plans played only a "modestly influential" role in the substance of the reform, and the president never really mobilized a partisan majority to support the tax reform legislation. "What actually drove tax reform forward was not Republican pressure in the face of Democratic resistance, but a process of interparty competition in which leaders of both groups first sought to win credit with the public for enacting reform and later competed to avoid blame for killing it." [25] Divided government in the case of tax reform (though not in most previous incremental approaches to tax policy) actually helped pass the legislation. With regard to the Economic Recovery Tax Act of 1981, both parties engaged in a bidding war to take credit for the huge tax cut. In this case, however, coherent tax policy and sound fiscal policy did not result from the fight for credit taking.

It Doesn't Matter

In an unusual departure from traditional scholarly debate on the topic of divided government, David Mayhew has convincingly argued that

> unified as opposed to divided control has not made an important difference in recent times in the incidence of two kinds of activity. These are, first, high-publicity investigations in which congressional committees expose misbehavior in the executive branch, and second, the enactment of a standard kind of important legislation.[26]

Mayhew takes a comprehensive look at "important" legislation passed between 1947 and 1988 and finds no consistent correlation between periods when party control of the government was unified or divided. His argument is made convincing by the care he takes in selecting which laws were important and which investigations were significant.

During some periods of American history (such as Reconstruction, the Progressive Era, and the New Deal) "ideological waves" dominated national policy making. Mayhew describes President Johnson's Great Society legislation as part of an ideological wave, but argues that much of this liberal agenda of the 1960s, contrary to conventional wisdom, extended into the Nixon and Ford years. "In retrospect, it seems in order to speak of an age of Johnson and Nixon. Johnson's role is familiar. Nixon variously acted as initiator, acquiescer, footdragger, and outright vetoer. But the bills kept getting passed under him and later Ford even though party control had switched to divided." The Nixon years "easily outstripped Truman's, Kennedy's, or Carter's as postwar generators of liberal legislation." [27]

In addition to "ideological waves," there is another indicator of successful governing: presidential success in passing coherent legislative proposals. This is the traditional measure of the responsible-party-government model. But even here Mayhew sees no correlation between presidential success and control of Congress by the president's party. "In fact, between 1946 and 1988, unified control supplied neither a necessary nor a sufficient condition for a President's success." [28] He notes that large-scale presidential legislative victories are relatively rare: Franklin Roosevelt's hundred days, Johnson's and the 89th Congress's spate of legislation, and Reagan's victories in his first year.

Mayhew does not argue that unified as opposed to divided party control makes *no* difference but that it makes "very little difference." He claims legislative activity is influenced more by electoral incentives, especially senators wishing to build a record to run for the presidency; the need to build broad coalitions to solve a problem; intense cleavages in public opinion that crosscut party lines; and public moods that seem to foster surges of lawmaking. Mayhew concludes: "Increasingly we seem to be stuck with divided party control in Washington, but that by itself does not seem to be any cause for alarm." [29]

Despite Mayhew's convincing argument, he does not solve the problem of incoherent policies and frustrated presidents. Roger Porter illustrates the problem of incoherence with a case study of policy making on trade issues. The Constitution, he explains, envisioned that Congress would determine trade policy for the United States, and in the 1920s and 1930s through the 1960s, Congress in fact did dominate trade policy. But with the growing complexity and magnitude of the international economy in the 1970s and 1980s, Congress has increasingly delegated trade policy to the executive branch. [30]

Trade policy making during the 1980s and divided government have produced outcomes that satisfy two important criteria of the U.S. political system. The policy-making system provides broad access to those of differing perspectives and gives them a chance to have an impact on trade policy. The process also produces results; that is, trade policy is made, and the system is not locked in stalemate. On other criteria by which policy is evaluated, however, the system fails. It does not produce policies that are consistent or coherent, and this is a source of considerable frustration to those concerned with trade policy. [31]

In addition to the problem of incoherent policies is the second problem, that of frustrated presidents. Presidents become frustrated when they cannot produce what they believe they were elected to produce, when they cannot deliver on their campaign promises. For Mayhew, this is not the main point: "who cares whether the President got what he wanted? That is not the right question. For purposes here, the question should be: is the system capable of generating important legislation? . . . In principle it does not make any difference." [32] But it does make a difference to presidents who feel that their elections have given them mandates for action. According to Terry Moe, presidential frustration results from high public expectations about presidential performance: "the expectations surrounding presidential performance far outstrip the institutional capacity of presidents to perform. This gives presidents a strong incentive to enhance that capacity." [33] Centralization and politicization of the presidency result. In addition, presidential frustration can easily lead to overreaching on the part of presidents and produce constitutional crises, such as Vietnam, Watergate, and the Iran-contra scandal.

Despite Mayhew's argument that divided government can produce periods of consistent legislation over long periods of time, such as the Johnson and Nixon years, those policies do not necessarily produce coherent government. Liberal legislation was passed during the Nixon years, but the government remained in crisis, with the president and Congress fighting each other over constitutional prerogatives. Mayhew's important contention that divided government does not matter very much in the long run offers little comfort to presidents or to opposing congressional majorities. And the presence of legislation or investigations does not necessarily mean consistent action or coherent policy. In this sense it *does* matter whether the president gets his way and can work with Congress to produce coherent governance rather than stalemate.

What Is to Be Done?

Those who come to different judgments about the consequences of divided judgment also have different prescriptions for solving the "problem." Possible responses to the problem include doing nothing, restoring responsible party government, creating bipartisan commissions or automatic devices, and giving more power to the president.

Do Nothing

Those who fear concerted action by a potentially oppressive majority are not anxious to "improve" the system. In their minds if a crisis is sufficiently evident, there will exist enough of a consensus to create agreement on a policy that will work its way through the political system. Short of that they might agree that "that government is best which governs least."

Others, who may not necessarily agree with all of the policy outcomes of this system, feel that structural tinkering is not desirable. Historian Arthur Schlesinger, Jr., argues that American history progresses in cycles, and that the proposals for structural changes made by political scientists who want to make the U.S. system more like a parliamentary system are shortsighted. Schlesinger sees the problem as one of personnel. If you do not like stalemate, elect better presidents.[34]

The lack of coherent policy direction may reflect ambivalence or deep divisions within the electorate. When the president and Congress cannot agree on deficit reduction or foreign policy toward Central America, they are reflecting disagreement within the electorate. In this situation any change that allowed one side or the other to impose its own solution would lead to further conflict, not concerted action.

Restore Responsible Party Government

The traditional solution to the problem of presidential-congressional deadlock since Woodrow Wilson has been to try to reinforce responsible party government. The consensus among political scientists in the midtwentieth century, formalized by the Committee on Political

Parties of the American Political Science Association, has been the responsible party model. Sundquist summarizes the consensus:

> By the 1960s, political science had developed a dominating theory as to how the American constitutional system should—and at its best, did—work. The political party was the institution that unified the separated branches of the government and brought coherence to the policy making process. And because the president was the leader of his party, he was the chief policy maker of the entire government, presiding directly over the executive branch and indirectly working through and with his party's congressional leadership over the legislative branch as well. . . . This established theory presupposed one essential condition: there would in fact be a majority party in control of both branches of government.[35]

Sundquist argues that the era of divided government is "simply an accident of the electoral system" in which a minority of ticket splitters imposes divided government on the majority of voters who vote a straight party ticket. He argues that the only way to restore accountability and the ability to act is to restore the responsible party model. Unlike Schlesinger, Sundquist thinks it is better to let one party lead the country in the direction it chooses, even if it is an unwise direction and opinion in the country is split. If the voters do not like that direction, they can elect the other party at the next election. At least major policy problems will be addressed, and someone can be held accountable.

Sundquist has proposed a number of legislative and constitutional changes to strengthen the party system and allow more concerted action by the majority party. They include

- the team ticket, which would force voters to vote for a president and for House and Senate candidates as one slate.
- four-year House terms and eight-year Senate terms, which would give the president time to make changes without the pressure of midterm congressional elections.
- special elections to enable the reconstitution of a "failed government."
- concurrent service in Congress and in the executive branch.[36]

The Committee on the Constitutional System was organized in 1982 to examine alternative constitutional arrangements. Chaired by Douglas Dillon, Lloyd Cutler, and Sen. Nancy Kassebaum, the committee in 1985 agreed that fundamental change ought to be considered seriously. Even though it did not directly endorse any specific remedies, the committee agreed that constitutional reform was necessary to reform the system.[37]

The likelihood of such basic structural changes is quite small. As Sundquist admits, "it only takes a split second of reflection to convince anyone that politically and practically it cannot be done." How, then, can the American political system be changed to make it work more effectively? Sundquist poses the challenge: "Needed: A Political Theory for the New Era of Coalition Government in the United States." [38]

Bipartisan Commissions and Automatic Devices

An American tradition since the Progressive Era is to turn contentious political problems over to "experts" to solve and to reduce the role of politics by creating bipartisan commissions. Examples include the Civil Service Commission created in 1883 and the regulatory commissions formed in the early decades of this century. The intention, if not the result, was to take politics out of policy making. Similarly, the purpose of automatic mechanisms written into law (such as the 1985 Gramm-Rudman-Hollings law that mandated the reduction of the federal budget deficit by fixed amounts each year) is to enable politicians of both parties to avoid blame for the effects of the laws they enact. In recent years these techniques have been used to break stalemates between the two parties and the two branches.

Members of an ad hoc bipartisan commission are selected by the president and Congress and charged with making the compromises needed to solve a specific problem. The main purpose of this technique is the opposite of the purpose of the responsible-party-government model, which is, in John C. Calhoun's words, "a well-connected chain of responsibility." [39] The party model assigns accountability so that voters can reward or punish the party and officials who are responsible for public policies. But the intent of bipartisan commissions and automatic devices is just the opposite: to break Calhoun's chain of accountability. The point is to leave no "fingerprints" on difficult policy decisions—not "look, ma, no hands" but rather "who, me?"

Bipartisan commissions in the 1980s addressed a number of contentious issues. The most successful was the Greenspan commission, which in 1983 formulated a compromise solution to the Social Security financing crisis. Other Reagan administration commissions were convened on MX-missile basing modes, U.S. policy in Latin America, and the shutdown of military bases nationwide. Congress also created the National Economic Commission. Its purpose was to propose a grand budget compromise that could be used to reduce the deficit after the 1988 election. But the winning candidate, George Bush, decided to ignore the commission, and its efforts came to naught.

Automatic devices to solve political problems have not been notably successful either. The proposal of the Quadrennial Commission to increase the pay of top officials of the three branches of government in 1988 turned into a political disaster because the proposed increases were overwhelmingly opposed by the public. Probably the most disruptive of the automatic devices was the Gramm-Rudman-Hollings act. Its requirements resulted in a plethora of budget gimmicks to achieve the appearance of deficit reduction, while the fiscal reality of huge deficits remained. All in all, the use of automatic devices and bipartisan commissions has had mixed results and has not presented any real solutions to the problems of divided government.

More Power to the President

For some time executivists have advocated another approach to the problem of deadlock in the system. Their solution is to give more power to the president and less power to Congress. Over the years Congress has come under attack for a variety of reasons, some having to do with its inherent nature as a fragmented organization with parochial constituencies, some stemming from its disagreements with individual presidents.

James Sundquist believes that Congress has some inherent weaknesses: "Representation produces individualism and parochialism. Individualism produces fragmentation and dispersion of authority within the Congress." This undermines the will to govern and the ability to lead, and as a result Congress lets power "drift to the executive branch." [40] The unwillingness of Congress to assume responsibility has made it also willing to delegate more of its own authority to the president. Only the constitutional infringements of President Nixon galvanized Congress to reassert itself, but the fundamentals of the relationship were not altered.

Other scholars have been critical of Congress as an institution. Morris Fiorina views Congress as a major part of the problem in public policy making. "Today the system has become an end in itself. It enables congressmen and bureaucrats to achieve their most dearly held goals by giving the appearance of satisfying the goals of the American people. In reality, public policy in this country is hostage to the personal goals of congressmen and the bureaucracy." [41]

Michael Mezey argues that Congress, because of its fundamental nature, is better suited to debate issues and play a representative role than to assert policy control. Legislatures tend to be open to influence, collegial in nature, and unspecialized. In contrast executives, and the presidency, tend to be specialized, hierarchical, and thus better able to make coherent and effective public policy.[42]

Despite the undisputed increase of presidential power over the past half century, conservatives have begun to worry about the "fettered presidency" being dominated by the "imperial Congress." [43] Robert H. Bork contends that "the president of the United States has been significantly weakened in recent years and that Congress is largely, but not entirely, responsible. Some recent presidents have failed to defend their office's prerogatives.... This is a deeply worrisome development." [44]

Jeane Kirkpatrick argues that "by accepting ... legislation such as the War Powers Act, the Boland amendments and the most recent contra aid bill ... presidents have made Congress's standards their own. They have acquiesced in demands incompatible with the responsibilities of the presidency." Moreover, the demand for clarity, certainty, and control before committing U.S. troops to hostilities makes the United States unable to take advantage of "fast breaking, unplanned opportunities." [45]

The implication of these executivist arguments seems to be that presidents should not accept laws, such as the Boland amendments, that prohibit them from using U.S. funds for certain purposes. This would limit Congress's "power of the purse," spelled out in Article I of the Constitution. Certainly consultation with Congress makes it more difficult for presidents to act quickly in committing the United States to hostilities in foreign countries (though not in the cases of the invasions of Panama or Grenada or the attacks on Libya). The problem is in agreeing upon what is an "opportunity." What the Reagan administration considered an opportunity in Nicaragua was not seen in the same light in Congress. The question is whether the Congress ought to have a say in U.S. military actions that may escalate into broader hostilities or war. By giving Congress the right to declare war, the Framers clearly expressed their intent that Congress play an important role in these matters. But thoughtful analyses of the inherent strengths and weaknesses of Congress and the search for an appropriate executive-legislative balance have too often given way to attacks on the legitimacy of Congress's very role in national policy making.

Policy disagreements have led to fierce attacks on the motives of members and on the legitimacy of the institution itself. Former Reagan appointee Paul Craig Roberts thus lambasted the congressional investigation of the Iran-contra affair: "Contragate is a case of the Congress protecting an enemy government in order to strike at an American president." Former Reagan White House aide Patrick Buchanan charged that Congress is guilty of "complicity in permitting the enemies of the United States to consolidate a military beachhead on the mainland of North America." [46] Conservative consultant Richard

Viguerie intended to make partisan use of the criticism of Congress when he predicted that "the number one conservative issue for the next couple of years will be this anti-Congress mood." [47]

Members of Congress have always criticized the institution of Congress, but recent attacks have been much more executivist in tone than in the past. Republican representative Newt Gingrich likened the 100th Congress (1987-1989) to "the despotic institution about which James Madison and Thomas Jefferson wrote. It is an imperial Congress reigned over by an imperial Speaker enacting special-interest legislation. . . . The present-day Congress has become the most unrepresentative and corrupt of the modern era. It is a Congress that lusts for power but evades responsibility for its actions." [48]

So weakened has the president become, concluded Bork, that he "must make a public issue of congressional attempts to control his legitimate powers, perhaps by refusing to accept some restrictions even at the risk of political damage." [49] So much for taking care that the laws be faithfully executed.

The rush of contemporary conservatives to embrace executive supremacy bothers some Republicans, among them Rep. Mickey Edwards of Oklahoma. "Unfortunately, many modern conservatives have become New Age monarchists, advocating ever greater concentrations of power in a new kinglike President. . . . What have we gained if we become the majority by becoming the party of centralized government?" Edwards asks. [50]

Conclusion

The range of alternatives suggested so far does not solve the problem of how to strike an executive-legislative balance of mutual restraint and comity. Despite the easing of relationships between the two branches after Bush succeeded Reagan, frustration continues over the government's inability to deal with crucial issues, like the deficit, before they reach the crisis stage. Basic structural change or constitutional amendment is unlikely, and the commission option is a limited tactical device that can be successful only in special circumstances.

Those who favor giving more power to the president have not fully accepted the legitimate role that the Framers gave Congress in domestic and foreign policy. The challenge is how to maintain a system of separated powers that can accommodate historical change. But those champions of Congress who decry presidential usurpation of legislative powers must admit that presidential leadership is still needed. The institutional reforms in Congress in the 1970s may have given Congress the tools and capacity to act, but they did not create the will to act. Institutional timidity, constituency responsiveness, and fragmented power still keep Congress from challenging the president and offering coherent alternatives. The new tools of the Congressional Budget Act of 1974 did not generate congressional alternatives to presidential budgets. Presidential leadership is still needed to formulate a budget.[51]

Since 1973, when Congress passed the War Powers Resolution, there have been few clear-cut situations in which the president was forced to comply with the automatic provisions of the law. The resolution states that the president must

> (1) consult with Congress before introducing U.S. troops into hostilities, (2) report any commitment of forces to Congress within forty-eight hours, and (3) terminate the use of forces within sixty days if Congress does not declare war, does not extend the period by law, or is unable to meet.[52]

President Reagan's compliance with these requirements was ambiguous in the 1980s when the United States attacked Grenada and Libya, put Marines in Lebanon, and provided protection for Kuwaiti oil tankers in the Persian Gulf. In situations where it was not obvious when the sixty-day clock began to tick, Congress was unwilling to act decisively.

But just because Congress has not always acted decisively or wisely is no reason to discount Article I of the Constitution. The reason that Congress should continue to play a major role in national policy, domestic and foreign, is not that it is best equipped by structure or disposition to make decisions, nor that it is always wiser than the president. One of its primary functions is to act as a constraint on the president and to raise constituency concerns that the president might otherwise ignore. The Framers intended to sacrifice some efficiency in order to prevent abuse of power.

The problem is how to enable presidents to act, yet prevent them from overreaching their power as happened in some important aspects of Vietnam, Watergate, and the Iran-contra affair. But just as the executive is not without fault in the exercise of power, neither is Congress. Congress sometimes asserts its oversight powers in ways that impinge on the executive's ability to manage the government effectively.

For example, the War Powers Resolution is probably not the best formula for letting Congress exercise its legitimate right to have a say in national security affairs. Decisions on weapons systems are often as affected by constituency concerns as by judgments about what the appropriate U.S. force structure ought to be. Speaker James Wright, as he later admitted, did infringe on the president's legitimate diplomatic and foreign policy prerogatives in his talks with the leaders of Nicaragua.

There are examples of a middle ground in which the differing interests of the two branches can be accommodated. One example is the aftermath of the 1983 Supreme Court decision in which the separation of powers purists won a Pyrrhic victory. The Court in *Immigration and Naturalization Service v. Chadha* declared that the legislative veto was unconstitutional. Since that decision there have been more than one hundred uses of the legislative veto.[53] It is a useful device that allows Congress to make relatively broad delegations of power to the executive branch while still retaining enough control to ensure that it can intervene if necessary. Thus, the executive branch continues to go along with its use.[54]

Other accommodations might be worked out. In the case of the war powers, the problem is how to preserve Congress's authority to declare war (Article I, section 8) in the present era when major wars are undertaken without a formal declaration. The War Powers Resolution allows Congress to force the president to cease hostilities by its own inaction. So far, experience with the resolution has not been satisfactory to either branch, and no president has admitted to its constitutionality. One possibility would be to amend the resolution to reverse the presumption, allowing the president to continue hostilities unless Congress by joint resolution (subject to presidential veto) calls for the withdrawal of troops. Congressional authority to determine whether the United States should engage in a war would be preserved, but the war-making initiative of the president would be protected, and the presumption would be that the president's actions were legitimate, absent a formal congressional vote. Congress could not force withdrawal of troops by inaction, and it would be forced to go on record and be held accountable.[55]

In the case of budget powers, impoundment, and the proposed line-item veto, Congress's power of the purse, as provided in Article I, should be preserved. But it is difficult for Congress to make budget cuts on its own. Rather than giving the president an item veto (and requiring Congress to come up with a two-thirds majority in order to compel expenditures), why not reformulate the rescission procedure? The law could be changed to allow the president to send a budget line item back to Congress with the provision that Congress would have to take a vote within a certain number of days in order to compel expenditure. In contrast to the current rescission process, Congress would not be able to force release of the funds by inaction. Such a process should not require an extraordinary majority but would allow the president to express formally differing spending priorities and force Congress to go on record over the issue.

The preceding examples—continuing the use of the informal legislative veto, modifying the War Powers Resolution, and changing the rescission process—provide for some accommodation of conflicting interests. They would refine the checks and balances system a bit. The proposals are based on the assumption that major constitutional changes are unlikely and undesirable.

These proposals also recognize that there is no mechanical fix. There is no substitute for leadership, trust, and comity. If the political will does not exist, automatic mechanisms or procedural reforms cannot force executive-legislative agreement. The experience with the Gramm-Rudman-Hollings bill demonstrates this and illustrates why a balanced budget amendment would not accomplish the task either.

If the system of shared powers is to allow effective governance, especially during an era of divided government, an appropriate attitude of respect and comity between the two branches is needed. As J. William Fulbright observed in the 1970s, "Our proper objective is neither a dominant presidency nor an aggressive Congress but, within the strict limits of what the Constitution mandates, a shifting of the emphasis according to the needs of the time and requirements of public policy." [56] A decade later George Shultz, then secretary of state, agreed: "We have this very difficult task of having a separation of powers that means we have to learn how to share power. Sharing power is harder, and we need to work at it harder than we do. But that's the only way." [57]

Notes

1. See Hugh Heclo, "Executive Budget Making," in *Federal Budget Policy in the 1980s,* ed. Gregory Mills and John Palmer (Washington, D.C.: Urban Institute, 1984), 255-291.
2. See Lester G. Seligman and Cary R. Covington, *The Coalitional Presidency* (Chicago: Dorsey Press, 1989).
3. See Theodore Lowi, *The Personalized President* (Ithaca, N.Y.: Cornell University Press, 1985), chap. 4.
4. Terry Moe, "The Politicized Presidency," in *The New Direction in American Politics,* ed. John Chubb and Paul Peterson (Washington, D.C.: Brookings Institution, 1985), 246.
5. James Sundquist, *The Decline and Resurgence of Congress* (Washington, D.C.: Brookings Institution, 1981), 94.
6. See James P. Pfiffner, *The President, the Budget, and Congress: Impoundment and the 1974 Budget Act* (Boulder, Colo.: Westview Press, 1979).
7. See Robert J. Spitzer, *The Presidential Veto* (Albany: State University of

New York Press, 1988).
8. See Charles O. Jones, *The Trusteeship Presidency: Jimmy Carter and the U.S. Congress* (Baton Rouge: Louisiana State University Press, 1988).
9. See the presidential support calculations for 1981 through 1988 in *Congressional Quarterly Weekly Report,* January 7, 1989, 1-12.
10. See George C. Edwards III, *At the Margins: Presidential Leadership of Congress* (New Haven, Conn.: Yale University Press, 1989), 40.
11. James Sundquist, "Needed: A Political Theory for the New Era of Coalition Government in the United States," *Political Science Quarterly* 103 (Winter 1988-1989): 629.
12. Ibid., 613.
13. See Edwards, *At the Margins,* 163; and *Congressional Quarterly Weekly Report,* July 8, 1989, 1716.
14. *Congressional Quarterly Weekly Report,* July 8, 1989, 1710-1716.
15. See Edwards, *At the Margins,* 151; and George C. Edwards III, *The Public Presidency* (New York: St. Martin's Press, 1983).
16. Quoted by Lloyd N. Cutler, "The Cost of Divided Government," *New York Times,* November 22, 1987.
17. James MacGregor Burns, *The Deadlock of Democracy* (Englewood Cliffs, N.J.: Prentice-Hall, 1967), 324-325.
18. Douglas Dillon, Address at Tufts University, May 30, 1982, in *Reforming American Government: The Bicentennial Papers of the Committee on the Constitutional System,* ed. Donald L. Robinson (Boulder, Colo.: Westview Press, 1985), 24, 29.
19. Sundquist, "Needed: A Political Theory," 629.
20. Lloyd Cutler, "To Form a Government," *Foreign Affairs* 59 (Fall 1980): 127.
21. Michael L. Mezey, *Congress, the President, and Public Policy* (Boulder, Colo.: Westview Press, 1989), 125, 143. See also Michael L. Mezey, "The Legislature, the Executive, and Public Policy: The Futile Quest for Congressional Power," chap. 6 of this volume.
22. James Sundquist, *Constitutional Reform and Effective Government* (Washington, D.C.: Brookings Institution, 1986), 75.
23. Sundquist, "Needed: A Political Theory," 627.
24. *Roll Call,* April 19, 1984, quoted in Sundquist, *Constitutional Reform,* 4.
25. See Timothy J. Conlan, Margaret T. Wrightson, and David R. Beam, *Taxing Choices: The Politics of Tax Reform* (Washington, D.C.: CQ Press, 1990), 237. They also cite scholars who see this useful form of party competition in environmental policy. See E. Donald Elliot, Bruce A. Ackerman, and John C. Millian, "Toward a Theory of Statutory Evolution: The Federalization of Environmental Law," *Journal of Law, Economics, and Organization* 2 (Fall 1985): 313-340.
26. David Mayhew, "Does It Make a Difference Whether Party Control of the American National Government Is Unified or Divided?" (Paper presented at the annual meeting of the American Political Science Association, Atlanta, Ga., September 1989), 5.

27. Ibid., 63, 64, 71.
28. Ibid., 75.
29. Ibid., 85, 122, 134.
30. Roger Porter, "The President, Congress, and Trade Policy," *Congress and the Presidency* 15 (Autumn 1988): 167-168.
31. Ibid., 165-184.
32. Mayhew, "Does It Make a Difference?" 32.
33. Moe, "Politicized Presidency," 269.
34. Arthur M. Schlesinger, Jr., "After the Imperial Presidency," in *The Cycles of American History* (Boston: Houghton Mifflin, 1986), 277-336.
35. Sundquist, "Needed: A Political Theory," 623-624.
36. Sundquist, *Constitutional Reform*, 240-241.
37. Robinson, *Reforming American Government*, xi-xii.
38. Sundquist, "Needed: A Political Theory," 631.
39. Quoted in Charles O. Jones, "Congress and the Constitutional Balance of Power," in *Congressional Politics*, ed. Christopher Deering (Chicago: Dorsey Press, 1989), 322.
40. Sundquist, *Decline and Resurgence of Congress*, 457.
41. Morris Fiorina, *Congress: Keystone of the Washington Establishment*, 2d ed. (New Haven, Conn.: Yale University Press, 1989), 76.
42. See Mezey, "The Legislature, the Executive, and Public Policy," chap. 6 of this volume. For a critique of Mezey, see Joseph Cooper, "Assessing Legislative Performance: A Reply to the Critics of Congress," *Congress and the Presidency* 13 (Spring 1986): 21-40. See also Mezey, *Congress, the President, and Public Policy.*
43. L. Gordon Crovitz and Jeremy A. Rabkin, eds., *The Fettered Presidency: Legal Constraints on the Executive Branch* (Washington, D.C.: American Enterprise Institute, 1989); and Gordon S. Jones and John A. Marini, *The Imperial Congress* (New York: Pharos Books, 1988).
44. Robert H. Bork, "Foreword," in *Fettered Presidency*, ix.
45. Jeane Kirkpatrick, "The Coup Game," *Washington Post*, October 16, 1989, A19.
46. Quoted by Norman Ornstein, "The Blame Game: Look Who's Bashing America Now," *Washington Post*, July 26, 1989, B1.
47. Quoted by E. J. Dionne, Jr., "Politics," *New York Times*, May 23, 1989.
48. Newt Gingrich, "Foreword," in *Imperial Congress*, ix-x.
49. Bork, "Foreword," in *Fettered Presidency*, xiv.
50. Quoted by Michael Oreskes, "An 'Imperial Congress' in Conservatives' Sights," *New York Times*, May 27, 1989, B13.
51. See James P. Pfiffner, *The Strategic Presidency* (Pacific Grove, Calif.: Brooks/Cole, 1988), chaps. 6 and 7; and James P. Pfiffner, "The President's Legislative Agenda," *The Annals of the American Academy of Political and Social Science* 499 (September 1988): 32-35.
52. Roger H. Davidson and Walter J. Oleszek, *Congress and Its Members*, 3d ed. (Washington, D.C.: CQ Press, 1990), 404.
53. The usefulness of the device was vividly illustrated in 1987, when James

C. Miller III, director of the Office of Management and Budget, objected to a provision in the foreign assistance appropriations bill that disallowed the transfer of funds among accounts without written permission from the Appropriations Committee. Miller said that the provision violated the constitutional principles established in *Chadha*. The alternative, of course, was to require OMB to go through the full legislative process whenever it wanted to shift appropriated funds among accounts. When this was pointed out, Miller withdrew his objection and the language remained. See Louis Fisher, "Micromanagement by Congress: Reality and Myth," in *Fettered Presidency*, 146-149; and Louis Fisher, "Congress as Micromanager of the Executive Branch," in *The Managerial Presidency*, ed. James P. Pfiffner (Pacific Grove, Calif.: Brooks/Cole, 1990).

54. President Bush and Congress were able to set aside the most contentious foreign policy issue of the 1980s when they agreed to provide the Nicaraguan contras with humanitarian aid for a fixed period of time, with the provision that after November 1989 four committee chairs in Congress would have to agree that the aid was indeed humanitarian in order for the aid to continue into 1990. As the president's counselor, C. Boyden Gray, pointed out, this was in effect a legislative veto, even if it was not written into the legislation. Instead of the informal legislative veto agreement, the administration could have returned to Congress to seek passage of a new piece of legislation, but it clearly preferred to accept the compromise. As Louis Fisher has observed, these provisions "are not legal in effect. They are, however, in effect legal." Fisher, "Micromanagement," 148.

55. See the discussion of this kind of option by Robert Katzman in "War Powers: Toward a New Accommodation," in *A Question of Balance*, ed. Thomas E. Mann (Washington, D.C.: Brookings Institution, 1990), 67.

56. Quoted in Sundquist, *Decline and Resurgence of Congress*, 461.

57. Quoted in Hedrick Smith, *The Power Game: How Washington Works* (New York: Random House, 1988), 726.

4. THE PRESIDENCY AND
THREE ERAS OF THE MODERN CONGRESS

Roger H. Davidson

The legislative workload is a major determinant of the structure and substance of legislative-executive relations. The Constitution and the political history of the United States make this clear. Articles I and II, after all, are largely devoted to the interleaved lawmaking responsibilities of the two branches—from initiation ("He [the president] shall from time to time . . . recommend to their [Congress's] consideration such measures as he shall judge necessary and expedient") to implementation ("He shall take care that the laws be faithfully executed"). Beginning with George Washington, activist presidents have always inserted themselves into the legislative process. Franklin D. Roosevelt and his successors institutionalized "the legislative presidency": today's chief executives are expected to present Congress with their legislative agendas and to provide their allies on Capitol Hill with guidance and leadership.

As for Congress, one attribute sets it apart from virtually all of the world's other national assemblies: it is a working body that writes, processes, and refines its own products, relying to a large degree on "in-house" resources. Until quite recently scholars paid scant attention to legislative business as a research topic. Yet Congress's agenda and workload shape not only the behavior and operations of the Senate and House of Representatives but also the two chambers' relationships with the executive branch. What is more, the legislative workload reminds us of "what Congress actually does and how it does it, with all its duties and all its occupations, with all its devices of management and resources of power." [1]

Today both the president and Congress confront a number and variety of demands unmatched in all but the most turbulent years of the past. "What is equally true, as the history of [Congress] readily demonstrates, is that the volume of output demands, as well as the degree of their complexity, uniformity, and volatility, vary greatly over time." [2] Aggregate legislative statistics from the post-World War II period show how variable these workload measures can be.

Legislative activity is, of course, only one aspect of interactions between presidents and Congresses. The number of executive communications to Congress, for example, has risen impressively over the past two generations. There are now almost as many executive communications referred to congressional committees as legislative proposals similarly referred. Making federal appointments is another legislative-executive interaction that has become ever more burdensome at both ends of Pennsylvania Avenue. Implementation and oversight, not to mention administrative and judicial rulemaking, are functions that also repeatedly propel the president and Congress into joint action. Given the breadth and reach of modern government, oversight remains burdensome even when few new statutes are produced. Yet it bears a close relationship to lawmaking: it flows from previously enacted statutes and it influences how these statutes are implemented and revised.

Anyone using legislative statistics should be aware of their limits.[3] Definitions of terms are neither simple nor self-evident. Data collection, moreover, requires making decisions, sometimes arbitrary, on methods to be followed—what sources to rely on, what dates to use as benchmarks, and so forth. If legislative statistics are interpreted as indicators of demands or workloads, extra caution must be exercised. A shift in numbers may indicate changing demands; alternatively, it may signify innovative management of those demands by politicians. Finally, data convey only a partial picture of the scope and volume of legislative activity. Despite these caveats, a careful study of trends can reveal a great deal about contemporary relations between the branches of government.[4]

Overall Legislative Trends

One workload indicator is the number of bills and resolutions introduced in Congress. In both chambers bill introduction showed long-term growth from the mid-1940s until the late 1960s, followed by gradual and then precipitous decline. A portion of the recent decline of introduced House bills and resolutions can be traced to changes in cosponsorship rules in 1967 and again in 1978. The general pattern in the House and Senate, however, is similar: gradual buildup, then a period of extraordinary legislative activity in the 1960s and early 1970s followed by a rather sudden and striking contraction.

Bill introduction and sponsorship vary widely among individual senators and representatives. Some lawmakers are inveterate sponsors of bills and resolutions; others shy away from sponsoring measures. From 1947 to 1949 (80th Congress), House members on average authored eighteen bills or resolutions compared with thirty-three for senators. In the late 1960s figures peaked at about fifty measures per representative and forty-nine measures per senator. Then in the 1970s and especially in the 1980s, the figures plummeted. Today's lawmakers introduce fewer measures than at the beginning of the period—about thirty per senator and sixteen per representative.

Legislators today are doubly disadvantaged: not only do they introduce fewer bills and resolutions, but their proposals are less likely to be approved by the full chamber. A Senate bill or resolution introduced in the immediate postwar years had better than an even chance of passage; the odds are now about one in four.[5] A House bill or resolution used to have a 25 percent chance of passage; today the odds are half that. This trend, as will be seen, stems in large part from the introduction of fewer administrative or noncontroversial measures.

Overall workload levels reverberate, to a greater or lesser degree, in the committee rooms of the two houses. To be sure, every committee is unique, as Richard F. Fenno, Jr., reminds us; one committee's jurisdiction may soar while other panels are looking for work.[6] Yet most committees conform more or less to the overall workload pattern I have sketched, in terms of bills and resolutions referred to them.[7] In the boom years of the 1970s, activity levels reached modern-day peaks. After about 1978 committee workload indicators declined markedly. From 1985 to 1987 (99th Congress), for example, the number of measures referred to House committees was only one-third what it had been a decade earlier. In the Senate, referrals to committees were down 30 percent.

Five of the House committees studied by Fenno in the early 1970s were reexamined in three selected Congresses: the prereform 90th (1967-1969), the reform 94th (1975-1977), and the postreform 98th (1983-1985).[8] Committee activity and workload soared in the 1970s, as a full policy agenda found a newly decentralized power structure that offered multiple channels for initiative and action. In the mid-1970s the number of measures referred to the committees rose more than 20 percent, despite the fact that House rules by this time permitted cosponsorship of measures. The five committees scheduled more than twice as many hearing days as they had a decade earlier. By the mid-1980s the trend was reversed: referrals were cut almost in half, while days of hearings were down about one-third.

One panel that compiled extensive records throughout this period was the House Committee on Energy and Commerce (until 1981, the Committee on Interstate and Foreign Commerce). Though by no means an "average" committee (if such a thing exists), Energy and Commerce is nonetheless a good barometer of workload trends. The panel is a major player in domestic policy making: its jurisdiction, expansive and jealously guarded by its chairman and staff, brings it nearly a tenth of all measures referred to House committees. Incoming demands—for example, bills referred and issues covered—peaked in the 93d Congress (1973-1975); committee activity—for example, days of hearings, hours of sitting, and pages of testimony—peaked later in the decade.[9] Although the committee is regarded as one of the most aggressive and active on Capitol Hill, it spent 40 percent fewer hours in hearings in the 98th Congress than in the 95th, and 45 percent fewer hours in mark-up sessions. Its activity record, in short, parallels the overall cyclical pattern I have outlined.

Recorded votes on the House and Senate floor underscore these shifts in legislative activity. The numbers of recorded votes remained quite low in the 1940s and 1950s, accelerated in the 1960s, and then exploded in the 1970s.[10] The rise in floor activity is linked directly to changes in rules and procedures that made it easier for members to offer floor amendments and to gain recorded votes. This shifted power perceptibly from the committee rooms to the chambers themselves.[11] In postreform Congresses, the number of recorded votes has stabilized at about eight hundred per chamber, slightly more than half the rate for the peak Congresses of the 1970s.

Finally, consider the end product of lawmaking: bills and resolutions that survive the labyrinthine legislative process to become law. Working in tandem, Congress and the executive branch strictly regulate the flow of legislative outputs. Of the nearly ten thousand bills and resolutions introduced in the House and Senate in a given Congress, only about 6 percent find their way into the statute books. The size and shape of the legislative product are a function not only of political support or opposition but also of changing rules specifying which matters must be resolved by statute and which must be handled by other means.

Overall legislative output figures—measures passed by the two chambers, measures signed into law—are quite different from the input and activity figures described thus far. There was no great upsurge during the activist era of the 1960s and 1970s; nor has there been a steep decline in more recent Congresses. The number of public bills enacted began at a high level after World War II, peaking in the mid-1950s.[12] Levels have descended gradually since then. The number of private bills enacted has slowed to a trickle. In the early postwar period, private bills typically equaled or exceeded public laws in number; today they are rare.

Legislative output is shaped by periodic decisions to include or exclude matters from legislative consideration. The burgeoning legislative agenda produced by the Great Depression and World War II, for example, led to demands for simplification and streamlining. As George

B. Galloway, staff director of the 1945-1946 Committee on the Organization of Congress, described the legislative branch predicament:

> Still functioning for the most part with the machinery and facilities inherited from the simpler days of the mauve decade, its calendars and committees became increasingly congested, its councils confused, and its members bewildered and harassed by multiplying technical problems and local pressures.[13]

Not surprisingly, one of the objectives of the 1946 Legislative Reorganization Act was to trim and systematize the legislative agenda. Minor or administrative questions were delegated to administrative agencies or tribunals.

The 1946 act's goal of shrinking the legislative workload, though initially frustrated, eventually came to pass. The most dramatic development was the long-term decline of private bills—mostly private immigration and claims cases. This trend remained relatively steady over the past forty years.

Categories of administrative matters have also gradually been jettisoned. More than half of all public laws produced in the late 1940s and 1950s addressed administrative matters rather than general policy questions.[14] Examples include Native American tribal claims settlements, land conveyances, interstate compacts, legislative housekeeping matters, pay adjustments, and income disbursements. Less than 40 percent of the laws concerned major or general policy decisions—appropriations, authorizations, or even substantive amendments to authorizations. Fewer than one of twenty laws were commemorative—that is, established commemorative days, weeks, or months; authorized commemorative stamps, medals, or coins; or named federal buildings or other facilities. During the 1960s the proportions of public laws were roughly as follows: substantive, 45 percent; administrative, 40 percent; commemorative, 5 to 8 percent. By 1977-1978 nearly three-quarters of all public laws were substantive, with administrative and commemorative measures accounting for 15 percent and 10 percent, respectively.

The most dramatic shift in the 1980s was the growth of commemoratives at the expense of substantive laws. Commemoratives came to represent nearly half of all statutes produced in a given Congress, whereas substantive laws accounted for about 30 percent and administrative matters 20 percent. The shrinkage in the volume of substantive legislation was no doubt related to the increasingly common stratagem of packaging legislative proposals into massive measures—for example, continuing resolutions, reconciliation bills, tax reform measures, and broad-scale reauthorizations. This is attested by the steady growth in the length of public statutes, despite the upsurge in brief commemorative measures. In the late 1960s more than two-thirds of all public laws took up no more than a single page; in the 1980s fewer than half of all laws were that brief.[15] And the proportion of truly long enactments—twenty-one pages or more—grew threefold from the late 1960s to the mid-1980s. Legalistic verbosity is only partly to blame; legislative packaging is also at work.

These statistical trends, especially the activity and workload figures, lend strong support to the thesis that contemporary lawmaking has passed through three distinct stages or eras. The first was a relatively static era dominated by a bipartisan conservative coalition (roughly 1937-1964); the second was an era of reform and liberal activism (1965-1978); and the third was an era of contraction, of fiscal restraint and stalemate (1979 to the present). Legislative-executive relations were likely to follow different patterns in each of these three periods.

Like any artifacts of historical categorization, these three eras are bound to arouse debate over their precise definitions and boundaries, and perhaps even over their validity or utility in illuminating legislative-executive relations. Historical developments, after all, are continuous and multifaceted, rarely yielding unambiguous boundaries. Although my primary data sets begin in 1947, I have extended the first era back to the second Roosevelt administration by relying on fragmentary statistical indicators and a wealth of qualitative data. The boundaries of the second, reformist, era are especially problematic: Reformist skirmishes broke out over a period of years starting in the late 1950s; by the time the climax occurred in 1974-1975, the era's energy was already waning. The period of the 1980s, too, eludes definition because of its very nearness.

Despite these caveats, it is intriguing how closely these three eras coincide with changing journalistic and scholarly understandings of the legislative process. The "textbook" account of Congress that emerged from the first era was well researched and descriptively persuasive; the same can be said for the reform era, which still dominates journalistic and textbook treatments of the subject.[16] There has even emerged a measure of scholarly consensus on the nature and characteristics of the recent postreform era. Fashionable theoretical paradigms have shifted roughly in tandem with changing legislative characteristics. Explaining these three eras, then, promises to illuminate our understanding of policy making and presidential-congressional relations.

The Era of the Strong Committee Chairmen
(1937-1964)

In the period of strong committee chairmen, which lasted roughly from the second Roosevelt administration through the mid-1960s,

Congress was dominated by an oligarchy of senior leaders, sometimes called "the barons" or "the old bulls." Whichever party was in power, congressional leaders overrepresented safe one-party regions (the Democratic rural South, the Republican rural Northeast and Midwest) and reflected the limited legislative agenda of the bipartisan conservative coalition that controlled so much domestic policy making. This created a hostile environment for activist presidents and their ambitious legislative agendas. " 'For God's sake,' a congressional spokesman telephoned the White House in April 1938, 'don't send us any more controversial legislation!' " James MacGregor Burns recounted this anecdote from Franklin Roosevelt's second term and summed up legislative-executive relations as "deadlock on the Potomac." [17]

Harry Truman's clashes with Congress began early and continued throughout his administration. "Except for the modified Employment Act of 1946," relates Robert Donovan, "the [Democratic] Seventy-ninth Congress had squelched practically every piece of social and economic legislation Truman had requested." [18] Truman's other Congresses were equally frustrating, though in different ways. The Republican 80th Congress "gave [Truman] his most enduring image. Facing an opposition-controlled legislative body almost certain to reject any domestic program he proposed, he adopted the role of an oppositionist." [19]

Truman campaigned successfully in 1948 by excoriating the "awful, do-nothing 80th Congress." Yet the Democratic 81st Congress rejected virtually all his Fair Deal initiatives, and the 82d, marked by depleted Democratic majorities and the Korean War stalemate, was even more hostile to new domestic legislation.

The 1950s were years of outward quiescence accompanied by underlying, yet accelerating, demands for action and innovation. President Dwight D. Eisenhower, whose legislative objectives were far more modest than Truman's, was increasingly placed in the position of offering scaled-down alternatives to programs launched on Capitol Hill by coalitions of activist Democrats and moderate Republicans.

The legislative workload throughout this era was, accordingly, relatively stable and manageable from year to year. A large proportion of the bills and resolutions were routine and concerned matters not yet delegated to the executive branch for resolution—for example, immigration cases, land claims, and private legislation. Demands were building, however, for new legislation to address civil rights and other concerns of urban and suburban voters. The important committees (the taxing and spending panels plus House Rules) were cohesive groups—"corporate," to use Fenno's term—with firm leadership and rigorous internal norms of behavior.[20] They kept a tight lid on new legislation, especially in fiscal affairs. The appropriations committees in particular served as guardians of the Treasury, holding in check the more rapacious inclinations of the program-oriented authorizing panels.

Few members of today's Congress participated in that bygone congressional era. As the decade of the 1980s ended, no more than two dozen representatives and only half a dozen senators had been in office during that time. The reminiscences of this remnant often betray bitterness at how they were initially treated by the barons. As members' memories of this era fade, however, there survive many colorful anecdotes and stories, some of them no doubt apocryphal, about the exploits and foibles of the old bulls—among them Speaker Sam Rayburn, D-Texas; Ways and Means Chairman Wilbur Mills, D-Ark.; Senate Minority Leader Everett M. Dirksen, R-Ill.; and, most of all, Senate Majority Leader Lyndon B. Johnson, D-Texas.

Journalists and political scientists closely studied this era of the strong committee chairmen. Borrowing research concepts and techniques from sociology and anthropology, behaviorally trained political scientists, in particular, illuminated Congress's workings through close personal observation, interviews, and statistical analysis. The Senate of this era was admiringly described by journalist William S. White and systematically analyzed by political scientist Donald R. Matthews.[21] Richard F. Fenno, Jr., produced powerful, detailed accounts of committee operations and the budgetary process.[22] To do justice to the many scholars who examined the workings of the postwar Congress would require a lengthy listing of names and citations.

The picture of the postwar Congress that emerged from the behaviorists' assault upon Capitol Hill was so persuasive that one scholar labeled it "the textbook Congress." [23] According to the leading intellectual framework, the institution was viewed as an interlocking pattern of personal relationships in which structure and function worked in rough equilibrium. Ironically, by the time observers got around to completing this coherent picture of a tight, closed, internally coherent congressional world, that world was already being turned upside down. Pressures for change mounted, heralding a prolonged period of reformist politics.

The Reform Era (1965-1978)

The cozy domains of the barons were eventually pulled apart by what journalist Hedrick Smith called a "power earthquake." [24] The metaphor is attractive but imprecise. Although many observers (Smith included) associate the changes with the post-Watergate "class of 1974" and the subsequent overthrow of three House committee chairmen, these events signaled the climax rather than the zenith of the era of legislative activism and procedural reforms. It would require a sophisticated understanding of plate tectonics to provide a more accurate geophysical metaphor for these developments.

The boundaries of the reform era, like those of the other eras, are somewhat imprecise. The process of change began in earnest after the 1958 elections, when the Democrats enlarged their ranks by sixteen senators and fifty-one representatives, many of them urban and suburban liberals. The elections had an immediate effect in both chambers. Senate Majority Leader Johnson's autocratic rule softened perceptibly; in the House a small band of liberal activists formally launched the Democratic Study Group, which subsequently spearheaded the efforts for procedural reforms. Two years later Johnson relinquished the Senate majority leadership to the mild-mannered, liberal Mike Mansfield, D-Mont., while Speaker Rayburn struggled to break the conservatives' control of the powerful Rules Committee. The reform era approached its climax in the mid-1970s with successive waves of changes in committee and floor procedures and, in 1975, the ouster of three of the barons from their committee chairmanships.

One underlying cause of the upheaval was the policy demands of urban and suburban voting blocs as well as minority groups—demands heeded by activist presidents.[25] The spirit of the era was reflected in the popular "movements" that came to prominence: civil rights, environmentalism, consumerism, and opposition to the Vietnam War. Longer range causes of reform included reapportionment and redistricting, widened citizen participation, social upheaval, and technological innovations in transportation and communications.

The resulting changes pointed Congress in the direction of a more open and participatory legislative process: greater leverage for individual lawmakers and dispersion of influence among and within the committees. More leaders existed than ever before, and more influence could be exerted by nonleaders. More staff aides were on hand to extend the legislative reach of even the most junior members.

Individual senators and representatives, while enjoying their enhanced legislative involvement, were obliged to devote increasing attention to their constituents back home. No longer was frantic constituency outreach confined to a few senators from large states and a few representatives from swing districts; it was practiced by all members (or their staffs), in order to purchase electoral security in an age of dwindling party support. In their home styles, members tended to exchange the role of workhorse, or legislative specialist, for that of showhorse, becoming legislative generalists and credit seekers. The reforms were propelled by, and in turn helped to facilitate, an ambitious and expansionary presidential agenda, as the themes "the

New Frontier" and "the Great Society" suggest. This era witnessed a host of landmark enactments in civil rights, education, medical insurance, employment and training, science and space, consumer protection, and the environment, not to mention five new cabinet departments and four constitutional amendments. Legislative activity soared by whatever measure one chooses to apply—bills introduced, hearings, reports, hours in session, floor amendments, recorded floor votes, and measures passed.[26] The processing of freestanding bills and resolutions became the centerpiece of committee and subcommittee work.

Much of the decentralization of the 1960s and 1970s was accompanied by a weakening of the appropriations committees' grip over spending and by a strengthening of the power of the authorizing committees (for example, Agriculture, Banking, Commerce) to influence federal spending practices. The authorizing committees made ingenious use of "backdoor spending" provisions—such as contract authority, budget authority, direct Treasury borrowing, and especially entitlements—to strip the appropriations panels of much of their former fiscal guardianship role.[27] According to John Ellwood, three-quarters of the domestic spending growth between 1970 and 1983 occurred in budget accounts lying outside annual appropriations—that is, beyond the appropriations committees' reach.[28]

The procedural autonomy of another prereform power center, the House Ways and Means Committee, was not breached until nearly the close of the reform period. "During the congressional revolution of the 1970s," wrote Abner Mikva and Patti Saris, "the Ways and Means Committee became a 'bastille' that symbolized the inequities of the old order." [29] The panel's independence was reduced not only by chamberwide reforms (caucus ratification of committee chairmanships, modified or open rules for floor deliberation, open committee meetings) but also by provisions aimed explicitly at the committee (enlargement of the committee, transfer of Democratic committee assignments to the Steering and Policy Committee, jurisdictional encroachments, and, finally, mandated subcommittees). By this time Chairman Mills's House career was drawing to a close, and he was followed by far weaker leaders.

Like the earlier period, this reform era was well documented by journalists and scholars.[30] The most popular scholarly paradigm of the era was drawn from economics, and it conveyed the decentralization and fragmentation of the period.[31] Lawmakers are viewed not as role players in a complex system of interactions in equilibrium but as individual entrepreneurs in a vast open marketplace that rewards self-interested competitiveness with little or no regard for the welfare of the whole.

The Postreform Era (1979-)

During the 1980s Congress again faced an environment that departed in significant ways from what had gone before. Although the shift is popularly associated with the Reagan administration, it was under way by 1979-1981 (the 96th Congress).

The advent of what economist Lester Thurow called the "zero-sum society" no doubt lay at the root of the changed political atmosphere.[32] The economy no longer seemed to support the federal government's array of services, many of them enacted during the reform period. The sluggish economy was marked by "stagflation," a coexistence of high inflation and high unemployment. Meanwhile, the government's costly and relatively impervious system of entitlements, coupled with President Reagan's 1981 scheme of tax cuts and program reallocations, turned the "fiscal dividends" of the postwar era into "structural deficits."

Intellectual fashions and political realities repudiated the notion that government could solve all manner of economic and social ills. Disenchantment with the results of government programs, many of which had been shamelessly oversold to glean support for their enactment, led to widespread demands for a statutory cease-fire: disinvestment, deregulation, and privatization. At the same time, "bracket creep" raised the marginal and real tax rates of millions of citizens and spurred a series of tax revolts that swept through the states to Washington.

In the 1980s the president and Congress were fixated on resolving fiscal and revenue issues, rather than on designing new programs or establishing new agencies in response to constituent preferences or national needs. In the domestic realm, the emphasis was on reviewing, adjusting, refining, or cutting back existing programs. "There's not a whole lot of money for any kind of new programs," remarked Sen. Thad Cochran, R-Miss., "so we're holding oversight hearings on old programs ... which may not be all that bad an idea." [33] Accordingly, fewer individual members were tempted to put forward their ideas as freestanding bills or resolutions. Such new ideas as were salable were more likely to be contained in amendments to large-scale legislative vehicles: reauthorizations, continuing appropriations, and debt limit or reconciliation bills.

The environment of constraint in the 1980s reversed the previous era's liberal activism. Government revenues were curtailed by lagging economic productivity, exaggerated after 1981 by tax cuts, program reallocations, and soaring deficits. Few new programs were launched, and few domestic programs were awarded additional funding. Although the public continued to expect Congress to take action to solve problems, there was equal sentiment for cutting back "big government" and reducing public sector deficits. Public faith in government capacity to solve problems plummeted in the wake of criticisms of waste and ineffectiveness of government programs.

Economists, true to form, disagreed widely on the seriousness of the deficit. Politicians, for their part, resorted to creative bookkeeping to give the appearance of balancing revenues and outlays and trimming the deficit as required by the 1985 Gramm-Rudman-Hollings law. For some politicians, the deficit problem even seemed advantageous. Conservatives seized upon revenue shortfalls as a way of controlling demands for new programs and new spending. Liberals blamed the situation on the failures of the Reagan and Bush administrations.

When all is said and done, however, the economic predicament severely curtailed legislative productivity. "Rarely in peacetime has a single issue dominated politics here the way the budget deficit is doing now," observed a *New York Times* correspondent. "The most important legislative measures of the year—tax cuts, expansion of child-care benefits, changes in Medicare and Medicaid and many others—are paralyzed." [34] In some cases zero-sum politics was practiced literally, as members bartered such programs as congressional mailing costs for pressing demands for spending on eastern Europe or the war on drugs. Senate Majority Leader George J. Mitchell, D-Maine, characterized the deficit dilemma as "the whale in the bathtub that leaves no room for anything else." [35]

The results of "cutback politics" characterize the postreform Congress in at least six ways. First, fewer bills are sponsored by individual senators and representatives. Second, key policy decisions are packaged into huge "megabills," enabling lawmakers to gain support for provisions that would be unlikely to pass as freestanding measures. Third, lawmakers employ techniques of "blame avoidance"—for example, in closing military bases—to protect themselves from the adverse effects of cutback politics. Fourth, more noncontroversial "commemorative" resolutions are passed—nearly half of all laws produced by recent Congresses. Fifth, party-line voting on Capitol Hill, driven by budgetary concerns, has soared to modern-day highs. Finally, leadership in the House and Senate is markedly stronger now than at any time since 1910. Today's leaders benefit not only from powers conferred by reform-era innovations of the 1960s and 1970s; they also respond to widespread expectations that they are the only people who can, and should, untangle jurisdictional overlaps and orchestrate the legislative schedule.

The House Ways and Means Committee mirrors the shifts of the postreform era in Congress as a whole. Randall Strahan has described the changed agenda that the committee faced after 1978. Following the reform-era assaults on the committee and hiatus in leadership, Chairman Dan Rostenkowski, D-Ill., set about systematically to strengthen the panel's position.[36] According to Allen Schick, the chairman's efforts succeeded in the main: "Ways and Means has regained its status and effectiveness by resorting to a simple formula that worked for it in the past: the committee is successful when it controls the House and when the chairman controls the committee." [37]

The Committee's exhaustive bicentennial history explains that the chairman "centralized control over staff and substantially diminished the autonomy of subcommittee chairs." [38] Rostenkowski's personal leverage was enhanced by his influence over Democratic assignments to the panel as well as his selective use of sanctions. To promote cohesiveness, he scheduled more closed meetings and arranged for weekend retreats and seminars to discuss policy questions.[39] The panel's internal politics settled somewhere between the extremes of bipartisan consensus of the prereform Mills era and the reform period's divisive partisanship.[40]

Confronted by a lagging economy, divided government, and the public's doubts about the efficacy of public programs, the president and Congress in the postreform era changed the way they approached the legislative workload. Presidents trimmed their agendas and hampered congressional initiatives through a combination of curtailed revenue and veto threats. Congress, for its part, moved away from the decentralized system established during the 1960s and 1970s to facilitate that era's frenetic legislative activity. A knowledgeable British scholar put it this way: "There can be little doubt that the Congress of the mid-1980s differed from that of the late 1970s in terms of its emphasis on parliamentary reform, legislative activity, constituency attentiveness and distribution of power." In sum, "the reform orientation of the New [or reform-era] Congress [was] left far behind." [41]

Consider the kinds of institutional innovations made by the postreform Congress. Beginning in the late 1970s, Congress confronted an altered set of demands for legislative action. The political agenda shrank, narrowing the prospects for new programs or spending priorities. While many of the structural innovations of the earlier reform era remained intact, procedures were adjusted to cope with the altered environment. Committee and floor agendas contracted. Important decisions were more apt to be folded into lengthy omnibus vehicles, often processed by more than one committee and typically superintended by party leaders. Members and committees explored new categories of policy making, or rather they exploited existing categories—for example, oversight, commemoratives, indexing, and symbolic measures—that were well suited to the immediate policy environment.

Conclusion

This foray into the thicket of legislative activity and productivity reveals two general truths about modern-day politics and policy making. First, legislative productivity does not necessarily coincide with the tenure of individual presidencies. Second, legislative productivity is less determined by party control of government than many scholars contend.

Presidencies and Legislative Productivity

The conservative coalition era outlasted several presidents of widely varying goals and skills. Roosevelt failed after 1936 to keep Capitol Hill safe for New Deal initiatives and, after 1940, was preoccupied with the war effort. Truman repeatedly broke his lance in efforts to push legislation through conservative Congresses—most memorably in housing, labor-management relations, civil rights, and medical care. In the 1950s Eisenhower's modest, moderately right-of-center legislative instincts fit in with the obstructionism of the conservative coalition that ruled Capitol Hill. More aggressive than Eisenhower, Kennedy enjoyed considerable legislative success at a time when the old order in Congress was crumbling.

The reformist era, with its huge working majority of liberals in both chambers of Congress, spanned the presidencies of Lyndon Johnson, Richard Nixon, Gerald Ford, and (in part) Jimmy Carter. Johnson's presidency was perhaps the most productive in history, legislatively speaking. Yet the flow of legislation hardly abated during the presidencies of Nixon and Ford. A recitation of legislative high points from the Nixon years suggests that the mutual hostility between the Republican president and the Democratic Congress did not stand in the way of significant legislative enactments. These laws included a comprehensive tax code revision, the National Environmental Policy Act of 1969, major air and water pollution control measures, endangered species protection, a comprehensive organized crime bill, postal reorganization, urban mass transit and rail reorganization plans, the Occupational Safety and Health Act of 1970 (OSHA), the Consumer Product Safety Act, the Comprehensive Employment and Training Act (CETA), the Federal Election Campaign Act, coastal zone management, the trans-Alaska pipeline, the War Powers Resolution of 1973, and the Congressional Budget and Impoundment Control Act of 1974—not to mention the Twenty-Sixth Amendment giving eighteen-year-olds the right to vote and the proposed twenty-seventh amendment on equal rights for women.

The liberal juggernaut continued for at least two reasons. First, Nixon saw his primary mission to be in foreign affairs and diplomacy, leaving his aides in the domestic departments relatively free to negotiate as best they could with Capitol Hill majorities. Second, the Nixon and Ford Congresses attempted extraordinarily high numbers of veto overrides, often succeeding in their efforts.[42] Nixon may have been a conservative president, but the legislative record of his administration is expansive and liberal. It bears careful, dispassionate reexamination by historians and political scientists.

The most recent legislative era spans part or all of the presidencies of Jimmy Carter, Ronald Reagan, and George Bush. The advent of zero-sum, stalemate politics is popularly associated with Reagan, who took office in 1980, pledging to cut taxes, domestic aid, and welfare programs. To be sure, his election was interpreted at the time as a sea change in American politics; some of Reagan's early initiatives— especially the 1981 revenue cuts and his repeated threats to veto new domestic spending or taxes—helped to curtail the legislative agenda. A deteriorating economy and the public's disenchantment with big government, however, had already caused President Carter to begin to limit his legislative agenda.[43] By the 96th Congress (1979-1981) the altered environment had led to a decline in legislative workload. Had Carter been reelected in 1980, it is likely that he, and Congress, would have traveled down the road toward zero-sum politics.

Party Control and Legislative Productivity

Party control determines policy outputs. No proposition is more widely accepted among scholars and other observers. Many would further contend that "things go better" when the same party controls both the executive and legislative branches and that divided government is a prescription for confusion, delay, and deadlock. Policy outputs are, to be sure, affected by party control. Certainly presidents are more apt to achieve their legislative goals if their partisans comfortably control both chambers.

Equally to the point, shifts in Capitol Hill partisan ratios can yield meaningful changes in policy outputs, quite apart from any questions of party control or alignment. The recession-driven influx of Democrats in 1959-1960, the Johnson landslide class of 1964, the Watergate class of 1974, and the GOP shift of 1981-1983 involved important changes in partisan strength on Capitol Hill that led in turn to policy redirections and procedural innovations. These changes apparently went beyond underlying changes in attitudes or voting habits within the electorate as a whole, not to mention any long-term partisan realignment.

Yet party control is an incomplete guide to legislative activity and productivity. The administrations of Roosevelt, Truman, and Carter testify to the fact that party control of both branches is no guarantee of legislative productivity. By the same token, the Nixon-Ford period and the first year of the Reagan administration saw productivity far beyond what would be expected from divided government.

Legislative activity and workload, in short, fit imperfectly with conventional political thinking that stresses presidential leadership or the locus of party control of the two branches. The record of the past two generations casts doubt on the assumptions that unified party control raises legislative productivity and that divided government leads to stalemate.

Notes

1. Woodrow Wilson, *Congressional Government* (1885; reprint, Baltimore: Johns Hopkins University Press, 1981), 56.
2. Joseph Cooper, "Organization and Innovation in the House of Representatives," in *The House at Work*, ed. Joseph Cooper and G. Calvin Mackenzie (Austin: University of Texas Press, 1980), 332.
3. Roger H. Davidson, "The Legislative Work of Congress" (Paper presented at the annual meeting of the American Political Science Association, Washington, D.C., August 28-31, 1986), 5-6.
4. This essay rests on statistical data compiled by the author, his former colleagues at the Congressional Research Service, and other investigators. Although no tables or charts are presented here, interested readers are invited to consult original sources such as Roger H. Davidson, "Congressional Committees as Moving Targets," *Legislative Studies Quarterly* 11 (February 1986): 19-33; Davidson, "The Legislative Work of Congress"; Roger H. Davidson and Carol Hardy, "Indicators of Senate Activity and Workload," Congressional Research Service Report 87-497S, June 8, 1987; Roger H. Davidson and Carol Hardy, "Indicators of House of Representatives Activity and Workload," Congressional Research Service Report 87-136S, June 8, 1987; and Norman J. Ornstein, Thomas E. Mann, and Michael J. Malbin, *Vital Statistics on Congress, 1989-1990* (Washington, D.C.: CQ Press, 1990).
5. Davidson and Hardy, "Indicators of Senate Activity," 31.
6. Richard F. Fenno, Jr., *Congressmen in Committees* (Boston: Little, Brown, 1973), 280.
7. Davidson and Hardy, "Indicators of Senate Activity"; and Davidson and Hardy, "Indicators of House Activity."
8. Davidson, "Congressional Committees as Moving Targets," 28-29.
9. House Committee on Energy and Commerce, *Report of the Committee on Energy and Commerce*, H. Rept. 99-512, 99th Cong., 2d sess., April 8,

1986, 286.

10. Ornstein, Mann, and Malbin, *Vital Statistics,* 150-151, 158.

11. Steven S. Smith, *Call to Order: Floor Politics in the House and Senate* (Washington, D.C.: Brookings Institution, 1989).

12. Davidson, "Legislative Work of Congress," 26-27.

13. George B. Galloway, *Congress at the Crossroads* (New York: Crowell, 1946), 53.

14. Davidson, "Legislative Work of Congress."

15. Ibid., 29.

16. Kenneth A. Shepsle, "The Changing Textbook Congress," in *Can the Government Govern?* ed. John E. Chubb and Paul E. Peterson (Washington, D.C.: Brookings Institution, 1989); and Roger H. Davidson, "The New Centralization on Capitol Hill," *Review of Politics* 50 (Summer 1988): 345-364.

17. James MacGregor Burns, *Roosevelt: The Lion and the Fox* (New York: Harcourt, Brace, 1956), 337, 339.

18. Robert J. Donovan, *Conflict and Crisis: The Presidency of Harry S Truman, 1945-1948* (New York: Norton, 1977), 260.

19. Alonzo L. Hamby, "The Mind and Character of Harry S Truman," in *The Truman Presidency,* ed. Michael J. Lacey (Cambridge: Woodrow Wilson International Center for Scholars and Cambridge University Press, 1989), 46.

20. Fenno, *Congressmen in Committees,* 279.

21. William S. White, *Citadel: The Story of the U.S. Senate* (New York: Harper & Brothers, 1956); and Donald R. Matthews, *U.S. Senators and Their World* (Chapel Hill: University of North Carolina Press, 1960).

22. Fenno, *Congressmen in Committees;* and Richard F. Fenno, Jr., *The Power of the Purse: Appropriations Politics in Congress* (Boston: Little, Brown, 1966).

23. Shepsle, "Changing Textbook Congress." By the 1970s and 1980s, however, this view had been supplanted by a revised reform era "textbook" view that stressed the institution's decentralization and fragmentation. For an expression of this view, see Hedrick Smith, *The Power Game: How Washington Works* (New York: Random House, 1988).

24. Smith, *Power Game,* chap. 2.

25. James L. Sundquist, *Politics and Policy: The Eisenhower, Kennedy, and Johnson Years* (Washington, D.C.: Brookings Institution, 1968).

26. Davidson and Hardy, "Indicators of Senate Activity"; and Davidson and Hardy, "Indicators of House Activity."

27. Allen Schick, *Congress and Money: Budgeting, Spending and Taxing* (Washington, D.C.: Urban Institute Press, 1980), 424-436.

28. John W. Ellwood, "The Great Exception: The Congressional Budget Process in an Age of Decentralization," in *Congress Reconsidered,* 3d ed., ed. Lawrence C. Dodd and Bruce I. Oppenheimer (Washington, D.C.: CQ Press, 1985), 315-342.

29. Abner J. Mikva and Patti B. Saris, *The American Congress: The First*

Branch (New York: Franklin Watts, 1983), 292.

30. Roger H. Davidson and Walter J. Oleszek, *Congress Against Itself* (Bloomington: Indiana University Press, 1977); Sundquist, *Politics and Policy;* and Leroy N. Rieselbach, *Congressional Reform* (Washington, D.C.: CQ Press, 1986).
31. David R. Mayhew, *Congress: The Electoral Connection* (New Haven, Conn.: Yale University Press, 1974).
32. Lester Thurow, *The Zero-Sum Society* (New York: Basic Books, 1980).
33. Quoted in' Helen Dewar, "Congress Off to Slowest Start in Years," *Washington Post,* May 13, 1989, A4.
34. David E. Rosenbaum, "Why the Deficit Is Paralyzing Congress," *New York Times,* October 22, 1989, E1.
35. Quoted in Helen Dewar, "At Finish of Slow-Starting Session, Lawmakers End Up Eyeball to Eyeball," *Washington Post,* November 21, 1989, A18.
36. Randall Strahan, "Agenda Change and Committee Politics in the Postreform House," *Legislative Studies Quarterly* 13 (May 1988): 185-194.
37. Allen Schick, "The Ways and Means of Leading Ways and Means," *Brookings Review* 7 (Fall 1989): 17.
38. U.S. House of Representatives, *The Committee on Ways and Means: A Bicentennial History, 1789-1989* (Washington, D.C.: U.S. Government Printing Office, 1989), 369.
39. Ibid., 370-372.
40. Schick, "Ways and Means," 21.
41. Christopher J. Bailey, "Beyond the New Congress: Aspects of Congressional Development in the 1980s," *Parliamentary Affairs* 41 (April 1988): 246.
42. Ornstein, Mann, and Malbin, *Vital Statistics*, 153, 162.
43. Charles O. Jones, *The Trusteeship Presidency: Jimmy Carter and the U.S. Congress* (Baton Rouge: Louisiana State University Press, 1988), chap. 7.

5. THE CONTEXT OF
CONGRESSIONAL POLICY MAKING

Walter J. Oleszek

"The genius of the American system has been its ability to adapt to change," remarked Senate Majority Leader George Mitchell, D-Maine, in early 1989.[1] Although there are few iron laws of politics, change is certainly one of them. Congress is constantly adapting to change. New procedures, processes, or practices come into being in response to diverse conditions and circumstances. Some innovations are incorporated formally in House or Senate rules or public laws; others evolve informally. Variable, too, is the relationship between the political parties, between the House and Senate, and between Congress and the White House. Needless to say, the larger political environment significantly affects House, Senate, and executive branch politics and priorities.

The decade of the 1980s was a tumultuous period for members, for both chambers of Congress, and for legislative-executive relations. For example, Republicans gained control of the Senate for the first time in twenty-six years and remained the majority party for six consecutive years (1981-1987). Procedural innovations and unconventional law-making, such as the use of megabills hundreds of pages in length, became almost commonplace and highlighted the flexibility and respon-siveness of Congress's decision-making processes (sometimes in ways that permitted legislators to avoid blame from constituents for making unpopular choices).

In the wake of soaring federal deficits, the politics of resource scarcity led to repeated clashes between Congress and the president over spending and revenue issues. Each used ingenious gimmicks, or "smoke and mirrors," to meet the statutory targets for deficit reduction prescribed by the Gramm-Rudman-Hollings law passed in the mid-1980s (see Chapter 8). Congress sometimes supplied the smoke and presidents the mirror (or vice versa). Another behavioral change involved an intense, short-term focus: meeting annual deficit targets. Still a third concerned the development of domestic programs that cost little or no money or did not create more federal bureaucracy. Constrained by budget limits, yet keen on sponsoring new initiatives, members began to mandate that the cost of their ideas be either shared or borne by businesses, state and local governments, or program beneficiaries.

Many of these changes in congressional policy making during the 1980s are likely to endure throughout the 1990s. This chapter focuses on three gradual shifts in Congress's external environment—agenda changes, flux in the party system, and divided government—and how they influence the way Congress makes decisions.

Congress and Agenda Change

Politics is sometimes called the art of the possible. It might also be called the art of defining the possibilities. As the nations of the world become increasingly interdependent, the U.S. Congress is confronting a host of new issues that challenge its capacity for defining the possibilities. Far-reaching global changes in the environment, in economics, and in diplomacy, and startling changes in U.S. demographics, are reshaping Congress's agenda and political discourse.

The Environment

Once perceived as largely a local or regional concern, the environment is now viewed by many as an urgent planetary challenge. The contemporary press and media are filled with stories about oil spills, ozone layer depletion, the greenhouse effect, acid rain, toxic wastes, and deforestation—as well as related topics such as population growth, energy consumption, scientific know-how, and economic development. One scientist put it this way:

> When my grandfather was born, environmental concerns were almost all based on housekeeping and trash in the back yard. By the time I was born there were demonstrable regional impacts. The birth of my children coincided with entire river systems and airsheds being affected. Now . . . major global systems, upon which society depends for its welfare, are being destroyed.[2]

Some commentators have even suggested that the global environment "may become the overarching issue for the next 40 years in the way the Cold War defined our worldview during the last 40 years." [3]

Economics

The United States is part of an increasingly competitive world economy. While the often discussed budget and trade deficits occupy a lot of Congress's and the White House's time, another "deficit" arouses common concern: building competitive industries and building a competitive society. "The problem here," explained Rep. Patricia Schroeder, D-Colo., "is we don't think internationally. In Denver, where I come from and where I talk to business groups, they think international trade is sending Coors beer to Texas." [4]

Congress and the president worry about numerous other economic issues, such as the exchange value of the dollar in the global marketplace, the huge foreign debt of many Third World nations, and foreign investment in the United States. As Senate President Pro Tempore Robert C. Byrd, D-W.Va., stated, "The Congress does not even have the basic data to make judgments about the ownership of our economy: where the dangers of foreign ownership are, where the benefits are, how we control the mix, and what kinds of measures we should be taking when things have gone too far in one industry or another." [5]

Diplomacy

Diplomatically and militarily, international relations are entering a post-Cold War era. The dramatic political changes in the Soviet Union under Mikhail Gorbachev, and in Germany and Eastern Europe, have challenged long-held assumptions about the communist menace and opened new possibilities for peace. Policy makers are understandably cautious in evaluating Soviet intentions; still, the changed international landscape has prompted reexamination of our nation's diplomatic objectives and military requirements. "We live," remarked Deputy Secretary of State Lawrence Eagleburger, "in a time of transition, one of risks and opportunities." [6] One of those opportunities may be better legislative-executive cooperation in international decision making (for example, the Bush agreement at the start of the 101st Congress on U.S. aid to the Nicaraguan contras, an issue that had sharply divided the branches during Ronald Reagan's presidency).

Demographics

There are scores of significant demographic changes influencing public attitudes about Congress's agenda. The aging of the population and the changing structure of the American family (working women and single-parent families, for example) have raised new issues. Child care, parental leave, nursing and home health care for the elderly, child poverty, and the shrinking pool of young workers are among the concerns of the electorate.

Legislative Implications

What are the legislative implications of these sorts of agenda changes? First, as already noted, new, complex, interdependent, and not easily resolvable issues—especially in an era of scarce resources—are being added to an already heavy congressional schedule. In addition to the regular items that appear on Congress's agenda (the annual money bills, measures requiring reauthorization, emergency legislation, and bills and amendments advanced by entrepreneurial members), House and Senate leaders and chairmen are now obliged to find some way to accommodate even more legislative business.

Second, legislators' schedules are long, fragmented, and unpredictable. Representatives and senators work, on average, at least an eleven-hour day. With their time splintered into tiny bits and pieces, how will members find the time to think, read, and learn about so many new issues? Washington is so filled with movers and shakers, remarked Norman Cousins, that there is hardly any room for thinkers: "We have everything we need except the most important thing of all—time to think and the habit of thought. We lack time for the one indispensable for safety." [7] Perhaps as members reflect on the interconnectedness of many issues (dubbed "intermestic," after international and domestic, by one scholar), they will begin to broaden their representational focus to encompass a "home style" that includes transnational constituencies.

Third, lobbying by or for foreign governments, corporations, or interest groups has greatly increased. In 1988, for instance, 152 Japanese companies and government agencies hired 113 American firms to represent them in Washington. The cost exceeded $100 million, "more than the combined budgets of the U.S. Chamber of Commerce, the National Association of Manufacturers, the Business Roundtable, the Committee for Economic Development and the American Business Conference—the five most influential business organizations in Washington." [8]

The surge in foreign lobbying stems in part from Congress's more assertive role in international affairs and the issues on the legislative agenda. Among them are trade imbalances, joint ventures in manufacturing, foreign investments in the United States, and conflicts between national security and the export of sophisticated technology. One study pointed to a related issue that needs legislative attention: "use of former Federal officials by foreign governments to lobby the Executive Branch." [9] Part of the reason that this lobbying activity may require special attention is the lack of sufficient information on the extensiveness of the practice.

Finally, Congress has increasingly relied on ad hoc devices to address new concerns. Party leaders now employ a wide variety of informal mechanisms—working groups, leadership amendments, task forces, outside commissions, or study groups—to consider complex substantive and fiscal issues. Procedural devices are also used. During the 100th Congress, Senate Democratic Leader Byrd explained how he promoted an integrated approach to the issue of trade:

I have worked closely with nine committee chairmen to develop a comprehensive, bipartisan approach to international competition. In place of a series of individual bills, we adopted an omnibus approach in which different legislative initiatives were knitted together into a consistent whole. It is ... a procedural departure that has helped the existing Senate committee structure deal with a new and complex challenge.[10]

To address contemporary issues, rank-and-file members frequently form ad hoc caucuses (the Congressional Competitiveness Caucus, the Senate Anti-Terrorism Caucus, and the Third World Debt Caucus, for example). These entities, which are often bicameral and bipartisan, provide members with the organization, ideas, and votes to influence legislation. In sum, two questions seem especially relevant: Can the institution of Congress skillfully and purposefully adapt to new agenda demands? Or will those demands eventually overload or overwhelm its policy-making capabilities?

Internal power fluctuations in Congress (the distribution of influence between committee chairmen and individual members, for example) and legislative assertiveness in nearly every policy arena (triggered in part by enhanced analytical capability and distrust of the executive branch) have lessened Congress's reliance on the president's traditional agenda-setting role. The irony may be that the more open, responsive, individualistic, and less manageable Congress becomes, the more it may require the "focusing" skills of the president. To be sure, competition in agenda setting will continue to characterize relations between the legislative and executive branches. This need not be a formula for stalemate, however. As former senator J. William Fulbright, D-Ark., once counseled: "Our proper objective is neither a dominant presidency nor an aggressive Congress but, within the strict limits of what the Constitution mandates, a shifting of the emphasis according to the needs of the time and the requirements of public policy." [11]

Flux in the Party System

In 1972 journalist David Broder wrote a book entitled *The Party's Over;* thirteen years later two political specialists wrote *The Party Goes On.*[12] Whether one believes that political parties are undergoing decline, dealignment, realignment, or resurgence, it seems clear that the two-party system is in ferment. With the decline of machine politics, patronage, and voter loyalty of the past, both parties are adjusting to new circumstances. Democrats, long the advocates of an activist national government, appear to recognize the limitations of government. Republicans, long-time proponents of the private sector, seem to appreciate the government's role in accomplishing certain social tasks.

The aging of the electorate and the addition of new immigrant groups (Asians and Latinos, for example) are forcing both parties to reshape their message, appeal, and demographic base. Technology has also changed the parties. Candidates often rely more on computer software than on shoe leather to win elections. Professional campaign consultants provide an enormous range of services, including fund raising, polling, and media advertising, which enable candidates to reduce their reliance on party organizations. Candidate-centered elections (whether a response to weakened parties or a cause of weakened parties) are generally replacing party-centered elections.

These changes in the party system strongly influence the institutional environment in the House and Senate. At least three areas in this connection are worth exploring: the nature of the membership, the effect of the campaign "money chase" on legislative business, and members' heightened stress on constituency service.

Nature of the Membership

The membership of today's Congress differs from that of earlier Congresses in an especially important regard: the number of Democratic seats that come from the South. Regionally, the Democratic "lock" on the South has been eclipsed by the rise of competitive partisan politics. The Republican party has emerged as a competitive force, especially in presidential politics. More voters identify with that party, and Republicans have increased their share of southern seats in the House and Senate. In short, congressional strength in this region has evolved from the "Solid South" to the rather competitive environment of the 1980s.

Changes in the South (economic, electoral, social, and demographic) produced significant legislative repercussions. Not only did the Democratic share of southern seats decline, but the South sent a new breed of Democrat to Congress. These southern Democrats vote more like their northern colleagues on a wide range of issues. In Kenneth Shepsle's words, there has been a "northernization of the South." "What you're seeing now in the modern South is that we're no longer monolithic," said Mississippi Republican senator Thad Cochran. "There's a political mix here that looks more and more like the rest of the country." [13]

There are policy consequences associated with this new "political mix." Southern Democrats are more likely to vote with a majority of their own party than with the so-called conservative coalition, a voting alliance of southern Democrats and Republicans. The coalition used to form on 20 to 30 percent of all roll-call votes in the Senate between the mid-1960s and 1980. In 1987 the "coalition appeared on only 7.6 percent of the Senate votes, an all-time low." [14] And even when southern Democrats join with Republicans to form a majority, as occurred in September 1989 on the capital gains fight in the House, that combination is more likely to reflect concerns about specific issues than a return to a consistent coalitional pattern.

The Money Chase

There is no question that it costs a lot to win and hold House and Senate seats. Election expenditures have escalated in the past few election cycles. Inflation, the expense of hiring professional consultants, and the costs of campaigning in the age of television account in large part for the increases. In 1976, for example, the winner of a Senate seat spent on average $610,000; in 1986 the cost was a little more than $3 million. And two years later the "average cost to win a seat in the U.S. Senate," noted Sen. David Boren, D-Okla., "was $4,083,308." [15] (The average House race in 1988 cost $393,000.) It is a political fact of life in the 1980s, wrote a commentator, "that those in the Congress, and those who aspire to be in it, need money." [16]

This financial reality affects the scheduling of House and Senate business. Members' fund-raising activities take more and more of their valuable time, which has increasingly led to scheduling conflicts. Members cannot "chase money" and debate and vote on legislation at the same time. To minimize the conflicts between electoral and lawmaking activities, explained former senator Charles Mathias, R-Md.,

> the practice has grown up in the last several years of providing "windows" in the Senate schedule. A window is a period of time in which it is understood that there will be no roll-call votes. Senators are assured that they won't be embarrassed by being absent for a recorded vote. Windows usually occur between six and eight in the evening, which is the normal time for holding fundraising cocktail parties.[17]

"They'll never admit it," noted one Washington political consultant, "but certainly some members [of the House] and some Senators spend a majority of their time raising money." [18]

As long as large sums of money are required to get elected, public and congressional debate about money and policy making will continue. Legislators, lobbyists, and citizens sometimes question the propriety of fund-raising practices. Members are concerned about the implied obligation when they accept money from political action committees

(PACs). Lobbyists resent pressure from members to buy tickets to their fund raisers. And citizens are concerned that the tie between lobbyists and money raising pushes Congress to enact laws that benefit the few and not the many.

Finally, the money chase affects the somewhat mysterious process of selecting party leaders. Not only are party leaders selected by secret ballot in closed-door party sessions, but the choice involves many intangible factors, such as a candidate's parliamentary shrewdness, media presence, and skill in coalition building. To these qualities can be added a host of others, including the leader's fund-raising capabilities. Party leaders are expected to raise and contribute campaign money for partisan colleagues. The three Democratic candidates for the job of majority leader in the 101st Congress (George Mitchell, D-Maine; Daniel Inouye, D-Hawaii; and J. Bennett Johnston, D-La.) all participated in fund-raising activities for their colleagues. As one observer noted, "the job of fundraiser is becoming more important to senators' expectations of what a majority leader should do. The candidates thus are not trying to buy votes so much as to demonstrate how well they can fulfill that role." [19]

It is worth noting that two of the top congressional leaders in the 1980s—Senate Majority Leader Mitchell and former House majority whip Tony Coelho, D-Calif.—previously headed their party's campaign committee and reportedly performed extraordinarily well in that capacity. In the 1988 majority leadership race, Senator Mitchell won the support of many Democrats elected in 1986, the election cycle in which he headed his party's campaign committee. Mitchell, according to press accounts, "became an overnight Democratic hero when he led the 1986 campaign that resulted in his party regaining Senate control." [20]

Constituency Service

To maintain popularity back home is not always easy. "I'm competing to represent my district against the lobbyists and the special interests," declared Rep. Mike Synar, D-Okla.[21] Lobbyists and their PAC affiliates can raise large sums of money for candidates. They can employ sophisticated new techniques to generate grass-roots pressure campaigns. They can combine with other groups to form potent electoral alliances. Thus Representative Synar and other legislators complain they are competing to represent their state or district against the information distributed there by interest groups.

Furthermore, legislative actions are scrutinized more closely by the media than in the past. Consequently, members may be less able or willing to make compromises or modify their positions once they have been expressed in public. Constituents, too, are far better educated than ever before. "The effects of this educational transformation are profound," explained Horace W. Busby. "[A] more self-reliant populace is less attracted to Government intervention and, at the same time, is more disposed to be independent of party dictates." [22] The party, as a result, no longer acts as the main bridge or mediator between the elected leader and the voter. Instead, voters learn about their members of Congress from media accounts. Conversely, legislators base their assessments of constituency opinion not simply on what local political leaders tell them but on what the legislators' own personal visits reveal.

It is small wonder that legislators create their own personal party organizations back home. Attentiveness to voter interests is crucial to political survival even in a "power of incumbency" era. The paradox is that incumbent members seem safer than ever, yet they are sometimes reluctant to take positions that may be controversial back home. Part of the explanation for this is the speed with which "instant constituencies" can be aroused to make life difficult for and electorally threatening to incumbents.

The effect of these diverse developments (sophisticated grass-roots lobbying, better educated constituents, and heightened media coverage) is greater attention to constituency service, even in the Senate. Richard Shelby, D-Ala., elected in 1986, highlighted the expanded notion of constituency service:

> Many freshmen view their role differently than 25 years ago, when a Senator was only a legislator. Now a Senator is also a grantsman, an ombudsman and a caseworker.... When we are asked by our constituents to help, we can't say we don't have time because we are focusing on national and international issues. [23]

Travel to the states is another indicator of constituency attentiveness. "Two trips a year," recalled Sen. Strom Thurmond, R-S.C., was about how frequently senators went home in the 1950s. [24] Today senators, like House members, travel to their states to meet with constituents much more frequently. Democratic senator Wendell Ford said he averaged about forty-eight weekends a year in Kentucky. [25] One consequence of this constant travel is some loss of collegiality. The Senate "is no longer a group of guys who get together and socialize, who go to [each] other's offices after a vote, sit down and have a few drinks.... Instead, we're on planes back to our home states," explained John McCain, R-Ariz. [26]

The Senate instituted in 1988, and continued in 1989 and 1990, "a three week—one week" schedule. During every month, the Senate is in session three weeks (Monday through Friday) and off one week.

The purpose of this reform was to enable senators to plan and conduct their constituency-related business and other work with greater certainty. Some House members are now urging their party leaders to adopt the Senate system. "By having three full five-day weeks ... for legislative business and one week off for constituency business, a variety of positive results would likely result," argued Reps. Barbara Kennelly, D-Conn., Thomas Tauke, R-Iowa, and Matthew McHugh, D-N.Y.[27]

Other indicators of the emphasis today on constituency service include the greater number of staff aides working in members' districts or states, the surge in commemorative bills (designating special days, weeks, or months of the year for local interests and activities), and the increase in franked mail. In short, the parochial nature of much congressional activity may help to account for the proclivity of voters to split their tickets and create the "split personality" government that has been common since the 1950s.

Divided Government

In recent years scholars and commentators have examined divided government (split party control of the national elective branches) with renewed interest. Nationally known journalist David S. Broder, for example, headlined the topic in a September 4, 1989, article in the *Washington Post:* "Scholars Debate Government's Division by Party." Heightened interest in divided government stems from at least three factors: its near permanent condition in recent decades; its probable meaning (a weakening of the parties' traditional role in promoting public accountability and some degree of unity in the U.S. system of separated powers); and its encouragement, in the judgment of some analysts, of "trench warfare" between the legislative and executive branches and political "gridlock" in addressing important national issues. As Dan Rostenkowski, D-Ill., chairman of the House Ways and Means Committee, said about raising revenue: "The politics are that we shouldn't do all the dangerous work alone, allowing [Republican president George Bush] to protest that those devilish Democrats made him do it." [28]

There are two overlapping, yet different, types of divided government. The first is split party control of Congress; the second is one party in charge of Congress and the other in charge of the White House. Each will be discussed in turn to illuminate some of their policy, political, and procedural implications. Either variant of divided government may be perceived as another informal "check" in the system of separated powers. Three decades ago Douglass Cater observed that a "sizeable body of public opinion appears to believe that a President of one party and a Congress of the other can do a better job of keeping tabs on each other. In an era of big and irrevocable decisions, why not add this new check to the numerous ones already written into the Constitution?" [29] Cater's question about the value of divided government is still debated by today's commentators.

Split Party Control of Congress

Until the 1981-1987 period, only twice during this century had there been divided party control of Congress: the 62d Congress (1911-1913) and the 72d Congress (1931-1933). One explanation for split party control of the House and Senate involves the staggered terms of senators. The entire House faces reelection every two years; only one-third of the Senate is thus exposed. This means that the Senate is apt to be more resistant than the House to short-term electoral tides that occasionally sweep the nation and slower to respond to longer term trends. Particularly when one party has a large "cushion" over the other, a single senatorial election is unlikely to transform the majority senatorial party into one of minority status.

During the 1981-1987 period, split party control of Congress affected bicameral and legislative-executive relations in at least four broad ways. First, President Reagan needed the support of some House Democrats to pass his proposals (as President Bush needs the support of Democrats in both houses today). Particularly in 1981, Reagan's successes in the House resulted from disunity in Democratic ranks and unity among House Republicans. Democrats held nominal control of the House, but real control on important issues rested with an ideological majority that consisted of conservative Democrats and Republicans.

Second, the Senate played a pivotal role during the 1981-1987 period by accelerating action on the Reagan agenda (pressuring House Democrats in the process), blocking unwanted Democratic proposals, or seizing the initiative on issues when the White House failed to do so. For instance, national efforts to curb the deficit often emanated from the GOP Senate, led by Majority Leader Bob Dole of Kansas. It often fell to the Senate, acting as gatekeeper, broker, facilitator, or referee, "to find and open the door to compromise when confrontation between Reagan and the House threat[ened] to disrupt the government's business." [30]

Third, conference committees assumed greater importance as each chamber sought to enact its own version of disputed legislation—often packaged in the aforementioned megabills—or to draft the law in conference (the case with the 1985 Gramm-Rudman-Hollings deficit reduction statute). The use of massive bills, an unconventional form of lawmaking that continues to flourish in an era of cutback budgeting, led to massive conferences. Often hundreds of conferees were involved in resolving interchamber disagreements on crucial legislation. (The largest conference in history met on the Omnibus Reconciliation Act of 1981. More than 250 House and Senate conferees, meeting in more than fifty subconferences, settled over three hundred matters that were in disagreement.)

With omnibus bills frequently short-circuiting normal floor routine, conference committees became the penultimate policy maker for Congress. "Let the conference decide" was an often heard refrain. And with the partisan division accentuating the natural rivalry between the House and Senate, conference committees were not "just reconciling the differences between the two houses of Congress," but also "the differences between two political parties." [31]

Finally, bicameral maneuverings became more complex as a result of Democratic control of the House and Republican control of the Senate. For example, when House Republicans became frustrated in advancing their policy goals, they turned on occasion for legislative aid to their partisan Senate colleagues. Yet bicameral discussion of Congress's agenda typically involved the two majority parties rather than members of the same party. As one account noted, "House Democratic and Senate Republican leaders have developed a closer relationship with each other than with their party colleagues in the other chamber, leaving some feeling of isolation among House Republicans and Senate Democrats." [32]

Split Party Control of Congress and the White House

This second type of divided government has characterized the political system for many years (see Table 5-1). Since 1956, the first time in this century that a newly elected president (Republican Dwight D. Eisenhower, who was beginning his second term) faced a Congress controlled by the opposition party, the GOP has won the White House in six of nine presidential elections. Also beginning in the mid-1950s, Democrats have always controlled the House—and usually the Senate as well. It is hardly surprising that Republicans today are increasingly viewed as the "executive party" and Democrats as the "legislative party."

Why this partisan division persists confounds many analysts, especially since the Reagan presidency encouraged broad segments of the electorate, particularly young voters, to identify with the Republican party. And despite Reagan's general popularity, which contributed to the Republican takeover of the Senate in 1980, the GOP is no stronger today in the House than when Reagan began his presidency. Two key factors appear to account for this: the 1982 economic recession

TABLE 5-1 Divided Government in the Twentieth Century

President	Party	Congress	House control	Senate control
Taft	R	62d (1911-1913)	D	R
Wilson	D	66th (1919-1921)	R	R
Hoover	R	72d (1931-1933)	D	R
Truman	D	80th (1947-1949)	R	R
Eisenhower	R	84th (1955-1957)	D	D
Eisenhower	R	85th (1957-1959)	D	D
Eisenhower	R	86th (1959-1961)	D	D
Nixon	R	91st (1969-1971)	D	D
Nixon	R	92d (1971-1973)	D	D
Nixon	R	93d (1973-1974)	D	D
Ford	R	93d (1974-1975)	D	D
Ford	R	94th (1975-1977)	D	D
Reagan	R	97th (1981-1983)	D	R
Reagan	R	98th (1983-1985)	D	R
Reagan	R	99th (1985-1987)	D	R
Reagan	R	100th (1987-1989)	D	D
Bush	R	101st (1989-1991)	D	D

and the 1986 "six-year itch" election, so-called because the party that occupies the White House for six consecutive years traditionally loses seats (even control) in the House and Senate. (Ironically, the longer the Republicans control the White House, the more difficult it might become for them to win seats in Congress, especially the House. Alternatively, the notion of "trickle-down Republicanism" may eventually erode Democratic control of Congress.) [33]

Explanations. Numerous theories purport to explain truncated partisan control of Congress and the White House. One suggests that Republicans enjoy a majority "lock" on the electoral college because their partisan strength is concentrated in growing geographic areas that are increasingly congenial to the GOP. People are moving from the central cities, which have been traditionally Democratic, to Republican communities surrounding the cities. In addition to these suburbs, states in the South, West, and Southwest are generally presumed to be more sympathetic to the GOP than to the Democratic party.

Another theory holds that the ticket-splitting electorate of the United States prefers divided government because it wants different things from Congress and the White House. Republican presidents are accorded high marks for their handling of national priorities concerning the economy and defense. Democratic Congresses act to protect the social programs that citizens want and to advance group interests in health care, housing assistance, farm subsidies, and many other diverse areas. In short, voters expect GOP presidents to promote peace and prosperity and Democratic Congresses to deliver particularized benefits to constituents and groups.

Another explanation is that the power of incumbency promotes divided government. Given the advantages of incumbency, such as name recognition, fund-raising ability, and staff resources, it is extraordinarily difficult for challengers to defeat Democratic or Republican incumbents, especially in the House. Democrats are the beneficiaries of the incumbency factor because, by political skill or luck, they were in the majority in Congress when this reelection factor took hold. In the November 1986 and 1988 elections, nearly 99 percent of the House members who sought reelection won. (Senate incumbents are more easily defeated than their House counterparts in large part because there are fewer problems in recruiting credible and adequately financed Senate challengers.) After thirty-five straight years in control of the House, Democrats appear to have a "lock" on that chamber. The Senate, on the other hand, may function as the "swing" branch of government. "In terms of our recent political experience," said former senator Thomas Eagleton, D-Mo., "we are left with the Senate as the only part of our governmental structure that may swing with change in voter attitude." [34]

Still another view highlights the general inability of Republicans to recruit experienced challengers to take on House Democratic incumbents. "A major reason for the failure of Republicans to win more congressional seats is the simple fact that often Democrats field candidates with good track records in politics, business or community life, while [GOP] candidates fall short in these areas," explained Rep. Mickey Edwards, R-Okla., chairman of the House Republican Policy Committee.[35] More Democrats than Republicans run unopposed in the general election; this pattern highlights the lack of incentive for GOP candidates to run for the House where, even if they should win, Democrats will still dominate the lawmaking process. Conversely, Democrats seem unable to nominate presidential candidates who can win the White House. Each party, in brief, faces different political circumstances: Democrats have a "bottoms up" problem and Republicans a "top down" dilemma.

Finally, it is worth noting that the Constitution permits divided government. Voters separately choose candidates for the House, the Senate, and the White House. Perhaps more surprising than the recent occurrence of divided government is its comparative absence during much of U.S. history. Today's voter, it seems, cares less about party label and more about the qualities of the candidates. This tendency has led to "coalition government" and produced several political and policy consequences that merit some mention.

Consequences. However one views divided government, it seems plain to many that the "split level" arrangement contributed to heightened partisanship in the 1980s. "I never want to see divided government again in my lifetime," declared Sen. Robert C. Byrd, D-W.Va., when he was majority leader of the 100th Congress.[36] His sentiment reflects the partisan warfare and legislative-executive conflict that characterized much congressional policy making during the decade.

There are many instances that show evidence of greater partisanship. One was the election of Ronald Reagan as president. He advanced an ideologically charged and controversial agenda that aroused strong congressional opposition. A skilled partisan leader, Reagan often battled Congress, especially its Democratic leaders, in numerous policy areas (no cuts in defense or no tax hikes, for instance) and publicly blamed Congress when it frustrated his initiatives. (Interestingly, the Democratic leaders of the 101st Congress—Speaker Thomas Foley and Senate Majority Leader Mitchell—often seem frustrated with President Bush's affable approach toward the legislative branch, which has kept Democrats on the defensive and strengthened GOP control of the nation's agenda.) Split party control of Congress also fostered partisanship as Senate Republicans often functioned as an instrument of the GOP White House.

Another indicator of heightened partisanship was the parliamentary warfare that erupted periodically, even in the Senate where party conflict is often muted. Senators criticized each other personally, party leaders clashed heatedly on the floor, and legislators traded charges of partisan excesses. No wonder many senators became concerned about the decline of comity in the Senate. As the glue of personal and political camaraderie began to dissolve, and as many new senators pushed their individual agendas to the detriment of institutional obligations, the atmosphere of the Senate shifted from cooperative politics to confrontation politics.

The trend toward confrontation politics is particularly evident in the House, where the rules emphasize majority rule (Senate rules are biased toward minority rights) and where Republicans have been in the minority for nearly four decades. "Each new day that I serve," lamented Minority Leader Bob Michel of Illinois, "I am setting a new record for having served longer in consecutive years as a member of the minority party than any other man or woman in history." [37] Not only are House Republicans frustrated at their long minority status, but they are bitter at what they perceive to be majority party abuses, such as distorted committee membership and staffing ratios, the partisan scheduling of measures, "gag" rules that restrict floor amendments, the mishandling of election recounts, and proxy voting in committees.

The result of such frustrations has been an aggressive GOP posture toward the Democratic-led House. Through a combination of parliamentary, public relations, and political guerrilla warfare strategies, Republicans have confronted the Democrats on a host of issues. "Confrontation fits our strategy," said then House GOP whip Richard Cheney (now secretary of defense). "Polarization often has very beneficial results. If everything is handled through compromise and conciliation, if there are no real issues dividing us from the Democrats, why should the country change and make us the majority?" [38] House Democrats dispute Republicans' charges that House procedures treat them unfairly. The real GOP complaint is "not to House procedures," Speaker Foley wrote when he was majority leader, "but to the policies achieved with those procedures." [39]

The issue of ethics has become a weapon of partisan warfare in the House. In June 1989 Speaker Jim Wright, D-Texas, became the first Speaker ever to be forced to leave the House because of charges of financial irregularities. The charges against Wright were brought by House GOP whip Newt Gingrich of Georgia. Arkansas Democrat Bill Alexander then brought ethical charges against Gingrich; these charges were later dropped by the House ethics committee.

House Republicans have tried to dislodge the Democrats from their party status by attacking them on the issues and calling them "liberals." They also used the issue of ethics in some 1990 House races. The campaign objective was to charge that arrogant, entrenched (through gerrymandering), and corrupt (through fund-raising tactics) Democrats had held control of the House too long:

> The idea is to accuse the Democrats of ruling the House through a
> system of entrenched corruption. If people see enough corruption,
> they will get the idea that the whole system has to be overthrown—
> and the Democratic majority will be swept away.[40]

Needless to say, polls indicate that voters doubt that Republicans are more ethical than Democrats.

Another manifestation of heightened partisanship is in legislative-executive relationships. There appears to be a new partisan overlay to the constitutional separation of powers: "Republicans have come to support expansion of presidential power, and the diminution of congressional power. The Democrats have come to support expansion of congressional power and have sought to undermine and place limitations on presidential power." [41] This marks a shift in partisan perspectives. Republicans used to lament the power of Democratic presidents, such as Franklin Roosevelt, and to stress congressional prerogatives. The Senate's rejection of President Bush's nominee to be secretary of defense, former GOP senator John Tower of Texas, perhaps reflected the new separation of powers. "The Tower fight [was] not about character or competence, or even about ideology," explained scholar Everett Carll Ladd. "It [was] about entrenched Democratic congressional power challenging entrenched Republican executive power." [42] The longer each party controls either Congress or the White House without much prospect of capturing the other, the greater will be the intensity of the "showdown" between the branches.

Heightened partisanship also affects policy making. Chances for gridlock increase because each branch may block or delay action wanted by the other. "We expend so much energy and effort here seeking to gain and retain tactical partisan advantage," stated Senate Majority Leader Mitchell, "that it is often difficult to keep a focus on what our central objective is, and that is to deal with [national problems] in a responsible way." [43] Elective officials understand, too, that policies and votes can be framed to promote political retribution back home. One result: risk-averse politicians are reluctant to make hard choices.

Yet for all its allegedly negative consequences, divided government produced a large number of policy successes in the 1980s. One example is the Tax Reform Act of 1986, the most sweeping overhaul of the Internal Revenue Code since World War II:

> Ironically, the fact that government was split in 1985 and 1986—with the GOP controlling the White House and the Senate, and the Democrats controlling the House—proved to be a boost to the passage of tax reform. Tax reform's progress reflected a continuous fear on the part of one party that the other party would steal the issue from them. It was that competition that helped keep tax reform alive.[44]

The Democratically controlled 100th Congress (1987-1989) was one of the most productive since the mid-1960s. It passed significant legislation on health, welfare, immigration reform, trade, deficit reduction, and defense. As one scholar noted, the 100th Congress gave "the lie to the notion that the system can't produce" during a president's lame-duck years.[45]

Other post-World War II presidents who faced Congresses controlled by the opposition party—Harry S. Truman, Dwight D. Eisenhower, and Richard Nixon, for example—also achieved major successes, such as the Marshall Plan, civil rights legislation, and the normalization of relations with China. And some presidents who had their party in control of both houses of Congress, such as Democrat Jimmy Carter, encountered significant difficulties in getting their proposals through the legislative branch. "So there is something more than just having your party in power in all three places," noted one analyst. "You've got to know [how] to build political coalitions that work, that pull together, that sustain policies that you as President effectively articulate." [46] In short, while same-party control of Congress and the White House might be better for policy making and account-ability, divided government, despite its drawbacks, can be made to work.

Conclusion

Our constitutional system of shared powers, reinforced today by heightened partisanship, presents challenges and opportunities. Still, the White House and Congress are capable of adjusting to contempo-rary political reality and to the societal circumstances and values that give their activities direction. Whether institutional leaders achieve a harmony of purpose often depends on whether there is consensus among the citizenry for purposeful action. As Rep. Lee Hamilton, D-Ind., said about Congress and policy making:

> When the nation clearly wants change, the Congress can respond decisively. But when public opinion is more mixed, the legislature responds with delay and inaction. The Congress can often work out compromises of conflicting interests and act on the basis of a national consensus, but it cannot impose a consensus where none exists.[47]

An important issue, then, is how to advance legitimate national purposes when short-term politics seem more popular than long-term perspectives.

Notes

1. *Congressional Record*, daily ed., January 25, 1989, S88.
2. Ibid., daily ed., March 21, 1989, E878.
3. William Schneider, "Welcome to the Greening of America," *National Journal*, May 27, 1989, 1334.
4. David Crook, "Schroeder's Pep Talk to Hollywood," *Los Angeles Times*, pt. 6, August 2, 1983, 7.
5. *Congressional Record*, daily ed., September 28, 1989, S12037.
6. Lawrence S. Eagleburger, "Uncharted Waters Ahead: U.S. Needs a New

Compass," *Los Angeles Times,* September 24, 1989, pt. 5, 2.

7. Norman Cousins, "Take Time to Think," *Christian Science Monitor,* September 26, 1989, 18.

8. Pat Choate, "How Foreign Firms Buy U.S. Clout," *Washington Post,* June 19, 1988, C1.

9. *Congressional Record,* daily ed., September 19, 1989, S11301.

10. Ibid., daily ed., April 19, 1988, S4216.

11. J. William Fulbright, "The Legislator As Educator," *Foreign Affairs* 58 (Spring 1979): 726.

12. David Broder, *The Party's Over* (New York: Harper & Row, 1972); and Xander Kayden and Eddie Mahe, Jr., *The Party Goes On* (New York: Basic Books, 1985).

13. Macon Morehouse, "Conservative Coalition: Still Alive, but Barely," *Congressional Quarterly Weekly Report,* November 19, 1988, 3345. To be sure, southern Democrats and Republicans are often wary of becoming too closely identified with the views of their Washington-based national parties.

14. Norman J. Ornstein, Robert L. Peabody, and David W. Rohde, "Change in the Senate: Toward the 1990s," in *Congress Reconsidered,* 4th ed., ed. Lawrence C. Dodd and Bruce I. Oppenheimer (Washington, D.C.: CQ Press, 1989), 16.

15. *Congressional Record,* daily ed., February 22, 1989, S1609.

16. Andy Plattner, "The High Cost of Holding and Keeping Public Office," *U.S. News & World Report,* June 22, 1987, 30.

17. Quoted in Philip M. Stern, "The Tin Cup Congress," *Washington Monthly,* May 1988, 4.

18. Michael Oreskes, "Congress," *New York Times,* July 11, 1989, A17.

19. Stephen Gettinger, "Potential Senate Leaders Flex Money Muscles," *Congressional Quarterly Weekly Report,* October 8, 1988, 2776.

20. Helen Dewar, "Senator Mitchell Elected Majority Leader," *Washington Post,* November 30, 1988, A1, A8.

21. *New York Times,* January 24, 1980, A16.

22. Horace W. Busby, "The New Politics of Who We Are," *New York Times,* September 9, 1984, E25.

23. Richard Cohen, "Assertive Freshmen," *National Journal,* May 2, 1987, 1061.

24. Peter Osterlund, "The Senate's Business As Usual Just Isn't What It Used to Be," *Christian Science Monitor,* April 22, 1988, 1.

25. *Congressional Record,* daily ed., October 1, 1985, S12343.

26. Helen Dewar, "Defeat of Tower Reflects Dramatic Changes in Senate," *Washington Post,* March 13, 1989, A6.

27. See *The View from Capitol Hill: Lawmakers on Congressional Reform* (Washington, D.C.: Center for Responsive Politics, 1989), 43.

28. Elizabeth Wehr, "Tax Options for 1989: Higher Rates on Gasoline," *Congressional Quarterly Weekly Report,* January 7, 1989, 27.

29. Douglass Cater, "Split Personality of the Voter," *New York Times*

Magazine, January 24, 1960, 71.

30. "GOP Senate Plays Gatekeeper Role in 1983," *Congressional Quarterly Weekly Report,* December 3, 1983, 2548.
31. This observation was made by a top aide to Thomas P. O'Neill, Jr., former Speaker of the House. Steven V. Roberts, "The Nitty-Gritty of Conference," *New York Times,* July 17, 1985, A18.
32. Richard E. Cohen, "A Congress Divided," *National Journal,* January 18, 1986, 131.
33. Kim Mattingly, "Centrist Democrats Warned 'Trickle-Down Republicanism' May Defeat Them in 1992," *Roll Call,* March 20-26, 1989, 8.
34. *Congressional Record,* daily ed., April 6, 1989, S3402.
35. Quoted in Tom Kenworthy, "Inability to Recruit Strong Candidates Hinders GOP Efforts to Regain House," *Washington Post,* December 26, 1989, A4.
36. Helen Dewar, "Full Plate of Leftovers Awaits Hill, Reagan in 1988," *Washington Post,* December 23, 1987, A6.
37. *Congressional Record,* daily ed., September 12, 1989, E3000.
38. Fred Barnes, "On the Hill, Raging Representatives," *New Republic,* June 3, 1985, 9.
39. *Roll Call,* June 19, 1988, 5.
40. William Schneider, "Jim Wright's Capitol Punishment," *Los Angeles Times,* pt. 5, June 4, 1989, 1.
41. Benjamin Ginsberg, "A Post-Electoral Era?" *PS,* March 1989, 19.
42. Everett Carll Ladd, "The New Workings of Separation of Powers," *Christian Science Monitor,* March 3, 1989, 19.
43. *Congressional Record,* daily ed., October 5, 1989, S12721.
44. Alan S. Murray and Jeffrey H. Birnbaum, "Lawmakers, Lobbyists, and the Unlikely Triumph of Tax Reform," *Congress & the Presidency* (Autumn 1988): 190.
45. Charles O. Jones quoted in Janet Hook, "100th Congress Wraps Up Surprisingly Busy Year," *Congressional Quarterly Weekly Report,* October 29, 1988, 3117.
46. Hedrick Smith, "Considerations on the Power System," *Presidential Studies Quarterly* (Summer 1988): 497.
47. *Congressional Record,* daily ed., March 15, 1989, E805.

6. THE LEGISLATURE, THE EXECUTIVE, AND PUBLIC POLICY: THE FUTILE QUEST FOR CONGRESSIONAL POWER

Michael L. Mezey

In recent years an impressive body of research concerning the policy-making relationship between the president and Congress has made important methodological and substantive contributions to our understanding of the interactions between these institutions.[1] These studies share a crucial yet largely unexamined premise: they accept as a given that the U.S. Congress should have a central policy-making role. With one significant exception, neither the consequences of such a role for the quality of public policy nor alternative formulations of the legislature's role are seriously considered.[2]

In this chapter I begin from a theoretical perspective by identifying five criteria necessary for optimal public policy and four characteristics essential to legislative institutions. I argue that because of these characteristics legislatures will be unlikely to produce public policy that meets the proposed criteria of optimality. The idea that the legislature should nonetheless be central to the policy-making process is premised on an activist legislative model, which demands more from the legislature in regard to policy making than it is institutionally capable of delivering. To support this position, I examine the U.S. Congress's performance as a policy-making body and then propose an alternative representation model that carries with it a different, more appropriate policy-making role for the legislature than does the activist model. In conclusion, I suggest that some of what has been interpreted as a resurgence of Congress in the past two decades has in fact been movement toward the representation model.[3]

Definitions

Any assessment of the performance of a political institution in making public policy must begin with an understanding of what constitutes good public policy. Although there is no scholarly consensus on what distinguishes good public policy from bad, we can perhaps agree that public policy optimally should meet at least five criteria: it should be informed, timely, coherent, effective, and responsive.

By informed I mean that public policy should be based on the best information available. By timely I mean that policy should not be delayed to the point where it exacerbates the problem it addresses, with adverse consequences for the political system. By coherent I mean that policy should fit with other policies currently in force and that it should not seek internally contradictory goals. By effective I mean that policy should be designed to accomplish the goals for which it is created. By responsive I mean that policy should satisfy the major constituencies to whom it is relevant and serve the broader but more diffuse public interest as well.[4]

When a legislature fails to make public policy that meets these criteria of optimality, its poor performance is often attributed to particular characteristics of that legislature. Recent policy failures of the U.S. Congress, for example, have been connected with the increased internal fragmentation that resulted from the reforms of the 1970s.[5] Similarly, the problems of Third World legislatures have sometimes been traced to the amateurism and opportunism of their members.[6]

The thesis of this discussion is that the policy-making performance of a legislature is most often determined by characteristics generic to *all* legislatures rather than to the quirks and traits of specific institutions. These generic characteristics stand in marked contrast to the characteristics of other political institutions, particularly the executive branch. Legislatures worldwide are collegial, representative, open, and non-specialized, while executives tend to be hierarchical, less representative, closed, and specialized.[7]

By collegial I mean that legislatures are collective bodies whose members are formally equal in voting power and who take their decisions through simple or extraordinary majority votes. Although executive behavior does demonstrate some collegial aspects, a formal hierarchy characterizes its operation to the point where decisions need not be made through a voting process.

By representative I mean that the legislature is elected by a larger public to whom it is formally responsible and in whose interests it acts. Political executives such as prime ministers and presidents are often elected and are, in that sense, representative, but their appointees and the permanent bureaucracy are neither elected nor composed in a way designed to make them representative of a broader population.

By open I mean that the legislature meets publicly and keeps a record of its deliberations. Conventionally, the executive operates in a closed policy-making arena. Cabinet and staff meetings are not open to the public, and documents produced within the executive branch are not normally made public.

By nonspecialized I mean that the legislature requires of its members no special training nor expertise in public policy matters. Although the same is true for political executives, special qualifications are usually required of those who hold appointive positions and of all who hold positions within the permanent bureaucracy.

These four characteristics of the legislature are the traditional strength of the institution. The collegiality of its members allows the legislature to accommodate a heterogeneous society by providing seats for diverse regions, groups, and interests, all of whom are allowed the same opportunity to participate in the deliberations of the body. The representative nature of the legislature has constituted the institution's claim to legitimacy, enabling it to assert that it acts for the people of the country and with their express consent. Its openness is essential to its legitimacy, because it invites those whom it claims to represent to view and evaluate the record of its accomplishments; the constituents may judge for themselves the efficacy of the representation they are receiving. Finally, the nonspecialized nature of the legislature follows from its representativeness and attests to the right of citizens to decide upon the qualifications of their representatives and the capacity of "the collective, nontechnical mind" to bring to bear "insights and sensitivities that are likely to go beyond the perception and ken of any group of experts." [8]

Legislatures as Policy-Making Institutions

These defining characteristics of the legislature, as they contrast with those of the executive, have consequences for the capacity of each institution to contribute toward public policy that will meet the criteria of optimality.

Informed Public Policy

In acquiring information, modern legislatures are at a disadvantage because their nonspecialized members must depend on the information generated by the specialists in the bureaucracy. This is particularly true in the areas of foreign policy and defense policy, where secrecy is likely to be considered legitimate.

Although committee systems and professional staff can enhance the legislature's ability to gain expertise, committees have been able to acquire significant policy expertise in only a few legislatures. [9] Furthermore, if staff resources are dedicated to the personal and political needs of legislators rather than to their policy needs, a large staff may not increase legislators' access to information. Even devoting staff time to policy matters may well make no difference if legislators must depend on bureaucrats who work for the legislature rather than those who work in the executive branch. In both cases, a strong staff may dominate the elected representatives in the legislature with their superior knowledge and expertise about a particular topic.[10]

Legislatures do have some advantages over executives in generating information. Because of the representative nature of the legislature, a wider spectrum of views is likely to be found there than in the less representative executive bureaucracy. Although such an environment may not produce expertise, it can produce, on nontechnical matters, the perspectives and arguments that can help to identify the best policy alternatives. This advantage is fostered by the openness of the legislature and by the articulation of contrary views that it encourages. The more closed and less representative environment of the executive branch may inhibit the expression of deviant viewpoints.

On balance, then, the legislature is less likely than the executive branch to generate the technical and expert information upon which public policy should rest, but the diversity of views expressed within it can broaden the information base upon which policy alternatives are generated and selected.

Timely Public Policy

Legislatures are notoriously slow-moving institutions because they are collegial, open, and representative. Collegial bodies resist leadership. With each member formally equal in power, a relatively large number of members must want to act before the legislature can act. Hierarchically organized bodies need agreement from a relatively small number of participants in order to act. The larger the number of people from whom agreement is required, the longer it takes for them to arrive at agreement.

In the legislature, simply providing a hearing for the multiplicity of interests represented is time-consuming. The process of accommodating different views, of coming to positions acceptable to significant numbers of members, takes even longer. Situations arise, too, that consume a great deal of time but yield no agreement. The openness of the legislature fosters other delays. Representatives acting on behalf of special interests may find it difficult to concede or compromise those interests publicly. The openness of the legislature therefore can put a premium on posturing rather than on policy making, and sometimes legislators may prefer having no policy rather than one unacceptable to those whom they represent. In more closed executive arenas, it is easier for agreements to be reached and for policy to advance.

On the other hand, the greater diversity of opinion in the open legislative arena may mean that the legislature can prod the executive into action when the latter, for one reason or another, is reluctant to act.

The legislature may articulate policy needs that may not be apparent from the capital or to those who need not, as a condition for retaining their positions, respond to public pressure. It may thereby generate publicity and pressure, compelling more expeditious action than the executive, left to its own devices, would be willing to undertake.

Thus, legislatures can encourage others to act, but they cannot act in as timely a fashion as the executive. It can be argued that policies that are unable to secure legislative agreement should not be pursued and that much can be gained from delay and caution; however, the costs of action delayed or not taken also can be high.

Coherent Public Policy

Legislative action often appears to be incoherent. Policies approved on one day may be inconsistent with those approved previously. Calls for lower budget deficits may be followed by appropriations and revenue legislation that makes large deficits inevitable. A policy to discourage citizens from smoking may coexist with a policy of price supports for tobacco growers.

Although incoherence can characterize public policy emanating from any source, the nonspecialized, collegial, and representative nature of the legislature seems to make such policies more likely to emerge from that institution. Those who are not experts in a policy area are less likely than those who are experts to see how a proposal fits or fails to fit with the extant body of public policy. Furthermore, an institution that is representative of diverse interests and that operates largely through compromise may view an incoherent yet consensual policy as more desirable than a coherent policy for which sufficient support cannot be generated. Stated differently, legislators are likely to be more process-oriented than policy-oriented, more willing to view the gaining of an agreement rather than the coherence of the policy embodied in the agreement as the end to be sought.

This is not to say that the executive branch is immune to similar pressures. Presidents and prime ministers too must conciliate people with diverse views, and negotiation and compromise are as much a part of bureaucratic life as of legislative life. Nonetheless, the representativeness of the legislature makes it less receptive than the executive to the systematic analysis necessary to produce coherent public policy.

Effective Public Policy

Producing policy that achieves the goals it is designed to achieve depends in part upon the quality of the information that the policy maker has and in part on the timeliness of the policy. The debilities of the legislature in regard to information and timeliness therefore adversely affect the legislature's capacity to produce effective public policy. In addition, the process-oriented nature of legislative activity may work against policy effectiveness since there may be a tension between the policy that will win the widest agreement and that which is most likely to solve the policy problem at hand. To the extent that legislatures seek policy alternatives that will reconcile widely disparate views, they risk producing policy that, while broadly supported, simply does not work.

Again, this observation is not meant to suggest that the executive is invulnerable to the temptation of consensual rather than effective policies. Even bureaucrats must seek support for their policy initiatives from various constituencies. A consensual policy, by virtue of that characteristic, can be more effective than one that is not consensual because supported policies may be more likely to succeed than unsupported policies. Consensual policies, however, also must be judged on their capacity to accomplish goals, and legislatures often seem unwilling to make that evaluation—not because legislators are incompetent or uncaring individuals but because the legislative process is slanted more toward achieving policy agreement than toward policy effectiveness.

Responsive Public Policy

The difficulties experienced by the legislature in arriving at effective public policies suggest its strength in arriving at responsive public policies. The compromises that often frustrate effective policy stem from the representative and open nature of the legislature, traits that encourage responsiveness to the policy issues of immediate concern to members' constituencies. Such responsiveness often culminates in a policy that is least offensive to the largest number of people.

This view of responsiveness is limited, however. Although it is important that policy be responsive to the short-term wishes of the people, it is also important that it be responsive to their long-term wishes. For example, a policy that defers maintenance on public facilities so that tax increases can be avoided or so that the money can be diverted toward more immediate ends may be responsive to popular wishes until the very time that the infrastructure of public facilities collapses and the population experiences the consequences of deferred maintenance. The point is that the public expects its political system to be well run, and responsiveness to this expectation may require a degree of nonresponsiveness to some immediate demands. Because legislative terms are short and because constituents may want visible indications of their representatives' effectiveness, legislatures may be oriented more toward short-term than long-term responsiveness. Similarly, legislators, because of their status as representatives, may be more responsive to the narrow interests of their constituencies than to a broader national interest.

Two Legislative Models

So far, the point of this discussion is that legislatures sometimes enhance but are more likely to diminish the prospect of achieving public policy that meets the criteria of optimality. It is often assumed that such an uneven contribution from the legislature is inevitable and that the institution's failings must be tolerated in order to preserve the positive contributions that it makes.

This position arises from what might be termed an *activist model* of the legislature. An activist model assumes that the job of the legislature is to initiate, deliberate, and decide upon public policy. In James Burnham's words, "the primary business of a legislature in a democratic republic is to answer the big questions of policy." [11] The executive branch in such a model is at most a policy-making partner of the legislature, but the legislature is a "significant independent law-making institution, capable of legislative innovation and able to undertake the creative act of law-making without executive leadership if necessary." [12]

The argument for an activist model of the legislature usually incorporates an appeal to democratic values. Unless the legislature functions as a powerful policy-making force,

> the road to a bureaucratic state and a kind of monarchic government will be opened up.... [T]he major problems for the country will be handled in ways that will become excessively majoritarian, often arbitrary, usually collectivist.[13]

Legislatures that conform to the activist model are rare indeed. Aside from the U.S. Congress, perhaps some American state legislatures, and possibly at one time the congresses of the Philippines, Chile, and Costa Rica, no other legislature has approximated the requirements of the activist model.

Standing in contrast to the activist model is the *representation model* of the legislature, which assumes a primary policy-making role for the executive and a secondary policy-making role for the legislature. Under such a model, legislators affect policy through the vigorous performance of representational activities such as articulating constituency and group demands, seeking solutions to the problems of individual constituents, and otherwise serving as a conduit between popular and mass views and those who make policy. Legislatures operating under this model can, through discussion and debate, affect public policy by setting the parameters within which the executive operates, by modifying executive initiatives, and by overseeing the implementation of public policy.

Although Jean Blondel did not use those categories, he distinguished between the activist model and the representation model in these terms:

> The yardstick by which to measure the significance of legislatures should not be whether the legislature "really" passes all the statutes, or even most of the rules of the country, and whether it is in a "real" position to make and unmake governments. These simply are not the "functions" of legislatures. The function of the legislature is to provide a means of ensuring that there are channels of communication between the people and the executive, as a result of which it is possible for demands to be injected into the decision-making machinery whenever they exist and for the executive decisions to be checked if they raise difficulties, problems, and injustices.[14]

Representation legislatures are relatively numerous compared with activist legislatures. Most continental European parliaments and legislative institutions in more open developing nations generally conform to the representation model.[15]

I maintain that the activist model is incompatible with the generic characteristics of legislatures and the representation model is compatible with them. If this assertion is true, it means that activist legislatures ordinarily will fail to produce public policy that meets the criteria of optimality.

Congress as an Activist Legislature

The argument that activist legislatures will be unlikely to produce good public policy can be supported by examining the policy-making performance of the U.S. Congress—an institution that uniquely exemplifies the activist model[16]—against the five criteria of optimal public policy defined above.

Informed Public Policy

During the 1960s the consensus of scholarly opinion was that poor information was one of the elements that seriously limited Congress's capacity to make public policy.[17] John Saloma summarized several categories of information problems confronting Congress; these included dependence on the executive bureaucracy, executive secrecy, decentralized information within the legislature, and multiple channels of information.[18]

The information problems of Congress received much attention during the reform era of the 1970s. The sizes of committee and subcommittee staff increased 250 percent between 1970 and 1983, while the personal staff of members increased 60 percent. The Congressional Budget Office and the Office of Technology Assessment were established, and the staff of support agencies such as the Congressional Research Service and the General Accounting Office doubled.[19] By the end of the decade it was possible to conclude that Congress had "successfully established its independence of the executive branch for information, policy analysis, program evaluation, and legislative advice." [20]

Congressional independence from the executive in information matters does not mean that Congress has solved its information problems, however. Michael Malbin has argued that members of Congress have become overly dependent upon committee staff, who negotiate the details of legislation and whose work results in "increasingly inclusive, increasingly complex legislation that can only be understood by an expert." [21] The question is whether a Congress overwhelmed by the bureaucracy and expertise of its own staff is better informed than a Congress dependent upon the executive's bureaucracy.

Malbin and others also note that congressional staff has increased the workload of members by instigating more legislative proposals and by tying up the legislators' time in staff supervision.[22] As a result legislators may have less time to come to grips with the information generated by their staff. The real issue may be whether legislators, even with the best information sources, are able or willing to use all the data they receive. As one report prepared for the Senate noted:

> Senators do not feel a lack of information. What they are missing, however, is the ability to place the information they have in broader contexts. . . . [T]he distinction must be made between information or data, and knowledge.[23]

Put differently, if Congress has failed its failure has not been in "upgrading its capacity to elicit information from the federal bureaucracy, but in failing to create a structure within Congress that can act on this information in a decisive and coherent manner." [24]

Whether or not Congress will want to create such a structure is debatable. The pressures that legislatures experience because they are representative institutions may discourage their members from using the information they receive. Robert Reischauer, writing about the economic information at Congress's disposal, says that Congress is

> capable of ignoring the information when it contradicts powerful political forces. Whether Congress chooses to use information or

not is a political question. The answer reflects the strengths and weaknesses of Congress as an institution, not the limitations of the advice or of the information-gathering system.[25]

In discussing Congress's regulatory activities, Mark Nadel reaches a harsher conclusion:

> Congress is almost completely impervious to systematic policy analysis, particularly in the short run. . . . [T]he dominant factor in the use of analysis is not whether it is correct or technically competent but which side it supports.[26]

Although Congress has improved its information sources, it has yet to demonstrate that a representative and nonspecialized body can use this information to produce better and more informed public policy.

Timely Public Policy

There is no evidence that Congress is moving more expeditiously on public policy questions now than it has in the past. Congressional rules and procedures continue to allow legislators bent upon delaying or stopping legislation to engage in what Bruce Oppenheimer calls the "new obstructionism." [27] James Sundquist traces this phenomenon to the representative nature of Congress:

> [A] congressman is expected to struggle to the end and, if necessary, go down battling for his constituents. Out of this fact of life comes the foot-dragging, the sluggishness, the evasion of hard questions that are indelible elements of the congressional image.[28]

The representative nature of the legislature causes its members to devote much of their time and their staff's time to servicing the particular demands of their constituencies.

Congressional reluctance to act is also attributable to the open nature of the institution. Naomi Caiden suggests that the "politics of subtraction" involved in reducing government budgets work more effectively in countries where the issues are "fought out primarily behind the scenes in the closed world of cabinets and bureaucracies," while in the United States the problems are exacerbated because "the budget drama is played out in the public arena of Congress." [29] With the eyes of constituents and lobbyists constantly on the legislator, and "with a larger number of effective participants . . . coalition building is even more difficult, time consuming, and expensive." [30] Although not a perfect indicator, the fact that legislation has been getting longer supports a perception that more people are being accommodated with amendments and certainly implies that legislation is taking longer to pass.[31] The basic issue concerning time is the collegiality of the legislature. In a deliberative assembly of formally equal members, it takes time to accommodate everyone, or even to accommodate a majority. Recent congressional reforms have made Congress an even more collegial body in the sense that many more participants are now involved in every legislative decision.[32] Norman Ornstein advises that if a president is to prevail over Congress he must accept this premise: "he will be required to know and to deal regularly with a much wider array of players in the process, members and staff."[33] If time was a concern in the "old Congress," it is a major problem in the reformed Congress.

Coherent Public Policy

Even those who have admired the U.S. Congress have noted occasions when it seemed to be moving simultaneously in opposite directions. For example, one observer wryly suggests that members of Congress

> feed their enthusiasm for certain programs by reporting authorizations from their legislative committees and guiding them through the House. They feed their belief in economy by supporting the Appropriations Committee when it cuts appropriations for various programs, including some of the very same ones that they have previously supported.[34]

Sundquist tells us what is wrong with this system; he notes that objectives will conflict, but

> the opposing considerations must be balanced.... The government's programs must support its goals, functional or sectoral policies must be brought into consistency with broad objectives, decisions that affect one another must be related so that the totality makes sense.[35]

Pursuing these goals requires a capacity to plan and to integrate policy. The lack of capacity of a fragmented legislature to perform these functions is one of the major weaknesses of Congress.[36]

Here again the problem lies with Congress's collegial nature, which, compared with the more hierarchical arrangements characteristic of the executive branch, increases its likelihood of producing incoherent policy. This is not to say that incoherence never characterizes policy that emanates from the executive, but "the fact remains that the executive branch does have the capability of being more decisive than the legislative branch when it has to be, and of bringing its policies into a more consistent whole, simply because it is a hierarchy."[37]

The structural manifestation of collegiality in the legislature—the decentralized subcommittee system—ensures that "the problems of leadership, coordination, and policy surveillance" will be exacerbated.[38]

With each subcommittee and its associated subgovernmental structure of interest groups and bureaucrats virtually an autonomous world unto itself, it is difficult to "orchestrate the work of the disparate work groups into some semblance of an integrated whole." [39] Policy in Congress therefore proceeds in unconnected chunks.

Effective Public Policy

Congress's ability to develop effective policies is diminished because the compromises necessary for creating a winning coalition are not always congruent with the demands of effective policy. Catherine Rudder, in her analysis of the passage of the 1981 tax bill, puts it this way:

> the primary interest of participants was in winning, that is, writing a bill that could attract a majority of votes in Congress. Absent were careful deliberation, a sense of limits, an ability to say no to claimants, and an overriding concern for the quality of the bill and for the integrity of the tax code. [40]

The problem is attributable to both the openness and the representative nature of Congress. As Rudder argues in an earlier analysis, the reforms of the 1970s that opened up the writing of tax bills—a process that had hitherto taken place behind the closed doors of the House Ways and Means Committee—increased the responsiveness of members to special interest groups but decreased the chances of responsible and effective tax legislation. [41] She suggests that the Senate in 1982 enacted more responsible tax legislation in part because the majority leader operated in a more closed environment that excluded the public and the press. [42]

The effectiveness of distributive programs depends upon who gets what. The representative nature of Congress impels it to answer that classic question with formula grants. Formula grants generalize programs so that as many states and districts as possible reap the benefits. "This tendency to universalize the particular does not necessarily result in good public policy," Arthur Maass gently suggests. [43] Writing about entitlement programs, John Ferejohn makes a similar point when he concludes that there is a "trade-off between the effectiveness of a transfer program in getting benefits to its intended targets and the support for the program within Congress." [44] And Douglas Arnold says that bureaucrats "are much more likely than congressmen to target funds according to need." Although bureaucrats too are concerned with political variables, "they are free to make individual project decisions" and "they are not faced with the task of writing blanket formulas suitable for every case." [45]

Responsive Public Policy

The previous discussion suggests that representatives, as they strive for legislative packages that can win majorities, often jeopardize the effectiveness of the policies involved. Congressional parochialism also can lead to a slighting of long-term national interests so that short-term constituency demands can be met.

The decentralized structure of Congress enables members to maximize their responsiveness to constituency pressures, thereby virtually ensuring their reelection.[46] Members seek and are granted committee assignments where they can best represent these interests, and then

> whole committees become special pleaders for segmental interests. Agriculture committees are profarmer, interior committees pro-West, labor committees prolabor, veterans committees proveteran, armed services committees promilitary, and so on.[47]

This arrangement allows members to protect their individual political interests, but the general public interest is often ignored. As Sundquist concludes: "a body made up of individuals looking out for themselves cannot, as a collectivity, act responsibly. It cannot govern." [48]

Congress's experience with supply side economics during the first administration of Ronald Reagan is a case in point. John Ellwood describes how legislators disregarded clear evidence that the supply side doctrine would not work, focusing rather on an apparently painless way to cut taxes, maintain funding for programs popular in their constituencies, and lower both inflation and unemployment. The result was that the laws of mathematics and economics prevailed, and the largest deficits in history appeared.[49]

As the supply side debacle demonstrates, the executive also may act irresponsibly. The point is that the executive has what Congress lacks: the "structural capacity" to "rise above the pressure of local and narrow interests." [50]

The Representation Model

Congress shows a disturbing tendency—not always, but often enough—toward ignorance, delay, incoherence, ineffectiveness, and irresponsibility as it grapples with public policy challenges. These failures can be traced in large measure to the generic legislative characteristics of Congress: its representativeness, its collegiality, its openness, and the nonspecialized nature of its membership. The viability of the activist model to which Congress ostensibly conforms is therefore called into question.

The legislative policy-making role incorporated in the representation model, however, is more likely to contribute to the formulation of optimal public policy than is the activist model. The representation model redefines the policy-making responsibilities of the legislature by conceding to the executive the dominant role in the policy-making process. Although the representation legislature can and will, in extraordinary situations, say no to the executive, ordinarily the executive will have its way on most issues most of the time. The legislature will establish the parameters within which the executive acts and will seek to modify proposals designed for the most part by the executive.

This concession of primary policy-making authority to the executive assumes that, compared with the legislature, the executive is better able to achieve public policy that meets the criteria of optimality. Because the executive branch is staffed by more specialists than the legislature, it is capable of more informed policy making. Because it is hierarchically rather than collegially organized, it is capable of more timely and more coherent public policy. Because it is a more closed institution, it is capable of more expeditious and more effective policies. And because it is a less representative institution than the legislature, it can make more effective policies that may be less responsive to short-term demands and more responsive to long-term national interests.

Obviously, there are dangers when so much power is vested in the executive branch. Bureaucrats may fail to see how policies affect ordinary people. Hierarchies may not accord the same full consideration to divergent views that a collegial body would. Closed and nonrepresentative institutions are suspect by the standards of democracy, and from a practical standpoint they may not be open to the different perspectives from which an intelligent conception of the national interest must come. For these reasons the representation model does not eliminate the legislature from the policy-making process.

Debate

The ability of representation model legislatures to influence policy turns upon their capacity to engage in open debate on the policy issues of the day. Although this role of discussion may be close to the original concept of parliament as a place to talk (that is, *parler)*, there is often a tendency to view such activity, in the absence of a frequently exercised legislative capacity to reject executive proposals, as nothing more than talking.[51] Talking may have the latent function of venting anger and legitimizing executive actions, but it can be argued that it has no real consequences for the policies that are ultimately adopted.[52] The executive, virtually certain that it will for the most part prevail, will feel free to ignore legislative discussions and proceed on its own information and at its own pace. Although executive behavior can follow this direction, the process is likely to be more complex.

To the extent that legislative debates are publicized and to the extent that the legislature is broadly representative of public opinion, the executive will ignore what is said in the legislature at its peril. In one sense, the prospect of adverse reaction in the legislature to executive policy-making initiatives may dissuade the executive from going ahead, even if the authority or the votes to do so are available. David Mayhew observed that "public opinion has policy effects without any laws being passed; presidents, bureaucrats, and judges, anticipating trouble with Congress, take action to avoid it." He reminds us that after the Tet offensive of 1968 congressional opinion rather than congressional action contributed to a change in the policy of Lyndon B. Johnson's administration.[53]

In another sense, legislative debate can encourage timely public policy decisions by prodding the executive into action. In late 1985, discussion in Congress, along with threatened actions, evoked substantial changes in the publicly pronounced policies of the Reagan administration in regard to both South Africa and trade policy. In neither case did Congress act, but congressional discussion and its influence on public opinion caused the president to change his policy course.

Legislative discussion also may expand the information base upon which decisions are taken. As the views and opinions in the nation are articulated in the legislature, the responsiveness of public policy to public opinion may be increased. The representation model presumes that the executive, freed from viewing the legislature solely as an adversary, will use the opinion of the legislature either to alert it to political or technical problems in what it proposes to do or to guide it toward more efficacious means for doing so. In discussing how national policy planning in the United States might be improved, Michael Reagan proposes exactly such a role for Congress:

> [I]f coherence is a prime criterion for planning, congressional participation in the goal setting stage should be for the purpose of criticizing executive plans, proposing alternatives to stimulate public discussion and clarify party choices for the voters . . . and limiting presidential action to what the interests and constituents congressmen see themselves as representing will stand.[54]

In this sense, debate in representation legislatures may place de facto limits upon executive action that are nearly as effective as the de jure limits upon which activist legislatures for the most part rely.

Finally, legislative discussion also can provide the data upon which to build a conception of the national interest. John Stuart Mill long ago defined the proper function of the legislature as the nation's "Congress of opinions—an arena in which not only the general opinion of the nation but that of every section of it . . . can produce itself in full light and challenge discussion." [55] Maass emphasizes this same point in his "discussion" model of Congress, which, in many respects, is similar to the representation model. Maass says that the "Executive's role is leadership—to initiate and impel." He suggests that among the roles of Congress are facilitating discussion and providing "the breadth of view" upon which the public interest is based.[56]

Oversight

A second category of activities engaged in by representation legislatures involves the oversight of the executive branch. In Mill's view, "to watch and control the Government" was the "proper office" of the legislature as compared with the governing function, for which he thought the legislature "radically unfit." [57] The representative breadth and openness of the legislature make it an ideal arena within which the executive branch can be held accountable for its policy actions. Acting as a forum for executive accountability is common to nearly all legislatures, but it is crucial to the success of representation legislatures. Because the representation model cedes so much policy-making authority to the executive, it assumes that aggressive performance of legislative oversight activities, by ensuring that the executive will account publicly for its actions, will prevent abuses of this power. Finally, oversight can increase the effectiveness of policy by enlarging the information base upon which decisions to revise policies can be reached.

Linkage

The representative nature of the legislature means that its members will bring to the executive branch problems that individual constituents have with policies and will work to resolve them. Providing constituents with this service, as well as lobbying on behalf of the constituency as a whole for its share of distributional programs, is a nearly universal function of legislatures.[58] These activities inject an element of responsiveness into the policy-making process. The executive can be expected to respond to such requests because by so doing it may prevent open hostility from legislators and because the executive, as noted earlier, has an interest in generating support for its policies. Thus, the legislature is able "to provide a complement to the views of the President so that their interaction in both administration and legislation results in a more valid refinement of community consensus than would otherwise be the case." [59]

In sum, the representation model discourages the legislature from viewing itself as the incubator and designer of public policy—something that it does poorly—and instead encourages the legislature to do what it can do well—to publicly discuss policy problems and alternative solutions, to aggressively oversee the development and implementation of public policy by the executive, and to represent to the executive the needs and demands of individual constituents as well as the constituency as a whole. These activities contribute to optimal public policy in two ways: they improve the information base, and they encourage timely and responsive policy but without significantly detracting from these qualities or from the coherence and effectiveness of public policy.

Congress and the Future

For more than two hundred years the U.S. Congress has stood at the center of this nation's policy-making system; its involvement in the policy-making process has been greater than that of any other legislature in the world. This involvement is due less to any particular merit in the design or performance of the institution than to the unique structure of the American political system and the environment within which the system has operated during most of its history. The Madisonian design of decentralizing political power among the different branches of the national government ensured that at the national level neither the executive nor the legislative branch would consistently be able to force its will upon the other. In other nations political party organizations arose to bridge similar institutional divisions between the legislative and the executive branches, but in the United States a weak and decentralized political party system, rooted for the most part in the fragmentation of political power imposed by the federal system, proved incapable of performing this function.

This constitutional plan of "separated institutions sharing power" has been the major source of Congress's policy-making prerogatives.[60] Except for brief periods of extraordinary presidential ascendancy, the U.S. Congress has compelled presidents to deal with the legislature. Congress has always had the capacity to force, and has often been able to win, confrontations with the president. These congressional victories have most often meant that Congress stops the president from carrying out his policy plans, less often that Congress is making alternative public policy, and even less frequently that Congress is introducing better policy alternatives.[61]

The literature on relations between the legislative and the executive has for the most part ignored these policy consequences of our peculiar arrangement of presidential-congressional power. The focus has been on the question of whether the president or Congress has been the dominant player. The scholarly consensus has been that, while the executive's role is frequently overestimated and Congress's role often underestimated, the executive has generally taken the lead in major policy developments, and in the long term the trend will continue in the direction of the president and away from Congress.[62]

Only occasionally has the question of whether the president or Congress is in control been connected to the issue of Congress's capacity to produce good public policy. Lawrence Dodd has argued that the American political system will experience increasing difficulty in making effective public policies.[63] Under pressure from a variety of external environmental factors, both domestic and international, Congress—and American political institutions more generally—will continue to have difficulty responding, thus threatening a crisis of legitimacy unless major structural reform is undertaken. In the short run, says Dodd, presidential domination of Congress will be the norm. James Sundquist found some hopeful signs in the resurgent Congress of the 1970s, but he too concluded that congressional authority will not be restored because "the new assertiveness of the Congress has not been fully matched by new capability, by institutional forms that would assure responsibility in the more aggressive exercise of power." [64] Like Dodd, Sundquist predicts a renewed period of presidential domination. Even with divided government, presidential domination of Congress seems likely to be the norm into the 1990s.

The conclusions reached by Dodd and by Sundquist fit with my discussion of congressional policy failings and with the studies upon which that discussion has been based. Certainly, stalemate between the president and Congress, or confrontations that produce the policy preferences of the winning side but do not necessarily elicit effective policies, simply will not do. Political systems must have the capacity to act. The system as it now operates seems designed to act only when it is confronted with either crisis or consensus. Although consensual policies may on some scores be more desirable than nonconsensual policies, consensual policies are not necessarily effective, timely, coherent, informed, or even responsive to the short-term or long-term interests of the American people, particularly if such a consensus represents simply the lowest common denominator of multiple conflicting views.

To create the capacity to develop public policy that meets the criteria of optimality, it is necessary to cut the constitutional knot of shared congressional and executive policy-making power and more sharply delineate the roles of Congress and the president. The representation model seems the most realistic division, building as it does upon the characteristics of the executive and the legislative branches that are the strengths of each institution. Freed from its futile quest for machinery that can help it to develop effective and coherent policy alternatives independent of the president and the bureaucracy, Congress can concentrate on what it can do: it can increase its capacity to watch and control the executive, it can refine its techniques for representing interests so that the general as well as the particular wills of the people can be heard, and it can check the propensity of bureaucrats to ignore the people as they make public policy.

For the representation model to work, we must encourage dialogue between the president and Congress in a context that presumes executive action and a congressional response that establishes, through discussion and debate, the parameters within which the executive will act. In this sense, it is possible to interpret the resurgence of Congress in the 1970s that Sundquist discusses as constituting a movement toward the representation model. Although the reformed congressional budgetary process, the War Powers Resolution of 1973, and the legislative veto may be viewed by some as mechanisms for recapturing power from the president, it should be noted that each is predicated upon and triggered by previous executive action. (See Chapters 8, 9, and 10.) These acts may therefore be viewed as concessions to executive domination and as mechanisms for ensuring forms of congressional involvement that are compatible with the requisites of a representation model.

The budget reforms, for example, promised the capacity for presidential leadership in bringing coherence to the budgetary process, at the same time protecting the congressional power of the purse. As Allen Schick notes, the reconciliation process used in 1981 "forced Congress to consider the budget whole and on the president's terms." [65] Although subsequent budgetary experiences have not followed the 1981 model, according to Schick a negotiating relationship has been established between the White House and Congress. He goes on to say that "it is in the long-term interest of the White House to improve the budget capacity of Congress" and that this capacity need not conflict with a "presidentially oriented" budget system. [66]

As for the War Powers Resolution, the jury is still out in regard to how real are the restrictions that it places on the president and exactly how much consultation with Congress it requires. [67] The probability of consultation between the president and Congress on matters of military intervention has certainly been increased by the resolution's provisions, and, at least in the Lebanese crisis of 1984, dialogue did take place.

The legislative veto, while certainly subject to both constitutional questions and congressional abuse, has, as Maass says, "great significance as a device for improving congressional oversight and at the same time improving presidential leadership by allowing for, while at the same time controlling, necessary executive discretion." [68] Joseph Cooper agrees, arguing that the legislative veto encourages executive responsiveness and "permits the two essential yet conflicting needs of the modern democratic state, executive leadership and legislative control, to be reconciled and mutually satisfied." [69]

Although these developments suggest that Congress has, perhaps tacitly, begun to make its peace with the representation model, the problem, as Maass observes, is that Congress does not always talk as it behaves and its reformers continue to discuss the need to restore Congress's role as an independent policy maker.[70] Such "restoration" efforts are bound to fail because they ignore the fundamental point that legislatures are not designed to make policies that approach the criteria of optimality discussed in this chapter. Thus, Congress may succeed in restoring its power, but it also will fail to govern.

Notes

This chapter was first published in *Congress and the Presidency* 13 (Spring 1986): 1-20. The journal is a joint publication of the Center for Congressional and Presidential Studies and the U.S. Capitol Historical Society. The chapter is reprinted with only copy editing changes. An expanded and revised statement of the argument can be found in Michael L. Mezey, *Congress, the President, and Public Policy* (Boulder, Colo.: Westview Press, 1989).

1. For recent scholarly literature on the traditional issues of constitutional principle and precedent, see Louis Fisher, *The Politics of Shared Power: Congress and the Executive* (Washington, D.C.: CQ Press, 1981). For literature dealing with the usual empirical question of which institution actually dominates, see George C. Edwards III, *Presidential Influence in Congress* (San Francisco: Freeman, 1980); and Richard Fleisher and Jon R. Bond, "Assessing Presidential Support in the House: Lessons from Reagan and Carter," *Journal of Politics* 45 (August 1983): 745-758. New discussions of presidential strategies for dealing with Congress can also be found in Paul C. Light, *The President's Agenda: Domestic Policy Choices from Kennedy to Carter* (Baltimore: Johns Hopkins University Press, 1982); and Charles O. Jones, "Presidential Negotiation with Congress," in *Both Ends of the Avenue: The Presidency, the Executive Branch, and Congress in the 1980s,* ed. Anthony King (Washington, D.C.: American Enterprise Institute, 1983). For detailed accounts of the relationship between the president and Congress during the early years of the Reagan administration, see Norman J. Ornstein, ed., *President and Congress: Assessing Reagan's First Year* (Washington, D.C.: American Enterprise

Institute, 1982); and Barbara Sinclair, "Agenda Control and Policy Success: Ronald Reagan and the 97th Congress," *Legislative Studies Quarterly* 10 (August 1985): 291-314. At least one excellent analysis of the pre-Reagan decade can be found in James L. Sundquist, *The Decline and Resurgence of Congress* (Washington, D.C.: Brookings Institution, 1981). For a review of some of this literature, see Michael L. Mezey, "The President and the Congress: A Review Article," *Legislative Studies Quarterly* 10 (November 1985): 519-536.

2. The major exception is Sundquist, *Decline and Resurgence of Congress.* As will become apparent, my analysis owes a great deal to his work.

3. In an earlier discussion, I used the term "policy-making model" rather than "activist model" to refer to a legislature with a central role in the policy-making process. See Michael L. Mezey, *Comparative Legislatures* (Durham, N.C.: Duke University Press, 1979), 13-17.

4. This view of what constitutes good public policy is heavily influenced by what Charles E. Lindblom calls the rational-comprehensive approach to public policy making. Lindblom contrasts that approach with the method of successive limited comparisons, or incrementalism, as it is now more commonly called. See Charles E. Lindblom, "The Science of Muddling Through," *Public Administration Review* 19 (Spring 1959): 79-88; and Charles E. Lindblom, *The Intelligence of Democracy* (New York: Free Press, 1964).

5. Lawrence C. Dodd and Richard L. Schott, *Congress and the Administrative State* (New York: Wiley, 1979).

6. Mezey, *Comparative Legislatures,* 253.

7. These legislative characteristics are incorporated in most definitions of legislatures. See Norman Meller, "The Identification and Classification of Legislatures," *Philippine Journal of Public Administration* 10 (October 1966): 308-319; Gerhard Loewenberg, "The Role of Parliaments in Modern Political Systems," in *Modern Parliaments: Change or Decline,* ed. Gerhard Loewenberg (Chicago: Aldine-Atherton, 1971); Fred W. Riggs, "Legislative Structures: Some Thoughts on Elected National Assemblies," in *Legislatures in Comparative Perspective,* ed. Allan Kornberg (New York: McKay, 1973); Nelson W. Polsby, "Legislatures," in *Handbook of Political Science,* ed. Fred I. Greenstein and Nelson W. Polsby (Reading, Mass.: Addison-Wesley, 1975), vol. 5; John E. Schwarz and L. Earl Shaw, *The United States Congress in Comparative Perspective* (Hinsdale, Ill.: Dryden Press, 1976); and Mezey, *Comparative Legislatures.* For a discussion of the contrasting characteristics of executives, see Anthony King, "Executives," in *Handbook of Political Science,* vol. 5.

8. Arthur Maass, *Congress and the Common Good* (New York: Basic Books, 1983), 12.

9. John D. Lees and Malcolm Shaw, eds., *Committees in Legislatures: A Comparative Analysis* (Durham, N.C.: Duke University Press, 1979).

10. Gerhard Loewenberg and Samuel C. Patterson, *Comparing Legislatures*

(Boston: Little, Brown, 1979), 164.

11. James Burnham, *Congress and the American Tradition* (Chicago: Regnery, 1959), 349.

12. Samuel C. Patterson, "The Semi-Sovereign Congress," in *The New American Political System*, ed. Anthony King (Washington, D.C.: American Enterprise Institute, 1978), 125.

13. Alfred DeGrazia, "Toward a New Model of Congress," in *Congress: The First Branch of Government*, ed. Alfred DeGrazia (Garden City, N.Y.: Doubleday, 1967), 16.

14. Jean Blondel, *Comparative Legislatures* (Englewood Cliffs, N.J.: Prentice-Hall, 1973), 134.

15. See Mezey, *Comparative Legislatures*, 36, 282-284.

16. This view of what the role of Congress should be has been referred to as the "literary theory"; see Roger H. Davidson, David M. Kovenock, and Michael K. O'Leary, *Congress in Crisis: Politics and Congressional Reform* (Belmont, Calif.: Wadsworth, 1966), 17-25. Another scholar has referred to it as the "whig" or "congressional supremacy" model; see John S. Saloma III, *Congress and the New Politics* (Boston: Little, Brown, 1969), 45-47.

17. See Kenneth Janda, "Information Systems for Congress," in *Congress: The First Branch of Government*, 405-412.

18. Saloma, *Congress and the New Politics*, 212-216.

19. Norman J. Ornstein et al., *Vital Statistics on Congress, 1984-1985* (Washington, D.C.: American Enterprise Institute, 1984), 121, 124, 127.

20. Sundquist, *Decline and Resurgence of Congress*, 407-408.

21. Michael J. Malbin, *Unelected Representatives: Congressional Staff and the Future of Representative Government* (New York: Basic Books, 1979), 250.

22. Sundquist, *Decline and Resurgence of Congress*, 409ff.

23. Norman J. Ornstein and David Rohde, "Resource Usage, Information, and Policymaking in the Senate," in *Congress and Public Policy*, ed. David C. Kozak and John D. Macartney (Homewood, Ill.: Dorsey Press, 1982), 310.

24. Dodd and Schott, *Congress and the Administrative State*, 273.

25. Robert D. Reischauer, "Getting, Using, and Misusing Economic Information," in *Making Economic Policy in Congress*, ed. Allen Schick (Washington, D.C.: American Enterprise Institute, 1983), 59.

26. Mark V. Nadel, "Making Regulatory Policy," in *Making Economic Policy in Congress*, 246.

27. Bruce I. Oppenheimer, "Congress and the New Obstructionism: Developing an Energy Policy," in *Congress Reconsidered*, 2d ed., ed. Lawrence C. Dodd and Bruce I. Oppenheimer (Washington, D.C.: CQ Press, 1981).

28. Sundquist, *Decline and Resurgence of Congress*, 454.

29. Naomi Caiden, "The Politics of Subtraction," in *Making Economic Policy in Congress*, 105.

30. Steven S. Smith, "New Patterns of Decisionmaking in Congress," in *The*

New Direction in American Politics, ed. John E. Chubb and Paul E. Peterson (Washington, D.C.: Brookings Institution, 1985), 218.

31. The average number of pages per statute rose from 3.8 pages in 1971-1972 to 9.2 in 1981-1982. See Ornstein et al., *Vital Statistics on Congress, 1984-1985,* 150. See also Barbara Sinclair, "Coping with Uncertainty: Building Coalitions in the House and the Senate," in *The New Congress,* ed. Thomas E. Mann and Norman J. Ornstein (Washington, D.C.: American Enterprise Institute, 1981), 220.
32. Smith, "New Patterns of Decisionmaking in Congress."
33. Norman J. Ornstein, "The Open Congress Meets the President," in *Both Ends of the Avenue,* 204.
34. Maass, *Congress and the Common Good,* 146.
35. Sundquist, *Decline and Resurgence of Congress,* 427.
36. Ibid.
37. Ibid., 428.
38. Dodd and Schott, *Congress and the Administrative State,* 128.
39. Roger H. Davidson and Walter J. Oleszek, *Congress and Its Members* (Washington, D.C.: CQ Press, 1981), 438.
40. Catherine E. Rudder, "Tax Policy: Structure and Choice," in *Making Economic Policy in Congress,* 206.
41. Catherine E. Rudder, "Committee Reform and the Revenue Process," in *Congress Reconsidered,* 1st ed., ed. Lawrence C. Dodd and Bruce I. Oppenheimer (New York: Praeger, 1977), 124-126.
42. Rudder, "Tax Policy: Structure and Choice," 207.
43. Maass, *Congress and the Common Good,* 169.
44. John Ferejohn, "Congress and Redistribution," in *Making Economic Policy in Congress,* 152.
45. R. Douglas Arnold, "The Local Roots of Domestic Policy," in *New Congress,* 285.
46. David R. Mayhew, *Congress: The Electoral Connection* (New Haven, Conn.: Yale University Press, 1974).
47. Sundquist, *Decline and Resurgence of Congress,* 451.
48. Ibid., 456.
49. John W. Ellwood, "Budget Control in a Redistributive Environment," in *Making Economic Policy in Congress,* 90. See also James A. Thurber, "The Impact of Budget Reform on Presidential and Congressional Governance," chap. 8 of this volume.
50. Sundquist, *Decline and Resurgence of Congress,* 451.
51. See Loewenberg and Patterson, *Comparing Legislatures,* chap. 1.
52. See Robert Packenham, "Legislatures and Political Development," in *Legislatures in Developmental Perspective,* ed. Allan Kornberg and Lloyd Musolf (Durham, N.C.: Duke University Press, 1970).
53. Mayhew, *Congress: The Electoral Connection,* 107.
54. Michael Reagan, "Toward Improving National Policy Planning," in *Congress and the President: Allies and Adversaries,* ed. Ronald C. Moe (Pacific Palisades, Calif.: Goodyear, 1971), 81.

55. John Stuart Mill, *Considerations on Representative Government* (1861; reprint, New York: Liberal Arts Press, 1958), 82.
56. Maass, *Congress and the Common Good*, 13, 18ff.
57. Mill, *Considerations on Representative Government*, 81.
58. Mezey, *Comparative Legislatures*, chap. 10.
59. Maass, *Congress and the Common Good*, 12.
60. Richard E. Neustadt, *Presidential Power* (New York: Wiley, 1960), 33.
61. This will strike some readers as extreme in the sense that it minimizes the importance of congressional policy leadership. See, for example, James L. Sundquist, *Politics and Policy* (Washington, D.C.: Brookings Institution, 1968), 389ff., concerning the policies generated by Congress during the Eisenhower administration, and Roger H. Davidson, "Senate Leaders: Janitors for an Untidy Chamber," in *Congress Reconsidered*, 3d ed., ed. Lawrence C. Dodd and Bruce I. Oppenheimer (Washington, D.C.: CQ Press, 1985), 232, in regard to congressional policy initiation during the Nixon administration. In mitigation, it may be wrong to generalize the events of the Eisenhower years on the presumption that "passive Presidents may be a vanishing breed"; see James David Barber, *The Presidential Character*, 3d ed. (Englewood Cliffs, N.J.: Prentice-Hall, 1985), 124. As for the Nixon period, it should be said that when Congress prods the executive into action—which was often the case during this period—it is performing in perfect consonance with the representation model.
62. See Mezey, "President and the Congress"; David E. Price, *Who Makes the Laws?* (Cambridge, Mass.: Schenckman, 1972); Gary Orfield, *Congressional Power: Congress and Social Change* (New York: Harcourt, Brace, 1975); Edwards, *Presidential Influence in Congress;* Dodd and Schott, *Congress and the Administrative State;* and Sundquist, *Decline and Resurgence of Congress.*
63. Lawrence C. Dodd, "Congress and the Quest for Power," in *Congress Reconsidered*, 1st ed.; and Lawrence C. Dodd, "Congress, the Constitution, and the Crisis of Legitimation," in *Congress Reconsidered*, 2d ed.
64. Sundquist, *Decline and Resurgence of Congress*, 483.
65. Allen Schick, "How the Budget Was Won and Lost," in *President and Congress: Assessing Reagan's First Year*, 26.
66. Allen Schick, "The Budget as an Instrument of Presidential Policy," in *The Reagan Presidency and the Governing of America*, ed. Lester M. Salamon and Michael S. Lund (Washington, D.C.: Urban Institute Press, 1984), 122-125.
67. Graham T. Allison, "Making War: The President and Congress," in *The Presidency Reappraised*, 2d ed., ed. Thomas Cronin and Rexford Tugwell (New York: Praeger, 1977); and Sundquist, *Decline and Resurgence of Congress*, 238ff.
68. Maass, *Congress and the Common Good*, 202.
69. Joseph Cooper, "Legislative Veto in the 1980s," in *Congress Reconsidered*, 3d ed., 379.
70. Maass, *Congress and the Common Good*, 55.

7. LEGISLATORS, REGULATORS, AND THE OMB: THE CONGRESSIONAL CHALLENGE TO PRESIDENTIAL REGULATORY RELIEF

Christopher H. Foreman, Jr.

Martial's ancient epigram "I can neither live with you nor without you" nicely captures the basic tension between the legislative and executive branches of government in the U.S. system of shared powers.[1] Each branch relies vitally on the other, but hesitancy, hostility, suspicion, and jealousy abound. Some aspects of this uneasy union are probed less often than they ought to be. Particularly rare is analysis of the consequences of congressional oversight of administration.[2]

This chapter examines an important new feature of legislative-executive relations: congressional response to cost-benefit regulatory review by the Office of Management and Budget (OMB) pursuant to two path-breaking executive orders issued during Ronald Reagan's first term as president. These orders would become particularly significant for health and safety regulatory policy (sometimes referred to rather less precisely as social regulation).[3]

Executive Order 12291, issued February 17, 1981, required (with a few explicit exceptions) that federal agencies base their rulemaking "on adequate information concerning the need for and consequences of proposed government action," that regulatory decisions weigh costs against benefits, that regulatory objectives "maximize the net benefits to society," and that the alternative selected for pursuing the objective reflect "the least net cost to society."[4] In addition, agencies were required to produce regulatory impact analyses justifying each "major" rule.[5] OMB was to review these analyses, along with proposed regulations, prior to promulgation, to ensure that the cost-benefit and cost-effectiveness criteria had been met. Within OMB the task fell to the Office of Information and Regulatory Affairs (OIRA). Outside OMB the principal partner in implementation was to be the Presidential Task Force on Regulatory Relief, chaired by then vice president George Bush. Executive Order 12498, issued on January 4, 1985, pushed OMB involvement in agency decision making several steps deeper. Essentially, any major effort to contemplate rules ("actions taken to consider whether to initiate rulemaking") would require the blessing of OIRA.

These two executive orders, and the broader regulatory relief effort they supported, created widespread discontent inside Congress. This, in turn, set the stage for Congress (or, at least, the House of Representatives) to threaten the administration with the ultimate weapon: a withdrawal of OMB funding. Once the administration had issued the first executive order and made clear its seriousness about vigorous implementation, a sustained interbranch clash became unavoidable. The combined institutional and policy stakes were simply too high.

What Is Oversight?

In this chapter the term *congressional oversight* is broadly construed and refers to two aspects of congressional activity: monitoring what the executive branch does and influencing what it does. These efforts, sometimes pursued in combination, may be formal or informal, may emanate from a variety of committees or congressional staff agencies, and may or may not involve lawmaking. The conventional textbook distinction between legislation and oversight is not made here because of the blending of activities and purposes that characterize the real world of Congress.[6]

Regulatory Relief in Context

Of course, institutional fragmentation and partisanship have always threatened presidential-congressional cooperation on a wide range of matters. Three additional features of the political context for social regulation are essential to an understanding of congressional oversight.

First, social regulation is riddled with conflict provoked by attentive interests outside government. At stake in issues such as pollution control and automotive safety are millions, even billions, of dollars in private sector costs. Regulated industries confront determined advocacy groups with strategic incentives to employ harsh rhetoric, to seek redress in a court of law or of public opinion, and to delay compromise. Oversight of social regulation is not a simple matter of policing programs for conformity with an established legislative intent. So unsettled is the policy area that postenactment congressional oversight is, in effect, a continuation of preenactment politics. Fixed and shared understandings about social regulation are conspicuously rare within Congress, much less between a Congress dominated by one party and a White House by the other.

Second, members of Congress today are very active in creating and implementing health and safety regulatory policy. Aided by committee staff, backed by motivated interests, and watched by an attentive press, they stand poised to object when presidents attempt to manage regulatory programs in unacceptable ways. Unpredictable agenda setters, these congressional entrepreneurs complicate relations between Congress and the White House by inserting themselves as advocates and roadblocks in the political process.

Third, much tension between the branches results when Congress, of necessity, cedes discretion to the executive branch without knowing precisely how it will be employed. In passing the Paperwork Reduction Act of 1980 (PRA), Congress created OIRA, which Reagan soon put to uses unintended by the Democratic Congress that voted for it.

To someone unfamiliar with the political battles that have characterized American regulatory policy, Reagan's executive orders might appear perfectly sensible, an unlikely source of controversy. Naturally enough, the administration labored mightily to create such an impression. Wendy Lee Gramm, the economist who headed OIRA in Reagan's second term, made these remarks about regulatory review:

> [I]t's plain good government. . . . Cost-benefit analyses are essential to make decisions in this world. It's how a business makes decisions. It's how you allocate resources efficiently. To suggest that one ought not to do it is to say one ought not think.[7]

As straightforward as regulatory review can be made to sound, its context and the concrete implications of such an intrusive OMB role made for political dynamite. While the Nixon, Ford, and Carter administrations had sought to inject a measure of presidential coordination and cost sensitivity into selected regulatory proposals, the Reagan administration reallocated power over a whole sphere of policy with enormous substantive and symbolic importance.[8] (Social regulation is an area of high public salience and one in which congressional policy entrepreneurs have often seized the initiative from the executive.)[9]

The context for this reallocation of power was widespread disenchantment with regulatory bureaucracies that had built up during the late 1970s. Business opposed what it deemed excessively costly rulemaking and intrusive enforcement. Dissatisfied with high-profile regulatory programs, Congress voted to curb the authority of the Federal Trade Commission (FTC) and used a series of appropriations riders in the 1970s to constrain the enforcement discretion of the Occupational Safety and Health Administration (OSHA). The Carter administration had briefly considered abolishing the Consumer Product Safety Commission (CPSC). Policy-focused economists criticized regulation as generally inefficient; in their view, business firms, the economy, and the public were bearing substantial unnecessary costs.

Regulatory flexibility and greater sensitivity to social costs were advocated.[10]

Although regulatory analysis had its legislative defenders, Congress had largely turned a deaf ear toward them. It was unwilling to stake regulatory programs on the kinds of "economizing" reforms being suggested, and it was suspicious of arguments that sounded too much like excuses for regulatory laxity. After all, even when the antiregulatory drumbeat was at its loudest, well-organized constituencies backed each major regulatory program, and they had strong voices in critical committees of Congress. The general idea of regulatory protection (especially in health and safety) remains popular with the mass public: poll data on environmental protection in particular are consistently and strongly supportive.[11]

On the other hand, Congress was very interested in reforms (such as the legislative veto) that appeared to offer it greater access to agency activity. It should surprise no one that a congressional power perspective on regulatory reform consistently proved more popular on Capitol Hill than economic efficiency. And the same institutional impulse that sustained this preference would haunt Reagan's regulatory relief initiatives.

The executive orders were the central procedural element in the Reagan administration's multisided challenge to the regulatory status quo. Unlike statutes, the executive orders could be issued by the president unilaterally and with widespread applicability. To imprint on the bureaucracy the preferred doctrine of regulatory relief, the administration also aggressively employed the more conventional tools of appointments, budgets, administrative reorganization, and shifts in enforcement emphasis. In these areas congressional opposition could be more directly effective than against executive orders. Because of its very scope and single-mindedness, regulatory relief naturally encountered congressional resistance.

Three Elements of Congressional Resistance

Congressional structure, resources, and political incentives combine to give oversight of regulatory relief a distinctive cast. Specifically, oversight is decentralized, diffuse, and opportunistic, a kind of legislative analog to guerrilla warfare.

Decentralization

Although scholars are beginning to focus on the collegial elements of the contemporary Congress, the dominant message of professional Congress watchers remains that the institution, unlike most parliaments, is profoundly decentralized.[12] For example, consider the legislative politics the Food and Drug Administration (FDA) must play. It must answer to the House Government Operations Committee, the Senate Governmental Affairs Committee, and authorization and appropriations committees in both houses. Although the agency has permanent authorization, the authorizing committees are free to critique its performance and to widen its responsibilities (which happened when Congress passed the 1976 Medical Device Amendments, the 1980 Infant Formula Act, and the 1983 Orphan Drug Act). The appropriations subcommittees with jurisdiction over the FDA budget are dominated by farm-state members of Congress who are ever alert to any activity that may affect their constituency. Particularly attentive to FDA matters in the House are the Energy and Commerce Committee's Subcommittee on Oversight and Investigations, chaired by the full committee chairman, John Dingell, D-Mich., and the Government Operations Committee's Subcommittee on Human Resources and Intergovernmental Relations, chaired by Ted Weiss, D-N.Y.[13] Regulatory agency activities also attract the attention of senators and representatives who are not members of the aforementioned committees. This leads to additional inquiry and comment. Given the multiplicity of units with a stake in agency programs, the decentralized reaction to regulatory relief was inevitable.

Diffusion

Moreover, the oversight weapon was aimed at diffuse targets. The multitude of committees and subcommittees with oversight responsibilities oversee not only agencies but also a far larger number of bureaucratic subunits, specific programs, and discrete decisions. The sheer magnitude and complexity of the oversight task made coordination and sustained attentiveness difficult. And yet the very scope and density of the bureaucratic state offered an important advantage to members anxious to highlight the perceived failings of Reagan's regulatory program.

The diffuseness of the bureaucracy dramatically increased the likelihood that some example of mismanagement, unwarranted OMB involvement, or decline in regulatory stringency would reach Congress's attention under conditions advantageous to the opponents of the new regime. (Indeed, disgruntled civil servants could and would provide a flow of information on the inner workings of the bureaucracy.) Thus, overseers might garner media attention and perhaps even challenge occasional decisions with an eye to reversing them.

Opportunism

Given these conditions, oversight of the OMB effort naturally was opportunistic, meaning enterprisingly selective. Many considerations inclined Congress to hammer at particular targets while largely ignoring others: members' constituencies and alliances, members' contacts inside the bureaucracy, the amount of staff investigative time available, and the more favorable political twist of some cases than others. Most of all, this selectivity quickly allowed overseers to supplement dry legal arguments with concrete regulatory shortcomings, which are of more interest to the general public.

OMB Under Fire

From the outset Executive Order 12291 proved unpopular among congressional Democrats, who continued to control the House of Representatives by a large margin, although they lost control of the Senate in the 1980 elections. Within the House, the earliest, most tenacious, and most focused objection to the OMB program emerged from Representative Dingell's Subcommittee on Oversight and Investigations. In mid-June of 1981, barely four months after the release of the first executive order, the subcommittee staged a hearing that highlighted serious objections.[14] At the same time the subcommittee also published a report by Morton Rosenberg of the Congressional Research Service that provided ammunition to Representative Dingell and then-representative Albert Gore, Jr., D-Tenn., a Dingell ally.[15] Because the regulatory relief program was so new, the subcommittee, drawing on Rosenberg's study, concentrated on a largely prospective attack, rooted in procedural, institutional, and constitutional anxieties. Congressional (and other) critics of the executive order asserted that it displaced proper institutional authority, contained questionable review criteria, gave OMB an opportunity for inappropriate secrecy, and increased OMB's oversight responsibilities without sufficiently increasing its analytic expertise. All of these shortcomings, critics charged, would facilitate delay and reduced stringency in particular rules issued.

Displacement of Authority. The Rosenberg report suggested that the order seemed "to establish a formal, comprehensive, centralized and substantively oriented system of control of informal rulemaking that is without precedent."[16] This scheme of review might conflict with the Administrative Procedure Act, removing discretion from agency heads and undermining congressional intent.

Questionable Review Criteria. Where, Chairman Dingell would repeatedly ask over the years, did Congress authorize the subjugation of regulatory decision making to cost-benefit review? And how would human lives be weighed against other factors?

Unrecorded Influence Over Decisions. Might the OMB or the Presidential Task Force on Regulatory Relief serve as channels of unseen influence and ex parte communication from interested parties? In the June 1981 hearing, for example, Rep. Mike Synar, D-Okla., commented on a speech that task force counsel C. Boyden Gray had given before the U.S. Chamber of Commerce. In this speech Gray highlighted the informal appellate role the administration envisioned for the task force.[17]

Analytic Expertise. Would OMB have adequate staff to conduct competent and timely reviews of the regulations that agencies would submit? Moreover, would the agencies be able to meet OMB's analytic demands? Representative Gore complained, "[T]he analytical resources of agency after agency are being cut, just as the demands placed on them by OMB are increased." [18]

Delay and Reduced Stringency. Underlying all of these complaints was the fear that protective rules would be delayed and weakened, thus jeopardizing public health and safety. The evidence led Representative Gore to conclude that "this administration's real goal is simply to stop regulation. If this is indeed the goal, it would be best to say it outright." [19]

Even if stopping regulation in its tracks had been the administration's goal, the June 1981 hearing would have been a rather weak political counterpunch. Dingell and his staff were well aware that the procedural and institutional questions raised during the hearing were unlikely to generate the degree of press attention or public outrage that concrete "horror stories" could trigger. Fortunately for congressional Democrats, the broad array of specific programs affected by the executive order, controversial appointments, budget cuts, and enforcement actions would soon transform the Reagan program into a more inviting target. Even where OMB review was not the immediate focus of inquiry and criticism, overseers were indirectly tarnishing its luster, generating a political climate inhospitable to regulatory relief as a whole. Individual members opposed to OMB's heightened role took every opportunity to remind their constituents of the dreaded "black hole" of review that was undermining basic protections. The tactics and effects of congressional oversight are vividly illustrated at two agencies: the Environmental Protection Agency (EPA) and the Food and Drug Administration.

Oversight at EPA

The 1982-1983 scandal at EPA resulted in the departure of no fewer than thirteen top officials in only seven weeks, five of them in a single day.[20] EPA administrator Anne Burford resigned and Rita Lavelle, assistant administrator for solid waste and emergency response, was fired. Congressional overseers managed to generate a media barrage that provoked a full-blown political crisis for the Reagan administration. While Dingell's subcommittee was the first and most aggressive in the oversight effort, other Democratic subcommittee chairmen in the House piled on, ultimately creating what might be described as "pack oversight." All in all, five House subcommittees investigated wrongdoing at EPA.[21]

Action by the administration in late 1982 set the stage for the confrontation. Claiming executive privilege, a claim it would later drop, the administration refused to provide documents that congressional committees had requested. When Administrator Burford refused to honor a subpoena issued by the Public Works and Transportation Committee's Subcommittee on Investigations and Oversight, chaired by Georgia Democrat Elliott Levitas, the full committee, and then the entire House, voted her in contempt of Congress. This was prosecutorial oversight at its most assertive. By the time the smoke cleared in the spring of 1983, the White House had brought back to EPA respected former administrator William Ruckelshaus as a symbol of its commitment to the environment.[22]

Waffling by the Reagan administration on regulatory policy concerning hazardous wastes also prompted criticism by Congress:

> On February 25, [1982,] the EPA proposed to reverse previous rules . . . that prohibited the burying of hazardous liquids in drums at waste disposal landfills. . . . The agency said it was suspending the ban for a ninety-day period, in part because it was unworkable and because industry had complained about the cost of complying with the previous regulations. . . . Rep. James Florio (D-N.J.), Chairman of a House subcommittee with jurisdiction over hazardous waste policy, characterized EPA actions as "a wholesale retreat" from the efforts to clean up hazardous waste disposal practices. . . . On March 19, 1982, the EPA reversed its three-week-old decision and established an interim rule prohibiting the burial of any container in which toxic liquids are standing in observable quantities. . . . [And on April 12, 1982,] the EPA reversed a much-criticized decision made in October 1981, and said that an estimated 10,000 hazardous waste disposal facilities would now have to obtain liability insurance protecting people from chemical contamination.[23]

In January 1986 pressure from Dingell's subcommittee prodded EPA to propose an immediate ban on some asbestos products and a ten-year phase-out of remaining asbestos uses.[24] Remarkably, this came a year after the acting deputy administrator, James Barnes, announced the agency's intention to defer its authority over the substance to OSHA and the Consumer Product Safety Commission. (Section 9 of the Toxic

Substances Control Act allows EPA to refer a substance elsewhere for regulatory action.)

Barnes's announcement sparked a political firestorm. After an investigation, Dingell's subcommittee concluded that Barnes had succumbed to unlawful OMB pressure.[25] Critics inside and outside Congress (and in EPA as well) argued that EPA's deferral of authority was unjustified, a cover for Reagan administration insensitivity to the environment and public health. Five weeks after the Barnes announcement, EPA placed the decision on hold pending further study. Nine months later EPA reaffirmed its original intent to move aggressively against asbestos.

In this instance congressional overseers were in an unusually favorable position to engage in what I call "tipping."[26] This occurs when an agency decision has worked its way to the point of final execution only to be delayed by last-minute disagreement. At this point timely howling by congressional watchdogs may be a sufficient catalyst for final promulgation of the regulation.

A similar situation (this time with congressional Republicans doing the prodding) seems to have occurred in 1985, when EPA hesitated on the verge of publishing recommended maximum containment levels (RMCLs) for forty chemicals under the 1974 Safe Drinking Water Act. The statute required that, after sufficient laboratory and field research, RMCLs be established that were adequate to prevent adverse health effects. The agency would then mandate a maximum containment level (MCL) that came as close to the health goal as available technology permitted. As is often the case with complex regulatory mandates, however, progress had been slow.

In April 1985 EPA submitted a proposal for RMCLs to OMB for review. OMB held onto the proposal well beyond the sixty days specified in Executive Order 12291. Congress complained, and loudly. The Senate Committee on Environment and Public Works sent two letters to OMB asking that the RMCLs be released, but it received no answer.[27] Then, on September 19, Sen. Dave Durenberger, R-Minn., introduced an amendment to the Comprehensive Environmental Response and Liability Act (Superfund) requiring that OMB release the RMCLs for *Federal Register* publication within three weeks. The Durenberger amendment cleared the Senate, and within a few days OMB released the RMCLs (more than five months after their original submission for review).[28]

Oversight at FDA

At the FDA, which is perhaps second only to EPA as a focus of congressional interest in health and safety regulation, one finds similar instances of successful oversight tipping in opposition to the Reagan administration.

The Dingell subcommittee was singularly effective in at least three instances. When a batch of vitamin-deficient infant formula was discovered in early 1982, the subcommittee used the occasion to denounce the administration on regulatory relief. Quality control and recall regulations implementing the 1980 Infant Formula Act had been slowed by OMB review. FDA commissioner Arthur Hull Hayes conceded that had the proposed regulations been in force and had they been followed by the offending firm, the defective formula would not have reached the market. The regulations were promptly issued.[29]

More than two years later a regulation intended to strengthen requirements for manufacturer reporting of harmful episodes involving medical devices was held up in the office of Margaret Heckler, the secretary of Health and Human Services. Dingell announced a hearing in the wake of deaths caused by improperly functioning anesthesia machines and used this as leverage to get Heckler to speed the regulation; he was prepared to grill her in public about the delay. Within a few days Heckler got the regulation out.[30]

And in March 1985 OMB released a labeling rule for sulfite content in processed foods. The preservative had been linked to several deaths and hundreds of cases of severe allergic reactions. In this case a major roadblock to final release had been an assistant secretary at Health and Human Services who remained unconvinced of the regulation's merit. A congressional hearing appears to have helped pressure the administration into yielding on the issue.[31]

Congress as Naysayer

Given the Reagan administration's antiregulatory stances, Congress had few occasions to play one of its favorite roles in regulatory oversight—that of naysayer. Congressional advocates of regulation could seldom threaten the administration with budget cuts, for example, since doing so would play directly into the hands of political appointees who wanted their agencies to give business more freedom. For the same reason, Congress was not well positioned to block offensive regulations in most cases; the problem for program advocates was to induce action, not retard it.

On occasion, however, when the administration wanted to take actions that offended congressional and constituency sensitivities, traditional blocking action proved feasible. Congress effectively blocked action on the recommendation of FTC chairman James C. Miller III to close ten regional offices of the Federal Trade Commission. In a controversial report on the FTC to the administration's transition team, Miller

> characterized the regional offices' efforts as "misguided" and "mismanaged" and suggested that trivial cases made up a dispro-portionate share of the caseload. The "geographic and psychologi-cal" distance between these offices and Washington headquarters was cited as an obstacle to the kind of effective, centralized control the Reagan administration sought. . . .
>
> Congress . . . was not receptive to Chairman Miller's propos-als—rejecting out of hand his initial suggestion to close all ten. In April 1982, responding to severe proposed budget cuts by both Miller and OMB, the agency's commissioners voted to close four of its ten regional offices, but congressional opposition forced a suspension of the plan; in December 1982, Congress provided additional funds to the agency to keep seven regional offices open for the remainder of the fiscal year.[32]

Perhaps the most sweeping collective challenge to OMB before 1986 came outside the area of social regulation. Congress voted in late 1983 to bar OMB from reviewing agricultural marketing orders, government supervised arrangements under which competition in certain commodities is severely restricted in the interest of market stability. The farm constituency and its congressional allies wanted to prevent what they perceived as inappropriate OMB meddling. An appropriations rider to this effect was passed as part of a massive continuing resolution when the regular funding bill containing OMB appropriations failed to emerge from Congress.[33]

Political Implications

Notwithstanding these examples of narrowly targeted congres-sional oversight, most decisions by OMB during Reagan's presidency were probably little influenced by congressional monitoring. After all, EPA alone has "approximately two hundred to two hundred and fifty regulations under development at any given time," and they vary widely in their visibility and vulnerability inside Congress.[34] Nor would OMB be especially concerned with the vast majority of these regulations. But by aggressively challenging the Reagan administra-tion's regulatory relief effort on many fronts and over several years, overseers played a crucial role in undermining political support for it. To be sure, Congress was not the only vehicle for this challenge. Scholars, journalists, and activists eager to safeguard regulatory pro-grams played important roles, as did the courts.[35] Congress, however, was a needed forum for the expression of reservations about regulatory relief by these other players.

This political climate has two discernible effects. Inside Congress, the spotlight trained on regulatory relief helped to create a suspicion of the program that was both bicameral and (to a limited degree) bipartisan, even during the 97th, 98th, and 99th Congresses (1981-1987), when Reagan enjoyed a Republican majority in the Senate. Republican moderates often proved uncomfortable with the scope and thrust of regulatory relief. Outside Congress, the regulatory relief effort contended with the ever-present clamor for health and safety protections. Congressional Democrats were convinced that this constituted a chink in Reagan's political armor, a chink that they meant to widen.[36]

Although it began with much fanfare and promise, the regulatory relief program was transformed into something of a political liability for the administration by mid-1983.[37] To be sure, the White House trumpeted concrete accomplishments: a 25 percent decline in the number of regulations, an annual reduction of more than three hundred million in paperwork burden hours, and a cost savings of approximately $150 billion projected over ten years.[38] (Responsible analysts later found these dollar savings to have been grossly inflated through various kinds of accounting legerdemain.)[39] Although the administration proclaimed regulatory relief to be a success, this message was muted by the political fallout of the EPA scandal, the public's perception of Interior secretary James Watt as an antienvironmental extremist, and persistent congressional opposition to OMB initiatives.

Attack on the Institutional Core: OIRA

The White House remained committed to the basic OMB review mechanism (as noted earlier, the least politically vulnerable element of its regulatory effort). On January 4, 1985, it issued Executive Order 12498, which gave OMB's Office of Information and Regulatory Affairs the responsibility of overseeing any "actions taken to consider whether to initiate rulemaking." Compared with the first executive order, however, this one downplayed regulatory relief as a goal. This objective crops up fifth after coordination, priority setting, accountability of agency executives, and presidential oversight of regulation. In Executive Order 12291, issued February 17, 1981, reducing "the burdens of existing and future regulations" had led the list.

Inside Congress, frustration with OMB meddling continued to mount despite the deemphasis on regulatory relief. Many in Congress perceived in OMB review a continuing antipathy to both legislative intent and public protection. (Indeed, the major regulatory reform bill of 1982, which passed the Senate with nary a dissenting vote, ran aground in the House Rules Committee as committee chairmen trooped forward to voice the fear that the measure would endanger programs dear to the hearts of many members while enhancing the power of OMB at Congress's expense.)[40] By 1983, as the Paperwork Reduction Act of 1980 neared reauthorization, there was strong sentiment for action to tame OMB. In particular, accusations of delay and unseen (and hence unfair) access for regulated interests continued to tarnish the program's image. The major regulatory reform bill considered by the House Judiciary Committee in 1983 (H.R. 2327) stated that the director of OMB "may not participate in any way in deciding what regulatory action, if any, [an] agency will take in any rulemaking proceeding." The director could establish guidelines for agency implementation of the reform statute only "after the public has been afforded notice and an opportunity to comment thereon . . . consistent with the prompt completion of rulemaking proceedings." The bill also stipulated that the director's written comments on rules be included in the rulemaking file.[41]

Meanwhile, OIRA's initial authorization expired in October 1983. Despite House passage of a reauthorization bill (the Paperwork Reduction Act Amendments of 1983, H.R. 2718), the Senate failed to act on its companion, S. 2433. For three years, from October 1983 to October 1986, OIRA would function without an authorization, funded from OMB's general yearly appropriations.[42]

During that period, determined opponents of OMB used means other than traditional legislative authorizations to undermine regulatory relief. In mid-1985 the chairmen of five standing committees in the House (Energy and Commerce, Judiciary, Government Operations, Education and Labor, and Post Office and Civil Service) filed an amicus curiae brief in the U.S. Court of Appeals of the D.C. Circuit, challenging the legitimacy of OMB's role in regulation. The brief came in support of a petition by the Public Citizen Health Research Group. The group asserted that OMB had significantly weakened a proposed OSHA rule intended to limit hospital workers' exposure to ethylene oxide, a suspected carcinogen.[43] Dingell's subcommittee, anxious to see what agencies were submitting to OMB, wrote to the departments of Energy and Transportation and to EPA, demanding to see draft proposals of regulations.[44] On May 30, 1985, the Environmental Defense Fund sued OMB on the grounds that review of an EPA rule on the tank storage of hazardous waste conflicted with a statutory deadline under the 1984 Hazardous and Solid Waste Amendments, a conflict that was supposed to exempt rules from OMB scrutiny under the first executive order.[45] In late November the Public Citizen Health Research Group won a decision in U.S. District Court (later lost on appeal) against the Department of Health and Human Services. The decision obligated agencies to make public their regulatory log documents, disclosing what regulations were under OMB review and for how long.[46]

By 1986, however, the congressional temperature on OMB, and OIRA specifically, had been turned up several degrees. In the House a group of committee chairmen, taking advantage of the lack of formal authorization for OIRA, moved to "defund" OIRA pending renewal of the Paperwork Reduction Act. The move, which had the support of Appropriations Committee Chairman Jamie Whitten, D-Miss., would have prohibited the use of any OMB funds for OIRA and regulatory review until formally authorized by statute.[47]

In the Senate, OIRA met with somewhat less hostility. Sen. Dave Durenberger, chairman of the Government Affairs Subcommittee on Intergovernmental Relations, was frustrated with the agency's behavior but apparently did "not question the basic framework of OMB regulatory review and want[ed] to maintain a working relationship with the White House office."[48] OMB Watch, a close (but hardly disinterested) observer of these deliberations, asserted that Durenberger

> was willing to make a deal that would get OMB to provide more public disclosure of OIRA's regulatory review process in exchange for his Subcommittee reporting out a Paperwork Reduction reauthorization bill.
>
> OMB was willing to make concessions because the combination of new OMB public access procedures and a PRA reauthorization bill would take the sting out of the "defunding" effort. Moreover, by all accounts, OMB demanded a "clean" reauthorization bill—unencumbered with regulatory review restrictions, organizational changes, or revisions to its paperwork clearance process.[49]

While Durenberger and his colleague on the full committee, Carl Levin, D-Mich., sought conciliation and greater agency openness, their approach drew the opposition of some senators, such as Tennessee Democrat Albert Gore, Jr., who refused to concede the conciliators' basic premise: OMB review was legitimate in principle, but flawed in execution.[50] This very opposition, combined with the House "defunding" drive, may have prodded OMB to make greater concessions than it otherwise might have made.

The result was that OMB accepted a deal it refused overtly to acknowledge.[51] In a June 13, 1986, memorandum, the agency set forth new procedures. Agency draft submissions to OIRA under Executive Orders 12291 and 12498 would be available upon written request.[52] Moreover, the line agencies could request that OIRA forward copies of written materials that had been received from nongovernmental parties relating to pending rules. The line agencies would be advised of oral communications of the same kind. And agency representatives would be invited to scheduled meetings on rules with outside parties.[53]

Durenberger and Levin were pleased with this apparent break-through, but OMB Watch remained dissatisfied:

> In specific, OIRA did not give an inch on four critical issues: (1) It will not publicly disclose its communications with agency personnel during regulatory reviews; (2) It will not even reveal the status of current review of agency activities; (3) It maintains that there is no need for judicial review of OIRA actions because they do not affect the substance of agency rules; and (4) It will not acknowledge it has no statutory authority to engage in regulatory review.[54]

OMB's adversaries in the House also were not placated. The move to deny OIRA funding continued. Barely a month after the deal was announced, the House Appropriations Committee's Subcommittee on Treasury, Postal Service, and General Government met in closed session and agreed by voice vote to cut off the $5.4 million that sustained OMB regulatory review. Not surprisingly, given Chairman Whitten's support and the Appropriations Committee's tradition of deference toward its subcommittees, the full committee went along with the "defunding" by voice vote.[55]

The White House made clear early on that it would stand firm against the threat of a funding cutoff. James C. Miller III, at that time OMB director, promised to relocate the review process elsewhere within the executive branch to keep it alive, declaring the issue "a matter of the president's constitutional power and authority." [56] Miller also threatened a veto of the entire appropriation bill.[57] After much maneuvering by congressional supporters of the Paperwork Reduction Act (notably by Democratic senator Lawton Chiles of Florida), the act (and OIRA) won reauthorization for three years as part of a massive continuing resolution. (Purists will note that Congress thus legislated on a spending bill, something it is supposed to avoid as a matter of procedure.)[58]

The reauthorized law attempted to constrain OIRA by forbidding the use of funds for regulatory review under the executive orders while permitting "paperwork" reviews (that is, approval of forms and information collection requirements) of regulations. But sharp distinctions between the two would remain elusive. The new version of the Paperwork Reduction Act also required that future heads of OIRA be subject to Senate confirmation.[59] In the end, the effort to rein in OIRA through its reauthorization failed. Review continued as before.

Looking Ahead

Suspicion of OMB in Congress and elsewhere carried over from the Reagan years into the Bush administration.[60] The Paperwork Reduction Act came up for renewal in 1989, and again congressional critics talked about rewriting it to guarantee more restricted and accessible regulatory review. The new administration debated whether and how to restructure such review (or at least how to refurbish its political cover). OMB director Richard Darman attempted to blunt congressional hostility by pledging expeditious process; no longer, he promised, would delay be used to resolve policy disputes.[61]

Since opponents of regulatory relief did not limit their efforts to Congress and the executive branch, it was no surprise to find the Supreme Court drawn into the fray. In June 1983 the Court ruled unanimously that the Department of Transportation would have to reconsider its earlier revocation of a regulation requiring the installation of "passive restraints" (air bags) in automobiles.[62] And in February 1990 the Court ruled 7-2 that the Paperwork Reduction Act did not allow OIRA to review regulations mandating the disclosure of information to "third parties" (in this case industrial workers).[63] Although clearly a victory for organized labor in its long struggle to win a tough "hazard communication" standard from OSHA, the Supreme Court decision appeared to be a setback for OMB within the narrow, if substantively important, sphere of disclosure regulation. The decision was by no means a mortal blow for OMB review; it dealt only with the PRA and not the executive orders. More efforts to get the Court to weigh in against elements of the program can surely be expected.

OMB will continue to have paperwork review as a potential stalking horse for regulatory review. As the executive director of OMB Watch, Gary D. Bass, explained during Senate testimony in 1989:

> Regulatory review under the two Executive Orders is not always OMB's only route into the substance of rulemaking. When regulations call for information to be collected ... OIRA gets to review the regulatory paper.... By eliminating the distinction between regulatory paperwork and non-regulatory paperwork, Congress established something akin to a "regulatory sunset" provision. The reason: since OIRA can approve paperwork for a maximum of three years, it means that regulatory paperwork must pass an OIRA screening at least every three years—subjecting the regulation to scrutiny. Furthermore, since the 1986 reauthorization extends the "public protection" clause to regulatory paperwork, OIRA can virtually nullify a regulation through its paperwork.[64]

Given the political volatility inherent in social regulation, especially in the context of divided government, continued legislative-executive conflict over OIRA's role is likely. Any agreement hammered out between the branches will be fragile. That became particularly evident in the spring of 1990, when senior White House staffers provoked the ire of House Government Operations Committee Chairman John Conyers, D-Mich., by asserting that the 1986 deal to restrain OIRA was an invalid infringement on presidential authority.[65]

Ideological retreat and political restraint by Congress or the president would facilitate interbranch cooperation, but the incentives for such behavior are weak. Presidents of either party are likely to find some form of centralized regulatory review attractive. The institutional and policy stakes for presidents on major regulatory decisions, and the variety of constraints they face, make unilateral mechanisms and strategies appealing.[66]

Congressional Democrats will continue to have a hard time chaining the beast they unwittingly set loose when they passed the Paperwork Reduction Act in 1980. For six years thereafter, President Reagan enjoyed a Republican Senate (bouts of dissent within his own party notwithstanding). Even with both houses of Congress firmly in Democratic hands since 1986, the White House can very likely put together a coalition of members disinclined, for various reasons, to scale back the president's power on a matter of broad and intense operational concern to him. Any bill designed to undercut or eliminate White House review instantly becomes Grade Á veto bait. Ironically, some of the legislators most strongly opposed to OMB review are reluctant to curb it formally for fear that doing so might lend legitimacy to the executive orders.[67]

For their part, therefore, Democrats in Congress will likely continue with their present, often defensive, efforts. These will include keeping a Republican president at bay in the process of reauthorizing and appropriating for substantive regulatory programs; dramatizing perceived assaults on the public health and safety through oversight directed at discrete cases; and permitting the president, though grudgingly, to introduce cost concerns into decision making through the only central mechanism currently available for this purpose, namely, OMB.

Notes

1. Martial, *Epigrams,* Book xii, ep. 47.
2. On the lack of attention to oversight as an independent variable, see Bert A. Rockman, "Legislative-Executive Relations and Legislative Oversight,"

in *Handbook of Legislative Research,* ed. Gerhard Loewenberg, Samuel C. Patterson, and Malcolm E. Jewell (Cambridge, Mass.: Harvard University Press, 1985), 582.

3. The scope of the term *social regulation* has varied somewhat. I use it here in a fairly restrictive sense, as a catchall for programs intended to protect workers, consumers, and the environment. For usage akin to mine, see Lester B. Lave, *The Strategy of Social Regulation: Decision Frameworks for Policy* (Washington, D.C.: Brookings Institution, 1981).

4. The major exceptions include foreign policy making, the military, and the independent regulatory commissions. The White House sought the voluntary cooperation of the commissions with its regulatory program. All quotations are taken from section 2 of Executive Order 12291.

5. According to section 1 of the executive order, a major rule was one that would likely create either an "annual effect on the economy" of at least $100 million, a "major increase in costs or prices," or "significant adverse effects" on competition, jobs, investment, productivity, innovation, or national competitiveness.

6. Christopher H. Foreman, Jr., *Signals from the Hill: Congressional Oversight and the Challenge of Social Regulation* (New Haven, Conn., and London: Yale University Press, 1988), 11-14. See also Lawrence D. Brown, *New Policies, New Politics: Government's Response to Government's Growth* (Washington, D.C.: Brookings Institution, 1983), 33. A comprehensive recent study that retains the conventional distinction between legislation and oversight is Joel D. Aberbach, *Keeping a Watchful Eye: The Politics of Congressional Oversight* (Washington, D.C.: Brookings Institution, 1990), 217-219.

7. Quoted in Margaret E. Kriz, "Kibitzer with Clout," *National Journal,* May 30, 1987, 1406-1407.

8. Efforts during the Nixon, Ford, and Carter administrations are described in George C. Eads and Michael Fix, *Relief or Reform? Reagan's Regulatory Dilemma* (Washington, D.C.: Urban Institute, 1984), chap. 3.

9. On the political salience of regulatory programs and the initiative taken by Congress, see David E. Price, "Policy Making in Congressional Committees: The Impact of 'Environmental' Factors," *American Political Science Review* 72 (June 1978): 548-574.

10. Eugene Bardach and Robert A. Kagan, *Going by the Book: The Problem of Regulatory Unreasonableness* (Philadelphia: Temple University Press, 1982).

11. William Schneider, "The Environment: The Public Wants More Protection, Not Less," *National Journal,* March 26, 1983, 676-677.

12. See Steven S. Smith, *Call to Order: Floor Politics in the House and Senate* (Washington, D.C.: Brookings Institution, 1989). Smith takes pains to acknowledge the powerful appeal that the decentralized process still holds for members of Congress.

13. See Foreman, *Signals from the Hill,* 45-55.

14. House Committee on Energy and Commerce, *Role of OMB in Regula-*

tion, hearing before the Subcommittee on Oversight and Investigations, 97th Cong., 1st sess., June 18, 1981.

15. House Committee on Energy and Commerce, *Presidential Control of Agency Rulemaking: An Analysis of Constitutional Issues That May Be Raised by Executive Order 12291,* 97th Cong., 1st sess., June 15, 1981.
16. Ibid., 70.
17. House Committee on Energy and Commerce, *Role of OMB in Regulation,* 53.
18. Ibid., 5.
19. Ibid. Regulatory review is much more effective at slowing or blocking rules than at improving their overall quality. See Marshall R. Goodman and Margaret T. Wrightson, *Managing Regulatory Reform: The Reagan Strategy and Its Impact* (New York: Praeger, 1987), 106.
20. Howard Kurtz, "Five EPA Officials Resign; Reagan Calls Departures Voluntary," *Washington Post,* March 26, 1983, A2.
21. The five subcommittees in the House were Energy and Commerce's Subcommittee on Oversight and Investigations, chaired by John Dingell of Michigan; Government Operations' Subcommittee on Environment, Energy, and Natural Resources, chaired by Mike Synar of Oklahoma; Public Works and Transportation's Subcommittee on Investigations and Oversight, chaired by Elliott Levitas of Georgia; Energy and Commerce's Subcommittee on Commerce, Transportation, and Tourism, chaired by James Florio of New Jersey; and Science and Technology's Subcommittee on Natural Resources, Agriculture Research, and Environment, chaired by James Scheuer of New York.
22. A reasonably thorough if strongly adversarial recounting of the scandal is Jonathan Lash, Katherine Gillman, and David Sheridan, *A Season of Spoils: The Story of the Reagan Administration's Attack on the Environment* (New York: Pantheon, 1984), chap. 1.
23. Richard Riley, "Toxic Substances, Hazardous Wastes, and Public Policy: Problems in Implementation," in *The Politics of Hazardous Waste Management,* ed. James P. Lester and Ann O'M. Bowman (Durham, N.C.: Duke University Press, 1983), 39-40.
24. Statement by EPA administrator Lee M. Thomas, January 23, 1986.
25. House Committee on Energy and Commerce, *EPA's Asbestos Regulations: Report on a Case Study on OMB Interference in Agency Rulemaking,* 99th Cong., 1st sess., October 1985.
26. Foreman, *Signals from the Hill,* 187.
27. *Congressional Record,* September 19, 1985, S11785.
28. Senate Committee on Environment and Public Works, *Office of Management and Budget Influence on Agency Regulations,* 99th Cong., 2d sess., May 1986, 26.
29. House Committee on Energy and Commerce, *Infant Formula: The Present Danger,* hearing before the Subcommittee on Oversight and Investigations, 97th Cong., 2d sess., March 11, 1982, 7, 11. See also *HHS News* (press release), April 5, 1982.

30. House Committee on Energy and Commerce, *Anesthesia Machine Failures,* hearing before the Subcommittee on Oversight and Investigations, 98th Cong., 2d sess., September 26, 1984.
31. Cristine Russell, "Rule to Label Food for Allergenic Sulfites Wins Out," *Washington Post,* March 29, 1985, A21.
32. Eads and Fix, *Relief or Reform?* 157-158.
33. "Treasury/Postal Service Bill Fails to Clear," *Congressional Quarterly Almanac, 1983* (Washington, D.C.: Congressional Quarterly, 1984), 531-536.
34. Memorandum dated November 3, 1987, from A. James Barnes, EPA deputy administrator, to a panel on regulatory negotiation, sponsored by the Federal Bar Association, District of Columbia Bar Association, and American Bar Association, 1.
35. See, for example, Susan J. Tolchin and Martin Tolchin, *Dismantling America: The Rush to Deregulate* (Boston: Houghton Mifflin, 1983).
36. Steven V. Roberts, "Democrats Press the 'Safety' Issue," *New York Times,* June 3, 1986, B6; David S. Broder, "Tony Coelho: The Triumph of the Democrats," *Washington Post,* June 8, 1986, F7; and Tom Kenworthy, "Democrats Assail Deregulation Under Reagan," *Washington Post,* August 10, 1988, A17.
37. This is also the judgment rendered in Eads and Fix, *Relief or Reform?* 4. See also "A Bipartisan Swing Back to More Regulation," *Business Week,* May 30, 1983, 74-75.
38. White House, *Highlights of the Regulatory Relief Accomplishments During the Reagan Administration,* August 1983, 1.
39. Eads and Fix, *Relief or Reform?* 237-245.
40. Diane Granat, "Rules Committee Fails to Act; Regulatory Reform Stalled," *Congressional Quarterly Weekly Report,* December 11, 1982, 3029.
41. H.R. 2327, subchapter II, subsection 624, 98th Cong., 1st sess.
42. *Congressional Record,* October 15, 1986, H10896.
43. Sara Fitzgerald and Peter Perl, "Hill Panel Chiefs Hit OMB," *Washington Post,* July 2, 1985, A15.
44. Henry Boyd Hall, "Expansion of OMB Power Decried," *Washington Post,* August 7, 1985, A17.
45. Senate Committee on Environment and Public Works, *Office of Management and Budget Influence on Agency Regulations,* 26-27.
46. Loretta Tofani, "Agencies Must Disclose Data on Proposed Rules," *Washington Post,* November 28, 1985, A17.
47. For this account, see OMB Watch, *Regulatory Review: OMB's New Public Disclosure Rules,* June 1986, 3-5.
48. Ibid., 3.
49. Ibid. See also Goodman and Wrightson, *Managing Regulatory Reform,* 192.
50. OMB Watch, *Regulatory Review,* 4.
51. Both OMB Watch and the press, however, understood the agency action

for what it was. See Judith Havemann, "No 'Shade Drawn' Dealings for OMB," *Washington Post,* June 17, 1986, A21.

52. Drafts submitted for OMB review under Executive Order 12291 are accessible only after a rule has been published in the *Federal Register.* Drafts submitted under Executive Order 12498 are available once the annual *Regulatory Program of the United States* has been published.

53. General Accounting Office, *Information on OMB's Review Process,* July 1989 (GGD-89-101FS), 17.

54. OMB Watch, *Regulatory Review,* 9.

55. Judith Havemann, " 'Defunding' OMB's Rule Reviewers," *Washington Post,* July 18, 1986, A17; and Judith Havemann, "House Moves to Wipe Out OMB Unit," *Washington Post,* July 31, 1986, A23.

56. Havemann, " 'Defunding' OMB's Rule Reviewers," A17.

57. Havemann, "House Moves to Wipe Out OMB Unit," A23.

58. OMB Watch, *Paperwork Reduction: The Quick Fix of 1986,* November 1986. For a detailed account of the wrangling over the Paperwork Reduction Act reauthorization, see Goodman and Wrightson, *Managing Regulatory Reform,* 191-194.

59. Making an existing position subject to Senate confirmation is an obvious and attractive way to challenge administration policies and to sensitize incoming executives to congressional concerns. Congress took this action in 1988 for future heads of FDA.

60. David C. Vladeck, "O.M.B.: A Dangerous Superagency," *New York Times,* September 6, 1989, A25.

61. David Hoffman, "Will the White House Take the Initiative on Regulatory Decisions?" *Washington Post,* February 3, 1989, A23. See also Judith Havemann, "OMB's Pledge: No More Foot Dragging," *Washington Post,* July 4, 1989, A21.

62. "High Court's Air Bag Ruling May Affect Other Deregulation Moves," *National Journal,* July 2, 1983, 1371, 1404-1405.

63. *Dole, Secretary of Labor, et al. v. United Steelworkers of America, et al.* (1990).

64. Statement of Gary D. Bass before the Subcommittee on Government Information and Regulation of the Senate Governmental Affairs Committee regarding reauthorization of the Paperwork Reduction Act, June 16, 1989, 11-12.

65. Neil A. Lewis, "Regulatory Review Office in Dispute," *New York Times,* May 5, 1990, 10.

66. James T. O'Reilly and Phyllis E. Brown, "In Search of Excellence: A Prescription for the Future of OMB Oversight of Rules," *Administrative Law Review* 39 (Fall 1987): 427-444. See also Terry M. Moe, "The Politicized Presidency," in *The New Direction in American Politics,* ed. John E. Chubb and Paul E. Peterson (Washington, D.C.: Brookings Institution, 1985), 235-271.

67. Letter dated April 24, 1990, from Gwen Rubinstein, senior program associate at OMB Watch, to the author.

8. THE IMPACT OF BUDGET REFORM ON PRESIDENTIAL AND CONGRESSIONAL GOVERNANCE

James A. Thurber

Decisions about the federal budget are at the heart of American politics. The Constitution gives Congress the power of the purse: the authority to establish revenue policy and to authorize and appropriate funds for the president and the executive branch of government. The president can tax and spend only to the extent allowed by Congress. Budgets reveal the degree of cooperation and conflict between the president and Congress over public policy priorities. The give and take between Congress and the president over federal spending, revenues, deficits, and debt affects the economy, national security, and many other crucial issues that are addressed by government.

Although the Constitution granted Congress the power of the purse, it did not prescribe the budgetary system to be used. Consequently, the system Congress has developed for itself and the president is based on its own rules, statutes, and legislative traditions. Over the past two hundred years, Congress has alternatively delegated significant budgetary powers to the president and tried to control the president's spending authority. This oscillation between budgetary delegation and control, between cooperation and conflict, has led to major changes in the way budgets are formulated.

Congress enacted the Budget and Accounting Act of 1921 to control presidential spending power. This act required the president to submit an annual budget for the federal government, but it also gave him the power to control and coordinate agency budget requests and to monitor spending through the Bureau of the Budget (renamed the Office of Management and Budget in 1970). From the Great Depression of the 1930s through the Vietnam War and Great Society legislation of the 1960s, there was an unprecedented escalation of program growth and federal spending. By the late 1960s the deficit had begun to increase, and a variety of seemingly uncontrollable deficit budgetary problems besieged Congress. Delayed action on appropriations bills caused alarm inside and outside the legislative branch. President Richard Nixon criticized members of Congress as being irresponsible big spenders, and he impounded appropriated funds for popular programs.

To regain from the president some of its budgetary power and to improve the way it made spending and revenue decisions, Congress passed the Budget and Impoundment Control Act of 1974 (Public Law 93-344, Titles I-IX). The act required Congress to adopt two budget resolutions setting spending and revenue levels and estimating deficits each year. In practice, however, Congress has adopted only a single budget resolution every year since 1983, and often late at that. Moreover, since the early 1980s, legislative-executive "gridlock" over the deficit has further disrupted the budget process and revealed serious problems in presidential-congressional relations.

In late 1985, in response to widespread frustration over the budget deficit, Congress passed the Balanced Budget and Emergency Deficit Control Act (Public Law 99-177). This act is usually referred to by the names of its sponsors: Senators Phil Gramm, R-Texas; Warren B. Rudman, R-N.H.; and Ernest F. Hollings, D-S.C. The GRH legislation mandates a set of deficit targets for each fiscal year. If the president and Congress cannot agree on a budget that comes within $10 million of the annual deficit target, a mechanism is triggered that reduces expenditures automatically to meet the deficit target. The original act called for a balanced budget in 1991. It set out to eliminate the deficit by imposing limits that shrank every year. A revision of the original act, the Balanced Budget and Emergency Deficit Control Reaffirmation Act of 1987, calls for a balanced budget in 1993. The strain of deficit reduction has led to further proposals to reform the congressional budget process, but no clear consensus has been reached within Congress or between Congress and the president on what should be done.

With the Budget and Impoundment Control Act of 1974 and the GRH legislation, Congress sought to recapture power over the budget process. But by failing to achieve annual deficit targets, thus triggering the GRH automatic budget-cutting mechanism, Congress effectively limited its own power. The main purpose of this chapter is to evaluate the effect of these reforms on congressional-presidential relations.

The Origins of Congressional Budget Reform

Before 1974 Congress considered the president's annual budget in a decentralized, piecemeal manner. Authorizations for federal agencies and programs were considered separately by congressional authorizing committees. Appropriations of funds for these agencies and programs were considered by the House and Senate appropriations committees working through subcommittees.

Revenue policies were handled in the House by the Ways and Means Committee and in the Senate by the Finance Committee. Congress never evaluated the relation between total expenditures and total revenues or the economic consequences of these disconnected budgetary decisions.

Moreover, interest groups and agencies strongly influenced the legislative process. The president's budget reflected the power of these interests more than a central fiscal policy. At no point was there an orderly review of the total budget by a single congressional committee or by the House and Senate as a whole. The budget was not even visible until all of the appropriations subcommittees' bills were passed, and frequently they were not passed before the beginning of the fiscal year. To compound the problem, supplemental appropriations bills were often passed in the middle of a fiscal year, making the size of the budget a moving target. Congress had neither budget committees nor skilled budget experts nor a comprehensive system to bring discipline to the budget-making process and to challenge the president's budget.

The Budget and Impoundment Control Act of 1974 established several major institutions and procedures that changed congressional-presidential relations.[1] The act created separate House and Senate Budget committees, responsible for setting overall tax and spending levels.[2] Most important, it required Congress each year to establish levels of expenditures and revenues, and it prescribed procedures for arriving at those spending and income totals. The procedures, later revised by GRH, included three important elements: (1) a timetable for action on budget-related legislation to ensure completion of the budget plan before the start of each fiscal year; (2) a requirement to adopt concurrent budget resolutions (which do not require presidential approval) for total budget authority, budget outlays, and revenues for the upcoming fiscal year; and (3) a reconciliation process to conform revenue, spending, and debt legislation to the levels specified in the budget resolution.[3] The 1974 legislation also created the Congressional Budget Office, which provides Congress with independent information and analysis on the budget. Title X of the act limited presidential use of two kinds of impoundments: deferrals and rescissions.[4] *Deferrals* are presidential requests to Congress to postpone or delay spending for a particular program for up to twelve months. *Rescissions* are presidential requests to abolish funding permanently for a program.

The GRH legislation, as noted earlier, established a procedure to reduce deficits to annual maximum levels through mandatory sequestration of funds when Congress did not reduce the deficit through legislation.[5] If the deficit limits are not met, the Office of Management and Budget (OMB) will make automatic spending cuts, using a congressionally mandated formula.[6]

In summary, the budget legislation passed in 1974, 1985, and 1987 has greatly influenced congressional-presidential cooperation and conflict over budgetary decisions.[7] What has been the specific effect of the reforms? To answer that question, this chapter focuses on six hypotheses: (1) that budget votes dominate roll-call voting in Congress; (2) that the president is an increasingly important cue in budget votes; (3) that congressional influence over presidential budget priorities has increased; (4) that Congress has more control over presidential impoundments; (5) that decision making in Congress on the budget has become more centralized, thus changing the budgeting power of presidents, agencies, committees, congressional leaders, and interest groups; and (6) that Congress has greater control over federal spending than it did before 1974.

Congressional Budget Voting

The same important questions about the federal budget confronted members of Congress annually: how much money should be spent on national security? how much for social programs? how much for grants to state and local government? what should be the revenue policy of the federal government? what deficit should be allowed? These macro-budgetary decisions are perceived by legislators to be an increasingly unpleasant fact of congressional life. Credit taking with constituents, interest groups, and government agencies is difficult, if not impossible, when members are voting on the entire federal budget. Republicans and Democrats alike find it difficult to justify to constituents their votes for large deficits and even more difficult to explain cutbacks on programs affecting their electors. Moreover, members complain, understandably, that the debate and votes on budgets take up too much time and push aside other legislative responsibilities.

Since 1980 more than half of all roll-call votes in Congress have been on budget-related bills, with a high of 56 percent in the House and 71 percent in the Senate (see Table 8-1). Because of a two-year budget agreement in 1987, the number of budget-related votes dropped dramatically in 1988 (32 percent in the Senate and 34 percent in the House). Since 1975, however, budget votes have dominated congressional voting, and members are increasingly exasperated with the amount of time spent on spending issues.

Presidential Influence on Budget Votes

Models of voting behavior by individual legislators suggest that legislators have imperfect knowledge about the decisions before them because their time and resources are limited. James G. March and Herbert Simon argue that everyone is routinely forced to make decisions without all the relevant facts, a phenomenon of "bounded rationality." [8] Members of Congress follow voting cues from trusted

TABLE 8-1   Budget-Related Roll-Call Votes in the Senate and House, 1980-1988

Measure	1980	1981	1982	1983	1984[a]	1985	1986	1987	1988
Senate									
Authorizations	82	55	31	58	62	67	33	84	30
Appropriations	128	130	109	107	76	59	74	66	67
Tax legislation	10	56	30	13	21	7	26	0	15
Budget resolutions	50	26	35	34	1	39	14	17	11
Reconciliation bills	4	63	18	2	1	23	12	8	0
Debt ceilings	6	12	19	15	7	29	14	17	0
Miscellaneous	3	2	30	9	1	6	10	3	0
Total budget-related roll calls	283	344	272	238	169	230	183	195	123
Total roll calls	531	483	465	381	292	381	359	420	379
Percentage budget-related	53	71	58	62	58	60	51	46	32
House									
Authorizations	105	70	71	129	119	95	112	118	84
Appropriations	111	85	79	112	76	82	93	86	60
Tax legislation	14	7	3	9	5	11	3	0	3
Budget resolutions	30	13	36	4	10	10	8	8	6
Reconciliation bills	6	12	18	2	5	10	10	6	0
Debt ceilings	7	2	0	3	6	11	4	7	0
Miscellaneous	4	7	8	3	1	1	1	2	1
Total budget-related roll calls	277	196	215	262	222	220	231	227	154
Total roll calls	604	353	459	498	408	439	451	488	451
Percentage budget-related	46	56	47	53	54	50	51	47	34

Source: Adapted from Norman J. Ornstein, Thomas E. Mann, and Michael J. Malbin, *Vital Statistics on Congress, 1989-1990* (Washington, D.C.: Congressional Quarterly, 1990), 183, 184.

[a] Includes the Deficit Reduction Act on which there were 47 votes in the Senate (authorizations, 27; tax legislation, 19; miscellaneous, 1) and 4 votes in the House (tax legislation, 3; reconciliation bills, 1).

sources when making most of their decisions, including how they should vote on budget bills.[9] Three important cues are party, ideology, and loyalty to the president, although there has been no study of the relative importance of these factors on budget-related roll-call votes, which are high profile and usually controversial. In such high-profile voting are party, ideology, and the president still significant influences on members' voting behavior? Does the president dominate budget voting? I attempt to answer these questions by using simple descriptive statistics and a multiple regression analysis.

Party Affiliation

The best predictor of how a legislator will vote is his or her party affiliation.[10] Herbert Weisberg's "simple party model" predicts House votes based solely on an individual legislator's party. He found that the average proportion of votes cast with the party majority from 1957 to 1974 was 82 percent. In a three-party system (Republicans, northern liberal Democrats, and southern conservative Democrats) the average is 85 percent.[11] These percentages are useful baselines against which to compare the importance of party in budget votes. As Keith Poole states, "No one questions that the primary explanatory variable in congressional voting is party." [12] But what is meant by *party support,* and is it an explanatory variable for budget votes as it is for other roll calls?

The great importance of party as a predictor of votes on House budget resolutions can be seen in Table 8-2. Since fiscal 1976, House votes on budget resolutions have been sharply divided between the parties. House Republicans stood firmly together: approximately 95 percent voted against adoption of the budget resolutions during the 1976-1981 period. In fiscal 1982 and 1983, Republicans in the House and Senate dominated the budget process, and most of them voted in favor of the Reagan administration's budget resolutions. In addition, a core of conservative southern Democrats voted with House Republicans during those two years, to pass the resolutions by narrow margins (for example, 206-200 for the fiscal 1982 second budget resolution).

House Democrats were less cohesive than the Republicans. At various times significant numbers of Democrats from both the northern and southern wings of the party opposed the position taken by their colleagues. Nevertheless, during the 1976-1981 period, House Democrats supplied enough votes to pass the budget resolutions, although on two occasions, the first resolution for fiscal 1978 and the second resolution for fiscal 1980, passage occurred only after the initial versions were rejected. In voting on the 1982 and 1983 budget resolutions, most House Democrats (except southern conservatives) opposed President Reagan's position and, when their view was rejected, voted against adoption of the budget resolution.

From 1975 to 1981, the Senate, unlike the House, displayed a bipartisan voting pattern on budget resolutions (see Table 8-3). This coalition of Republicans and southern conservative Democrats ensured passage of the resolutions by wide margins. After 1981, the two parties became polarized (except for their vote on the fiscal 1984 budget, when a pattern of bipartisanship again emerged). Growing Democratic

TABLE 8-2   House Votes on Adoption of Budget Resolutions, by Party, Fiscal 1976-1989

Fiscal year	Budget resolution	Total		Demo-crats		Southern Demo-crats		Northern Demo-crats		Repub-licans	
		Yes	No	Yes	No	Yes	No	Yes	No	Yes	No
1976	1st	200	196	197	69	46	36	151	33	3	127
	2d	225	191	214	68	52	37	162	31	11	123
1977	1st	221	155	208	44	49	24	159	20	13	111
	2d	227	151	215	38	61	22	154	16	12	113
	3rd	234	143	213	36	57	19	156	17	21	107
1978	1st [a]	213	179	206	58	64	19	142	39	7	121
	2d	199	188	195	59	56	27	139	32	4	129
1979	1st	201	197	198	61	46	36	152	25	3	136
	2d	217	178	215	42	61	17	154	61	2	136
1980	1st	221	184	211	50	64	17	146	33	10	134
	2d [a]	212	206	212	51	55	27	157	24	0	155
	3rd [b]	241	174	218	44	59	24	159	20	23	130
1981	1st	225	193	202	62	75	8	127	54	23	131
	2d	203	191	200	45	67	12	133	33	3	146
1982	1st	270	154	84	153	61	17	22	136	186	1
	2d	206	200	70	150	45	27	25	123	136	50
1983	1st	219	206	63	174	47	30	16	144	156	32
1984	1st	229	196	225	36	57	30	168	6	4	160
1985	1st	250	168	229	29	70	16	159	13	21	139
1986	1st	258	170	234	15	74	7	160	8	24	155
1987	1st	245	179	228	19	74	8	154	11	17	160
1988	1st	230	192	230	19	71	9	159	10	0	173
1989	1st	319	102	227	24	75	7	152	17	92	78

Source: The Inter-University Consortium for Political and Social Research.

Note: These votes are on passage of the resolutions in the House, not on adoption of the conference report. From fiscal 1983 to fiscal 1989, Congress adopted only one budget resolution each year, rather than the two originally prescribed by the Budget and Impoundment Control Act of 1974.

[a] The first-round budget resolution did not pass; the table presents votes on second round.

[b] The third resolution for fiscal 1980 was part of the first resolution for fiscal 1981, but it was voted on separately in the House.

opposition was matched by increasing Republican support for the resolutions. The party split has made it almost as difficult to pass budget resolutions in the Senate as in the House. Since 1983 the margin of approval in the Senate has narrowed. For the 1986 budget the vice president had to vote to break a tie in the Senate, an event that has happened only once since implementation of the budget act. This highly charged partisan environment delayed passage of the budgets, increased

TABLE 8-3 Senate Votes on Adoption of Budget Resolutions, by Party, Fiscal 1976-1989

Fiscal year	Budget resolution	Total		Demo-crats		Southern Demo-crats		Northern Demo-crats		Repub-licans	
		Yes	No	Yes	No	Yes	No	Yes	No	Yes	No
1976	1st	69	22	50	4	14	3	36	1	19	18
	2d	69	23	50	8	9	8	41	0	19	15
1977	1st	62	22	45	6	13	2	32	4	17	16
	2d	55	23	41	5	14	2	27	3	14	18
	3rd	72	20	55	3	15	3	40	0	17	17
1978	1st	56	31	41	14	5	11	36	3	15	17
	2d	63	21	46	8	13	4	33	4	17	13
1979	1st	64	27	48	8	13	4	35	4	16	19
	2d	56	18	42	6	12	3	30	3	14	12
1980	1st	64	20	44	5	15	1	29	4	20	15
	2d	62	36	45	14	17	2	28	12	17	22
1981	1st	68	28	49	6	18	1	31	5	19	22
	2d	48	46	33	21	12	7	21	14	15	25
1982	1st	78	20	28	18	14	1	14	17	50	2
	2d	49	48	2	44	1	13	1	31	47	4
1983	1st	48	43	3	41	2	13	1	28	45	2
1984	1st	50	49	29	17	5	9	24	8	21	32
1985	1st	41	34	1	31	0	8	1	23	40	3
1986	1st [a]	49	49	1	45	0	14	1	31	48	4
1987	1st	70	25	38	6	12	2	26	4	32	19
1988	1st	56	42	53	0	17	0	36	0	3	42
1989	1st	69	26	44	6	14	2	30	4	25	20

Source: The Inter-University Consortium for Political and Social Research.

Note: These votes are on passage of the resolutions in the Senate, not on adoption of the conference report. From fiscal 1983 to fiscal 1989, Congress adopted only one budget resolution each year, rather than the two originally prescribed by the Budget and Impoundment Control Act of 1974.

[a] The vice president voted to break tie.

the number of continuing resolutions, and created the setting for passage of the Gramm-Rudman-Hollings act calling for the automatic reduction of the budget deficit.

Party Unity, Ideology, and Presidential Support

Although party affiliation is a significant predictor of budget votes in the House and Senate, three other influences may cut across party lines. To what extent do party unity (a member's propensity to vote with his or her party), ideological orientation, and loyalty to the president influence congressional budget voting? To answer this question, I analyzed roll-call votes on final passage of twenty-eight budget resolutions in the House and twenty-one budget resolutions in the Senate between 1975 and 1982. All amendments voted on before final passage of the budget resolutions were evaluated for inclusion in the study and were excluded because it was determined that they measured the same behavior as the votes on the final resolutions. Roll-call votes, party unity scores, ideology scores, and presidential support scores were made available by the Inter-University Consortium for Political and Social Research (ICPSR).

Party unity votes are votes in which a majority of voting Democrats oppose a majority of voting Republicans. Party unity votes as a percentage of all votes in the House dropped from 55 to 35 percent during Lyndon B. Johnson's administration. All House roll-call votes produced a party split of approximately 35 percent under Presidents Richard Nixon and Gerald Ford—compared to 50 percent under Dwight D. Eisenhower, 40 percent under Jimmy Carter, and 37 percent under Ronald Reagan in his first year in office.[13] From 1983 to 1987, however, party unity votes in the House surged to all-time highs of 56, 47, 61, 56, and 64 percent.

Since the mid-1950s Senate party unity scores have averaged 45 percent; they were higher under Carter and Reagan than under any president since John F. Kennedy. Until 1982, in both the House and Senate, party cohesion was lower for Democrats than for Republicans. This had been true since the late 1930s, when issues began to bring together southern Democrats and Republicans, pitting them against northern Democrats. "[T]his conservative coalition has proved itself a formidable opponent to Democratic presidents." [14] On many issues the Democratic party in Congress was really two political parties, one northern and one southern. The Reagan years, from 1981 to 1988, saw a dramatic shift in this situation, however: House Democratic party unity scores were higher than Republican party unity scores. This certainly has been true on many budget votes, as Tables 8-2 and 8-3 show.

Ideology is the second independent variable in the model. The liberal/conservative dimension of ideology has been found to structure congressional voting generally.[15] For example, Keith Poole and Howard Rosenthal found that a single ideological dimension correctly classified approximately 82 percent of all House and Senate voting in the 1919-1985 period.[16] Poole argues that "political parties per se are not the primary variable; rather, the fundamental dimensions of belief (ideology) that give rise to parties are the primary variable." [17] Conservative coalition support scores (ranging from 0 to 100) have proven to be a reliable measure of a member's ideology for voting studies.[18] These scores are defined as the percentage of votes on which members agree with the position of the conservative coalition. The higher the score, the more conservative the legislator.

Conservative coalition votes are those in which a majority of northern Democrats oppose the stand taken by a majority of southern Democrats and Republicans (the conservative coalition). The percentages are adjusted to eliminate the effects of those not voting. During the Reagan years the percentage of votes won by the coalition ranged from 71 to 88 percent in the House and from 89 to 95 percent in the Senate. The success of the coalition after the 1980 elections stemmed mainly from the increase in the number of Republicans in the House and Senate and to the greater conservatism of the Senate Republicans.[19]

The third factor in the model is a member's propensity to vote in support of the president's position. *Presidential support scores* (adjusted to remove the effects of absences) represent the percentage of recorded votes on which members voted in agreement with the president's announced position. Congressional Quarterly (CQ) presidential support scores were used for the analysis. CQ determines what the president's stand is by his messages to Congress, press conference remarks, documents, and other public statements. Presidential support scores on budget votes indicate the relative influence of the president in the congressional budget process. Obviously, the party affiliation of the president and of a member of Congress helps to explain most votes. When the same party controls Congress and the presidency, presidential success never drops below 75 percent. With divided government, presidential roll-call success drops sharply: Ford, 58 percent; Nixon, 64 percent; and Eisenhower after 1954, 67 percent.[20]

Multivariate Analysis: Results and Interpretations

To assess the relative importance of the three independent variables—party unity scores, conservative coalition scores, and presidential support scores—multivariate analysis is used. Tables 8-4 and 8-5 report the results of multiple regression analysis of House and Senate budget votes for fiscal 1976 through 1983 using these three variables. The data used in the analysis were for votes on final passage and conference reports for first and second budget resolutions. The three independent variables were not found to be highly intercorrelated; thus, they were considered to be independent of each other. Logit analysis found similar signs and significance for the three independent variables and budget voting in the model as did the multiple regression.[21] Therefore, to allow for comparability with previous roll-call voting studies, multiple regression was used even though the dependent variable is dichotomous, a single budget vote for each resolution.

The amount of variance explained in budget votes by party unity scores, conservative coalition scores, and presidential support scores during the 1976-1983 period ranged widely from 7 to 74 percent for the Senate and from 20 to 70 percent for the House. At no time does the tripartite model explain as much variance as does the simple party affiliation model for all roll-call votes. The pattern of variance is still respectable, however, given the number of random factors likely to affect a vote on a macropolitical issue of such importance—namely, the federal budget. The average variance for the eight years under study is 45 percent for the House and 40 percent for the Senate. It is highest under the Reagan presidency (an average of .56 in the House and .60 in the Senate; an average R square of .40 in the House and .30 in the Senate). This may reflect the fact that the Reagan White House took a more dominant and proactive role in the budget process, especially when David Stockman was director of the Office of Management and Budget, than did the Carter administration in its early years.

During Carter's last two years, the amount of variance explained by party unity, ideology, and loyalty to the president's program almost doubled in the House. This suggests that the Carter White House learned to be more effective and coordinated in its budget lobbying on Capitol Hill. It gave up micromanagement efforts, such as attempting to cut funding for eighteen popular water projects, an effort that had brought a sharp bipartisan negative reaction to the president's first budget. The standardized regression coefficients for presidential support increased from .27 in 1976 to .70, .76, .81, and .85, respectively, in the years from 1977 to 1980. These figures show some of the strongest relationships during the eight-year period of this study.

The Senate is a different story. Variance explained for budget votes in the Senate during the Carter years started out poorly and got worse toward the end of his presidency. The R squares were the lowest of any year in the study: .23 for the second budget resolution in fiscal 1980, .07 for the second budget resolution in fiscal 1981, and .10 for the second budget resolution conference in fiscal 1981 (see Table 8-5). The early Reagan years started moderately high in the Senate and moved quickly to the highest R squares for any year in the study (from .35 on the first budget resolution in fiscal 1982 to .74 on the first budget resolution in fiscal 1983). The White House took advantage of the Republican majority in the Senate and the conservative coalition in the House to build support for the president's budget priorities, as shown by the high R squares and the strong relationship between presidential support scores and budget voting.

TABLE 8-4 Regressions of House Budget Votes on Party Unity, Conservative Coalition, and Presidential Support Scores, Fiscal 1976-1983

Budget resolution	Fiscal year	R^2	Standardized Regression Coefficients		
			Party unity	Conservative coalition	Presidential support
FBR	1976	.45	.03	-.37 [a]	-.33 [a]
FBRC	1976	.48	-.06	.32 [a]	-.43 [a]
SBR	1976	.48	-.08	-.56 [a]	-.18 [b]
SBRC	1976	.56	.00	-.57 [a]	-.21 [a]
FBR	1977	.50	-.04	-.19 [c]	-.53 [a]
FBRC	1977	.49	-.06	.01	-.71 [a]
SBR	1977	.45	-.06	-.10	-.61 [a]
TBR	1977	.45	-.08	-.15	-.54 [a]
FBR	1978	.38	-.13 [b]	-.40 [a]	-.27 [a]
FBRC	1978	.20	-.16 [a]	.09	.38 [a]
SBR	1978	.40	-.07	-.38 [a]	.29 [a]
SBRC	1978	.41	-.11 [b]	-.42 [a]	.27 [a]
FBR	1979	.46	.01	-.44 [a]	.26 [a]
FBRC	1979	.24	-.22 [a]	-.26 [a]	.28 [a]
SBR	1979	.40	-.08 [c]	-.24 [a]	.43 [a]
SBRC	1979	.40	-.14 [a]	-.29 [a]	.40 [a]
FBR	1980	.49	-.16 [a]	-.16 [c]	.85 [a]
FBRC	1980	.23	-.21 [a]	.40 [a]	.76 [a]
SBR	1980	.51	-.01	-.20 [b]	.53 [a]
SBRC	1980	.49	-.05	-.01	.70 [a]
TBR	1980	.57	-.13 [a]	-.37 [a]	.47 [a]
FBR	1981	.42	-.31 [a]	.25 [a]	.81 [a]
SBR	1981	.47	-.11 [b]	.34 [a]	.24 [b]
FBR	1982	.70	-.17 [a]	.31 [a]	.50 [a]
FBRC	1982	.67	-.20 [a]	.24 [a]	.54 [a]
SBR	1982	.36	-.11 [b]	.34 [a]	.24 [b]
FBR	1983	.53	-.17 [a]	.65 [a]	.04
FBRC	1983	.52	-.21 [a]	.45 [a]	.23 [b]

Note: FBR = first budget resolution, FBRC = first budget resolution conference, SBR = second budget resolution, SBRC = second budget resolution conference, TBR = third budget resolution.

[a] Significant at the .001 level or less.
[b] Significant at the .01 level or less.
[c] Significant at the .05 level or less.

The standardized regression coefficients in Tables 8-4 and 8-5 show the explanatory importance of the three independent variables as predictors of budget votes. Party unity is negatively related to

TABLE 8-5 Regressions of Senate Budget Votes on Party Unity, Conservative Coalition, and Presidential Support Scores, Fiscal 1976-1983

Budget resolution	Fiscal year	R^2	Standardized Regression Coefficients		
			Party unity	Conservative coalition	Presidential support
FBR	1976	.49	-.24 [b]	-.56 [a]	-.12
SBR	1976	.38	-.01	-.85 [a]	.30
FBR	1977	.29	-.24 [c]	-.12	-.37
SBR	1977	.37	-.30 [b]	-.26	-.28
SBRC	1977	.45	-.37 [a]	-.31	-.29
TBR	1977	.54	-.30 [a]	-.40 [a]	.39 [a]
FBR	1978	.49	-.02	-.39 [a]	.38 [a]
SBR	1978	.38	-.15	-.18	.48 [a]
FBR	1979	.45	-.06	-.41 [b]	.30 [c]
SBR	1979	.39	-.03	-.45 [c]	.19
FBR	1980	.34	-.14	.22	.73 [a]
SBR	1980	.23	-.23 [b]	.54 [a]	.54 [a]
SBRC	1980	.30	-.02	.14	.65 [a]
FBR	1981	.25	-.12	-.24 [c]	.30 [b]
SBR	1981	.07	.00	-.11 [c]	.19
SBRC	1981	.10	-.11	-.21	.14
FBR	1982	.35	-.08	.54 [b]	.05
FBRC	1982	.48	-.06	.56 [c]	.14
SBR	1982	.69	.02	-.54 [a]	1.27 [a]
FBR	1983	.74	.01	-.49 [a]	1.26 [a]
SBR	1983	.73	.05	-.49 [a]	1.25 [a]

Note: FBR = first budget resolution, FBRC = first budget resolution conference, SBR = second budget resolution, SBRC = second budget resolution conference, TBR = third budget resolution (in fiscal 1977 only).

[a] Significant at the .001 level or less.

[b] Significant at the .01 level or less.

[c] Significant at the .05 level or less.

budget votes in the House, and the relationship is weak and not statistically significant in the Senate. Members of the House with high party unity scores (that is, those who vote with the majority of their party most of the time) are most likely to vote against budget resolutions. Party unity is the weakest variable in the model, with the standardized regression coefficients rarely exceeding .20 and with most of the relationships statistically insignificant in the Senate. The one exception to this generalization is the first two years of the Ford administration in the Senate. Party unity standardized regression coefficients during those years are statistically significant and are the most strongly related to budget votes at an average of -.24. During the bipartisan years of the budget process in the Senate, party unity was negatively related to support of the budget resolutions. In other words, voting with the party was not as important to senators as supporting the bipartisan agreements of the Senate Budget Committee.

Ideology proved to be an important predictor of budget votes. Voting on the budget is one of the few ways members can express their general economic philosophy, be it liberal or conservative. Other kinds of votes are not so clearly interpreted in ideological terms. Generally, the more conservative a member, the more likely that member is to vote against passage of budget resolutions, which usually include large deficits and significant levels of social spending. This relationship between conservative coalition scores and voting for budget resolutions is strong in the Senate: standardized regression coefficients ranging from -.12 to 1.85, with the average in the midforties. One exception is the positive relationship between conservative coalition scores and Senate votes for President Reagan's budgets in fiscal 1982 and 1983, when some of the basic elements of Reaganomics were established. (The standardized regression coefficients for those years were positive, in the midforties and higher.)

Presidential support scores hold the most explanatory power in the model. There is a strong positive relationship between presidential support scores and voting in favor of budget resolutions. Generally, the higher the presidential support score, the more likely it is that a member will vote in favor of the budget resolutions (with the exceptions of fiscal years 1976 and 1977, the first two years of the congressional budget process). Standardized regression coefficients for presidential support scores are statistically significant for all but one vote in the House and well over half the votes in the Senate. Some of the strongest relationships (regression coefficients of .85 and .81 in fiscal years 1980 and 1981, respectively) are shown in the House for the last two years of the Carter administration after the president's increase of military expenditures. Presidential support regression coefficients for the first two years of the Reagan administration are strongly related to voting for budget resolutions.

In sum, there is compelling evidence that the president is a critical and steady influence on budget votes of members of Congress. Although these exploratory findings are consistent with several recent studies of congressional roll-call votes in general, this study is only the first step in understanding votes on budget resolutions. More complex analytical models of budget voting need to be developed, using the rich descriptive literature on the congressional budget process. The test of those models should include budget-related votes after fiscal 1983.

Congressional and Presidential
Influence Over Budget Priorities

Advocates of the 1974 budget act argued for "an improved congressional system for determining relative funding priorities." [22] Many felt reform was needed to unify the disaggregated budgetary process in Congress and to create a mechanism for challenging and changing the president's budget priorities. The first chairman of the House Budget Committee, Rep. Brock Adams, D-Wash., stated it simply: "Perhaps the most important aspect of the budget resolution is the fact that it contains the budget of Congress and that of the president." [23]

Congressional-presidential spending priorities are often driven by a highly representative and decentralized system that makes distributive decisions in favor of strong interest groups, agencies, and congressional committees. The budget process is both pluralistic and incremental, with each agency and interest group zealously guarding its part of the budget. Past budgetary outlays are given preference over new spending requests. Congress has had to learn to "just say no" to major increases and new programs and to say it to presidents, interest groups, and constituents, an often distasteful and politically risky task. Indeed, GRH forces Congress to reaffirm existing budget priorities, thereby leaving few resources and little congressional energy to tackle new programs. Automatic across-the-board cuts in a sequester under GRH do not, by definition, change budget priorities; they simply set existing program preferences permanently in place. Change in budget priorities has come increment by increment or by exception, not through radical reordering of budget priorities based on new-found congressional budgetary power.[24]

From 1974 to 1990, federal budget outlays grew dramatically— from $538.7 billion to an estimated $1.2 trillion (in constant dollars). As a percentage of gross national product spent by the federal government, this represented an increase from 19 percent to more than 21 percent. During the same period, outlays for various budget functions changed only slightly. For example, from 1974 to 1988, expenditures for national defense dropped from 29.5 percent to 29.0 percent of outlays, and those for human resources dropped from 50.4 to 50.0 percent. The most dramatic shift in spending preferences was caused by the government's borrowing to pay interest on the federal debt. From 1974 to 1989, the interest increased from $21.4 billion to $165.7 billion, or from 8 percent to more than 14 percent of the budget.

The real growth in government spending happened almost automatically through pluralistic incrementalism. Interest groups, agencies, and committees have been as successful under the 1974 budget process in protecting their base funding and securing their fair share of increase as they were before Congress centralized budgetary decision making. No major groups have been significantly disadvantaged by budget reform. No major programs have been cut. No congressional committees have tried to abolish programs under their jurisdiction. Spending priorities have not greatly changed as a direct result of the 1974 budget process or GRH.

The budget act of 1974 and the GRH legislation have given Congress some means to compete with the president's policy agenda; however, the complexity of the process (including the entrenchment of its principal participants and the size of the federal debt) have led to evenly distributed spending cuts and budget accounting tricks by Congress rather than to dramatic changes in presidential spending priorities. Although the reforms potentially gave Congress more budgetary power, the power as exercised checked how much the president spent; it did not change what he spent it on. Ironically, the reforms gave the president the same power: the power to block but not to initiate major changes in spending outlays. Thus, whether the reforms have increased congressional influence over presidential budget priorities is still an open question.

Congressional-Presidential Relations and Impoundment Control

Have the reforms allowed Congress to control presidential impoundments? Is the president obligated to spend money appropriated by Congress? When President Nixon impounded funds already authorized and signed into law, he blatantly challenged the constitutional doctrine of separation of powers that delegates to Congress the power of the purse and to the president the duty of spending appropriated funds.

A major objective of the Budget and Impoundment Control Act of 1974 was to control presidential impoundments. The act established procedures to review two kinds of impoundments: deferrals, to postpone or delay spending, and rescissions, to cancel or take back authority to spend. When presidents propose deferrals of up to twelve months, Congress may disapprove of the deferral resolution (with no time limit), compelling the release of the affected funds. Before 1983 deferrals could be defeated only by a one-house legislative veto. The Supreme Court found this unconstitutional in *Immigration and Naturalization Service v. Chadha*,[25] but Congress has circumvented the constitutionality issue by voting on deferrals in both houses.

When a president proposes a rescission, Congress has forty-five legislative days during which it can pass a bill permanently canceling funds, thereby approving the presidential rescission. If Congress fails to act during this period, the president is required to make the funds available for expenditure.

The effect of the impoundment provisions on congressional-presidential relations has been profound. The provisions have regularized and set a legal foundation for presidential impoundments, while allowing Congress to overturn these cuts when it desires. Congress has control over presidential impoundments, with a latent consequence that presidents can legally use them to cut back on spending they deem unnecessary.

The approval rate for deferrals is high, more than 88 percent (Table 8-6). President Reagan's success on proposed deferrals through 1988 was almost 89 percent, an average similar to President Ford's (86 percent) and President Carter's (89 percent). More than $136 billion in deferrals was saved by presidents from 1975 through 1988. Ford successfully deferred $31 billion; Carter, $25 billion; and Reagan, $80 billion. The obvious conclusion: when the president wants to delay expenditures legally, Congress generally agrees.

Between 1975 and 1988, use of the rescission process varied sharply from year to year (see Table 8-6). In 1975 and 1976, President Ford proposed more than $6 billion in rescissions, but Congress cut only $529.6 million, for a 9 percent average rescission rate.

During the Carter administration, the rescission rate increased to almost 42 percent for a $2.4 billion savings. Reagan used rescissions to assist his budget cuts in 1981 and 1982, when he cut an unprecedented $16 billion (with a very high rescission success rate of almost 60 percent). After the first two years of the Reagan administration, however, the number of rescissions proposed and accepted dropped dramatically. Only $400 million was cut during the next six years, and the total rescission success rate for Reagan's tenure in office was 25 percent. In summary, from 1975 to 1988, almost $20 billion was cut through rescissions (a 25 percent congressional acceptance rate). Congress reviews the permanent cuts through presidential rescissions carefully.

In conclusion, the impoundment provisions of the 1974 budget act have allowed Congress to check presidential impoundment power, and these provisions have been implemented without major political confrontations during both Republican and Democratic administrations. The impoundment controls help Congress to reassert its constitutional power of the purse. The president clearly has lost unilateral power to cut appropriated federal dollars. He is now forced to cooperate with Congress to build bipartisan support for impoundments. When that is not done, few funds are cut.

TABLE 8-6 Deferrals and Rescissions, 1975-1988

Administration and year	Deferrals		Rescissions	
	Amount (in millions)	Approval rate (%)	Amount (in millions)	Approval rate (%)[a]
Ford				
1975	$ 15,954.8	63.0	$ 391.3	14.4
1976[b]	7,762.3	95.3	138.3	3.9
1977	7,048.1	100.0	0.0	0.0
Total/Average	$ 30,765.2	86.1%	$ 529.6	9.2%
Carter				
1977	$ 4,975.8	99.5	$ 711.6	39.8
1978	4,910.3	98.9	593.7	46.0
1979	4,676.9	99.8	593.7	46.0
1980	5,027.0	47.8	550.8	34.0
1981	5,670.4	100.0	0.0	0.0
Total/Average	$ 25,260.4	89.2%	$ 2,449.8	41.5%
Reagan				
1981	$ 3,452.7	90.5	$11,715.2	76.3
1982	7,853.4	95.6	4,364.7	55.2
1983	9,624.0	70.7	0.0	0.0
1984	7,919.5	99.8	55.4	8.7
1985	16,044.7	95.6	165.6	8.9
1986	14,690.0	59.3	143.0	1.4
1987	11,320.0	98.5	36.0	0.6
1988	9,320.0	100.0	0.0	0.0
Total/Average	$ 80,224.3	88.8%	$16,479.9	25.2%
Grand total/ Average	$136,249.9	88.1%	$19,459.3	25.3%

Source: Compiled by author from data provided by Office of Management and Budget, October 1985, October 1987, and October 1989.

[a] The average approval rate excludes years for which no rescissions were attempted.

[b] Includes transition quarter from July to September.

Centralization of the Budget Process

Before the budget act was passed, the stable roles, relationships, and routines of the president, OMB, executive branch agencies, congressional party leaders, congressional committees, and interest groups led to few surprises in the federal budget process. Predictable pluralistic incrementalism with a narrow scope and low level of political conflict predominated over distributive budgetary processes. Since 1974, when the reforms were passed, however, two oil crises, stagflation, high interest rates, and Reaganomics have changed the economy and destabilized the budget process. Reagan era tax cuts forced Congress to make redistributive budget decisions that widened the number of participants in the conflict over the budget and increased the conflict's visibility. President Reagan achieved his purpose "to limit the growth of . . . government by limiting the revenues available to be spent." [26] The 1974 budget reform and GRH placed restraints on spending by openly relating outlays to revenues and calling for a balanced budget. A latent consequence of both acts has been increased budgetary conflict, confusion, and stalemate between Congress and the president.

The budget reforms centralized budget decisions and caused some jockeying for jurisdictional turf between the budget committees and the other standing committees, especially the appropriations and taxing committees. The authorization committees have lost power because of the appropriations committees' right to cap new backdoor spending. There are three kinds of backdoor spending techniques: "*Contract authority* permits agencies to enter into contracts that subsequently must be liquidated by appropriations. *Borrowing authority* allows agencies to spend money they have borrowed from the public or the Treasury. And *mandatory entitlements* grant eligible individuals and governments the right to receive payments from the national government. . . . Entitlements, for Medicare, for example, establish judicially enforceable rights without reference to dollar amounts." [27] The 1974 budget reforms restricted the authorization committees' use of contract authority and borrowing authority. But pre-1974 entitlement programs and net interest payments continue to reduce the ability of both Congress and the president to control the budget.

The 1974 budget act requires all standing committees to estimate the cost of programs within their jurisdiction early in the budget cycle. These estimates of authorizations tend to limit the committees' freedom and that of executive agencies and interest groups, which have a natural tendency to push for new programs and higher authorizations. The committees are forced to state priorities and to make difficult choices among programs very early in the process; they are much less vulnerable to twelfth-hour lobbying by agencies and strong, well-organized interest groups. Before the 1974 reform program, authorization levels were commonly double and even triple the final appropriations. The authorization committees would often approve programs at very high levels to placate strong pressures from outside Congress, knowing full well that the appropriations committees would decrease the funding to more reasonable levels. After 1974 and GRH, the authorization committees could no longer play this game. The requirement to estimate program costs reduces the gap between authorizations and appropriations and puts a cap on the political pressures from agencies and interest groups.

White House staff now find it necessary to work the Hill continually in order to win spending battles. The process is relatively open and thus more burdensome for the president and executive branch officials, forcing them to bargain more openly with members of Congress and to monitor the budget process carefully. OMB staff attend budget hearings and mark-ups, and the director often sits at the bargaining table with budget committee leaders to negotiate the final budget resolutions.

House-Senate Comparisons

Budgetary power in the Senate has generally been firmly in the hands of the committee chairs. House party leaders have played a stronger role in the budget process than have their Senate counterparts. House leaders set budget figures and offer refining amendments in order to marshal support for the budget resolutions. One of the consequences of the budget reform on the House majority leadership is that it has forced centralization, coordination, and the construction of a Democratic coalition behind congressional budgets. The Senate budget is more bipartisan, and the Senate has less conflict than the House in building budget resolutions.

House and Senate leaders from both parties, however, have helped give the budget process an independence from the president but not always from the power and expertise of committee and subcommittee chairs, who put pressure on the budget committees for higher spending for their favorite programs. When constituency interests and budget-committee priorities confront each other, the substantive committees with strong support from interest groups and agencies usually win in the battle over the budget.

A major challenge to the independence of the congressional budget process came during President Reagan's first year in office. OMB director David Stockman, a former representative who had an excellent understanding of the congressional budget reforms, used the reconciliation process to make severe cuts in spending by congressional committees. Interest groups and their friends on committees and in agencies were taken by surprise when Stockman and his allies on Capitol Hill locked in spending ceilings in the first concurrent resolution, thus changing the focus of the budget debate from line items to the highly centralized reconciliation resolution. In support of President Reagan, Republicans and conservative Democrats joined to increase defense spending and worked through the reconciliation process to reduce nondefense expenditures over the 1981-1983 period. The cuts totaled $100 billion. Democratic opponents were unable to stop the massive cuts until they weakened the conservative coalition in the House and eventually recaptured the Senate. The budget confrontations in 1981 and 1982 showed that the president can use the budget process to his advantage. Since 1983 interest groups, committees, and executive branch agencies have regained their protectionist power over the budget.

The reconciliation process was President Reagan's way of achieving reductions in expenditures within the protected jurisdiction of the tax committees and the sacred turf of the appropriations committees. Louis Fisher estimates that more than half the spending reductions in the reconciliation acts were within the jurisdiction of the House Ways and Means and Senate Finance committees.[28] After 1983 Congress used the reconciliation process to challenge several presidential budgetary priorities.

In conclusion, budget reforms have the potential to limit the power of policy subsystems—that is, interest groups, committees, and agencies with jurisdiction over specific programs—by giving presidents and congressional leaders tools to coordinate and centralize budgeting on Capitol Hill. Yet strong interests continue to win and weak interests continue to lose in the battle of the budget, no matter how centralized and well coordinated the budget process has become.

Budget Control:
Congress Versus the President

Have the 1974 reforms tightened control of the federal budget? In 1974 approximately 70 percent of the budget was considered relatively uncontrollable, coming primarily from interest payments on the debt and indexed permanently authorized entitlements (such as Social Security, which is 21 percent of the budget). These areas cannot be directly controlled by the president and the appropriations committees on an annual basis. In 1988 OMB considered 77.5 percent of the budget uncontrollable, a 7.5 percent increase since 1974. This lack of budgetary control comes from payments for individuals (43.5 percent), fixed program costs (15.1 percent), and prior-year contracts and obligations (18.9 percent). If interest payments of 14.1 percent are added to the OMB estimates, more than 90 percent of the budget is relatively uncontrollable.

Levels of benefit are normally established in authorizing law rather than through appropriations of budget authority. Efforts by

Congress or the president to reduce spending on these entitlement programs require changing the authorizing legislation, which is politically very difficult. In the absence of such legislative changes, the payments are made automatically, and in many cases they are made from the budget authority that is available without appropriations action to finance the program. The rise in permanent budget authority—resulting largely from these various forms of pre-1974 backdoor spending—has diminished the connection between congressional budgetary decisions in any given year and the actual outlays for that year. In short, the budget reforms have not significantly improved the capacity of Congress to control the budget.

GRH has put increased pressure on Congress and the president to focus on the uncontrollables; however, there is little evidence that members of Congress and the president have the political will to reduce spending for popular entitlement programs such as Social Security. As Stockman's successor at OMB, James C. Miller III, explains: "Deficits create many winners and few losers. . . . Every legislator is in a position to try to confer benefits on his or her favorite constituencies, and the incentive for any individual legislator to refrain from such behavior is virtually nonexistent." [29] As a representative assembly, Congress finds it difficult to oppose well-organized national interest groups, such as those protecting the interests of Social Security recipients. Once a relatively closed process for financing government agencies, congressional-presidential budgeting has been transformed into an open process for providing benefits and contracts to Americans. The more open the congressional budget process has become, the more Congress and the president have increased the flow of benefits to outsiders.

The deficit could be reduced by changing entitlements, by cutting defense spending rapidly, or by raising taxes. All of these solutions, however, require tighter budget control and spell political, if not electoral, suicide for members of Congress and the president. There is little evidence that the reforms have created greater control over the budget; thus the hypothesis that Congress has greater control over federal spending than it did before 1974 cannot be confirmed. Congress does not have greater control of the budget, and neither does the president.

Conclusion

The Budget and Impoundment Control Act of 1974 and the 1985 and 1987 GRH legislation are some of the most important structural and procedural budgetary reforms adopted by Congress in the past fifty years. Their consequences for presidential and congressional governance, cooperation, and conflict are far-reaching. The reforms:

- created an environment in which budget votes dominate roll-call voting in Congress;
- created a congressional budget process more independent of the president;
- opened up the budget process and required the president and executive staff to work more closely with Congress;
- established a coherent and constitutional method of congressional review over presidential impoundments;
- centralized congressional budget decision making and limited the power of authorization committees—and potentially the power of interest groups and agencies—in the budget process; and
- focused public attention on macroeconomic and microeconomic trade-offs, but with little effect on the controllability of the budget.

Budgeting by the president and Congress has become more democratic yet more conflicted.[30] Frequently, the result is policy-making gridlock. Congress is fundamentally a representative institution. Because it responds to political pressures and public preferences, any effort to make the budget process more efficient is in direct conflict with its constitutional design and natural state. The struggle inside Congress vacillates between centralization and decentralization of authority, and it will continue to cause delay, deadlock, and even a breakdown in congressional-presidential budgeting until the American people wish something different. New budget reforms—such as a balanced budget amendment, a biennial budget, combined appropriations and authorizations committees, or the line-item veto—will be problematic and unlikely to work unless there is a clear public consensus for change.[31]

A major objective of the budget reforms was to force consensus where none had existed. Budgeting rules, however, have not changed the desire of presidents and members of Congress to represent and to be reelected. It is clear that the executive-legislative divisions over budget policy remain as entrenched as ever. Increased budgetary discipline by Congress and the president is not a simple matter of legislation. Congress and the president will continue to bargain and compromise over incremental spending changes no matter what new budget reforms are adopted.

Notes

1. James A. Thurber, "Congressional Budget Reform and New Demands for Policy Analysis," *Policy Analysis* 2 (Spring 1976): 198-214; James A. Thurber, "Assessing the Congressional Budget Process Under Gramm-Rudman-Hollings and the 1974 Budget Act" (Paper delivered at the annual meeting of the American Political Science Association, Washington, D.C., September 1986).

2. John W. Ellwood and James A. Thurber, "The New Congressional Budget Process: The Hows and Whys of House-Senate Differences," in *Congress Reconsidered*, ed. Lawrence C. Dodd and Bruce I. Oppenheimer (New York: Praeger, 1977), 163-192.

3. Allen Schick, *Reconciliation and the Congressional Budget Process* (Washington, D.C.: American Enterprise Institute, 1981).

4. James P. Pfiffner, *The President, the Budget, and Congress: Impoundments and the 1974 Budget Act* (Boulder, Colo.: Westview Press, 1979).

5. Elizabeth Wehr, "Congress Enacts Far-Reaching Budget Measure," *Congressional Quarterly Weekly Report,* December 14, 1985, 2604-2611.

6. Elizabeth Wehr, "Gramm-Rudman: Domenici Has His Doubts," *Congressional Quarterly Weekly Report,* September 19, 1987, 2234-2235.

7. Rudolph G. Penner and Alan J. Abramson, *Broken Purse Strings: Congressional Budgeting, 1974-88* (Washington, D.C.: Urban Institute, 1988); John Ferejohn and Keith Krehbiel, "The Budget Process and the Size of the Budget," *American Journal of Political Science* 31 (May 1987): 296-320; and Kenneth A. Shepsle, "The Congressional Budget Process: Diagnosis, Prescription, Prognosis," in *Congressional Budgeting: Politics, Process, and Power,* ed. W. Thomas Wander, F. Ted Hebert, and Gary W. Copeland (Baltimore: Johns Hopkins University Press, 1984).

8. James G. March and Herbert Simon, *Organizations* (New York: Wiley, 1958), 137-142. See also Duncan MacRae, Jr., *Dimensions of Congressional Voting* (Berkeley: University of California Press, 1958); Keith T. Poole and Howard Rosenthal, "A Spatial Model for Legislative Roll Call Analysis," *American Journal of Political Science* 29 (1985): 357-384; Sam Peltzman, "Constituent Interest and Congressional Voting," *Journal of Law and Economics* 27 (1984): 181-210; Sam Peltzman, "An Economic Interpretation of the History of Congressional Voting in the Twentieth Century," *American Economic Review* 75 (1985): 656-675; Morris Fiorina, *Representatives, Roll Calls, and Constituencies* (Lexington, Mass.: Heath, 1974); and Herbert B. Asher and Herbert F. Weisberg, "Voting Change in Congress: Some Dynamic Perspectives in an Evolutionary Process," *American Journal of Political Science* 22 (1978): 391-425.

9. Melissa P. Collie, "Voting Behavior in Legislatures," in *Handbook of Legislative Research,* ed. Gerhard Loewenberg, Samuel Patterson, and Malcolm E. Jewell (Cambridge, Mass.: Harvard University Press, 1985).

10. Keith T. Poole, "Recent Developments in Analytical Models of Voting in the U.S. Congress," *Legislative Studies Quarterly* 13 (November 1988): 117-133; and Keith T. Poole and R. Steven Daniels, "Ideology, Party, and Voting in the U.S. Congress, 1959-1980," *American Political Science Review* 79 (June 1985): 373-399.

11. Herbert F. Weisberg, "Theories of Roll-Call Voting," *American Journal of Political Science* 22 (1978): 554-575.

12. Poole, "Recent Developments," 119.

13. Norman J. Ornstein, Thomas E. Mann, and Michael J. Malbin, *Vital Statistics on Congress, 1989-1990* (Washington, D.C.: Congressional Quarterly, 1990), 198.

14. Ibid., 190.

15. Jerrold Schneider, *Ideological Coalitions in Congress* (Westport, Conn.: Greenwood Press, 1979).

16. Poole and Rosenthal, "A Spatial Model for Legislative Roll Call Analysis," 357-384.

17. Poole, "Recent Developments," 129.

18. MacRae, *Dimensions;* Poole and Daniels, "Ideology, Party, and Voting."

19. Norman J. Ornstein, Thomas E. Mann, and Michael J. Malbin, *Vital Statistics on Congress, 1987-1988* (Washington, D.C.: Congressional Quarterly, 1987), 200, 210.

20. Ibid., 198.

21. Although it is customary to use logistic regression analysis (logit) to test a hypothesis with a dichotomous dependent variable (for example, budget votes), I am using regression analysis because it is more widely understood. I was careful to compare the signs and magnitude of relationships of the logit and regression coefficients. They are the same and thus the conclusions from both statistical methods are the same. For information on logit analysis, see John H. Aldrich and Forrest D. Nelson, *Linear Probability, Logit, and Probit Models* (Beverly Hills, Calif.: Sage, 1984).

22. Thurber, "Congressional Budget Reform," 201.

23. Quoted in Lance T. LeLoup, *Budgetary Politics: Dollars, Deficits, Decisions* (Brunswick, Ohio: King's Court Communications, 1977), 126.

24. Allen Schick, *Congress and Money: Budgeting, Spending and Taxing* (Washington, D.C.: Urban Institute, 1980); and Allen Schick, "Budgeting as Administrative Practice," in *Perspective on Budgeting* (Washington, D.C.: American Society for Public Administration, 1980).

25. See *Immigration and Naturalization Service v. Chadha,* 462 U.S. 919 (1983). See also William P. Schaefer and James A. Thurber, "The Legislative Veto and the Policy Subsystems: Its Impact on Congressional Oversight" (Paper delivered at the annual meeting of the Southern Political Science Association, Atlanta, Ga., September 1980); Louis Fisher, "Impoundments: Here We Go Again," *Public Budgeting and Finance* (Winter 1986): 72; and House Rules Committee, *Legislative Veto After Chadha,* hearings before the House Rules Committee, 98th Cong., 1st sess., 1983, 2d sess., 1984.

26. Leroy N. Rieselbach, *Congressional Reform* (Washington, D.C.: CQ Press, 1986), 100.
27. Roger H. Davidson and Walter J. Oleszek, *Congress and Its Members,* 3d ed. (Washington, D.C.: CQ Press, 1990), 378-379.
28. Louis Fisher, "The Budget Act of 1974: Reflections After Ten Years" (Paper delivered at the annual meeting of the Midwest Political Science Association, Chicago, Ill., April 1985).
29. James Miller, "Miller Says Deficit Begets Spending" (Washington, D.C.: American Enterprise Institute, spring 1987, memorandum), 8.
30. For further discussion, see James A. Thurber, "The Dynamics of Policy Subsystems in American Politics," in *Interest Group Politics,* 3d ed., ed. Allan J. Cigler and Burdett A. Loomis (Washington, D.C.: CQ Press, forthcoming).
31. For an evaluation of recommended budget reforms, see James A. Thurber, "Governance and the Budget Process: Evaluating Proposals for Change" (Paper prepared for publication by the White Burkett Miller Center of Public Affairs, University of Virginia, Charlottesville, Va., October 11, 1989); and James A. Thurber and Samantha Durst, "Delay, Deadlock, and Deficits: Evaluating Proposals for Congressional Budget Reform," in *Federal Budget and Financial Management Reform,* ed. Thomas Lynch (Westport, Conn.: Greenwood Press, forthcoming).

9. CONGRESS, THE PRESIDENT, AND WAR POWERS: THE PERENNIAL DEBATE

Christopher J. Deering

In the context of the post-World War II international system, debates about declarations of war, the existence of standing armies, and the legislated provision for military forces in times of need are largely moot. The central issue today is who controls standing military forces and how these forces are used. Is the president provided with standing military forces in an essentially unfettered fashion? Some analysts have suggested that this is so, or at least that it ought to be so. Others have argued that the executive possesses military resources only to carry out policies established by Congress.

Almost no one disputes the power of the president to repel sudden attacks against the territory of the United States. Nor does anyone dispute the power of Congress to commit the United States to war. With power divided, then, what determines when these two branches will cooperate on so fundamental an issue as national security? And is conflict between the two branches on this issue truly dangerous? Clearly, the Founders assumed that cooperation rather than conflict would be the norm, but they provided mechanisms for institutional conflict to prevent one branch—particularly the executive—from dominating in matters of national security.

During the past two hundred years, the scope of the president's power has expanded substantially, progressing from the limited notion of the executive's prerogative to respond to sudden attacks on U.S. territory to a wider authority to protect, even on a preemptive basis, American lives and property abroad.[1] Because of this change, legislative-executive competition now focuses on control of the preemptive, protective, retaliatory, limited, and covert use of American military force. After World War II, Congress lost that control—indeed willingly gave it away for the most part—before determining that it had surrendered too much control to the executive.

Contemporary opinion is divided on whether this situation is desirable, but almost everyone agrees that the modern presidency has gained the upper hand. By 1973 the war in Southeast Asia and protests in the United States had rekindled active debate on the subject and generated unambiguous competition between the two branches. Although Congress could not act with one voice, it was sufficiently displeased with Richard Nixon's administration in 1973 to pass the War Powers Resolution. That act—which limited troop deployments in hostile situations, required prompt presidential reports to Congress, and required formal congressional approval of continued troop deployments—was intended to reassert Congress's role in war powers and to regain some control of the standing military establishment.

Rather than settling the debate, however, the War Powers Resolution seems to have made matters worse. By virtually all accounts the act has failed. Debate surrounding its passage uncovered serious disagreement regarding the constitutional rights and responsibilities—as originally intended and as currently needed—for the use of military force. As a result, the executive and legislative branches have reached an uneasy standoff.

As we enter the nation's third century, it is important to understand the roots of the episodic cooperation and conflict between Congress and the president where military policy is concerned. Because previous commentary has ignored, downplayed, or underestimated their importance, it is also important to revisit several points in the debate regarding the balance of constitutional power. Thus, while the precise points covered here are not new, my intention is to offer a different interpretation of them and to add new perspective to the ongoing debate.

The Context of the Debate

The American Constitution was written at an important historical breakpoint. Although discussions about war powers frequently mention this fact, comments are usually limited to a couple of points. For example, Nicholas deB. Katzenbach makes this observation:

> One of the difficulties then [when the Constitution was written] and since is simply that force is not the option of only one side to a controversy. A second is that force, or threat of force, *need not amount to the full-scale "war" which the members of the Constitutional Convention surely had in the forefront of their minds.* A "Declaration of War" in the late eighteenth and nineteenth centuries was a formal act which carried with it a massive change of legal relations with both the enemy and neutrals. It was not a step lightly taken nor an easy one from which to disengage.[2]

Katzenbach also observes that because of this state of affairs nations frequently used "some measure of force without declaring war." But this gives too little credit to the Constitution's authors. Surely the

Founders were familiar with such practices, at least insofar as they had developed at that time. This comment, it should be said, is a small part of an article with a broader and more contemporary focus. Nonetheless, the impression left in it—and elsewhere in similar discussions—is that the Founders were concerned only with formal declarations of war that *preceded* full-scale military action.

It is important to realize that the authors of the Constitution were aware of some changes that had occurred and were likewise aware of the diplomatic and military tenor of their times, but they could not predict some important changes that would shortly affect the international diplomatic system. The Founders were not backward in their thinking nor in their knowledge of world affairs, although we sometimes are tempted to view their time as less advanced than it was or to regard them as operating with a sixteenth- or seventeenth-century mentality rather than living at the brink of the nineteenth century. In this context, two points are significant.

First, those present at the Constitutional Convention were well versed in the evolving practices and principles of international law—including alliance formation, neutrality, declarations of war, and treaties of peace. They understood the monarchical and aristocratic character of European nation-states. And they knew that the advent of the nation-state in Europe in the middle of the seventeenth century had not been accompanied by the constitutional principles of citizenship that link people to their national governments.[3]

Therefore, the authors of the Constitution knew quite well that their new government—based on the liberal principles of life, liberty, and property—would be uniquely popular in character and distinctly different from other nations in the diplomatic community. But they consciously made the decision to establish a government of the people, by the people, and for the people—and at the same time required it to formulate foreign and military policies in accord with those same principles. Thus, it is unfair and incorrect to conclude today that the Founders failed to recognize the difficulty of adhering to democratic processes while operating in the international environment as it existed at the time. It would be equally erroneous to conclude or to argue that foreign and defense policy were somehow exempt from the precepts of popular government embodied in the Constitution.

In contrast, the Founders could not foresee with any precision the subsequent rise in nationalism attended by popular revolutions that would forge the links of citizenship between Europeans and their national governments. Nor could they foresee the advent of interventionism, international ideological disputes, and unstable balances of power that would create a need for full-time diplomatic efforts across a wider range of issues and with a larger number of sovereign powers than existed in the world of the late eighteenth century. It is important to recognize, however, that many of these developments made other nation-states more rather than less like the United States.

Second, and perhaps more importantly, the Founders knew that the "ceremony of a formal denunciation of war [had] fallen into disuse." [4] Consequent to that, they were also aware of the distinction between full-scale, declared wars ("perfect" wars) and more limited wars characterized by defensive or reprisal actions ("imperfect" wars).[5] They also knew that state armies were mercenary forces. What they could not predict was that small mercenary forces, at least in wartime, would soon be outmoded by two military developments: the French *levee en masse* (or conscripted citizen army) and the decline of limited wars that excluded most civilian targets.[6]

The first development is important because huge armies could not be maintained by relying on the sentiments of patriots or the selfishness of mercenaries. Absent popular forms of government, no patriotic link existed to induce pure volunteerism. Couple that with the absence of unlimited funding and the increasingly lethal nature of warfare, and mercenaries also became inadequate. Thus, additional inducements were needed to fill the ranks of large modern military organizations. That development is closely linked to the second. Although the American revolutionary forces frequently adopted guerrilla tactics, the most important battles of that conflict pitted opposing armies against one another in pitched battle—as at Yorktown, for example. Civilians and civilian property were neither the targets of war nor its objects, and the destruction of property typically resulted from tactical or strategic considerations (the burning of bridges or armories, for example). This also changed during the nineteenth century, first during the Napoleonic campaigns but even more decisively during the American Civil War.[7]

When the Founders drafted the Constitution, they could not, of course, envision these important changes that would take place, but they were fully aware of the conditions of their time. Thus, they reacted on the basis of the empirical evidence at hand, distrusting the military because it was an instrument of monarchical power rather than an instrument of democracy. Experience during the Revolutionary War and under the Articles of Confederation, however, convinced delegates to the convention that the national government needed greater military capacity. During the revolution, General George Washington frequently had suffered from insufficient or shoddy supplies and equipment. Troop quotas during and after that conflict, which were to be supplied in the form of state militia, frequently lagged behind requested and promised levels. The decentralized nature of the Articles of Confederation left the national government nearly powerless to raise revenues, formulate a common commercial policy, or establish even a small national military force. And finally, just before the convention, an alarming rebellion by debt-ridden Massachusetts farmers, Shays's Rebellion, provided on a small scale an example of the sort of bloody domestic conflicts that might grow from a perpetually weak national government.

Invitation to Struggle

On August 17, 1787, James Madison and Elbridge Gerry asked the Constitutional Convention to consider an amendment to Article I, section 8, that would strike out the word *make* and insert the word *declare* in the clause that establishes Congress's war power. The amendment passed by a vote of 7-2.[8] Hence, rather than "the Congress shall have Power . . . to make war," we have "the Congress shall have Power . . . to declare war." Madison's notes from the convention suggest that little discussion occurred: the executive would be left with the power to *repel* sudden attacks and the responsibility to *conduct* actual military operations.[9] It is fair to say, however, that no other change has engendered so much debate—indeed, a full two hundred years' worth. It is generally agreed that debate on foreign and military policy making was of secondary importance during the Constitutional Convention.[10] Nonetheless, debate did occur during the convention and more heatedly during the ratifying conventions. As with other debates at the convention, the issue of military policy making centered on differing opinions about the strength of the new national government.[11] Only later would these disputes form the basis of the perennial debates about the nature and extent of executive and legislative power. This point is worth reemphasizing. The Constitutional Convention, the *Federalist Papers,* and the ratifying conventions focused primarily on the strength of the national, federated government and its advantages relative to the confederation. Thus, the debate regarding military power was less concerned with executive versus legislative control than with national armies versus state militia.

Gerry and other Democratic-Republicans such as Thomas Jefferson, Richard Henry Lee, and James Madison of Virginia were frightened at the prospect of a standing army at the disposal of the national government. Consider, for example, the words of Richard Henry Lee in a letter to Madison in 1787:

> You are perfectly right in your observation concerning the consequence of a standing army—that it has constantly terminated in the destruction of liberty. It has not only *been* constantly so, but I

think it clear, from the construction of human nature, that it *will* always be so. . . .[12]

Opponents of the standing national army believed that such an institution lacked democratic control, drained the treasury, burdened the people, and invited war. The new government should not emphasize military might but should promote commercial development, neutrality, and the safeguarding of political liberties. These Democratic-Republicans almost certainly also believed, even if they did not say it, that a national army would undercut their own local militias, in which most politicians held commissions. Indeed, it has been argued that the vested interests in the local militia were as formidable a block to establishing a regular army as any of the philosophical arguments advanced at the time. Thus, in 1787 localism may have been as powerful a motive as liberal individualism in combating the forces that favored a stronger national government.[13]

The Federalists, led by Alexander Hamilton during the convention, believed that the new nation required a strong national government in order to achieve some degree of stability and continued independence from England, France, and Spain. Hamilton believed that a professional army and navy of at least modest proportions would be necessary to secure American interests:

> The steady operations of war against a regular and disciplined army can only be successfully conducted by a force of the same kind. Considerations of economy, not less than of stability and vigor, confirm this position. . . . War, like most other things, is a science to be acquired and perfected by diligence, by perseverance, by time, and by practice.[14]

In contrast to the Democratic-Republicans, Hamilton hoped to be the architect of a competitive national economy. As a realist he knew that many years would pass before America could seriously compete with the other trading and manufacturing nations of the world. In the interim the new country would need a regular army and navy to secure its financial interests from the intrusions of others.[15]

On balance, the Constitution came out closer to Madison's and Gerry's democratic point of view than to Hamilton's. As in other matters, the Founders erred on the side of limits rather than permissiveness. As ratified, their approach to military policy and policy making included several key components: (1) the Constitution clearly established civilian control of the military; (2) the military was to be created by Congress, the popular branch of government; (3) except during wartime the army would be limited in size; and (4) Congress would take the lead in determining when or whether the United States should enter into war.[16]

In this context, the president's role as commander in chief takes on a more limited mandate than is today commonly perceived.[17] When the Constitution was written, the term *commander in chief* had been in use for more than a century and a half. The position and the title were widely used by the American states and in Europe. More importantly, at the time of the Constitutional Convention and beyond, the title and the position were much more limited than they are today. Indeed, George Washington, before becoming commander in chief as first president of the United States, had already been commissioned "General and Commander in chief, of the army of the United Colonies." [18] Commanders in chief were frequently theater commanders, much in the same way that the U.S. military uses the term today (for example, CINCPAC, or Commander in Chief, Pacific). Even Hamilton points out that colonial governors were appointed (first by the Crown and later by state constitutions) to be commanders in chief of their respective state militia:

> But the constitutions of several of the states expressly declare their governors to be commanders-in-chief, as well of the army as navy; and it may well be a question whether those of New Hampshire and Massachusetts, in particular, do not, in this instance, confer larger powers upon their respective governors than could be claimed by a President of the United States.[19]

Commanders in chief, in most cases, were not field commanders. They might have been—and remain—theater commanders in chief, meaning they usually had an army and a navy under their command. But they would typically have been far removed from battle. As a result, at least one analyst has concluded:

> The meaning of [commander in chief] was that settled by a century and a half of usage: it designated the officer who stood at the apex of a military hierarchy. In British practice there were several such hierarchies, each with a separate commander in chief directly accountable to the Secretary of War. In the constitutional scheme there was a single hierarchy with a single commander in chief. But in all cases the commander in chief was under the direction of a political superior, a king or the Continental Congress or the national Congress. The term carried absolutely no overtones of any independent political authority.[20]

In sum, the Founders' view of the president's role as commander in chief was much more limited than contemporary commentators often suggest. As devised and understood at the time, and contrary to the wishes of participants such as Hamilton, the president's duty was to command a military establishment if it became necessary (to repel sudden attack or for other legislated purposes), when provided for by Congress, or pursuant to a declaration of war.

On balance, therefore, what Edward S. Corwin has called the Constitution's "invitation to struggle" was the product of three important factors: design, disagreement, and change. The Constitution explicitly set up a system of competition among the three branches of government. By preventing a concentration of power in a single branch and by establishing in each branch an "institutional will" to guard its prerogatives jealously, the Founders sought to avoid tyranny. In spite of this particular consensus supportive of the separation of powers, disagreement about emphasis and detail prevented the Founders from clearly locating the bulk of power in the new government. By compromising, they ensured that the debate would persist. At least in part because of the sheer novelty of the effort, they left some parts of the Constitution vague since they could not foresee every circumstance.

Regardless of the original intent of the Founders, the linchpin ultimately was the absence of a standing army, which, during peacetime, left the president nothing to command. Thus, the basic contours of the debate about executive-legislative relations were already in place when the Constitution was written. Since then the terms of that debate have changed little. What has changed, of course, are the circumstances within which the debate takes place. More than anything else, the presence of a sizable standing army and the civilian military establishment have shifted the balance of power in favor of the executive.

Diplomacy Versus Defense

In the contemporary world of nuclear deterrence, limited war, and covert actions, sharp distinctions between foreign and military policy are difficult to enunciate with clarity. It is sometimes suggested that because the Founders faced a simpler world they saw no need to make these distinctions. Moreover, arguments favoring an energetic and independent executive role where war powers are concerned frequently lump diplomacy and defense together. Yet it is not clear that the Founders, who addressed both of these areas in the Constitution, intended as much. In any case, they seemed to treat these problems in a more general fashion. The Constitution required careful drafting. It had to provide for a true national government that would overcome the weaknesses of the Articles of Confederation. At the same time, it had to be limited enough to satisfy the fears harbored by most of the Founders about centralized power *and* stand a chance of ratification. The Founders' solution was comprised of a policy of consolidated deterrence, a detailed list of congressional responsibilities, and a brief grant of executive authority. These are discussed in turn.

First, the Founders adopted an approach to foreign and defense policy that can be characterized as consolidated deterrence. Consolidated deterrence was a means of combining the new country's national strengths to deter foreign aggression and diminish its national weaknesses. John Jay aptly characterizes this concept:

> If [foreign nations] see that our national government is efficient and well administered, our trade prudently regulated, our militia properly organized and disciplined, our resources and finances discreetly managed, our credit re-established, our people free, contented, and united, they will be much more disposed to cultivate our friendship than provoke our resentment.[21]

For Jay, and for most of the other delegates at the Constitutional Convention, national security was best achieved through a common commercial policy, a stable and capable national government, and "discreetly" managed finances. The new, small, and indebted nation had no prospects for world domination and no appetite for international power. Separated from the rest of the world by a vast, unexplored frontier to the west and by a wide ocean to the east, its citizens hoped to thrive in relative isolation from the rest of the world. A strong, unified, national government and an attendant strength in commerce were the two most important requirements for safety from its British, French, and Spanish rivals. A well-organized militia and a competent navy provided added measures of security.

Second, the Founders enumerated for Congress, in Article I of the Constitution, an explicit and lengthy set of foreign policy and national security responsibilities. These responsibilities include the obvious—declaring war, establishing an army and a navy, controlling immigration, regulating foreign commerce—and the not so obvious—granting letters of marque and reprisal. In this discussion, the not so obvious is important.

The power to grant letters of marque and reprisal is probably the least considered aspect of Article I, section 8. And yet, given what has been said previously, it is not likely that the language was a careless carry-over from the Articles of Confederation. Letters of marque and reprisal had been a feature of European politics for at least five centuries. These letters, granted by state authority, legitimated private reprisals against subjects of other states; they might include seizures of property or individuals. By the early eighteenth century the authorization of private reprisals had nearly disappeared, but the reprisals by states on their own behalf continued—through the use of both public forces and privateers.[22] In several cases, in the period before the Constitutional Convention, these actions had resulted in war. The Founders, aware of these incidents, knew quite well that limited actions might easily lead to full-scale war. Thus, it is unlikely that the Founders would have given Congress sole discretion to declare "perfect" wars but withheld its power where "imperfect" wars were concerned. In arguing against the careless carry-over position regarding this passage, Charles A. Lofgren concludes:

> While the wording in question [Article I, section 8] admittedly spoke broadly of granting "letters of marque and reprisal," issuance of the *special* variety had passed out of fashion in peace time. The clause thus could easily have been interpreted as serving as a kind of shorthand for vesting in Congress the power of *general* reprisal outside the context of declared war. For someone in the late 1780s, this interpretation . . . would have given the phrase meaning and would have been consistent with history and the treatises [on international law]. Once accepted, this interpretation would have given increased plausibility to the view that Congress possessed whatever war-commencing power was not covered by the phrase "to declare war." [23]

Consider this interpretation but with a modern example. On April 14, 1986, the United States launched a series of presidentially authorized air strikes against Libya in retaliation for "terrorist attacks launched against American citizens." [24] President Ronald Reagan's decision to attack was applauded nearly unanimously, but his authority to attack without congressional consultation was not so readily accepted. The incident takes on a different coloration if it is considered in the context of marque and reprisal.

The Constitution contains only a single explicit limitation on Congress's power in this area: "no appropriation of money to [raise and support armies] shall be for a longer term than two years." [25] In sum, where national security is concerned, the Constitution gives to Congress a wide-ranging, clear-cut, and explicit grant of policy-making authority.

Third, in areas of foreign policy and national security the Founders provided the president with a brief, general, and undetailed grant of authority. The president's powers are stated in Article II, section 2; executive duties and responsibilities are in section 3. The only explicit national security power granted to the president consists of the following:

> The President shall be Commander in Chief of the Army and Navy of the United States, and of the Militia of the several States, when called into the actual Service of the United States. . . .[26]

In addition, the president is granted two diplomatic powers: the power to make treaties and the power to appoint ambassadors (each with the advice and consent of the Senate). The president is also vested with the "executive power." Section III adds the diplomatic responsibility of "receiving ambassadors and other public ministers" [27] and the responsibility to "take care that the laws be faithfully executed."

Thus, the Constitution gives Congress the bulk of powers necessary for assembling this early strategic triad of consolidated deterrence: defense, foreign commerce, and economic policy. The president is asked to execute these laws, to command the military if and when it is called into service, and perhaps to take the lead in national diplomacy. This division of power makes logical and historical sense. The Founders' profound distrust of monarchical power, especially when joined to military power, led them to circumscribe that combination. On the other hand, it was difficult for them to give the diplomatic functions to the "more popular branch"—hence, their practical concession to secrecy, dispatch, energy, and efficiency (to use terms frequently applied in the *Federalist Papers)* that were required in diplomacy.

This rough division between diplomacy and defense is generally overlooked today. The *Federalist Papers* scarcely mention the president's role as commander in chief.[28] In contrast, however, both Hamilton and Jay discuss the president's peculiar advantages in diplomacy. Indeed, it is sometimes forgotten that Jay's reference to secrecy and dispatch is a reference to the diplomatic requisites of treaty making and that it touches not at all on war making.[29] Hamilton extols those same virtues but without mentioning either diplomacy or defense: "Decision, activity, secrecy, and dispatch will generally characterize the proceedings of one man in a much more eminent degree than the proceedings of any greater number...." [30] Nonetheless, modern commentators have adopted Jay's language and applied it in a much broader fashion to describe the presidency's supposed advantages in defense as well as in diplomacy.[31]

Postconvention Precedents

In April 1793 President Washington issued a Proclamation of Neutrality, declaring that the United States would not take sides in the fight between France and Britain. Jefferson and his Democratic-Republican allies, who were pro-French, believed that Washington's proclamation was calculated to aid the British. For their part, Washington and Hamilton believed a neutral U.S. position would help to ensure safe shipping for American cargoes crossing the Atlantic. Regardless, the event precipitated the first major postconvention debate on executive power in foreign and military policy making—and with it came the first compromise.

Hamilton, writing as "Pacificus," argued that the conduct of foreign relations was by nature a function of the executive branch and that, absent specific exceptions, it should remain with the executive.[32] Further, he argued, Congress's possession of the power to declare war should not and did not diminish presidential discretion in utilizing powers granted by the Constitution. Madison, writing as "Helvidius," responded that the war-making power of Congress elbows aside the executive power of the president because of its importance.

This political battle ended in something of a compromise. Congressional primacy was upheld in 1794, when a formal act of neutrality was passed by Congress and signed by Washington. The act, however, enunciated several principles set down earlier by Washington's proclamation, giving the Federalists a policy victory.

Two aspects of this debate are noteworthy. First, in spite of its references to war powers, the debate focuses largely upon a diplomatic matter more in the realm of foreign affairs than of military policy. This focus is consistent with the idea mentioned earlier that the Federalists' concerns were with energy and efficiency in diplomatic endeavors. Second, this is but one of many subsequent examples in which policy positions became the animating features behind constitutional debates.

For a little more than two decades after the Constitution was ratified—into the Madison administration—the Federalists and their opponents seriously debated whether to establish a regular, professional national army and navy. That debate, with contours much like those outlined earlier, settled nothing. Supporters of congressional control—again Madison, Jefferson, and Gerry—argued that the executive's role as commander in chief was limited.[33] Money spent on the military, they asserted, robbed the economy of its vitality when growth was needed. A strong standing army would be an invitation for executives to seek foreign adventure. A strong standing army would threaten, and therefore would invite, preemptive attacks by other nations. But Hamilton and the Federalists could not agree. An investment in the military, they responded, would provide security for commerce. A vibrant commerce, in turn, would invite jealousy and interference from abroad. Congress would be slow to act in time of need. The executive, therefore, required the tools and the flexibility to act.

As they did in the neutrality debate, Federalist presidents George Washington and John Adams won compromise victories that resulted in small increases in regular army personnel—only to see most of the authorized troops never recruited—and the establishment of a separate

Navy Department in 1798—only to see its shipbuilding program halted after Jefferson was inaugurated. In succeeding years the political battle in Congress was won by the Democratic-Republicans and their presidents—Jefferson, Madison, Monroe, and Adams. But the victory did not indicate that a majority sentiment for a professional military was lacking; it reflected, rather, a rough three-way division of national political opinion. The interior states of the new nation opposed the navy and supported an army that could protect them from Indians. The coastal, commercially oriented Federalists stressed the need for a navy. In concert, these two factions might have formed a majority.[34] They remained at loggerheads, however, and the Democratic-Republican opponents of both a strong army and a navy were the beneficiaries. Whatever the immediate cause, the result was that throughout the nineteenth century the United States established an uninterrupted pattern of maintaining minimal military power during peacetime, hastily improvising for defense during war, and subsequently demobilizing. That practice has been altered since World War II.

Twentieth Century Developments

From the middle of the nineteenth century until after World War II, few serious legal or political doubts existed about the president's freedom to use American troops. Decisions by district courts and the Supreme Court adopted a decidedly Hamiltonian point of view, a trend that culminated in 1936 with Justice George Sutherland's infamous and expansive opinion in *United States v. Curtiss-Wright Export Corp.* In that opinion, Sutherland argued broadly that powers and responsibilities in foreign policy were inherent in national sovereignty, that even if not spelled out in the Constitution they would have been the responsibility of the national government, and that the president was peculiarly suited to this responsibility, which required a "degree of discretion and freedom from statutory restriction." [35]

Assuming Sutherland was correct—and many disagree—in order for a president to engage troops abroad, some means of raising the requisite number of troops and supplying them with equipment and transportation still had to be found. Presidential adventurism, if not legally prevented, was at least constrained by the lack of a large standing army and by the absence of substantial numbers of U.S. troops stationed abroad.[36] Thus, even if presidents could force Congress's hand, congressional participation was still required. For example, President Theodore Roosevelt recognized his need for congressional cooperation. But he determined to use politics and bluff as leverage to gain that cooperation in the early 1900s, when he sent the White Fleet on a world cruise in spite of congressional opposition. The president simply told Congress that if they wanted to bring the fleet back they would have to appropriate funds to do so.

Circumstances today are considerably different. The burden of proof now rests with Congress to demonstrate why executives should not be engaged in foreign military activities. Congress, having supplied the troops, agreed to the bases, appropriated funds for the equipment, and consented to the alliance structures necessary to pursue military policies abroad, is consequently reduced to a reactive role back home. Two modern developments have essentially defined this state of affairs: the post-World War II standing army and the establishment of an institutionalized national security presidency.

The Standing Army

In the decade before World War II, the active-duty military forces of the United States averaged 275,650 personnel per year.[37] From 1946 to 1950, the average was 1,826,900 personnel per year, 6.6 times the prewar level. (Before World War II, the largest increase in the standing military from a prewar to a postwar period had occurred after the Spanish American War. From 1866 to 1897, the number of personnel on average was 43,400. This figure rose to 132,400 personnel during the 1899-1916 interwar period, or three times the prewar size.) This expansion after World War II represented an unprecedented retention of sizable land, air, and naval forces. And it was fully authorized by the U.S. Congress. The peacetime establishment of a substantial standing army, with institutional and intelligence support in the context of firm treaty commitments, marked a significant break with Congress's 150-year practice of maintaining a small-to-moderate-sized standing army, adhering to a policy of neutrality, and creating only modest-sized civilian institutions for the military's support.

The maintenance of, and later increase in, the large standing army after World War II is typically traced to several related causes.[38] First, the United States was the only major industrial nation to survive the war intact. Second, the Soviets' maintenance of a large army forced the United States into a role as guarantor of peace in Europe. Third, in contrast to previous wars, world or otherwise, the United States had assumed a position of leadership among Western democracies that forced it center stage in international affairs. Finally, despite the end of the war, a series of hot and cold regional conflicts required the United States to maintain enough military might to fight limited wars without abandoning or weakening its commitments to Europe.

The most important practical effect of these changes on the United States was to reverse its traditional practice of frantic wartime troop expansions necessary to fight wars. When there was no standing army,

Congress always had to make a positive commitment in time of war. Short of an all-out conventional war, the president now has enough military resources at his command to commit the United States to a substantial "war," with or without congressional consent. Congress, should it be so inclined, is placed in the untenable position of having to take troops away from the president or of withholding appropriations if it desires to limit executive action. Thus, Congress's participation in military policy is no longer primarily positive, but negative.

Moreover, the president now has more flexibility in utilizing military force abroad than at any other time in American history. As of 1990 the United States had about one-quarter of its total troop strength stationed outside the country. Few dispute that these troops may be used to defend American interests and that such discretion rests with the president, but serious questions arise regarding what conditions warrant the president's discretion and what Congress's role is in ratifying such decisions.

The Institutionalized National Security Presidency

Decision, activity, secrecy, and dispatch, argued Hamilton, are much more likely to characterize the actions of a single leader than of many attempting to act in concert. Given current institutional arrangements, however, these functions may not be possible. On October 3, 1989, President George Bush provided U.S. support for a coup attempt in Panama against Gen. Manuel Antonio Noriega. Apparently, however, confusion about which roads were to be blocked by American personnel allowed Panamanian government troops to enter into Panama City and put down the coup. In the weeks after the attempt, Congress and the president engaged in a front-page shouting match about foreign policy prerogatives, unreasonable restraint, and constitutional balances of power. Although not all foreign or military policy initiatives are fated to be successful, this particular episode—and many others of recent years—raised questions about whether the unity envisioned by Hamilton has been lost, regardless of the balance of constitutional power. Put more pointedly, decision, activity, secrecy, and dispatch may well be desirable for the president, but they may now be mutually exclusive, since, given the nature of the modern presidency, activity compromises secrecy, dispatch compromises decision making, and so forth.

James Sundquist argues that the institutional presidency has been produced by an accretion of power:

> There are many institutional factors, moreover, that would deter a president from surrendering power, even should he choose to do so.

> As each new brick was added to the structure of the strong presidency, usually during the tenure of one of the aggressive occupants of that office, it was fixed in place by the mortar of institutionalization—statutes, organizational units, reporting requirements, executive orders, written and unwritten understandings governing behavior in both branches and the relations between them.[39]

Congress has contributed mightily to this process of institutionalization by passing the necessary legislation. For the most part the process benefited both individual members and Congress as a whole; hence, it was rational from the congressional perspective. Sundquist has nicely encapsulated the character of the modern presidency:

> The modern presidency is symbolized by, and embodied in, the Executive Office of the President, an apparatus of a dozen or so component offices erected as a composite policymaking, coordinating, and directing structure for the executive branch—and in many respects, in normal circumstances, for the government as a whole.[40]

Although this process of institutionalization is certainly not confined to national security, it is perhaps most obvious there. We have, as a result, an institutionalized national security presidency.

The landmark event in this process occurred in 1947, when Congress passed the National Security Act, which created a third military service (the Air Force), consolidated control of military affairs in the newly created Department of Defense, established the Central Intelligence Agency to gather national intelligence, and instructed the president to organize the National Security Council to coordinate executive branch policy affecting national security. Shortly afterward Congress consented to ratify several treaties that, for the first time in U.S. history, committed the nation to peacetime military alliances with other nations around the world. It also consented, pursuant to those treaties and others, to station large numbers of American troops abroad.

As with many legislative acts of the twentieth century, the creation of a large standing army and its accompanying civilian establishment worked to the disadvantage of Congress.[41] Put simply, it has shifted, on a de facto if not de jure basis, the war-making power to the executive and altered the longstanding constitutional balance of power between Congress and the president. The executive establishment is large, capable, and in place. The public generally expects its presidents to act decisively, not just to repel sudden attacks but to protect American interests, property, and citizens wherever they might be.

Current Perspectives in the Debate

In July, August, and September of 1987, the Senate Foreign Relations Committee's Special Subcommittee on War Powers held hearings to evaluate and improve the War Powers Resolution of 1973. Those hearings resulted in no substantial movement toward change in the law. The subtitle of the committee print of the hearings and accompanying documents—covering 1,428 pages of fact and opinion— may give some clue why. It reads: "Congress and the President at a Constitutional Impasse." There is, to be sure, an impasse, but it results more from an unwillingness on either side to press its case than from each having pushed its constitutional case to a logical limit without resolution.

The Executive Perspective

Since the War Powers Resolution was passed, each president has stated his opinion that it is an unconstitutional infringement of the inherent powers of the executive as commander in chief. A 1984 message from President Reagan to Congress typifies this opinion. For the first time since passage of the act, Congress initiated a formal statutory authorization (required by the act to keep U.S. forces in such situations beyond sixty days) for the deployment of U.S. troops in the peace-keeping force supervising a cease-fire between warring factions in Lebanon. Reagan signed the act but added this caution:

> I do not and cannot cede any of the authority vested in me under the Constitution as President and as Commander-in-Chief of the United States Armed Forces. Nor should my signing be viewed as any acknowledgement that the President's constitutional authority can be impermissibly infringed by statute, that congressional authorization would be required if and when the period specified in . . . the War Powers Resolution might be deemed to have been triggered and the period expired, or that [the eighteen-month authorization] may be interpreted to revise the President's constitutional authority to deploy United States Armed Forces.[42]

And yet no president has pressed the case for fear that the Court would refuse to adjudicate the question or that the executive's case would be lost. The unwillingness to challenge these alleged intrusions onto the presidency's constitutional turf has not been universally applauded. First, consider Robert H. Bork's comments in his foreword to a collection of essays and commentary largely critical of Congress's interventions into the affairs of the executive branch:

> The chapters contained in this volume demonstrate that the office of the president of the United States has been significantly

weakened in recent years and that Congress is largely, but not entirely, responsible. Some recent presidents have failed to defend their office's prerogatives, allowing Congress to establish easements across the constitutional powers of the presidency that time and use may make permanent. This is a deeply worrisome development, for America has usually prospered most in eras of strong presidents, and the state of today's world makes the capacity for strong executive action more important than ever.[43]

Then consider the remarks of Jeane J. Kirkpatrick, a contributor to that volume:

> In the earliest days of the Reagan administration we had serious discussions in the cabinet about the possibility of a legal challenge to the War Powers Act. A decision not to proceed was made on the grounds that it would be difficult to bring the question before a court on the appropriate issue. But I think we might have proceeded. . . . This administration should have made a head-on fight against congressional efforts to micromanage foreign policy, and the next administration should also fight this trend head on, for it is finally incompatible with all the requirements for effective American foreign policy.[44]

Rather than directly challenging the War Powers Resolution, all recent administrations have been content to criticize Congress's interference, to reject the resolution publicly, and to define a narrow role for Congress in national security policy. The presidents have acknowledged Congress's right to declare war, mindful that such declarations are essentially obsolete. They recognize Congress's power of the purse, asserting, however, that that power is circumscribed. Once appropriations have been made, they claim, the president is free to use the troops as he sees fit. Another statement by Bork is typical of this perspective:

> On the subject of the use of armed force, the Constitution suggests the poles of power but leaves most of the intermediate ground for political contention by the branches. The major decisions are reserved for Congress, as shown not only by its power to declare war but by its absolute control of spending. Although the president is commander in chief, Congress is under no constitutional obligation to provide him with a single private to order about. But once Congress provides the president with armed forces, it cannot interfere with his tactical decisions, and considering that the deployment of men and materiel is often crucial to the conduct of foreign policy, in the modern world "tactical decisions" may encompass a great deal.[45]

Recent presidents have chosen to put up with congressional micromanagement, while publicly proclaiming broad inherent powers for the executive office. What makes their claim increasingly problematic is the mingling of foreign and national security policy. As noted earlier, it is at least arguable that the Founders envisioned the president taking a lead role in diplomacy—although even this role demanded consultation. Since World War II, however, it has been increasingly difficult to disentangle foreign and military policy as U.S. troops, military advisers, and covert personnel have become the instruments of American foreign policy abroad. As efforts to define congressional and presidential power continue, this problem deserves special attention.[46]

The Congressional Perspective

On the question of war powers, as with other matters of institutional balance during the twentieth century, Congress has frequently been its own worst enemy. It should be clear that if Congress had refused to delegate powers to the president or had circumscribed them more carefully at each step, fewer problems would have resulted during the past forty-five years. Sundquist emphasizes this point:

> The modern aggrandizement of the presidency was the product of considered legislative decisions, neither acts of impulse by the Congress nor presidential coups d'état. The Congress had to consent, because it had to pass the laws. But more than that, much of the transfer of power was initiated by the legislative branch itself.[47]

At present, a majority in both houses of Congress may believe that the War Powers Resolution is constitutional, but the majority is not overwhelming. A substantial number of members (a majority of Republicans and a significant number of Democrats) have doubts about the constitutionality of the law and hold opinions of inherent power very close to those of recent presidents. For example, the current Senate majority leader, George J. Mitchell of Maine, expressed precisely these doubts about the War Powers Resolution during debate on President Reagan's initiative to reflag oil tankers and to provide convoy protection in the Persian Gulf in 1986 and 1987:

> [T]he War Powers Resolution extends Congress' power beyond that of declaring war; the Resolution allows Congress—without even casting a vote—to deprive the President of his authority to deploy and move troops in situations that may fall short of war.[48]

Like other members of Congress, Mitchell does not reject the War Powers Resolution totally, preferring instead to amend it. Thus, on May 19, 1988, he joined outgoing Senate majority leader Robert C. Byrd, D-W.Va., Senate Armed Services Committee chair Sam

Nunn, D-Ga., and Armed Services Committee ranking Republican John W. Warner, R-Va., in introducing S.J. Res. 323, which would amend the existing provisions of the War Powers Resolution. That resolution and several competitors were referred to the Senate Foreign Relations Committee. A rough three-way split in Congress prevents action on the legislation. One faction opposes the original resolution or any replacement resolution, believing it to be an unconstitutional infringement of the president's power. Another group thinks the proposed amendments are weak and give ground to the president. The centrist coalition is attempting to save the war powers act by amending it.

Congress, like the president, is generally unwilling or unable to confront the issue squarely. Instead, the issue crops up periodically, cloaked in constitutional arguments but aimed at some policy disagreement with the executive. Cecil V. Crabb and Pat M. Holt accurately describe this situation:

> What becomes clear from the post-World War II practice is that Congress pays much less attention to constitutional niceties or consistency than it does to pragmatic considerations. When Congress has agreed with the general thrust of a presidential policy, it has acquiesced in the use or even the enlargement of presidential power. When it has disagreed, it has asserted its own prerogatives.[49]

Ultimately, these three congressional perspectives lead to deadlock. As long as presidential power is viewed as legitimate—and that has been a majority opinion since World War II—there can be no serious confrontation between the branches. At the present time, however, a third perspective, the political, dominates.

The Political Perspective

One of the most important defining characteristics of government in our time is the politics of divided government. The tendency of the two major political parties to control different branches of government is now a fact of political life.[50] Elliott Abrams, an assistant secretary of state during the Reagan administration, described this partisan split:

> What is new, I would argue—and what makes the system in some respects not only different but much worse—is the infusion of ideology and partisan politics into the struggles between the legislative and executive branches, so that the struggle between the branches today is also, in many areas, a struggle between left and right. The reason for this is not hard to find. It is that the Democratic party essentially controls the legislative branch and has for quite a long time and the Republican party has controlled the

executive branch for sixteen of the past twenty years. A partisan balance has changed the situation for the worse.[51]

By themselves, however, partisan political differences do not explain the interbranch conflict, as Jimmy Carter's administration proves. After a long accumulation of practice and precedent, Congress finally determined to reassert its constitutional prerogatives in the aftermath of the Watergate affair and the war in Vietnam. But practice and precedent are inevitably difficult to overcome, as Jacob Javits, R-N.Y., a sponsor of the War Powers Resolution, acknowledged during debate before the legislation was passed in 1973:

> [B]ecause the Congress has not heretofore established rules for the initiation or continuation of military hostilities . . . in the absence of a declaration of war, it has fallen upon the commander in chief to exercise his executive discretion on an ad hoc, case-by-case, basis. This, in its cumulative effect over the years, has now led to great confusion and dissension in the nation, and has given rise to an anomalous and doubtful legal and constitutional situation.[52]

Similar statements might be made about the country's experience after sixteen years under the War Powers Resolution.

Because congressional reassertion came after the fact, however, the results fell far short of the constitutional impasse alluded to in the subtitle of the Senate committee's hearings. Instead, it has produced a political stalemate between the executive and legislative branches. This stalemate is both partisan and ideological, but it is also an institutional competition of the sort predicted by Madison. It may validate the position taken by Lawrence C. Dodd in 1979 that Congress tends to fall farther behind presidential power each time a cycle of decline and resurgence takes place.[53] As long as the War Powers Resolution remains the focus of debate, this competition is likely to remain.

Conclusion: Into the Third Century

The War Powers Resolution was the product of extraordinary political circumstances. Its passage came after a long-term accretion of power by the executive branch and a Congress confronting institutional developments of its own making. From before the Civil War until after World War II, the courts generally handed down decisions that endorsed the expanded definition of executive power.[54] From the early 1920s until the late 1960s, Congress constructed the imposing edifice of the institutionalized presidency. Throughout that period, chief executives, for the most part, gladly accepted the leadership role, the infrastructure provided by Congress, and the delegated powers. More often than not, public opinion supported presidential primacy.

Contemporary arguments about the war powers have frequently misread the historical circumstances of the drafting of the Constitution. They alter or ignore the original intent of the Founders and thus fail to recognize Congress's current predicament, namely, the accumulation of institutional structures and precedents of acquiescence that are largely of Congress's own making.

From the time of the U.S. evacuation of Saigon and Phnom Penh in 1975, through the incidents in the Persian Gulf in 1988, three American presidents have determined that U.S. military forces should be used to advance American interests. There is no reason to think that George Bush and his successors will escape similar controversies, as events in Panama have already shown. Few military planners, policy makers, or other analysts believe that a large-scale, protracted conventional military conflict is likely. Many do fear the possibility of an extended limited war. And most predict even more limited uses of American military power. Thus, the continued importance of questions about Congress, the president, and war powers is ensured. The current law has failed. Debate about its replacement is not only important but inescapable.

Notes

1. On this point, see Newell L. Highsmith, "Policing Executive Adventurism: Congressional Oversight of Military and Paramilitary Operations," *Harvard Journal on Legislation* 19 (Summer 1982): 333-335.
2. Nicholas deB. Katzenbach, "The Constitution and Foreign Policy," in *A Workable Government? The Constitution After 200 Years,* ed. Burke Marshall (New York: Norton, 1987), 63. (Emphasis added.)
3. This rise of the nation-state is typically associated with the Treaty of Westphalia in 1648.
4. Alexander Hamilton, *Federalist* no. 25, in *The Federalist Papers,* ed. Clinton Rossiter (New York: New American Library, 1961), 165.
5. This point is made by Arthur Schlesinger, Jr., *The Imperial Presidency* (New York: Houghton Mifflin, 1973), 21; and by Charles A. Lofgren, "War-Making Under the Constitution: The Original Understanding," *Yale Law Journal* 81 (1972): 689-697.
6. Navies were also mercenary forces, although they might also include dragooned, impressed, or shanghaied personnel.
7. For more on both of these developments, see James M. McPherson, *Battle Cry of Freedom: The Civil War Era* (New York: Oxford University Press, 1988), esp. chaps. 10, 15, and 20.
8. New Hampshire and Connecticut voted no, but in a footnote Madison indicates that Connecticut later switched to aye. James Madison, *Notes of*

Debates in the Federal Convention of 1787 (New York: Norton, 1987), 476n.

9. The opinions of only six delegates are mentioned in the treatment of the change, which barely exceeds one page in length (of 635 total pages). Two other delegates receive brief mention in Madison's footnote regarding the switch of Connecticut's vote from no to aye. Only Pierce Butler of South Carolina is recorded as speaking squarely for executive authority. See Madison, *Notes of Debates,* 475-476.

10. See, for example, Louis Smith, *American Democracy and Military Power: A Study of Civil Control of the Military Power in the United States* (Chicago: University of Chicago Press, 1951), 17-19.

11. At least one analyst has suggested that some of the strongest promilitary arguments, those of Alexander Hamilton, were aimed primarily at support for federal military capacity as opposed to state militia and were much less concerned with the question of the relative strengths of the national branches. See Lofgren, "War-Making Under the Constitution," 680.

12. Quoted in Charles Warren, *The Making of the Constitution* (Boston: Little, Brown, 1928), 484.

13. See Pendleton Herring, *The Impact of War: Our American Democracy Under Arms* (New York: Holt, Rinehart, & Winston, 1941), 30.

14. Hamilton, *Federalist* no. 25, in *Federalist Papers,* 166.

15. A good discussion of Hamilton's economic and military thought appears in Edward Mead Earle, "Adam Smith, Alexander Hamilton, Friedrich List: The Economic Foundations of Military Power," in *Makers of Modern Strategy: Military Thought from Machiavelli to Hitler,* ed. Edward Mead Earle (Princeton, N.J.: Princeton University Press, 1948), 117-154.

16. On the question of civil-military relations, see Smith, *American Democracy and Military Power,* 17-36.

17. This discussion is based on Francis D. Wormuth, "The Nixon Theory of the War Power: A Critique," *California Law Review* 60 (May 1972): 623-703.

18. Ibid., 631.

19. Hamilton, *Federalist* no. 69, in *Federalist Papers,* 418. Hamilton may have been engaging in hyperbole, but it is worth recalling that the most ardent and vocal opponent of standing armies, executive war powers, and indeed the entire federal Constitution—Elbridge Gerry—came from Massachusetts. Gerry makes no obvious complaint about the power of the Massachusetts governor in this regard. Because of his opposition, Gerry was not a delegate to the subsequent Massachusetts ratifying convention, although he was invited to answer questions as a nondelegate.

20. Wormuth, "Nixon Theory of the War Power," 635.

21. John Jay, *Federalist* no. 4, in *Federalist Papers,* 49.

22. Letters of marque and reprisal are now obsolete. In 1856 the European powers agreed to end privateering. As a general practice, nations no longer authorize private third parties to "exact justice." See Louis Henkin,

Foreign Affairs and the Constitution (New York: Norton, 1972), 68.

23. Lofgren, "War-Making Under the Constitution," 696-697.

24. Quote from the president's speech, April 14, 1986, in *Congressional Quarterly Weekly Report,* April 19, 1986, 881.

25. Article I, section 8, clause 12.

26. Article II, section 2, clause 1.

27. Hamilton describes this duty as "more a matter of dignity than of authority. It is a circumstance which will be without consequence in the administration of the government; and it is far more convenient that it should be arranged in this manner. . . ." (Hamilton, *Federalist* no. 69, in *Federalist Papers,* 420.)

28. Hamilton does touch on the president's role in *Federalist* no. 69 *(Federalist Papers, 417-418),* in which he characterizes the role as a limited one and compares it to similar grants of authority in existence at the time of the convention. He also may have remained silent on the issue for fear of raising a red herring. Either that or he experienced a sudden shift of opinion in his editorializing as "Pacificus" during the debate on neutrality only a few years later.

29. Jay, *Federalist* no. 64, in *Federalist Papers,* 392.

30. Hamilton, *Federalist* no. 70, in *Federalist Papers,* 424.

31. For example, in 1988 in a broad discussion of the War Powers Resolution before the Senate Foreign Relations Committee's Special Subcommittee on War Powers, Robert F. Turner included a section called "The Need for Secrecy." His discussion focuses primarily on foreign affairs, and he quotes at length from Jay's discussion of treaty making in *Federalist* no. 64. Turner makes a case for a tradition of congressional "deference to the President in foreign affairs." It is not at all clear that either Congress or the courts showed the same deference where defense policy was concerned. See Robert F. Turner, "Restoring the 'Rule of Law': Reflections on the War Powers Resolution at Fifteen," in Committee on Foreign Relations, *The War Power After 200 Years: Congress and the President at a Constitutional Impasse,* 100th Congress, 2d sess. (Washington, D.C.: U.S. Government Printing Office, 1989), 832-841. Another example, with a more pro-Congress bent, is Katzenbach, "Constitution and Foreign Policy," 59-75.

32. Hamilton's pseudonym is at least ironic, given his general philosophical bent, mercantilist leaning, and orientation in the debate at hand.

33. It is no small irony, given his general view, that Jefferson deployed an American naval squadron against the Barbary pirates and also signed the bill establishing the military academy at West Point. It is also ironic that Jefferson's attempts to consult with Congress on the matter of the Barbary pirates, actions consistent with his expressed beliefs regarding Congress's role, were paralleled by his more circumspect commands to the U.S. squadron. See Turner, "Restoring the 'Rule of Law,'" 819-822.

   To further muddy the waters, consider the following suggestion that Jefferson made in response to Madison's draft bill of rights: "I like it as far as it goes; but I should have been for going further. For instance the following alterations and additions would have pleased me. . . ." Here Jefferson inserted a full page of suggestions before adding Article 10, which states: "All troops of the U.S. shall stand ipso facto disbanded at the expiration of the term for which their pay and subsistence shall have been last voted by Congress, and all officers and soldiers not natives of the U.S. shall be incapable of serving in their armies by land except during a foreign war." See the letter from Thomas Jefferson to James Madison, August 28, 1789, reprinted in *The Origins of the American Constitution: A Documentary History,* ed. Michael Kammen (New York: Penguin Books, 1986), 378-379.

34. Harold and Margaret Sprout provide an enlightening analysis of the voting patterns in Congress during this period, primarily on naval bills. See Harold and Margaret Sprout, *The Rise of American Naval Power* (Princeton, N.J.: Princeton University Press, 1944), 25-72. Leonard D. White also discusses the effect of these three regional interests, particularly the disagreements between the Federalists and the Democratic-Republicans during this early period. See Leonard D. White, *The Federalists: A Study in Administrative History* (New York: Macmillan, 1948), esp. chaps. 1, 12, and 13.

35. *United States v. Curtiss-Wright Export Corp.,* 299 U.S. 304 (1936). The controversy in the *Curtiss-Wright* case arose when Congress passed a joint resolution in 1934 authorizing the president to establish an embargo on arms sales to belligerents involved in the so-called Chaco War in South America. President Franklin Roosevelt proclaimed the embargo, and subsequently legal action was taken against Curtiss-Wright for violating the law. Lawyers for the corporation challenged the law as an unconstitutional delegation of legislative power to the president. Sutherland's sweeping decision distinguished constitutional restraints that might apply to "internal" (domestic) affairs and a general lack of such constraints where "external" (foreign) affairs are concerned. Hence, the president required a "degree of discretion and freedom from statutory restrictions which would not be admissible were domestic affairs alone involved." For a list of additional cases offering broad delegation arguments, see Louis Fisher, "The Legitimacy of the Congressional National Security Role," in *The Constitution and National Security,* ed. Howard E. Shuman and Walter R. Thomas (Washington, D.C.: National Defense University Press, 1990), 258 n15.

36. I use the term *standing army* generically to refer to air, ground, and naval forces. The Founders feared a large standing ground army and limited appropriations for it to two years. There is no such restriction for a navy (or for an air force).

37. The figures here and following are from Christopher J. Deering, "Congress, the President, and Military Policy," *The Annals of the American Academy of Political and Social Science* 499 (September 1988): 136-147.

38. Nearly a million additional peacetime, active-duty personnel would be retained after the Korean War.

39. James L. Sundquist, *The Decline and Resurgence of Congress* (Washington, D.C.: Brookings Institution, 1981), 35.

40. Ibid.

41. These acts include, for example, the Budget Act of 1921, the Executive Reorganization Act of 1939, the Employment Act of 1946, and the Trade Expansion Act of 1962, plus the foreign policy resolutions that served to endorse the executive's military power: the Formosa Resolution of 1955, the Middle East Resolution of 1957, and the Tonkin Gulf Resolution of 1964. These legislative acts marked a continuous shift in power, by design and by default, to the executive during the twentieth century. See Sundquist, *Decline and Resurgence of Congress.*

42. Quoted in Cecil V. Crabb, Jr., and Pat M. Holt, *Invitation to Struggle: Congress, the President, and Foreign Policy,* 2d ed. (Washington, D.C.: CQ Press, 1984), 147.

43. Robert H. Bork, "Foreword," in *The Fettered Presidency: Legal Constraints on the Executive Branch,* ed. L. Gordon Crovitz and Jeremy A. Rabkin (Washington, D.C.: American Enterprise Institute, 1989), ix. For other views along the same lines, see Gordon S. Jones and John A. Marini, eds., *The Imperial Congress: Crisis and the Separation of Powers* (New York: Pharos Books, 1988).

44. Jeane J. Kirkpatrick, "Commentary by Jeane J. Kirkpatrick," in *Fettered Presidency,* 45.

45. Bork, "Foreword," in *Fettered Presidency,* xii.

46. Highsmith, "Policing Executive Adventurism," discusses the failures of the War Powers Resolution in this respect and examines what he regards to be the comparably better treatment of the use of congressionally provided personnel in 1980 amendments to the National Security Act.

47. Sundquist, *Decline and Resurgence of Congress,* 35.

48. Statement of Sen. George J. Mitchell, September 30, 1987, typescript, 3.

49. Crabb and Holt, *Invitation to Struggle,* 129.

50. See Charles O. Jones, "Congress and the Constitutional Balance of Power," in *Congressional Politics,* ed. Christopher J. Deering (Chicago: Dorsey Press, 1989), 322-337; and James P. Pfiffner, "Divided Government and the Problem of Governance," chap. 3 of this volume.

51. Elliott Abrams, "Commentary by Elliott Abrams," in *Fettered Presidency,* 38.

52. Jacob Javits with Raphael Steinberg, *Javits: The Autobiography of a Public Man* (Boston: Houghton Mifflin, 1981), 403.

53. Lawrence C. Dodd, "Congress and the Quest for Power," in *Congress Reconsidered,* ed. Lawrence C. Dodd and Bruce I. Oppenheimer (New York: Praeger, 1979), 269-307.

54. The most prominent exception is *Youngstown Sheet and Tube Co. v. Sawyer,* 343 U.S. 579 (1952). In this case the Supreme Court held that the president exceeded his constitutional powers when he ordered the

secretary of commerce to take possession of the nation's steel mills. The president promulgated his order during the Korean War, basing his decision on national security grounds.

10. WAR POWERS:
THE NEED FOR COLLECTIVE JUDGMENT

Louis Fisher

The War Powers Resolution of 1973, an effort to reconcile executive and legislative powers, has taken a heavy pounding in recent years. Critics have called for radical revision of the resolution or even outright repeal. Decisions on this issue depend in large part on how we understand the purposes of the 1973 statute. Was it enacted merely to "end Vietnams," and thus is it poorly suited for other kinds of military action?

The purpose of the War Powers Resolution is to provide for the "collective judgment" of Congress and the president before U.S. forces are sent into combat, particularly for long-term military commitments. The resolution allows the president to act unilaterally for short-term military actions, up to ninety days, but requires congressional approval for engagements beyond that point. Congress can also order the withdrawal of U.S. forces within the ninety-day period.

It is a mistake to view the War Powers Resolution solely within the context of the Vietnam War. No doubt the legislative history is dominated by that military conflict, and there is no shortage of evidence of partisan attacks on Richard Nixon and efforts to retaliate against the policies of Lyndon Johnson. Those motivations were present; however, the War Powers Resolution is more than a composite of partisan and personal politics. Looked at within a broader context of four decades, beginning in the early 1930s, it represents a serious and responsible bipartisan effort to recapture legislative authority that had drifted to the president. Only by understanding the forces behind this congressional effort, both constitutionally and institutionally, can we comprehend the significance of the War Powers Resolution. Without this understanding, we may mistake congressional involvement in the war powers as an encroachment on executive prerogatives.

When the Pendulum Stopped Swinging

We are all familiar with the cycle of presidential and congressional government. A series of strong executives, from Thomas Jefferson to Andrew Jackson to Abraham Lincoln to Woodrow Wilson, provoked Congress to reassert its powers. Strong presidents were succeeded by less successful chief executives: James Madison followed Jefferson, Martin Van Buren came into office after Jackson, Andrew Johnson was the unhappy successor to Lincoln, and Warren G. Harding represented a return to "normalcy" after Wilson. Even after major military conflicts, such as the Civil War and World War I, Congress was able to restore its place as a coequal branch.

Something different happened in the 1930s. The powers transferred to the president during the Great Depression and later during World War II did not return to Congress. What had been a temporary disequilibrium in earlier periods, quickly righted to begin a new cycle, now became a permanent fixture of executive-legislative relations. Congress recognized the radical nature of this transformation and made efforts, after World War II, to regain its stature.

It is with the administration of Franklin D. Roosevelt that one discovers fundamental changes in presidential power and influence. Emergency powers were exercised by the president in a manner that has no parallels in American history. The domestic economic crisis brought forth the full panoply of executive power, as though the country had been invaded by a foreign enemy. Indeed, Roosevelt's inaugural address in 1933 drew an analogy between the Great Depression and a time of war: "[I]f we are to go forward, we must move as a trained and loyal army willing to sacrifice for the good of a common discipline. . . ." The larger purposes "will bind upon us all as a sacred obligation with a unity of duty hitherto evoked only in time of armed strife." If Congress failed to face up to the emergency, Roosevelt threatened to seek broad emergency authority:

> It is to be hoped that the normal balance of Executive and legislative authority may be wholly adequate to meet the unprecedented task before us. But it may be that an unprecedented demand and need for undelayed action may call for temporary departure from that normal balance of public procedure.

The temporary departure became a permanent condition, in part through Roosevelt's initiatives, in part through worldwide forces beyond his control. Under Roosevelt's prodding, Congress delegated vast powers to him with regard to agriculture, public works, home mortgages, and banking and currency. Members of Congress occasionally chastised themselves for abdicating authority vested in them by the Constitution. When some legislators objected that Roosevelt had asked for dictatorial powers, Democratic senator Millard Tydings of Maryland countered: "Of course he did. Why? Because Congress itself refused to do its duty, to protect the integrity of the national credit." [1]

Emergency relief programs during the Great Depression set aside billions of dollars to be spent at Roosevelt's discretion. In 1935 Congress was about to give Roosevelt another $4.8 billion, to be used "in the discretion and under the direction of the President" (at a time when federal spending was less than $10 billion a year). Roosevelt could use the money for such open-ended purposes as "relieving economic maladjustments" and "alleviating distress." A little too general? Sen. Arthur Vandenberg, R-Mich., employed sarcasm to decry the absence of standards, suggesting that the bill could be vastly simplified by eliminating the text and substituting for it two brief sections:

SECTION 1: Congress hereby appropriates $4,880,000,000 to the President of the United States to use as he pleases.
SEC. 2: Anybody who does not like it is fined $1,000.[2]

The pendulum seemed about ready to swing back toward Congress after Roosevelt's reelection victory in 1936. Roosevelt had badly miscalculated in his effort to pack the Supreme Court and seize additional executive authority. Congress reacted by shelving his Court-packing plan and adding new restrictions to delegated power. In 1937, when Roosevelt asked for authority to reorganize the executive branch, Congress blocked the proposal. Legislators interpreted his move as part of a general effort to establish a "presidential dictatorship." Roosevelt's request for reorganization authority was put on the back burner until 1939, when a much weaker version passed.[3] By that time his appeals for emergency authority had worn thin. In 1939, after FDR had declared thirty-nine emergencies over a six-year period, Rep. Bruce Barton, R-N.Y., dryly noted: "Any national administration is entitled to one or two emergencies in a term of 6 years. But an emergency every 6 weeks means plain bad management."[4]

Congress was clearly poised to recapture power that had slipped to the president. The normal swings of presidential and congressional dominance were about to resume. At that very moment, however, the rumblings of war in Europe and in the Far East set the stage for continued executive dominance.

On September 8, 1939, after Germany invaded Poland, Roosevelt proclaimed a state of limited emergency. The following September he announced an agreement to exchange fifty "over-aged" destroyers with Britain in return for the right to use bases on British islands in the Atlantic and Caribbean. In April 1941 he signed an agreement with Denmark, pledging America's defense of Greenland in return for the right to construct and operate defense installations on the island. On May 27, 1941, he proclaimed the existence of an unlimited national emergency. Shortly thereafter he signed an agreement with Iceland to permit U.S. forces to land there in order to prevent Germany from occupying Iceland and using it as a naval or air base against the Western Hemisphere. On June 7, 1941, he seized an aviation plant in California and took over several other defense facilities. Three months before Pearl Harbor, he issued his "shoot-on-sight" orders to U.S. forces in defense waters, warning that German and Italian vessels entered those waters at their own risk.

When members of Congress appeared reluctant to grant powers that Roosevelt wanted, he told them he would act with or without statutory authority:

> I ask the Congress to pass legislation under which the President would be specifically authorized to stabilize the cost of living, including the prices of all farm commodities. The purpose should be to hold farm prices at parity, or at levels of a recent date, whichever is higher.
>
> I ask the Congress to take this action by the first of October. Inaction on your part by that date will leave me with an inescapable responsibility to the people of this country to see to it that the war effort is no longer imperiled by threat of economic chaos.
>
> In the event that the Congress should fail to act, and act adequately, I shall accept the responsibility, and I will act. . . .
>
> The responsibilities of the President in wartime to protect the Nation are very grave. This total war, with our fighting fronts all over the world, makes the use of executive power far more essential than in any previous war.[5]

In this same address, Roosevelt said that when "the war is won, the powers under which I act automatically revert to the people—to whom they belong." In fact, after the war was won, presidential powers did not revert at all, either to Congress or to the people. Emergency powers are not surrendered so easily. President Harry S. Truman announced the end of the war in Europe on May 8, 1945. On August 14 he announced the surrender of Japan. Nevertheless, in May 1946 he seized certain bituminous coal mines under authority of the War Labor Disputes Act, which empowered the president to take possession of any plant, mine, or facility as may be required for the "war effort." That authority remained in force until the president proclaimed the "termination of hostilities," a step Truman did not take until December 31, 1946, more than sixteen months after Japan's surrender. By proclaiming that hostilities had terminated, Truman relinquished certain wartime powers but retained others that remained available during "a state of war," or a "state of emergency." Truman stressed that "a state of war still exists."[6]

The judiciary supported this consolidation of executive power. The Housing and Rent Act of 1947 provided for an extension of wartime rent controls. In upholding this statute, the Supreme Court observed that the housing deficit, created by the demobilization of veterans and the reduction of residential construction during the war, had not yet been eliminated. The Court did concede that war in modern times affected the economy for years afterward and created a dangerous situation in which the war power "may not only swallow up all other powers of Congress but largely obliterate the Ninth and Tenth Amendments as well." [7]

In 1947 Congress terminated certain "temporary" emergency and war powers. Approximately 175 statutory provisions were involved, many dating back to the First World War. Even with that action, 103 war or emergency statutes remained in effect.[8] On April 28, 1952, Truman finally signed a statement terminating the state of war with Japan and the national emergencies proclaimed by Roosevelt in 1939 and 1941. Although actual hostilities had lasted for fewer than four years, Roosevelt and Truman exercised emergency and war powers for more than twelve years.

Congress Takes Stock

Toward the end of World War II, Congress reviewed what had happened to its prerogatives over the previous decade. The decline of parliamentary institutions throughout the world prompted some of the stocktaking, but there was a growing appreciation that Congress was no longer able to compete effectively with the executive branch. Congress was rapidly becoming a second-class, second-rate institution. The Joint Committee on the Organization of Congress, created in 1944, voiced its apprehension:

> [T]he decline of Congress in relation to the executive branch of our Federal Government has caused increased legislative concern. Under the Constitution, Congress is the policy-making branch of government. There are manifest growing tendencies in recent times toward the shift of policy-making power to the Executive, partly because of the comparative lack of effective instrumentalities and the less adequate facilities of the legislative branch. To redress the balance and recover its rightful position in our governmental structure, Congress, many Members feel, must modernize its machinery, coordinate its various parts, and establish the research facilities that can provide it with the knowledge that is power.[9]

The result of the committee's effort was the Legislative Reorganization Act of 1946, which restructured congressional committees and strengthened the analytical capacity of Congress. To assist Congress in maintaining control over the executive branch, standing committees were directed to exercise "continuous watchfulness" over executive agencies.[10]

Truman's initiative in sending troops to Korea in 1950 under-scored the now-permanent nature of executive power. The legality of his action has been debated for decades. What is not debatable is that the president, for the first time, had committed U.S. troops abroad into a major conflict on his own authority. He acted without a declaration of war or specific authorization by Congress. Significantly, the critics at that time were conservative Republicans, while Democrats generally rushed to Truman's defense.

The fact that Truman had used his prerogatives to commit the country to a major war in Korea magnified the impression that Congress was being overshadowed and overwhelmed. In 1951 Truman announced his intention to send ground forces to Europe without seeking congressional approval, possibly triggering military conflict with the Soviet Union. He believed that he did not need the approval of Congress to send additional troops to Europe, although he said it was generally his policy to consult with members of Congress before making any move in foreign affairs or domestic affairs.[11]

Truman's sending of troops to Korea and Europe finally precipi-tated a major confrontation with Congress. In an extremely powerful floor statement, Sen. Robert Taft, R-Ohio, delivered a ten-thousand-word speech to encourage Congress to defend its prerogatives. He argued that constructive criticism from Congress on foreign policy is essential to the safety of the nation. He repudiated the idea that a challenge to the administration's foreign policy "is an attack on the unity of the Nation, that it gives aid and comfort to the enemy, and that it sabotages any idea of a bipartisan foreign policy for the national benefit." He dismissed this mind-set as a dangerous fallacy that threatened the existence of the nation. Members of Congress, and particularly senators, had "a constitutional obligation to reexamine constantly and discuss the foreign policy of the United States." The trend toward secrecy on the part of recent administrations, combined with the failure to consult Congress and seek its advice, deprived members of Congress "of the substance of the powers conferred on them by the Constitution."[12] Taft feared that Truman, having embarked on a war in Korea without congressional authority, was about to do the same in Europe. These were the concluding remarks of "Mr. Republican," the leading conservative of his time:

> [T]he policy we adopt must be approved by Congress and the people after full and free discussion. The commitment of a land

army to Europe is a program never approved by Congress, into which we should not drift. The policy of secret executive agreements has brought us to danger and disaster. It threatens the liberties of our people.[13]

For three months in 1951 the Senate engaged in the "Great Debate." Throughout January, February, and March a long line of resolutions, speeches, and votes focused on the scope and limits of presidential power and on Truman's authority to send troops to Europe. The purpose of the principal resolution, S. Res. 99, was to support the sending of four additional divisions to Europe. The resolution was not legally binding, since it represented the views of a single house of Congress, but it gave senators an opportunity to debate in substantial detail the boundaries of congressional and presidential prerogatives.

Taft believed that Congress had the power to prevent the president from sending troops anywhere in the world to involve the United States in war. He felt it was "incumbent upon the Congress to assert clearly its own constitutional powers unless it desires to lose them." In what could be read as a precursor of the War Powers Resolution, Taft urged Congress to assert its powers in the form of a joint resolution.[14] An amendment by Sen. Kenneth Wherry, R-Neb., to replace the pending Senate resolution with a joint resolution, was ruled out of order.[15] Sen. John Bricker, R-Ohio, attempted to recommit the Senate resolution and have it resubmitted as a joint resolution, but his move failed, 31-56.[16]

At this stage of the debate, the Senate preferred to express its sentiment by a resolution rather than to present the president with a bill or joint resolution. Public opinion polls, however, suggested that Americans preferred stronger measures. A Gallup poll revealed that the public, by a margin of 64 percent to 28 percent, believed that presidents should not be allowed to send U.S. forces overseas unless Congress first granted its approval.[17]

The resolution debated by the Senate had many purposes. To Sen. Edward Thye, R-Minn., it highlighted the need to have "a closer relationship between the executive and legislative branches of our Government with reference to such questions as the assignment of troops abroad. Congress is close to the people and has a definite responsibility."[18] Sen. John McClellan, D-Ark., offered an amendment requiring congressional approval of future plans to send troops abroad. Although the amendment was initially rejected, 44-46, it was later accepted.[19] An amendment by Sen. Herbert Lehman, D-N.Y., simply calling for the "fullest collaboration" between Congress and the president on future troop actions, was decisively rejected, 35-55.[20]

The Senate passed its resolution by a vote of 69 to 21. It approved Truman's sending of four divisions to Europe but stated that "in the interests of sound constitutional processes, and of national unity and understanding, congressional approval should be obtained of any policy requiring the assignment of American troops abroad when such assignment is in implementation of article 3 of the North Atlantic Treaty," and that no ground troops in addition to the four divisions should be sent "without further congressional approval." [21]

Earlier in the session, Rep. Frederick Coudert, R-N.Y., introduced legislation to require the authorization of Congress before military forces could be send abroad.[22] After the Senate had completed action on its resolution, Coudert proposed that no part of the appropriations in the defense appropriations bill could be used for the cost of sending or maintaining additional ground troops in Europe. His amendment failed, 84-131.[23]

The 1951 debate provoked both houses of Congress to rethink the congressional role in foreign affairs and the war power. In 1951 the House Foreign Affairs Committee released a report on the use of U.S. forces in foreign countries. Without drawing conclusions, this document compiled a sophisticated collection of materials that focused on two issues: the extent of the president's power to commit the nation to military action and the extent of the legislative power to control the president.[24] This document is regularly updated. Also in 1951 the Senate committees on armed services and on foreign relations published an executive branch study on the president's power to send armed forces outside the United States.[25]

A House study in 1956 on the president's powers as commander in chief drew attention to the fact that the period since the 1930s signaled something fundamentally new in executive-legislative relations. The study concluded that "in no other period of 20 years of American history have so many different Presidents been called on to exercise this constitutional power [of commander in chief] in so many different kinds of situations, each one of major importance." [26]

The Brief Experiment with Cooperation

After these sharp collisions between President Truman and Congress, the Eisenhower administration avoided unilateral moves in dispatching troops abroad. Instead, President Dwight D. Eisenhower sought the enactment of area resolutions that would delegate congressional authority to the president. In 1955, in response to dangerous events in the Formosa Straits, Eisenhower appealed to Congress for joint action. Communist China had begun shelling the Quemoy island. It also mounted air attacks against other islands north of Formosa and seized the island of Ichiang. Rather than waiting for the United Nations to act, Eisenhower urged Congress "to participate now, by specific resolution, in measures designed to improve the prospects for peace. These measures would contemplate the use of the armed forces of the United States if necessary to assure the security of Formosa and the Pescadores." [27] While identifying his prerogatives as commander in chief, Eisenhower stated his much stronger preference to act jointly with Congress:

> Authority for some of the actions which might be required would be inherent in the authority of the Commander-in-Chief. Until Congress can act I would not hesitate, so far as my Constitutional powers extend, to take whatever emergency action might be forced upon us in order to protect the rights and security of the United States.
>
> However, a suitable Congressional resolution would clearly and publicly establish the authority of the President as Commander-in-Chief to employ the armed forces of this nation promptly and effectively for the purposes indicated if in his judgment it became necessary. It would make clear the unified and serious intentions of our Government, our Congress, and our people.[28]

Congress passed the Formosa Resolution in 1955, authorizing the president to employ U.S. forces "as he deems necessary" for the purpose of securing and protecting Formosa and the Pescadores against armed attack.[29] Eisenhower repeated this approach in 1957, asking Congress to pass a joint resolution authorizing him to employ armed forces in the Middle East. This time, however, legislators objected to giving the president a blank check. Congressional debate consumed several months and resulted in several restrictions on the delegated authority. For example, section 6 of the statute permitted Congress to terminate the authority by passing a concurrent resolution, which requires action by both Houses but is not presented to the president for his signature or veto.[30]

Eisenhower emphasized the importance of executive-legislative coordination: "I deem it necessary to seek the cooperation of the Congress. Only with that cooperation can we give the reassurance needed to deter aggression...." [31] He urged that "basic United States policy should now find expression in joint action by the Congress and the Executive." [32] In his memoirs, Eisenhower explained the choice between using executive prerogatives or seeking congressional support. On New Year's Day in 1957 he met with Secretary of State John Foster Dulles and congressional leaders of both parties. House Majority Leader John

McCormack, D-Mass., asked Eisenhower whether he, as commander in chief, already possessed power to carry out actions in the Middle East without congressional authorization. Eisenhower replied that

> greater effect could be had from a consensus of Executive and Legislative opinion, and I spoke earnestly of the desire of the Middle East countries to have reassurance now that the United States would stand ready to help. . . . Near the end of this meeting I reminded the legislators that the Constitution assumes that our two branches of government should get along together.[33]

Eisenhower's observation was extremely perceptive. He knew that lawyers and policy advisers in the executive branch could locate sufficient authorities and precedents to justify presidential action. It was his seasoned judgment, however, that a commitment by the United States would have much greater effect on allies and enemies alike if it represented the collective judgment of the president and Congress. Unilateral actions taken by a president who lacks the support of Congress and the people can threaten national prestige. Eisenhower's position was sound then and is sound now.

Eisenhower's experiment was short-lived. Unlike Eisenhower, President John F. Kennedy was prepared to act solely on his own constitutional authority. During the Cuban missile crisis, he did not request a joint resolution. He said as commander in chief "I have full authority now to take such action" militarily against Cuba.[34] In a news conference on September 13, 1962, he gave this revealing response:

> Q. Mr. President, you said in your opening statement that you now had full authority to act in the Cuban affair. In view of this, do you think there's any virtue in the Senate or the Congress passing the resolution saying you have that authority?
>
> THE PRESIDENT. No. I think the Members of Congress would, speaking as they do with a particular responsibility—I think it would be useful, if they desired to do so, for them to express their view. And as I've seen the resolutions which have been discussed—a resolution which I think Senator [Mike] Mansfield [D-Mont.] introduced and which Chairman [Carl] Vinson [D-Ga.] introduced in the House—and I would think that—I'd be very glad to have those resolutions passed if that should be the desire of the Congress.[35]

On October 3, 1962, Congress passed the Cuba Resolution, stating that the United States is "determined to prevent by whatever means may be necessary, including the use of arms, the Marxist-Leninist regime in Cuba from extending, by force or the threat of force, its aggressive or subversive activities to any part of this hemisphere." [36] This resolution did not authorize presidential action; it merely expressed the sentiments of Congress. Since no authority was delegated, there was no provision for termination by concurrent resolution.

When Kennedy acted on October 22 to interdict offensive weapons being delivered to Cuba, he based his action on "the authority entrusted to me by the Constitution as endorsed by the resolution of the Congress...." [37] The language in his proclamation read as follows:

> Now, THEREFORE, I, JOHN F. KENNEDY, President of the United States of America, acting under and by virtue of the authority conferred upon me by the Constitution and statutes of the United States, in accordance with the aforementioned resolutions of the United States Congress and of the Organ of Consultation of the American Republics.... [38]

Next came the fateful Southeast Asia Resolution of 1964, enacted in the middle of a presidential election year. After reported attacks against U.S. vessels in the Gulf of Tonkin, Congress passed legislation to approve and support "the determination of the President, as Commander in Chief, to take all necessary measures to repel any armed attack against the forces of the United States and to prevent further aggression." The United States was "prepared, as the President determines, to take all necessary steps, including the use of armed force...." [39]

Congress spent little time debating the resolution. The reported attacks had occurred on August 2 and 4. President Johnson requested the resolution on August 4. The Senate began debate on August 6 and passed the resolution the next day, 88-2. The House quickly passed the measure on August 7 by a vote of 414-0. One of the two opponents in the Senate, Wayne Morse, D-Ore., displayed an uncanny gift for prophecy: "Unpopular as it is, I am perfectly willing to make the statement for history that if we follow a course of action that bogs down thousands of American boys in Asia, the administration responsible for it will be rejected and repudiated by the American people. It should be." [40]

The Continuing Need for Collective Judgment

Mired in a land war in Southeast Asia and confronting huge American casualties, Congress began the slow process of reevaluating its role in twentieth-century wars. Even for conflicts on the vast scale of Korea and Vietnam, a declaration of war by Congress now seemed outmoded. What legislative checks could be placed on the president's decision to initiate military actions?

From 1969 to 1973, Congress declared its policy that commitments abroad required the concerted action of both branches. The National Commitments Resolution of 1969, as passed by the Senate, represents a significant breakthrough in congressional awareness. Beginning with draft resolutions in 1967, the Senate Foreign Relations Committee conducted extensive hearings that explored the need for obtaining congressional approval before committing U.S. economic and military resources to another country. The committee concluded that the concentration of power in the executive branch had progressed to such a point that "it is no longer accurate to characterize our government, in matters of foreign relations, as one of separated powers checked and balanced against each other. . . ." The president had acquired "virtual supremacy over the making as well as the conduct of the foreign relations of the United States." [41] Emergencies were not new to America, but, the committee noted, the crisis since 1940 "has been chronic." [42]

The Senate Foreign Relations Committee, which had reported the Tonkin Gulf Resolution favorably, now admitted that it had failed to discharge its constitutional duties:

> In adopting a resolution with such sweeping language, however, Congress committed the error of making a *personal* judgment as to how President Johnson would implement the resolution when it had a responsibility to make an *institutional* judgment, first, as to what *any* President would do with so great an acknowledgment of power, and, second, as to whether, under the Constitution, Congress had the right to grant or concede the authority in question.[43]

The National Commitments Resolution defines a national commitment as the "use of the armed forces of the United States on foreign territory, or a promise to assist a foreign country, government, or people by the use of the armed forces or financial resources of the United States, either immediately or upon the happening of certain events." Next, the resolution provided that "it is the sense of the Senate that a national commitment by the United States results only from affirmative action taken by the executive and legislative branches of the United States by means of a treaty, statute, or concurrent resolution of both Houses of Congress specifically providing for such commitment." [44] Passed in the form of a Senate resolution, the measure has no legal effect. It does, however, announce a vital principle of executive-legislative relations in foreign affairs. The resolution passed 70-16 with broad bipartisan backing. The Democrats supported it 43-3; the Republicans voted in favor 27-13.

Several long-term forces were clearly at work when Congress began drafting a war powers resolution. In 1970 the House of

Representatives passed a war powers resolution by a vote of 289-39. The House recognized that the president "in certain extraordinary and emergency circumstances has the authority to defend the United States and its citizens without specific prior authorization by the Congress." Congressional control would depend on consultation by the president with Congress ("whenever feasible"), reports by the president to Congress, and congressional action through the regular legislative process. The Senate did not act on the measure, regarding it as conceding too much power to the president.

In 1973, with the confrontation between President Nixon and Congress reaching fever pitch, the House and the Senate adopted a compromise product. President Nixon vetoed the War Powers Resolution, but both houses were able to override him, the House narrowly (284-135) and the Senate by a more comfortable margin (75-18). The House override reveals partisan calculations. Fifteen members of the House, after voting against the House bill and the conference version because it ceded too much power to the president, then voted to override.[45] If they regarded the bill as inadequate or unsound, why vote to make it public law?

Some of the legislators might have reversed positions because they feared that a failure to override Nixon would have lent support to the extreme views of presidential power expressed in his veto message. Yet it is clear that some legislators saw a veto override in the context of impeachment. Rep. Bella Abzug, D-N.Y., one of the fifteen to vote against the House bill and the conference version before voting to override Nixon, told her colleagues: "This could be a turning point in the struggle to control an administration that has run amuck. It could accelerate the demand for the impeachment of the President." [46]

The veto override also became entangled in the politics of Watergate. Nixon had vetoed eight bills during the 93d Congress; eight times the Democratic Congress failed to override. A number of legislators saw the War Powers Resolution as a way to reassert congressional power.[47] The "Saturday night massacre," which drove Special Prosecutor Archibald Cox, Attorney General Elliot Richardson, and Deputy Attorney General William Ruckelshaus out of the administration, occurred just four days before Nixon's veto of the War Powers Resolution. The political tension was further heightened by Spiro Agnew's resignation as vice president ten days before the "Saturday night massacre."

The War Powers Resolution calls for the "collective judgment" of both Congress and the president before U.S. troops are sent into combat. The resolution has been criticized as a usurpation of presidential power, reflecting an overactive Congress during the Vietnam era. But its basic principle was supported long ago by Senator Taft and President Eisenhower. Republicans and Democrats, conservatives and liberals, presidentialists and congressionalists have all understood the importance of joint action by Congress and the president. The Iran-contra affair during Reagan's second term illustrates the cost to the president, and to the presidency, of an administration's trying to act alone without congressional and public support.[48]

Henry Kissinger, a strong defender of executive power, had this to say in 1975 while serving as secretary of state:

> Comity between the executive and legislative branches is the only possible basis for national action. The decade-long struggle in this country over executive dominance in foreign affairs is over. The recognition that the Congress is a coequal branch of government is the dominant fact of national politics today. The executive accepts that the Congress must have both the sense and the reality of participation: foreign policy must be a shared enterprise.[49]

In his testimony before the Senate Foreign Relations Committee in 1988, Abraham D. Sofaer, legal adviser to the State Department, offered a similar perspective:

> This administration recognizes that Congress has a critical role to play in the determination of the circumstances under which the United States should commit its forces to actual or potential hostilities. No Executive policy or activity in this area can have any hope of success in the long term unless Congress and the American people concur in it and are willing to support its execution.[50]

The basic purpose of the War Powers Resolution seems eminently sound. Section 2(a) states that the introduction of U.S. troops into combat should have the "collective judgment of both the Congress and the President." That principle is the dominant lesson of the past four decades. No doubt there are occasions when presidents may have to act without congressional authority. I believe that President Gerald Ford had sufficient authority in 1975 to evacuate American citizens and foreign nationals from South Vietnam and Cambodia. Instead of acting immediately, he gave Congress nine days to provide him with statutory authority. Congress was unable to pass the legislation, and Ford eventually ordered the evacuations, which he should have done from the start.[51] Other situations might warrant unilateral presidential action, but commitments of U.S. troops into combat need the collective judgment of both branches.

Robert F. Turner, who recognizes a greater scope for presidential power than I do, nevertheless appreciates the need for executive-legislative cooperation. He expressed this position very eloquently in testimony before the House Foreign Affairs Committee in 1988:

> Although from a purely constitutional perspective the President in my view has a great deal of independent power in the making and conduct of foreign policy, in the long run those policies are almost guaranteed to fail if the Congress and the American people do not understand and support them. Regardless of the legal requirements, therefore, it is a political imperative that the two political branches of our Government cooperate—in a spirit of mutual respect and comity—if we, as a Nation, are to make a positive contribution to international peace with freedom.[52]

A Forbidden Legislative Veto?

What of section 5(c) in the War Powers Resolution, permitting a majority of both houses (by concurrent resolution) to direct the president to remove forces engaged in combat? Is that a legislative veto invalidated by *Immigration and Naturalization Service v. Chadha* (1983)? In *Chadha,* the Supreme Court held that any action by Congress that affects the legal rights, duties, and relations of persons outside the legislative branch must be done through the full legislative process, including action by both houses and presentation of a bill or resolution to the president for his signature or veto. A concurrent resolution is not presented to the president. In his testimony in 1988 Abraham Sofaer said that the concurrent resolution was "clearly" unconstitutional and should be repealed.[53] In a committee report in 1987, the Senate Foreign Relations Committee also stated that the concurrent resolution in the War Powers Resolution "has been effectively nullified" by *Chadha.*[54] Should the concurrent resolution be replaced by a joint resolution to comply with *Chadha*'s requirements for bicameralism and presentment?

I think not. The term "legislative veto" should be defined strictly as a condition placed on delegated power, such as the one-house veto that accompanied the delegation of reorganization authority to the president, or the two-house veto attached to rulemaking authority for the Federal Trade Commission. In the case of the War Powers Resolution, no power was delegated. No one argued that the war power belongs exclusively to the legislative branch and was being delegated to the president in the War Powers Resolution on the condition that Congress retain control by passing a concurrent resolution. Section 8(d)(2) expressly states that nothing in the War Powers Resolution "shall be construed as granting any authority to the President with respect to the introduction of United States Armed Forces into hostilities or into situations wherein involvement in hostilities is clearly indicated by the circumstances which authority he would not have had in the absence of this joint resolution."

The constitutional case for the concurrent resolution in the War Powers Resolution thus rests on quite different grounds from those for the legislative vetoes previously enacted by Congress. The disadvantages of replacing the concurrent resolution by a joint resolution, supposedly compelled by *Chadha,* are best illustrated by an incident in 1973. Congress added language to an appropriations bill to forbid the use of any funds to support combat activities in Cambodia or Laos. The language covered not only the supplemental funds in the bill but also funds made available by previous appropriations. Nixon vetoed the bill and Congress was unable to muster the two-thirds majority in each House for an override. As a result, the bill was revised to delay the cutoff of funds from June 30 to August 15, 1973, giving President Nixon forty-five more days to bomb Cambodia.

This compromise mooted a case in the Eastern District of New York. Democratic representative Elizabeth Holtzman had filed a suit to ask the courts to determine that the president could not engage in combat operations in Southeast Asia without congressional authorization. U.S. district judge Orrin G. Judd held that Congress had not authorized the bombing of Cambodia. The inability of Congress to override Nixon's veto, he said, could not be interpreted as an affirmative grant of authority. As Judd observed: "It cannot be the rule that the President needs a vote of only one-third plus one of either House in order to conduct a war, but this would be the consequence of holding that Congress must override a Presidential veto in order to terminate hostilities which it has not authorized." [55] His order was stayed by the U.S. Supreme Court because the August 15 compromise had broken the impasse between the two branches.[56] Eventually, Judd's decision was reversed by the Second Circuit, which treated the dispute as a political question.[57]

The concurrent resolution in the War Powers Resolution remains a useful and appropriate means for expressing congressional policy. If Congress were to pass such a resolution, the president could argue that it would have no legally binding effect and would be invalid under *Chadha.* In so doing, he would be announcing his determination to keep U.S. forces engaged in hostilities despite the opposition of a majority of each house of Congress. No doubt he could persist for a time in exercising his prerogatives, identifying any number of authorities to justify his actions. It is difficult, however, to think of a scenario in which a president would continue a war in the face of majority opposition in both houses of Congress. Enactment of a joint resolution exceeds what is necessary, constitutionally, and would put Congress in the position it was in in 1973: struggling to find a two-thirds majority in each house for an override, thereby allowing the president to continue a war simply by retaining the support of one-third plus one in a single house. Under these circumstances, and confining *Chadha* as it should be to questions of delegated authority, the appropriate vehicle for legislative action is the concurrent resolution.[58]

Congress must be prepared, and willing, to exercise the ample powers within its arsenal. When it acquiesces to executive initiatives, the record clearly shows that legislative inaction will not be cured by judicial remedies. Four times during the Reagan administration, members of Congress filed suit in federal court to have President Reagan's military actions in El Salvador, Nicaragua, Grenada, and the Persian Gulf held unconstitutional and illegal. Four times the federal courts gave Congress the same message: if you fail to challenge the president, don't come to us.[59] Justice Lewis Powell put it well in the treaty termination case of *Goldwater v. Carter* (1979): "If the Congress chooses not to confront the President, it is not our task to do so." [60] Congress has the constitutional power. It needs also the institutional courage and constitutional understanding to share with the president the momentous decision to send U.S. forces into combat.

Notes

1. *Congressional Record* 77 (1933): 270.
2. *Congressional Record* 79 (1935): 2014.
3. 53 Stat. 561 (1939). See Louis Fisher, *Constitutional Conflicts Between Congress and the President* (Princeton, N.J.: Princeton University Press, 1985), 165-166.
4. *Congressional Record* 84 (1939): 2854.
5. *Public Papers and Addresses of Franklin D. Roosevelt,* vol. 11 (New York: Harper & Bros., 1950), 364-365.
6. *Public Papers of the Presidents of the United States, 1946* (Washington, D.C.: U.S. Government Printing Office, 1962), 512-513.
7. *Woods v. Miller,* 333 U.S. 138, 146 (1948).
8. 61 Stat. 449 (1949); *Public Papers of the Presidents of the United States, 1947* (Washington, D.C.: U.S. Government Printing Office, 1963), 357.
9. S. Doc. 36, 79th Cong., 1st sess., 1945, 2.
10. 60 Stat. 832, sec. 136 (1946).
11. *Public Papers of the Presidents of the United States, 1951* (Washington, D.C.: U.S. Government Printing Office, 1965), 4, 19-22.

12. *Congressional Record* 97 (1951): 55.
13. Ibid., 61.
14. Ibid., 2987.
15. Ibid., 3065.
16. Ibid., 3199.
17. Ibid., 3015.
18. Ibid., 3041.
19. Ibid., 3082-3083, 3096.
20. Ibid., 3104.
21. Ibid., 3283 (para. 6).
22. Ibid., 34 (H.J. Res. 9).
23. Ibid., 9746.
24. House Committee on Foreign Affairs, *Background Information on the Use of United States Armed Forces in Foreign Countries,* 82d Cong., 1st sess., 1951, committee print.
25. Senate Committees on Armed Forces and Foreign Relations, *Powers of the President to Send the Armed Forces Outside the United States,* 82d Cong., 1st sess., 1951, committee print.
26. H. Doc. 443, 84th Cong., 2d sess., 1956, viii.
27. *Public Papers of the Presidents of the United States, 1955* (Washington, D.C.: U.S. Government Printing Office, 1959), 209.
28. Ibid., 209-210.
29. 69 Stat. 7 (1955).
30. 71 Stat. 4 (1957).
31. *Public Papers of the Presidents of the United States, 1957* (Washington, D.C.: U.S. Government Printing Office, 1958), 11.
32. Ibid., 12.
33. Dwight D. Eisenhower, *Waging Peace, 1956-1961* (The White House Years) (Garden City, N.Y.: Doubleday, 1965), 179.
34. *Public Papers of the Presidents of the United States, 1962* (Washington, D.C.: U.S. Government Printing Office, 1963), 674, 679.
35. Ibid., 679.
36. 76 Stat. 697 (1962).
37. *Public Papers of the Presidents, 1962,* 807.
38. Ibid., 810.
39. 78 Stat. 384 (1964).
40. *Congressional Record* 110 (1964): 18427.
41. S. Rept. 129, 91st Cong., 1st sess., 1969, 7.
42. Ibid., 8.
43. Ibid., 23. (Emphases in original.)
44. *Congressional Record* 115 (1969): 17245.
45. Fisher, *Constitutional Conflicts Between Congress and the President,* 298-299.
46. *Congressional Record* 119 (1973): 36211.
47. Thomas F. Eagleton, *War and Presidential Power: A Chronicle of Congressional Surrender* (New York: Liveright, 1974), 213-220.

48. Louis Fisher, "Foreign Policy Powers of the President and Congress," *The Annals of the American Academy of Political and Social Science* 499 (September 1988): 148; Louis Fisher, "How To Avoid Iran-Contras," *California Law Review* 76 (July 1988): 939.
49. *Department of State Bulletin* 72 (May 5, 1975): 562.
50. Senate Committee on Foreign Relations, *The War Power After 200 Years: Congress and the President at a Constitutional Impasse,* hearings before the Senate Committee on Foreign Relations, 100th Cong., 2d sess., 1988, 144.
51. Fisher, *Constitutional Conflicts Between Congress and the President,* 298-299.
52. House Foreign Affairs Committee, *War Powers: Origins, Purposes, and Applications,* hearings before the House Foreign Affairs Committee, 100th Cong., 2d sess., 1988, 56.
53. Senate Committee on Foreign Relations, *War Power After 200 Years,* 1061.
54. S. Rept. 100-106, 100th Cong., 1st sess., 1987, 6.
55. *Holtzman v. Schlesinger,* 361 F. Supp. 553, 565 (E.D.N.Y. 1973).
56. *Holtzman v. Schlesinger,* 414 U.S. 1304, 1316, 1321 (1973).
57. *Holtzman v. Schlesinger,* 484 F. 2d 1307 (2d Cir. 1973).
58. See G. Sidney Buchanan, "In Defense of the War Powers Resolution: *Chadha* Does Not Apply," *Houston Law Review* 22 (October 1985): 1155.
59. On El Salvador, see *Crockett v. Reagan,* 558 F. Supp. 893 (D.D.C. 1982), affirmed, *Crockett v. Reagan,* 720 F. 2d 1355 (D.C. Cir. 1983); on Nicaragua, see *Sanchez-Espinoza v. Reagan,* 568 F. Supp. 596 (D.D.C. 1983), affirmed, *Sanchez-Espinoza v. Reagan,* 770 F. 2d 202 (D.C. Cir. 1985); on Grenada, see *Conyers v. Reagan,* 578 F. Supp. 324 (D.D.C. 1984), dismissed as moot, *Conyers v. Reagan,* 765 F. 2d 1124 (D.C. Cir. 1985); on the Persian Gulf, see *Lowry v. Reagan,* 676 F. Supp. 333 (D.D.C. 1987).
60. *Goldwater v. Carter,* 444 U.S. 996, 998 (1979).

11. CONGRESS AND NICARAGUA: THE LIMITS OF ALTERNATIVE POLICY MAKING

Philip Brenner and William M. LeoGrande

On March 24, 1989, President George Bush announced an historic accord that marked the end of a war between two semisovereign powers. The announcement culminated four weeks of negotiations by Secretary of State James A. Baker and marked the administration's first foreign policy success. In these meetings, however, Baker was not representing the United States. He was the emissary of the executive branch, and the agreement was with the U.S. Congress over policy toward Nicaragua.

Few analysts of U.S. policy toward Nicaragua have ignored Congress, and several even have focused on congressional actions.[1] Indeed, it would have been difficult to overlook the role Congress played in policy making toward Nicaragua in the 1980s. The Iran-contra affair emanated directly from the congressional cutoff of aid to the Nicaraguan armed opposition, or contras: the ban forced members of the executive branch to use unconstitutional means when they chose to continue their contra funding.

The prevailing scholarly view, however, has been that Congress had a minor part in shaping U.S. policy. The framework into which most scholars have placed Congress relegates it to the category of elements that must be considered in explaining the twists and turns of U.S. policy. Though many might disagree with his judgment about the Iran-contra affair, Rep. Henry Hyde, R-Ill., in effect captured the conventional executive-oriented wisdom about Congress when he wrote:

> [T]he Founding Fathers intended to vest the general control of foreign affairs in the President.... [T]here are Members of the House and Senate who do not believe that communism in Central America is a grave threat to peace and freedom ...; there are Members who concede the threat in the abstract, but wish to do little about it beyond talking; and there are Members who acknowledge the threat and wish to challenge it.... The strange alliance between the unbelieving and the believing-but-unwilling has made a mockery of our foreign policy: we have had one policy

one year and another policy the next.... Too little have we acknowledged that our own convolutions have made the task of the Executive even more difficult.[2]

In contrast, Secretary of State Baker's negotiations on Capitol Hill seemed to evidence an appreciation for how much the role of Congress had evolved.[3] Rather than treating Congress as merely a source of influence, Baker implicitly acknowledged the legislative branch as an equal, with a distinctive policy. Indeed, for much of the 1980s the administration and Congress each had its own policy toward Nicaragua. Neither one quite prevailed, though each branch undertook extraordinary efforts to achieve its policy ends. Each influenced the other and thus contributed to the inconsistency that characterized both the legislature's and the executive's Nicaragua policies.

The notion that Congress might have its own foreign policy is consistent with, though different from, the now common observation that in the 1970s the legislature began to involve itself extensively in foreign policy making and to defer less to executive initiatives.[4]

Analysts have attributed the reorientation to several factors. Among them are a breakdown in the post-World War II consensus about the role of the United States in the world, precipitated by the Vietnam War; a series of relatively weak presidents; new members who came to Congress with an activist agenda; and the development in the legislative branch of mechanisms—such as improved information resources, increased staff, and subcommittees that could hold hearings and do independent investigations—that enhanced Congress's ability to initiate and shape policy.

These changes, along with major congressional initiatives on war powers, intelligence activities, covert action, human rights, and arms sales, led two observers in 1979 to describe Congress's new foreign policy-making role as a "revolution." [5] Yet the revolution seemed short-lived. The arrival of a strong president in 1981, and the subsequent congressional deferral to him on military spending, arms sales, human rights, and covert action, suggested that the pendulum had swung partially back, placing Congress in a decidedly secondary role.

Still, members of Congress were active on foreign policy issues in the 1980s, especially on policies toward Nicaragua, El Salvador, and southern Africa. But the view of Congress as secondary engendered the characterization that congressional activism was no more than interference in executive branch policy making. In its positive aspect, the caricature portrayed an image in which the legislature intruded to correct executive branch excesses or to help the executive branch avoid pitfalls.[6] As a criticism, it painted Congress as irresponsibly preventing the successful implementation of U.S. foreign policy, either through "micromanagement" or personal diplomacy.[7] In either case, U.S. policy was cast as the policy of the administration.

This framework would be adequate to explain congressional behavior with respect to Nicaragua until 1983. From then on, however, subgroups in the legislature developed alternative U.S. policies toward Nicaragua. As is the case with any plans that might be appropriately termed a policy, these policies included clear sets of goals, strategies for achieving the goals, and instruments to implement the strategies.

Congressional policy—that is, the policy of the institution as a whole articulated in its votes—was sometimes an expression of one or another of the subgroups' policies. At other times, when compromises were struck among the groups advocating alternative policies, it was an amalgam. And for about one and half years in mid-decade, congressional policy was coincident with the administration's, because Senate and House Republicans advocated positions that were essentially the same as the executive's, and they prevailed. Indeed, during the time that the Senate was controlled by the Republican party, it was the House that offered an alternative policy, and congressional policy was often a compromise between the administration and the House that did not always reflect a consistent relationship between goals, strategies, and methods.

The fact that a distinctive congressional policy toward Nicaragua was evident in voting does not indicate that there was a consensus in the legislature about the policy. Congress was polarized on the issue, and throughout the 1980s large blocs of members were absolutely consistent in their opposing positions.

Notably, Nicaragua policy generated divisions within the administration as well, though not with the extremes found in Congress. The conflicts between agencies over Nicaragua policy frequently meant that one agency's actions contradicted the efforts of another.[8] Even official pronouncements by President Ronald Reagan were not clear guides to U.S. policy. At times they were intended to mislead U.S. allies, the public, Congress, and the Nicaraguan government, and at other times they may have reflected the president's ignorance of what some administration officials were doing.[9] In effect, congressional policy may have appeared more fragmentary than the administration's only because members of Congress were so much more accessible and willing to speak openly to journalists and scholars than were administration officials.

Congress rarely sets out to develop its own foreign policy. Most members are content to let an administration lead and to reach a bipartisan compromise cooperatively. The Nicaraguan case was unusual in this regard, though it was not unique. Congress appears to have developed and pursued distinctive policies toward El Salvador and southern Africa as well, and an analysis of congressional policy toward Nicaragua may suggest why the legislature deviated from its normal pattern in those cases.

Our analysis will begin with a review of the growing conflict between the legislature and executive branch over Nicaragua. We will highlight how and why Congress came to develop its own policy and will indicate the limits the legislature confronted in fashioning an alternative to the administration's approach.

Congress and Contra Aid

During the 1980s the development of the congressional-executive conflict over Nicaragua proceeded in stages. In the first period, from January 1981 until the spring of 1983, the president set the policy agenda, and Congress acquiesced. The second period lasted approximately two years, during which time an increasing number of members opposed the administration's policy and began to develop alternatives. In the third period, from the spring of 1985 to the spring of 1986, one group among the Democrats came to ascendance, and their choice carried Congress. The fourth period lasted less than a year, ending with the close of the 99th Congress in January 1987. During this time Congress adopted a position that was essentially the same as the administration's. From January 1987 until March 1989, however, House Democrats defined a distinctive congressional policy, and this formed the basis of the settlement achieved with the Bush administration in March 1989. The 1989 bipartisan agreement took Nicaragua off the congressional agenda until after the February 1990 Nicaraguan elections. The surprise victory of opposition candidate Violeta Chamorro and the demobilization of the contras after her inauguration in April marked the end of the covert war.

January 1981 to Spring 1983

Though there was some debate inside the Reagan administration about Nicaragua policy, senior officials oriented the policy to the 1980 Republican platform's call for a struggle to "establish a free and independent government" in Nicaragua.[10] In Congress a large bloc of members were critical of the administration's policy. Most preferred the approach of the U.S. ambassador to Nicaragua, Lawrence Pezzullo, who was critical of the Nicaraguan government but advocated the maintenance of aid to Nicaragua in order to retain some leverage there.[11] Still, the majority in both chambers tolerated the new administration's antagonistic approach toward Nicaragua, which included the abandonment of efforts to induce "desirable" Nicaraguan behavior by holding out the carrot of assistance.

By the end of 1981, the administration had settled on a policy. Embodied in National Security Decision Directive 17, which the president signed on November 23, 1981, it involved a covert war against Nicaragua. NSDD 17 gave the CIA authority to create a contra army in Honduras and to work with foreign governments—principally Argentina—in training and maintaining these paramilitary commandos. It was not NSDD 17, however, but a presidential finding on December 1 that became the focus of subsequent congressional attention. The finding authorized financial and logistical support of a five-hundred-person force for the purpose of interdicting an alleged flow of arms from Nicaragua to El Salvador.[12]

The covert operation against Nicaragua was controversial from its inception. Some members of the House and Senate intelligence committees argued that it would inevitably entangle the United States with the remnants of former president Anastasio Somoza's hated National Guard—a futile alliance that would allow the Sandinistas to rally popular support. They also warned that efforts to depose the Sandinistas could spark a wider regional war, drawing the United States into direct military involvement. It was to assuage these concerns that CIA director William Casey promised the committees that the scope and purpose of the Nicaragua operation would be limited to the interception of arms.[13]

U.S. support transformed the contras from a ragtag assortment of raiding parties with only a few hundred men into a well-equipped, professionally trained army. As the contra force grew and the war widened—and the U.S. role became more central—both intelligence committees began to worry that the operation was spiraling far beyond the boundaries they had originally approved. In April 1982 liberal Democrats in the House committee failed in a bid to cut off funding for the covert war.[14] But, in an effort to hold the CIA to its stated objective of arms interdiction and to send the administration a message that members were concerned about the direction of policy, the House Intelligence Committee added language to the Classified Annex to the Fiscal Year (FY) 1983 Intelligence Authorization (Public Law 97-269) prohibiting U.S. aid to paramilitary groups "for the purpose of overthrowing the Government of Nicaragua or provoking a military exchange between Nicaragua and Honduras."

This language was not designed to bring the covert operation to a halt. On the contrary, it was intentionally crafted to register the committee's growing uneasiness without interfering with the operation. The Reagan administration interpreted the law to mean that U.S.

support for the contras could continue so long as the purpose of the United States was not one of those proscribed. It asserted that the intentions of the contras—whose leaders declared publicly they intended to overthrow the Nicaraguan government—were separable from U.S. intentions and were thus legally irrelevant. Although this construction irritated some members, Congress accepted the logic of the administration's contention.

In December 1982 the mild restriction on contra aid contained in the Classified Annex was reiterated publicly when the House voted 411-0 to attach it to the fiscal 1983 defense appropriations bill. Although its passage merely reaffirmed existing law, this first "Boland amendment"—so named because it was offered by House Intelligence Committee Chairman Edward Boland, D-Mass.—sent another warning to the administration that it had not eased congressional concerns.[15]

Spring 1983 to Spring 1985

The steady expansion of the covert war in 1983 convinced an increasing number of members that President Reagan's real intention was to overthrow the Nicaraguan government, which would be a violation of the Boland amendment.[16] Boland and the House Democratic leadership believed that Congress could not control or limit the covert war because Director Casey would not deal with them in good faith. From their perspective the administration's zealotry left Congress with only two choices: to endorse the war to overthrow the Nicaraguan government or to stop it. A middle ground no longer seemed viable, and inaction was tantamount to endorsement. This view was underscored by the removal of Assistant Secretary of State Thomas Enders, one of the few administration officials advocating a diplomatic approach toward Nicaragua. In the spring of 1983, the House intelligence and foreign affairs committees proposed the Boland-Zablocki bill (H.R. 2760) to prohibit funding, directly or indirectly, for military or paramilitary operations against Nicaragua.

Boland-Zablocki came to the House floor on July 27 and was bitterly debated for two days, finally passing by a vote of 228-195. Not surprisingly, the Republican-controlled Senate refused to take it up, but the House was not so easily dissuaded. On October 20 it voted for Boland-Zablocki again (227-194), this time adding it to the fiscal 1984 intelligence authorization bill (H.R. 2968). In November it included the ban on contra aid in the defense appropriations bill as well.

The Senate version of the intelligence bill authorized a continuation of the covert war by giving the administration its full funding request. A compromise was finally reached in conference, providing $24 million for the covert war—substantially less than the administration had requested—and prohibiting the president from supplementing that amount by using contingency funds or reprogramming.

The administration was free, of course, to come back to Congress with a supplemental request, which it did just a few months later in March 1984. Rather than following the normal procedure of submitting a request and having it referred to the relevant committees, however, the administration tried a legislative shortcut: attaching $21 million for the contras to an unrelated supplemental appropriation that had already passed the House. The administration hoped that once again a compromise between the House and Senate versions of the bill would produce at least part of the aid package it wanted. But the House conferees were unwilling to give in. On May 25, when the bill came back to the House in disagreement, the House voted 241-177 to add a provision banning the use of any funds appropriated in the bill for military or paramilitary operations against Nicaragua—the same "Boland" language ("Boland II") approved by the House the previous fall.

Between the time of the Senate vote on the supplemental appropriation in March and the House vote in May, the press revealed that the CIA had mined Nicaragua's harbors, damaging ships from nearly a dozen nations, most of them U.S. allies. The administration then compounded the political damage by refusing to recognize the jurisdiction of the World Court to hear a Nicaraguan complaint against U.S. support for the contras. The mining and the withdrawal from the Court were roundly condemned in Congress. Even the Senate, which had never denied an administration request for funding the covert war, approved by a vote of 84-12 a nonbinding resolution calling for a halt to the mining.

This was the atmosphere in the summer of 1984, when the Senate took up the conference report on the supplemental appropriation for child nutrition and summer jobs to which aid for the contras had been attached. Faced with the prospect of losing the popular summer jobs bill in an election year because of the Nicaraguan aid provision, the Senate leadership gave up the fight, receding to the House position. By that time the $24 million appropriated the preceding November had been exhausted, and so the legal expenditure of U.S. funds to aid the contras came to an end.

Having lost its bid for more aid during fiscal 1984, the administration shifted the fight to the pending legislation for fiscal 1985. The intelligence authorization for fiscal 1985 (H.R. 5399) passed the House with the Boland II language banning contra aid, but the Senate approved the administration's request for $24 million. In conference, the House refused to compromise. "We are not about to agree," Boland insisted. "The House has voted four times to stop this war in Nicaragua." [17] The most the House conferees would accept was a provision setting aside $14 million for contra aid, which the president could expend only if the new Congress approved it by a joint resolution after February 1985.

That settled the issue for the 98th Congress. Rather than waging a major battle over an unpopular policy in the midst of Reagan's reelection campaign, the administration postponed the fight, hoping that the 1984 election results would give it a stronger hand in 1985. [18] At the same time, Democrats anticipated that events in the region might bolster their campaign for a diplomatic solution.

Late in the summer, after eighteen months of negotiation, four countries on the periphery of Central America—Colombia, Mexico, Panama, and Venezuela—proposed a peace accord that they hoped would be signed by the five countries commonly defined as Central American—Costa Rica, El Salvador, Guatemala, Honduras, and Nicaragua. [19] Only Nicaragua agreed to sign it. The plan, called the Contadora proposals because the initial meetings took place on the island of Contadora, held out the promise of a diplomatic solution to the differences between Nicaragua and its neighbors, differences that seemed to be at the heart of the Reagan administration's concern about the Sandinistas. Democrats hoped that without the contras, and with a regional diplomatic initiative under way, the administration might be forced to settle for diplomatic pressure on the Nicaraguans. Yet the contras were kept solvent by a flow of cash from third countries, from private donors, and from the White House's arms sales to Iran, coordinated by National Security Council staff member Lt. Col. Oliver North. [20]

Soon after his second term began, President Reagan launched a bid to resume contra aid. On April 3, 1985, acting under the terms of the previous fall's compromise, he requested release of the $14 million. The Senate quickly approved the request, 53-46 (S.J. Res. 106).

In the House the Democratic leadership feared that the majority against funding the contras was eroding. Many Democrats indicated that they were reluctant to cut off contra aid without having some alternative program they could support. As a remedy, the leadership devised H.J. Res. 247, sponsored by Michael Barnes, D-Md., chair of the Western Hemisphere Subcommittee, and Lee Hamilton, D-Ind., Boland's successor as chair of the Intelligence Committee. The Barnes-Hamilton proposal continued the ban on military aid for the contras, but it also provided $10 million for international relief agencies to aid Nicaraguan refugees and $4 million to help finance the Contadora peace process.

The Republicans devised their own proposal. Sponsored by Minority Leader Robert Michel, R-Ill., it provided the contras with $14 million in nonlethal aid to be administered by the Agency for International Development rather than the CIA. The Republican leadership hoped that by limiting aid to nonmilitary supplies and prohibiting CIA involvement, they could regain enough votes to keep the war going.

The Democratic leadership won a solid victory against the release of the $14 million in military aid (248-180). But then its strategy began to unravel. The first vote on Barnes-Hamilton produced a much narrower victory than the Democrats expected, 219-206. Michel's substitute was just barely defeated, 213-215, with the winning margin provided by members changing their votes moments before the final tally was announced. Even this drama was surpassed on the vote for final passage of the underlying resolution (the second vote on Barnes-Hamilton). To everyone's surprise, it was overwhelmingly defeated (303-123) by a bizarre coalition of Republicans and liberal Democrats. Many liberal Democrats had voted for Barnes-Hamilton initially only to prevent the passage of the Republican proposal. But once the Michel amendment had been defeated and the choice was between Barnes-Hamilton or no aid at all, the liberals voted for no aid. The surprise defeat of Barnes-Hamilton left moderate and conservative Democrats embittered. The whole purpose behind the bill had been to give them an alternative that did not totally abandon the contras.

Republicans apparently preferred to live temporarily with no aid rather than to swallow the Barnes-Hamilton alternative. They seemed to have reasoned that their narrow defeat on the first Barnes-Hamilton vote meant that they would soon be able to produce a majority for contra aid. Since they needed to pick up only two votes to pass Michel's amendment, the prospects for nonlethal aid looked excellent. They looked even better the day after the vote, when the headlines reported that Nicaraguan president Daniel Ortega was on his way to Moscow.

Ortega's trip was a political disaster for opponents of contra aid. Reagan had charged that the Sandinistas were communists and Soviet puppets. Ortega's trip seemed to prove him right. Many members of Congress who had voted against the contras felt embarrassed and betrayed; they felt that they had gone out on a political limb for Nicaragua, and Ortega unthinkingly had cut it off. The trip left these members with the suspicion that the Sandinistas could not be relied upon to act with any political acumen. At any moment they were likely to do something that would make it politically untenable to be seen as their defender. The fact that Ortega went to the Soviet Union in search of desperately needed oil, and that the trip had been announced before the vote, was neither widely recognized nor particularly relevant to its political impact in Washington.[21]

In effect, it was during this period that the lines were drawn between Congress and the president. Having failed to moderate the administration, Democrats and a few Republicans began to develop an alternative policy. Consistent with the Contadora orientation, they focused on negotiations with Nicaragua to alter the alleged transgressions against its neighbors and to weaken its links to Cuba and the Soviet Union. They relied on the power of the purse—cutting off aid to the contras—to pressure the administration to pursue negotiations seriously. But most Republicans defended the president, and the GOP held a majority in the Senate. What emerged from the compromises between the two chambers, then, lacked coherence. The war was continued for much of the period but at a level below what the administration judged was necessary for success. Yet even when Congress cut off funds for the contras, it could not force the administration to negotiate seriously.

Spring 1985 to Spring 1986

In part as a response to Ortega's trip to Moscow after the April 1985 vote and in part as an indication of congressional resolve "to do something" about Nicaragua, several members of the House and Senate called upon the administration late in April 1985 to apply economic sanctions. On May 1, in a seeming bow to congressional demands, President Reagan issued an executive order declaring that Nicaragua's behavior was a "threat" to the "national security and foreign policy of the United States," which warranted the imposition of a trade embargo.[22] The embargo had been planned for two years, however, and culminated a series of economic actions taken to destabilize the Nicaraguan government.[23]

The administration then launched a new drive for contra aid in the Senate, hoping that victory there might produce a momentum that would carry over to the House. On June 6 the Senate adopted, 55-42, an amendment to the State Department authorization (S. 1003) by Sam Nunn, D-Ga., providing $38 million in nonlethal aid during fiscal 1985 and 1986.

On June 12 the issue was joined once again in the House on a series of amendments to a supplemental appropriation (H.R. 2577). It was a debacle for the House leadership, as the Democrats lost four successive votes by wide margins. The House rejected a proposal to extend the Boland amendment's ban on military aid to the contras, 196-232, and it again rejected the Barnes-Hamilton alternative, 174-254. A new version of the Michel proposal had been developed in negotiations between the Republican leadership and a group of conservative Democrats headed by Dave McCurdy, D-Okla. It provided $27 million in nonlethal aid for the contras so long as it was not delivered by the CIA or Department of Defense. The amendment passed, 248-184, getting 35 more votes than it had received in April. Shortly thereafter the legal flow of U.S. aid to the contras resumed for the first time in more than a year.

The $27 million approved by Congress in June 1985 extended only through the first half of fiscal 1986, and it was clear that a new fight over aid would emerge early in 1986. It was foreshadowed on February 3 by a letter to President Reagan from thirty-one House moderates, most of whom had previously voted for nonlethal contra aid. They called on the president to postpone any request for aid.[24] Their plea was prompted in part by a declaration in January from the eight Latin American countries involved in the Contadora process—the original four and Argentina, Brazil, Peru, and Uruguay. This so-called Caraballeda message (named for the town in Venezuela where the latter four countries met in January 1986 to discuss Central America) recommended the "termination of external support to the irregular forces operating in the region." It was endorsed by the presidents of the five Central American countries.[25]

Nonetheless, on February 25 President Reagan asked Congress for $100 million in additional contra aid, a package more than twice as great as any previous request. Moreover, the president sought repeals of the ban on lethal military aid and of the prohibition on CIA involvement in the war.

The fight over Reagan's request was cast as the final epic battle between President Reagan and House Speaker Thomas P. O'Neill, D-Mass., who had announced his intention to retire at the end of the session. O'Neill drew upon his considerable prestige to swing wavering members to the Democrats' side. The president spoke about Nicaragua constantly for several weeks, culminating his campaign with a nation-wide television address on the eve of the congressional vote. But the White House had overreached with such a large request. The aid package was rejected, 222-210, a major defeat for the administration in light of the attention and prestige President Reagan had invested. The price of victory for the House leadership, however, was a promise to McCurdy and other swing legislators that there would be an opportunity to vote within the next few months on McCurdy's compromise proposal.[26]

It had been the change in voting by the swing legislators that had reversed the House's position in 1985. After the June vote, they emerged as a key group to which both contra aid opponents and the administration appealed. They claimed to side with the majority Democratic position in seeking a negotiated solution, but they endorsed the post-1983 administration rationale for the war, which was to reform Nicaragua internally. In contrast to a majority of House Democrats, the swing legislators advocated the use of contra military pressure to extract concessions from Nicaragua. But they also sought to pressure the contras to democratize their organization and to reduce human rights violations.

In part, this group gained influence by claiming that only its approach could break through the stalemate between Congress and the president that had developed over Nicaragua. Its claim was bolstered by a June 1985 letter President Reagan sent to Congress—a letter drafted by McCurdy—in which the president promised to support negotiations and not to pursue the military overthrow of the Nicaraguan government.[27] By 1986 it became clear that the administration was not adhering to its promises, and this behavior served to vitiate the swing legislators' influence within Congress.

Spring 1986 to January 1987

As the next round of voting on contra aid approached in mid-1986, Congress discovered that the contras had been less than scrupulous about how they spent the $27 million in nonlethal aid given to them in 1985. An investigation by the General Accounting Office (GAO) revealed that over half of the $27 million could not be accounted for. The press supplemented the stories of contra corruption with reports of their involvement in drug smuggling and gunrunning.[28]

In view of such revelations, it seemed unlikely that anyone would have shifted to the administration's side on the merits of the issue. But the White House was in search of just seven votes. Enormous pressure was brought to bear on the sixteen Republicans who had voted against the president in March 1986. The White House cast the issue as one of party loyalty, hinting that this was a benchmark vote that the president (whose popularity stood at a peak of 68 percent) would remember when he was deciding which Republican candidates to help in the fall. Still, the White House whip count showed that it could not win without the support of some moderate Democrats. To woo them, the harsh partisan rhetoric that characterized the debate earlier in the year was replaced by a conciliatory call for bipartisanship.[29]

The administration's strategy worked. On June 25, 1986, the House voted 221-209 to approve the president's $100 million aid package for the contras. Yet another version of the Barnes-Hamilton proposal was defeated, 183-245. The Democrats' only solace came from the adoption (215-212) of an amendment prohibiting U.S. personnel from training the contras in Honduras or Costa Rica within twenty miles of the Nicaraguan border. After a brief filibuster attempt by liberal Democrats, the Senate approved the $100 million aid proposal, 53-47, and the United States was officially back in the war.

In effect, the administration had changed Nicaragua from a foreign policy issue into a domestic one: reelection. The vote came in an election year, and moderate members were shy of tackling the president. Negotiations in the region had broken down, and the distinctive congressional alternative appeared unrealistic to most members. Four years of battle also had left some important members and aides exhausted, and these considerations were enough to make the majority congressional position essentially the same as the administration's. A significant bloc of members, however, remained fixed in pursuit of what had been a congressional alternative to the administration's Nicaragua policy.

January 1987 to March 1989

In the wake of the Republicans' losses in the 1986 elections and the exposure of the Iran-contra scandal, the House majority that supported Reagan's Nicaragua policy evaporated. The House voted in March 1987 to deny release of the last $40 million from the $100 million package approved the previous year; the vote was 230-196. Since only a joint resolution (which requires presidential concurrence) could block release of the funds, opponents of contra aid had no hope of overriding a presidential veto. But even though the vote was largely symbolic and aid continued to flow, the emergence of a firmer congressional resolve against aid was evident.

During 1987 the administration delayed any further requests for military support of the contras to avoid voting in the midst of the congressional investigation of the Iran-contra affair. The White House and the House Democratic leadership did agree to provide $20.7 million in food and medicine during the first half of fiscal 1988.

Meanwhile, efforts emerged in the region to secure a negotiated solution to the Nicaraguan war. These began in December 1986 with a new proposal by Costa Rican president Oscar Arias. The Contadora process had been all but abandoned, even though Brazil, Ecuador, Peru, and Uruguay had added their backing in 1985. Arias's plan was narrower than the Contadora proposals and would not have required the United States to remove its forces or military aid from the region. But it called for the termination of aid to all guerrilla forces in Central America, including the contras. This plan was endorsed in principle by El Salvador, Guatemala, and Honduras on February 16. One month later the Senate lauded it by a 97-1 vote (S. Con. Res. 24). Then in

August the United States proposed a new diplomatic initiative endorsed by House Speaker Jim Wright and President Reagan. Their plan was quickly superseded by the Central Americans themselves. On August 7, 1987, all five Central American presidents—including Nicaragua's Daniel Ortega—signed the Esquipulas accord, which was in essence the same as the February Arias plan. (The accord was named after the location of the meeting, in Esquipulas, Guatemala.) Under the Esquipulas agreement the five countries were pledged to establish pluralist democracies, hold free elections, halt support for regional insurgents, and seek national reconciliation with their own armed opponents.[30]

Progress on the diplomatic front reduced Reagan's chances of winning new military aid. Members of Congress wanted to underscore their support for regional peace efforts by acting in accord with the call for a contra aid ban. But many also felt that the contras had been encouraged to fight by the United States and should not be summarily abandoned. The matter of funding them faced Congress squarely in 1988, when the administration reported that the guerrilla forces had run out of money. On February 3 the House narrowly defeated (211-219) President Reagan's request for $36.25 million in military and nonmilitary assistance. The president's request also included a number of hidden costs that brought the total value of the package to some $60 million.

The administration still hoped it might prevail in April, when the Democratic leadership brought its own aid package to the floor. Sponsored by Rep. David Bonior, D-Mich., it included $16 million in food and medicine for the contras and $14.6 million for aid to Nicaraguan children victimized by the war. The Bonior proposal was approved initially, 215-210, but was finally defeated, 208-216, by staunch supporters of the contras, who felt that the Bonior plan provided too little, and by a few staunch opponents of contra aid, who felt that the plan provided too much. A few weeks later, however, the Republicans acquiesced and accepted the Democrats' proposal, preferring it to no aid at all.

The House, in its final vote on contra aid during the Reagan administration, handily rejected an amendment to the fiscal 1989 intelligence authorization bill that would have enabled the administration to resume military aid by drawing on the CIA's contingency fund. At that point, on May 26, 1988, a clear majority wanted to support the peace process that was moving rapidly within Nicaragua.

On March 23 the Nicaraguan government had signed a sixty-day cease-fire agreement with the contra political leadership. The so-called Sapoa accord—named for the Nicaraguan border town where it was signed—included plans for negotiations aimed at a permanent cease-fire, amnesty for contra soldiers, and government guarantees of free expression. The agreement was to be supervised by the leading prelate in Nicaragua, Cardinal Miguel Obando y Bravo, and by the secretary general of the Organization of American States, Joao Baena Soares. The agreement specified that the contras could receive humanitarian aid through neutral international organizations such as the Red Cross.

The Sapoa agreement, particularly the section on humanitarian aid, significantly undercut the rationale and legitimacy of the Reagan administration's contra aid program. Though the cease-fire broke down several times in the next year and the contra military leaders seemed opposed to it, the peace process continued to move forward with an announcement of elections in Nicaragua, the creation of a powerful and legitimate electoral council, and the willingness of the Nicaraguan government to allow international observers to monitor the electoral process. It became more difficult for the administration to portray the Nicaraguan government as intransigent, belligerent, and totalitarian and to justify support for the contra war. In effect, Sapoa led to the March 1989 agreement between Congress and the Bush administration that brought the policies of the two branches into synchronization.

The Legislative Struggle for an Alternative

The congressional effort to fashion an alternative policy toward Nicaragua was extraordinary. It absorbed the energies of an unusually large number of members and staff, particularly when assessed in relation to the size of the region involved and the level of proposed expenditure. It also attracted considerable effort by the administration and interest groups. This attention suggests the importance that was attached to the issue, but it only begins to indicate how a distinctive congressional policy developed. Four factors contributed to the emergence of an alternative policy in Congress: internal congressional activities; executive branch activities; domestic, nongovernmental activities and events; and regional activities and events.

Internal Congressional Activities

House Democrats prepared themselves to engage the president over Nicaragua and El Salvador policies even before Ronald Reagan took office. They selected Michael Barnes to chair the Inter-American Affairs (subsequently renamed Western Hemisphere) Subcommittee over the sitting chair, Gus Yatron, D-Pa., because Barnes had Latin American expertise and a more liberal voting record. With the loss of several liberal senators in the 1980 election and the switch in party control in the other chamber, House Democrats reasoned that they would need to have strength in this important subcommittee in order to challenge aggressive administration policies in Central America.

As the executive's policy emerged through covert action and directives that had no need for legislative corroboration, the Western Hemisphere Affairs Subcommittee had to develop a role for itself. It did this by regularly focusing public and media attention on Nicaragua, through trips to the region, and through an increasing number of hearings, especially after 1982.

The intelligence oversight committees themselves were deeply involved in overseeing Nicaragua policy, though this proved frustrating for many members because of the necessary secrecy attached to the deliberations of these panels. Notably, the original Boland amendment was already law—unknown to most members because much of an intelligence authorization is secret—when the House approved it publicly in December 1982.

Senators and representatives outside the intelligence committees also wanted to be involved in shaping the policy, and their desires generated additional congressional activity. The total number of hearings about Central America in the House and Senate increased nearly 50 percent from 1982 to 1983 and more than doubled from 1983 to 1984. The number of hearings stayed at the 1984 level for the next three years.

From 1983 until 1988, more than one hundred senators and representatives traveled to Nicaragua to meet with government officials, to observe elections, and even to consult with the contras. The trips added to the level of knowledge about Nicaragua inside Congress, reinforced the members' interest in the war, and contributed to the sentiment that Congress was capable of developing its own Nicaragua policy.

Both Democrats and Republicans worked to develop alternatives through several informal panels. In 1985 House Chief Deputy Majority Whip David Bonior became chair of the Democratic Caucus's Task Force on Central America. The group held regular reviews of Nicaragua policy, and Bonior frequently acted as a party spokesperson on Nicaragua, traveled to the region with other members, and worked closely with those on committees who had responsibility for Nicaragua policy.

Caucus chair Richard Gephardt, D-Mo., also created a working group on Central America in 1985, under the chairmanship of Mel Levine, D-Calif., to fashion a policy on which members could campaign in 1986. Encompassing a broad base of the party, the working group included several members who were not on any foreign policy committee; this became their forum for reviewing Nicaragua policy. Though the Levine group report ultimately received little attention, the preparatory meetings provided legislators with a place to hammer out differences, share information, and discuss criticisms of the administration's Nicaragua policy.[31]

What came to be known as the McCurdy group, named for the Oklahoma Democrat who led it, brought together several moderates who had swung back and forth between support for and opposition to contra aid. It formed after the April 1985 vote against aid and included Michael Andrews, D-Tex., Ronald Coleman, D-Tex., Jim Cooper, D-Tenn., Glenn English, D-Okla., Jim Jones, D-Okla., Ike Skelton, D-Mo., Jim Slattery, D-Kan., John Spratt, D-S.C., and Wes Watkins, D-Okla.[32] Although the McCurdy group had no organizational structure and was essentially a loose coalition, its members tended to vote alike and to seek a common strategy before key votes on contra aid. It appeared to have some influence in 1985 and 1986, which is what led President Reagan to negotiate with McCurdy in the hope of picking up moderate votes for aid.[33]

One bipartisan and bicameral group, the Arms Control and Foreign Policy Caucus, provided credible ammunition for opponents of contra aid through reports from its Central America working group, headed by George Miller, D-Calif. One study, for example, became the basis for critics' charges that the contra military leadership was largely made up of former Somoza National Guard officers.[34]

Though the Republicans in Congress had formidable support from the administration, they did not rely solely on the White House to organize a congressional coalition in support of the contras. The House Republican Study Committee acted as an informal whip organization and was dominated by the far right of the party. Moreover, activist conservatives had formed their own organization—the Conservative Opportunity Society—led by Newt Gingrich, R-Ga., Connie Mack, R-Fla., Robert Walker, R-Pa., and Vin Weber, R-Minn. The Republican leadership in both chambers not only had to negotiate with the Democrats but often functioned as mediators between the administration and more extreme Republicans.

It was Speaker Wright, though, who played the most remarkable role in developing a congressional policy toward Nicaragua. Distrusted by liberals while he was House majority leader, he emerged in 1987 as a central figure when he spearheaded a diplomatic initiative that forced the administration to endorse the Esquipulas plan. As he involved himself in discussions with foreign leaders and forged a consensus among Democrats, he took on an unprecedented role for a Speaker as Congress's foreign policy spokesperson on Nicaragua.[35]

Executive Branch Activities

As Congress struggled to define a coherent policy toward Nicaragua, the most powerful external influence on its behavior was naturally the executive branch. The president made support of the contras the centerpiece of his entire foreign policy. He focused on them in several State of the Union addresses, in a speech before a joint session of Congress, and in numerous radio and television appeals. And he used his personal charm effectively to persuade some members of Congress—especially Republicans—to back contra aid.[36]

In its public campaign, the administration aimed its message at four audiences. First there was Congress itself, which held the power of the purse. Second, there was the public. If the White House could persuade the public to back administration policy, it would increase its leverage with Congress. The administration used a variety of techniques to sway the public, including the designation of an office in the White House to target interest groups with information; the hiring of public relations firms, allegedly in some instances with funds designated for other purposes; and the creation of an office in the State Department designed to produce anti-Sandinista propaganda and to sell administration policy.[37]

Nicaragua itself was the third target of executive branch bravado. Administration officials hoped that the apparent resolve of the president and his tough language would lead to discord within the Sandinista leadership and to lower morale among its followers.

The final audience consisted of U.S. allies.[38] As Peter Kornbluh explains, the effort "had a threefold purpose: to win the support of allied governments . . . ; to enhance President Reagan's international credibility; and to facilitate U.S. efforts to undermine the Sandinistas." [39] Had U.S. allies in Latin America and Europe supported the administration's policy, their backing might have had some effect on congressional deliberations. But the allies gave little succor to the administration. None, for example, joined in the embargo against Nicaragua, and several picked up the trade that the United States had abandoned.

Above all, the administration had the ability to seize the initiative in ways that forced Congress to respond. In 1984 it opened a seeming diplomatic offensive by sending a special envoy to negotiate with the Nicaraguan government, and in 1985 it unilaterally imposed economic sanctions. Its control of classified information enabled it to use selective leaks for maximum effect. And because it was responsible for the contra operation, it had considerable leverage over the actions taken by the guerrillas.

Yet the administration's actions were not well coordinated and contributed to a sense in Congress that the executive was in disarray over its Nicaragua policy. This sense provided an opening for Congress to assert itself. Members saw that while one administration official asserted that the United States was pursuing diplomatic avenues, another would disavow diplomatic efforts and threaten military intervention. Claims that the contras were only supposed to interdict arms were contradicted by officials who leaked information about a wider war.[40] Ultimately, the administration's credibility with Congress was eroded by years of obfuscation—from the 1984 harbor mining to the Iran-contra scandal—that in part resulted from various officials charting their own policies. Thus in 1988, when officials claimed that the administration sought a peaceful solution by sustaining the contras, few believed them. As House Majority Whip Tony Coelho, D-Calif., remarked, "Yesterday's vote [to deny funding] was the White House not understanding the power of peace." [41]

The Iran-contra scandal not only opened the most gaping hole in the administration's credibility, but it also indicated to Congress that the obsession with overthrowing the Nicaraguan government was tearing at the very fabric of the Constitution and was distorting U.S. objectives in other foreign policy areas. In part, the scandal grew out of the influence of true believers such as Director of Central Intelligence William Casey over Nicaragua policy. These zealots would brook no obstacle in their pursuit of victory.[42] But ultimately it grew out of a shared administration view that Congress was an enemy against which a domestic war had to be waged. This perspective led the administration to act so aggressively in trying to achieve its aims in Congress—or in trying to bypass Congress—that it did limit Congress's ability to achieve its policy objectives.

Domestic, Nongovernmental Activities and Events

In analyzing the major votes for contra aid from 1983 to 1988, we conclude that shifts in the congressional majority were produced by a combination of member replacement and conversion. Both sides had large blocs of members who voted consistently, and the narrow, winning coalitions thus hung on the votes of swing members and those brought in by elections. This situation encouraged extensive lobbying efforts by both opponents and supporters of contra aid and made the 1984 and 1986 elections major determinants in congressional policy toward Nicaragua.

The lobbying strategies of both sides were remarkably similar. Both focused on the House and within that chamber on the approximately fifty members who had voted inconsistently on contra aid and who thus indicated that they might be open to persuasion.[43] Supporters of aid were able to rely on the president and on administration officials such as Colonel North to provide clout. Administration officials even coordinated the activities of some groups, the most famous of which was the National Endowment for the Preservation of Liberty, headed by Carl R. "Spitz" Channell. Channell pleaded guilty in 1988 to the charge of using tax-exempt money to buy military equipment for the contras. Supporters also created grassroots networks in members' districts. The largest continuous effort was mounted by Citizens for Reagan, though several smaller groups such as the Council on Inter-American Security and the National Center for Public Policy Research sought to influence Congress through elite opinion makers.[44]

Opponents of aid worked through a variety of groups. A coalition of religious and human rights organizations formed the Central American Working Group, and it maintained continuous liaison with members of Congress. Church groups that had mounted education campaigns at the grassroots were an important element of this coalition. In Washington, their efforts were coordinated through the Inter-religious Task Force. Other groups, such as Countdown 1987, were short-lived, coming into existence to apply pressure on the votes in a particular Congress. One effort went into the development of a political action committee, Pax Americas, but its budget was far less than that of the National Conservative Political Action Committee (NCPAC).

Throughout the decade coalitions also tried to generate public awareness through large demonstrations. The most successful was the Mobilization for Justice and Peace in Central America and Southern Africa. It brought together trade unions and religious groups for the first time and spearheaded an April 1987 march on Washington with more than one hundred thousand people. But it paid little attention to Congress and was barely noticed there.[45]

Whether the lobbying campaigns had any effect on the media is uncertain. But the media themselves contributed to the development of congressional policy by helping to define a common wisdom about Nicaragua policy and aid to the contras. Editorials on contra aid in the *New York Times* and the *Washington Post* before major votes from 1983 to 1988 tended to be critical of the Nicaraguan government. Calling them "Nicaragua's leftist tyrants," the *Times* charged in 1986 that "the Sandinistas have ... installed a totalitarian security system. ... The Sandinista junta has also meddled in its neighbors' affairs. ..." The *Post* asserted in 1986 that unquestionably "the Sandinistas are communists of the Soviet or Cuban school." Editorials also were hostile toward the administration's policy. In 1985, for example, the *Times* declared that "there is nothing unpatriotic about this resistance to the contra war." The contras, it asserted a year later, were organized by the CIA and "offer little hope of a democratic redemption." Still, both papers favored some form of aid to the contras. For example, the *Post* called on Congress in April 1985 to stop military aid to the contras, but "if it is not going to support that cause with either indirect or direct military means . . . it ought to support it with other means: diplomatic, political and economic." [46]

It is important also to appreciate how the 1984 and 1986 elections affected aid to the contras. Although the 1984 Reagan landslide brought a few new members to Congress who could be counted on to support aid to the contras, it is notable that the president lost on his first contra aid vote in the second term. Yet the new members did contribute to the reversal in June 1985, when the House endorsed a $27 million aid package.

One explanation for the switch is electoral vulnerability. Some members were said to be troubled by their defiance of the clearly popular president and feared being labeled "soft on communism." [47] The members who switched from their stand in April, however, overwhelmingly had run ahead of the president in their districts. Only the six first-term members who switched might reasonably have felt vulnerable. Four of them barely ran ahead of the president, and two ran behind him. Moreover, new members are likely to feel greater vulnerability than more senior members, merely because they do not know from experience how a charged issue might affect their constituents. Thus electoral vulnerability falls short as a general explanation of congressional behavior on contra aid, though the first-termers' vote changes alone would have sufficed to produce contra aid, and vulnerability may have been important to them.

Vulnerability can be further discounted in light of senators' and representatives' experiences. Although NCPAC attempted to make support for the contras a litmus test issue in 1986—it labeled targeted legislators the "Ortega 33"—not one senator or representative lost a seat because of anticontra votes. In part, this can be explained by the issue's lack of salience among the public at large.

There was also consistent public opposition to contra funding and to U.S. military intervention against Nicaragua. [48] When pollsters first began asking about aid to the contras in early 1983, they found that about 60 percent of the public opposed aid and only about 25 percent favored it. These proportions remained unchanged over the succeeding years. In March and April of 1986, 62 percent of respondents opposed aiding the contras, and less than 30 percent were in favor, though a majority favored some effort to "prevent the spread of communism in Central America." Still, over time there was decreasing approval for the use of force, and polls taken in mid-1988 still showed 57 percent opposed and only 27 percent in favor of contra aid.[49]

Overall, the 1986 election had an even greater effect on congressional policy than the 1984 landslide did, and in the opposite direction. When the Democrats regained majority control of the Senate, the White House could no longer count on victories there. This dominance reinvigorated House Democrats, who envisioned that with majorities in both chambers they might be able to legislate the elusive congressional alternative to the executive's policy.

Regional Activities and Events

What continued to animate the congressional search for an alternative was, as many saw it, the inappropriateness of the administration's policy for the evolving situation in Nicaragua. Indeed, after 1983 the House in particular was sensitive to regional diplomatic initiatives to end the contra war. Many members repeatedly signaled their desire to avoid direct U.S. military involvement and to support negotiated solutions to the problems they perceived. When negotiations seemed to make headway, House majorities did pull back on contra aid. When they bogged down, House Democrats found it more difficult to muster a majority against contra military assistance.

Consider the 1984 mining of Nicaragua's harbors. This covert operation may have "pissed off" Sen. Barry Goldwater, R-Ariz., only because he was inadequately informed about it. But many other members expressed outrage at the action itself and at the subsequent U.S. stance before the World Court. These events led directly to the House cutoff of aid that fall. Movement in the Contadora process and boasts by a National Security Council staffer in September 1984 that the administration had scuttled the diplomatic efforts to achieve peace also created disquiet on Capitol Hill about the president's policy.[50] That fall the contra program was cut off by passage of the Boland amendment.

In March 1986 the House once again refused to fund the contras. Many considerations contributed to the outcome, especially Speaker O'Neill's determination. But the vote followed on the heels of the Caraballeda declaration and its endorsement by the five Central American presidents. By June, when Congress approved President Reagan's $100 million request, the regional diplomatic efforts seemed to be floundering with little hope of revival.

It was the Esquipulas plan that set in motion the final movement toward a congressional policy. That Speaker Wright had joined President Reagan in proposing a bipartisan alternative the day before the Central American presidents met and had quickly acceded to the

Esquipulas plan added an incentive for members to support a diplomatic approach to the achievement of their objectives for Nicaragua: their own leader now was heavily involved in the peace process. Although the initial plan was implemented only in part, members of Congress became extraordinarily sensitive to President Arias's interpretations of how well proposed contra aid plans would correspond to the August 1987 Esquipulas accords.

An Evolving Congressional Policy

Congress, like the White House, was aware that several audiences were watching its legislative struggle over Nicaragua policy. One was the Nicaraguan government, which members of Congress hoped would modify its behavior. As Bill Richardson, D-N.M., warned in April 1985, the Nicaraguans had better "clean up their act" or they would face a renewal of contra aid.[51] A second audience was the U.S. public. Hearings, speeches, and even symbolic votes were often no more than efforts to assuage potentially angry constituents. Some members on both sides also hoped they could educate and persuade the public in order to facilitate the development of congressional policy.

The final audience was the administration. Repeatedly, members tried to indicate to Reagan administration officials which proposals might be acceptable and which were out of bounds. Members who wanted some form of contra aid, but who also recognized that congressional sentiment was inclined against the overthrow of the Nicaraguan government, attempted to encourage the administration to develop diplomatic initiatives. Such congressional prompting in part led to the administration entering into talks with the Nicaraguans in Manzanillo, Mexico, in 1984. But by the end of 1985, those within the administration who advocated a diplomatic solution were gone.[52] Members of Congress had no official who would listen to their advice.

This was especially difficult for the Republicans in Congress. The congressional environment encourages negotiation and bargaining, and members tend to avoid conflict. Although the contra aid debate frequently had a partisan cast to it and often was quite heated, congressional Republicans were far more willing to negotiate compromises than were administration officials who advocated all or nothing strategies.[53] Indeed, Sen. Richard Lugar, R-Ind., who chaired the Foreign Relations Committee in 1985 and 1986, had made bipartisanship his principal goal. The Republicans were thus not mere puppets of the administration, willing to do whatever bidding the administration demanded. They were less heterodox than the Democrats, and they tended to follow the administration's general direction. But they supported the president "with doubts," as one Republican remarked during a 1987 interview. Despite themselves, in the process of seeking compromises, they helped to fashion what became a distinctively congressional policy toward Nicaragua.

Essential elements of the congressional policy—support for diplomatic and regional plans that would pressure the Nicaraguan government to reform internally—are evident in the accord signed by President Bush and congressional leaders on March 24, 1989. In it, the administration promised to support the negotiating efforts of the Central American presidents and to refrain from military pressure on the Sandinistas during the period leading up to Nicaraguan elections in February 1990. Congress agreed to extend nonlethal assistance to the contras in the form of food and medicine until February 28, 1990, with the proviso that aid could be cut off by Congress after November 30, 1989.[54]

As early as 1982 some members did advocate the approach evident in the bipartisan accord. But at that point a distinctive congressional policy did not exist. U.S. policy was essentially the policy of the president. The old adage prevailed: the president proposed and the Congress disposed. The House Intelligence Committee did specify that the contra war was to be limited to the interdiction of arms, but it was merely dictating that the administration implement its policy as stated. Moreover, members of Congress ranged across the spectrum in their views about policy toward Nicaragua from those who advocated aid to the Nicaraguan government and nothing for the contras to those who endorsed an all-out war to overthrow the Sandinista-led government. By 1985, however, the inclination was plainly evident to develop an alternative policy, one that went beyond negating the executive's pursuit of contra military aid and that embodied a different approach to Nicaragua. At that point members actively sought a common ground on which a congressional policy could be built.

Recall that a majority of the House repeatedly rejected the administration's approach between July 1983 and April 1985, though it could not settle on an alternative. By 1985 there was a widely shared belief that the administration wanted to use the contras and the CIA to overthrow the Nicaraguan government.[55] A majority of representatives sought, in contrast, to demilitarize, to find ways to pressure the Nicaraguans to increase the participation of non-Sandinistas, and to end alleged support for insurgencies in other countries. Even most liberals by this point expressed disapproval of the Sandinista-led Nicaraguan government, though they hoped to pressure the Nicaraguans through nonmilitary means.[56]

Slowly, over the next two years, as the factors outlined in the preceding section affected them, members experimented with policy formulations that might achieve the objectives a majority had begun to articulate. The twists and turns of congressional policy were not merely passive reactions to differing pressures and events. They were proactive efforts to forge a workable policy that could consistently command majority support. At the same time, a large minority bloc in the House consistently supported aid to the contras, which in most years included military assistance.

The outlines of the congressional policy are evident from public statements and interviews by a cross section of Congress and ultimately from the March 1989 bipartisan agreement. In effect, the policy supported by a majority of Congress stipulated four points:

1. The two primary goals of U.S. policy should be, first, to achieve a pluralist, democratic political system in Nicaragua but without overthrowing the Nicaraguan government by force of arms; and second, to prevent the Nicaraguan government from committing aggression against neighboring countries.
2. The United States should achieve its objectives by using diplomatic means. In this regard, the United States should encourage and support the countries in Central America in their efforts to develop regional mechanisms for the promotion and maintenance of peace.[57]
3. The United States, however, should maintain pressure on the Nicaraguan government to engage in an internal dialogue with the armed and unarmed opposition, to open up its political system to non-Sandinista groups, to implement regional agreements, to reduce the size of its military, and to reduce its links to the Soviet Union and countries in the Warsaw Pact and Council of Mutual Economic Assistance.[58]
4. In addition, because the poor economies of Central America contribute to instability and discourage regional cooperation, the United States should provide regional economic assistance and support regional development plans.

It was these basic points that were embodied in the 1989 bipartisan agreement. Notably, there had been disagreement between the administration and Congress on three of the four points. The Reagan administration sought to overthrow the Nicaraguan government by force of arms, it eschewed diplomatic approaches to a resolution of the war, and it saw the contras as essential in maintaining pressure on the Nicaraguan government. Until March 1989 both Congress and the executive had succeeded in achieving some aspects of their policies and had failed to achieve others. That neither branch consistently prevailed for much of the decade contributed to the sense of policy incoherence.

Congress was most successful in cutting off military aid—and at times all official U.S. aid—to the contras. This success did undermine much of the contras' war-making capability. Congress also determined where U.S. troops could be deployed and how U.S. forces might assist the contras. It placed restrictions on what the contras could do, and it pressured them to reform their organization and to reduce human rights violations. In a similar way, congressional threats to unleash the contras were aimed at encouraging the Sandinistas to institute reforms inside Nicaragua.

Congress also legitimated regional efforts to develop and implement peace plans and to negotiate a resolution of differences between the Sandinistas and the opposition. These efforts were especially notable because, by excluding the United States, they broke dramatically with 150 years of practice. For the first time, Latin Americans seized the initiative from the northern colossus. Congress encouraged this assertion of independence in two ways. First, in lauding the Central Americans— much as the Swedes did in awarding the Nobel Peace Prize to President Arias—members of Congress demonstrated that some politically influential North Americans would try to insulate Latin American countries from administration reprisals. Second, by crafting legislation in accord with regional plans, Congress indicated that a major U.S. institution favored the Central Americans' efforts. Through the Speaker and some individual members, Congress even carried on a kind of negotiation with regional leaders about what sorts of funding might be provided and withheld for the contras and for regional development.

Finally, congressional opposition to the use of U.S. military force provided an additional, and perhaps telling, blow to any hopes some administration officials had of invading Nicaragua. Invasion may never have been a live option, but it was implicitly threatened. The military reportedly opposed the use of U.S. forces against Nicaragua, in part because such an operation promised to bog the United States down in a long and intensive guerrilla war and in part because there was little public support for an invasion. Church groups threatened massive domestic demonstrations if Nicaragua were invaded, and U.S. allies discouraged the use of military force. Still, had Congress been willing to countenance an invasion, advocates of force within the executive branch might have been given sufficient succor for invasion plans to have proceeded.

The Limits of Alternative Foreign Policy Making

The executive branch, too, prevailed in significant ways. First, it was able to secure approximately $250 million for the contras from

1982 until 1989 and to help build up this insurgent force from a remnant of the National Guard to a fifteen-thousand-person army. The contra war forced the Nicaraguan government to divert scarce resources away from development into national defense and to create a state of emergency that led to repression and fueled discontent against the Sandinistas. Fighting disrupted the economy and engendered considerable migration, which further weakened the government.

Other elements of the so-called low-intensity war against Nicaragua were put in place, either with little congressional awareness, with congressional acquiescence, or with congressional endorsement.[59] The CIA provided the contras with logistical, training, and intelligence support and attacked strategic locations with their "unilaterally controlled Latino assets." [60] Military maneuvers off the Nicaraguan coast and in Honduras continually led the Sandinistas to believe a U.S. invasion was in the offing and helped to keep them off balance.[61] Economic sanctions, which included a reduction of the sugar quota, an embargo, and pressure on international financial institutions and commercial banks to deny loans to Nicaragua, contributed to the havoc that the Nicaraguan economy suffered.[62]

Ultimately, the administration's major achievement was that it set the policy agenda. It was able to define Nicaragua as a threat to U.S. security interests and to maintain that internal restructuring of the Nicaraguan polity was essential to protect the United States because the Sandinistas were Marxist-Leninists who could not be trusted to uphold any diplomatic agreement.[63]

In effect, the consensus that emerged in Congress embodied major elements of the Reagan agenda. Congress did resist funding a proxy war aimed at overthrowing the Nicaraguan government, but it agreed that the United States should try to influence the internal affairs of Nicaragua. The main question that vexed Congress was how to achieve this objective. In making this critical compromise, Congress ultimately bowed to the administration.

Congress was at first inclined to focus only on Nicaragua's foreign policy, where it was concerned about the alleged subversion of neighboring Central American countries. The first Boland amendment was cast in these terms and was aimed at holding the administration to its own stated intention of interdicting arms. A slow, evolutionary process led members of Congress to share the president's view that the United States should attempt to alter internal Nicaraguan politics. Whether or not the legislators recognized that this aim derived from a disputed set of assumptions about Nicaragua, they had ceased debating the assumptions by 1985. In part, this explains the phenomenon perceived by lobbyists both for and against the contras that members no longer wanted information about Nicaragua and that increased information contributed little to the outcome of votes in Congress.

In reality, events in the region continued to influence Congress. Members did not focus solely on domestic politics, but they had decided U.S. policy should have dual goals: to alter Nicaragua's foreign and internal politics. Although these goals were essentially similar to the president's, Congress differed with him about the degree of necessary reform in Nicaragua and about the means that should be used to achieve reform. Regional events shaped congressional judgments on these matters.

Nicaragua, however, may have felt that Congress played a minor role in shaping policy. By the time that Congress had all but forced the contras to disband, the war against Nicaragua had devastated the economy and contributed to an erosion of gains made in the early days after the revolution. Members often complained that the Sandinista leadership was insensitive to political pressures faced by Congress—as, for example, when President Daniel Ortega traveled to Moscow in 1985 or ended the unilateral cease-fire against the contras in October 1989. But the Nicaraguans perceived Congress as equally insensitive to their desperate circumstances. They privately complained that Congress had neglected or been left out of significant aspects of the war, apart from direct U.S. support of the contras. These areas included U.S. military threats, economic assaults, and encouragement of third-country contra funding. Sandinista officials at times may have been unresponsive to congressional demands, therefore, because it did not seem that Nicaraguan behavior mattered enough for legislators to alter U.S. policy toward that country.

An assessment of the limits of alternative congressional policy making thus depends on one's vantage point. If the focus is on means, the congressional policy was significant. Congress eventually determined that the contras would not be the instrument of policy and that diplomacy would take precedence over military means. It also reduced the likelihood that there would be direct U.S. military intervention in Nicaragua. With respect to policy aims, congressional policy departed less dramatically from the executive's. But Congress nonetheless helped to make U.S. policy aims accord with those of countries in the region. Notably, the Arias plan required internal as well as external changes in Nicaragua's politics. Finally, if an assessment were to focus on the effect of the policy on Nicaragua, it could well be argued that the administration's ability to act unilaterally overwhelmed Congress's will to restrain the executive. Congressional pressure may have influenced Nicaragua's decision to institute internal reforms, but the executive's low-intensity war had a greater direct effect on conditions in Nicaragua.

Whatever its limitations, however, the emergence of an alternative congressional policy toward Nicaragua was significant because the circumstances that led Congress to develop its own policy toward Nicaragua were not unique. In this case, Congress began to develop its own policy when the Reagan administration refused to accede to early congressional attempts to moderate the policy. Administration intransigence and persistence escalated the conflict between the branches, which was exacerbated by elements of deceit and obfuscation.

The Democrats might have simply used the congressional power of the purse to veto the executive's policy, but many moderate to conservative Democrats were concerned about Nicaragua's behavior and wanted the United States to remain involved in Central America. Others may have wanted merely to avoid appearing irresponsible and believed that by proposing an alternative they could escape the inevitable charge that they had abandoned Nicaragua to communists. Moreover, liberal and moderate Democrats feared that the administration's policy was leading toward a widening of the war and the direct involvement of U.S. troops. As the conflict with the administration persisted and Nicaragua policy remained a seemingly visible issue, Democrats felt ever more compelled to conceptualize a full-blown alternative to the administration's policy.

The Bush administration appears more accommodating than its predecessor, but it does not have the salve of the post-World War II consensus that was repeatedly able to smooth over differences between the branches in the 1950s and 1960s. Today, there is no consensus about the U.S. role in the world, about the way in which the United States should respond to developments in the Third World, or about which U.S. interests are vital and deserve military and paramilitary intervention. Differences over these fundamental issues are bound to arise again, as they did in the case of Nicaragua, and they are likely to prompt congressional efforts to modify administration behavior. This is the legacy of the 1970s foreign policy "revolution" in Congress: now members of Congress believe they should appropriately struggle with these issues. Until a new foreign policy consensus emerges between the executive and legislature, then, we are likely to witness efforts by legislators to develop distinctive congressional policies that contribute significantly to U.S. foreign policy.

Notes

We would like to thank Elizabeth Cohn and Kimberly Heimert for their research assistance on this chapter.

1. The most thorough examination of congressional activity on Nicaragua is Cynthia J. Arnson, *Crossroads: Congress, the Reagan Administration, and Central America* (New York: Pantheon, 1989). See also Morris J. Blachman and Kenneth E. Sharpe, "Central American Traps: Challenging the Reagan Agenda," *World Policy Journal* 5 (Winter 1987-1988): 1-28; Roy Gutman, *Banana Diplomacy: The Making of American Policy in Nicaragua, 1981-1987* (New York: Simon & Schuster, 1988); Victor Johnson, "Congress and Contra Aid," in *Latin America and Caribbean Contemporary Record, 1987-1988,* ed. Abraham F. Lowenthal (New York: Holmes & Meier, 1989); Peter Kornbluh, *Nicaragua: The Price of Intervention* (Washington, D.C.: Institute for Policy Studies, 1987); William M. LeoGrande, "The Contras and Congress," in *Reagan Versus the Sandinistas,* ed. Thomas W. Walker (Boulder, Colo.: Westview Press, 1987), 202-227; and Robert A. Pastor, *Condemned to Repetition: The United States and Nicaragua* (Princeton, N.J.: Princeton University Press, 1987).
2. House Select Committee to Investigate Covert Arms Transactions with Iran and Senate Select Committee on Secret Military Assistance to Iran and the Nicaraguan Opposition, *Report of the Congressional Committees Investigating the Iran-Contra Affair,* H. Rept. 100-433, S. Rept. 100-216, November 1987, 100th Cong., 1st sess. (Washington, D.C.: U.S. Government Printing Office, 1987), 668, 669. (Hereafter cited as *Iran-Contra Report.)*
3. Notably, Baker's meetings with congressional leaders occurred in Congress, and Baker engaged in the negotiations personally.
4. For example, see Philip Brenner, *The Limits and Possibilities of Congress* (New York: St. Martin's Press, 1983); Cecil V. Crabb, Jr., and Pat M. Holt, *Invitation to Struggle: Congress, the President and Foreign Policy,* 3d ed. (Washington, D.C.: CQ Press, 1989); I. M. Destler, "Executive-Congressional Conflict in Foreign Policy: Explaining It, Coping with It," in *Congress Reconsidered,* 3d ed., ed. Lawrence C. Dodd and Bruce I. Oppenheimer (Washington, D.C.: CQ Press, 1985); Thomas M. Franck and Edward Weisband, *Foreign Policy by Congress* (New York: Oxford University Press, 1979); Susan Webb Hammond, "Congress and Foreign Policy," in *The Congress, the President and Foreign Policy,* ed. Edmund S. Muskie et al. (Lanham, Md.: University Press of America, 1986); and Charles W. Whalen, *The House and Foreign Policy* (Chapel Hill: University of North Carolina Press, 1982).
5. Franck and Weisband, *Foreign Policy by Congress,* 3-9.
6. For example, Pastor, *Condemned to Repetition,* 275, writes that "Congress plays the role of balancer of U.S. national interests."

7. Dick Cheney, "Congressional Overreaching in Foreign Policy," in *Foreign Policy and the Constitution,* ed. Robert A. Goldwin and Robert A. Licht (Washington, D.C.: American Enterprise Institute, 1990), 106-108.

8. See Gutman, *Banana Diplomacy.*

9. Gutman, *Banana Diplomacy,* chap. 14; Kornbluh, *Nicaragua,* chap. 4; Bob Woodward, *Veil: The Secret Wars of the CIA* (New York: Simon & Schuster, 1987), 296-297, 389-390.

10. *Congressional Quarterly Almanac, 1980* (Washington, D.C.: Congressional Quarterly, 1981), 82B.

11. Woodward, *Veil,* 114-116. Presumably, a majority of Congress also had supported this approach in approving the aid in 1980, but Congress had permitted the president to withhold aid in the U.S. national interest. See Arnson, *Crossroads,* 35-40, 43-47.

12. Kornbluh, *Nicaragua,* 20-24; Gutman, *Banana Diplomacy,* 84-85; Don Oberdorfer and Patrick Tyler, "Rebel Army Swells to 7,000 Men," *Washington Post,* May 8, 1983. The National Security Act of 1947 and the 1974 Hughes-Ryan amendment to the Foreign Assistance Act of 1961 require that the president submit a "finding" to the intelligence committees of Congress whenever he initiates a covert operation. The intelligence committees are not empowered to approve or disapprove such findings, although they can refuse to authorize funds for any operation they oppose. For the applicable statutes, see House Permanent Select Committee on Intelligence, *Compilation of Intelligence Laws and Related Laws and Executive Orders of Interest to the National Intelligence Community,* 99th Cong., 1st sess., committee print (Washington, D.C.: U.S. Government Printing Office, 1985), 211-214. The December 1 finding on Nicaragua is reported and reproduced in redacted form in U.S. Congress, *Report of the Congressional Committees Investigating the Iran-Contra Affair,* Appendix C: Chronology of Events, H. Rept. 100-433, S. Rept. 100-216, November 13, 1987, 100th Cong., 1st sess. (Washington, D.C.: U.S. Government Printing Office, 1987), 1, 143. (Hereafter cited as *Iran-Contra Report Chronology.*)

13. Casey's plan reportedly was crafted as well to assuage critics within the Reagan administration. See Woodward, *Veil,* 171-177. See also Patrick E. Tyler and Bob Woodward, "U.S. Approves Covert Plan in Nicaragua," *Washington Post,* March 10, 1982, A1; and Alfonso Chardy, "How the U.S. Covert Campaign Against Sandinistas Originated," *Philadelphia Inquirer,* February 16, 1983.

14. John Felton, "Congress Sought to Place Limits Early on U.S. Covert Assistance to 'Contras,' " *Congressional Quarterly Weekly Report,* April 20, 1985, 710-711.

15. For interpretations of the Boland amendments, see Andrew W. Hayes, "The Boland Amendments and Foreign Affairs Deference," *Columbia Law Review* 88 (1988): 1566-1569.

16. Arnson, *Crossroads,* 101-103; Kornbluh, *Nicaragua,* 55; LeoGrande, "Contras and Congress," 205-206.

17. John Felton, "On Foreign Aid, More Stumbling Blocks," *Congressional Quarterly Weekly Report,* October 6, 1984, 2418.
18. Public opinion remained opposed to contra aid, though a majority of respondents at the time did not know against which country—Nicaragua or El Salvador—the United States was supporting an insurgency or which of the two countries had U.S. backing. See William M. LeoGrande, *Central America and the Polls* (Washington, D.C.: Washington Office on Latin America, 1987).
19. Adolfo Aguilar Zinser, "Negotiation in Conflict: Central America and Contadora," in *Crisis in Central America,* ed. Nora Hamilton et al. (Boulder, Colo.: Westview Press, 1988), 97-115; Bruce Michael Bagley and Juan Gabriel Tokatlian, *Contadora: The Limits of Negotiation,* Foreign Policy Institute Case Studies 9 (Lanham, Md.: University Press of America, 1987); William Goodfellow, "The Diplomatic Front," in *Reagan Versus the Sandinistas,* 148-152.
20. *Iran-Contra Report,* chaps. 6 and 7.
21. Arnson, *Crossroads,* 184-185.
22. Kornbluh, *Nicaragua,* 101-103. Congressional Quarterly reported that "conservative Democratic senators had led the call for Reagan to impose sanctions as an alternative to military support of anti-Sandinista 'contras.'" See John Felton, "Reagan Imposes Trade Embargo on Nicaragua," *Congressional Quarterly Weekly Report,* May 4, 1985, 828. See also Gutman, *Banana Diplomacy,* 285-287.
23. Kornbluh, *Nicaragua,* chap. 2; Michael E. Conroy, "Economic Aggression as an Instrument of Low-Intensity Warfare," in *Reagan Versus the Sandinistas,* 65-72.
24. John Felton, "Reagan Gets Conflicting Advice on 'Contra' Aid," *Congressional Quarterly Weekly Report,* February 15, 1986, 306.
25. Goodfellow, "Diplomatic Front," 152; Johnson, "Congress and Contra Aid."
26. Arnson, *Crossroads,* 193-195.
27. "Reagan Letter on Aid to Nicaraguan Rebels," *Congressional Quarterly Weekly Report,* June 15, 1985, 1173.
28. William Buzenberg, "Who Got the $27 Million Intended for the Contras?" *New York Times,* June 19, 1986.
29. The most inflammatory rhetoric had come from White House communications director Patrick J. Buchanan. In an op-ed piece he warned, "With the vote on contra aid, the Democratic Party will reveal whether it stands with Ronald Reagan and the resistance—or Daniel Ortega and the communists." See "The Contras Need Our Help," *Washington Post,* March 5, 1986.
30. John Felton, "The Peace Option to Get a Fresh Airing in Upcoming Talks on Regional Plan," *Congressional Quarterly Weekly Report,* March 14, 1987, 462-463; John Felton, "Arias' Plan Has Yet to Bring Real Peace to the Political Factions on Capitol Hill," *Congressional Quarterly Weekly Report,* August 15, 1987, 1892-1893.

31. House Democratic Caucus Task Force on Central America, "Peace, Democracy, and Development: A Democratic Alternative" (Washington, D.C.: House Democratic Caucus Task Force on Central America, 1986, mimeographed).

32. The members of the group were identified on the basis of interviews. For discussion of the origins of the McCurdy group, see Arnson, *Crossroads,* 184.

33. Arnson, *Crossroads,* 188-189; Gutman, *Banana Diplomacy,* 289-290; LeoGrande, "Contras and Congress," 211-213.

34. House Arms Control and Foreign Policy Caucus, "Who Are the Contras?" (Washington, D.C.: House Arms Control and Foreign Policy Caucus, April 18, 1985).

35. John Felton, "Nicaragua Peace Process Moves to Capitol Hill," *Congressional Quarterly Weekly Report,* November 14, 1987, 2789-2791.

36. Arnson, *Crossroads,* 197-198.

37. Kornbluh, *Nicaragua,* 160-166; Robert Parry and Peter Kornbluh, "Iran-Contra's Untold Story," *Foreign Policy* 72 (Fall 1988): 3-30; *Iran-Contra Report,* chap. 4.

38. Gutman, *Banana Diplomacy,* 282, asserts there was yet another target of the public relations: "The audience that mattered to North and Casey was Ronald Reagan himself, and he was impressed."

39. Kornbluh, *Nicaragua,* 184. See also Daniel Siegel and Tom Spaulding with Peter Kornbluh, *Outcast Among Allies: The International Costs of Reagan's War Against Nicaragua* (Washington, D.C.: Institute for Policy Studies, 1985); and Stuart Holland and Donald Anderson, *Kissinger's Kingdom: A Counter-Report on Central America* (London: Spokesman, 1984).

40. Gutman, *Banana Diplomacy,* chap. 7; Woodward, *Veil,* chap. 13.

41. John Felton, "Contra-Aid Denial Shifts Burden to Democrats," *Congressional Quarterly Weekly Report,* February 6, 1988, 237.

42. Philip Brenner, "Waging Ideological War: Anti-Communism and US Policy in Central America," in *Socialist Register 1984,* ed. Ralph Miliband et al. (London: Merlin Press, 1984).

43. From 1983 to 1988, there were 535 different members in the House. Of these, 377 voted consistently on nineteen major contra aid votes. Some of the remaining 158 members were inconsistent on only one or two votes. Generally, about 50 members in any one year were likely to be vulnerable to pressure. For an extended discussion of these findings, see William M. LeoGrande and Philip Brenner, "The House Divided: Ideological Polarization in the U.S. House of Representatives over Assistance to the Nicaraguan 'Contras,'" unpublished manuscript, December 1989.

44. Cynthia J. Arnson and Philip Brenner, "The Limits of Lobbying: Interest Groups, Congress and Aid to the Contras," in *Public Opinion and Policy Toward Central America: The Case of Aid to the Nicaraguan Contras,* ed. Richard Sobel (Lexington, Mass.: Lexington Books, forthcoming); Gutman, *Banana Diplomacy,* 331-334; Steven Pressman, "White House

on the Defensive: Massive Lobbying Campaign Waged over Aid for 'Contras,' " *Congressional Quarterly Weekly Report,* April 20, 1985, 715-716; *Iran-Contra Report,* 87-92; Paul Starobin and Jeremy Gaunt, "Campaign Charges: Activities of Pro-Contra Groups Come Under Scrutiny," *Congressional Quarterly Weekly Report,* December 20, 1986, 3096-3097.

45. Beverly Bickel, Philip Brenner, and William LeoGrande, *Challenging the Reagan Doctrine: A Summation of the April 25th Mobilization* (Washington, D.C.: Foreign Policy Education Fund, 1987), 39-42.

46. "The Nicaraguan Horror Show," *New York Times,* March 18, 1986, A26; "The President's Nicaragua Appeal," *Washington Post,* March 18, 1986, A10; "Contadora or Contra?" *New York Times,* April 23, 1985, A26; "Congress on Nicaragua," *Washington Post,* April 23, 1985, A14.

47. John Felton, "House, in Dramatic Shift, Backs 'Contra' Aid," *Congressional Quarterly Weekly Report,* June 15, 1985, 1140.

48. LeoGrande, *Central America and the Polls,* 25-29.

49. Ibid. See also Richard Sobel, "Public Opinion About United States Intervention in El Salvador and Nicaragua," *Public Opinion Quarterly* 53 (Spring 1989): 115; Gallup Organization, "U.S. Assistance to Nicaragua," *Gallup Report* (July 1988): 11.

50. National Security Council, "Background Paper for NSC Meeting on Central America," October 30, 1984, cited in Kornbluh, *Nicaragua,* 182; Arnson, *Crossroads,* 155-168.

51. John Felton, "In Major Defeat, Reagan Loses 'Contra' Aid," *Congressional Quarterly Weekly Report,* April 27, 1985, 781.

52. Gutman, *Banana Diplomacy,* 297.

53. Arnson, *Crossroads,* 141-142; Gutman, *Banana Diplomacy,* 280-281.

54. For the text of the agreement, see "Bipartisan Agreement Reached on Central America," *Congressional Quarterly Weekly Report,* March 25, 1989, 669. The congressional cutoff could have occurred if any of four committees—House and Senate Appropriations, House Foreign Affairs, and Senate Foreign Relations—voted to suspend aid.

55. Felton, "House, in Dramatic Shift, Backs 'Contra' Aid," 1139-1140; Pastor, *Condemned to Repetition,* 250-251.

56. Gutman, *Banana Diplomacy,* 289.

57. Though there was broad support for this general objective, conservative Democrats and Republicans diverged from the full implications of this goal. The Contadora treaties, for example, would have required the demilitarization of Central America, including a reduction in U.S. military aid and an end of the U.S. military presence there. Many Democrats, but not a majority of Congress, embraced this requirement as an objective of U.S. policy.

58. A broad underlying theme evident in congressional deliberations was that the United States should thwart the development of communism in Central America. Members rarely were clear about what this objective meant, however. For some, communism was a code word for the Soviet

Union and countries allied with it in military and economic pacts. For others, communism signified a system of state ownership or single party rule. To a small number of members, a state was communist merely if it exhibited anti-U.S. sentiments.

59. Peter Kornbluh, "Nicaragua: U.S. Proinsurgency Warfare Against the Sandinistas," in *Low Intensity Warfare,* ed. Michael T. Klare and Peter Kornbluh (New York: Pantheon, 1988), 136-157.

60. Woodward, *Veil,* 320.

61. Eva Gold, "Military Encirclement," in *Reagan Versus the Sandinistas;* Kornbluh, *Nicaragua,* chap. 3.

62. Peter Kornbluh, "Uncle Sam's Money War Against the Sandinistas," *Washington Post,* August 27, 1989; Conroy, "Economic Aggression as an Instrument of Low-Intensity Warfare."

63. Blachman and Sharpe, "Central American Traps," 8-13. See also Arnson, *Crossroads,* 173-174; Kornbluh, *Nicaragua,* 166-179; and Wayne S. Smith, "Lies About Nicaragua," *Foreign Policy* 67 (Summer 1987): 87-103. Notably, members of Congress disagreed about the nature of the Sandinistas. Some agreed with the administration that the Sandinistas could not be trusted to implement an accord. For these members, restructuring meant the Sandinistas could not control the Nicaraguan military or government, even if they permitted non-Sandinistas a significant measure of political power. A majority of Congress ultimately agreed with regional negotiators that neither removal of the Sandinistas nor assurance of them being placed in only minor posts was a necessary precondition of an accord.

12. CONGRESS AND THE REMOVAL POWER

Louis Fisher

The gulf between judicial doctrines and political practice often runs wide and deep. There are many opinions by the U.S. Supreme Court that broadly uphold the president's power to remove officials within the executive agencies and independent commissions. Quite different interpretations have been advanced by Congress or through accommodations reached between the executive and legislative branches. Compare two conflicting positions on the removal power: one by a jurist, the other by an administrator. In 1926 Chief Justice William Howard Taft declared that the power to remove executive officers "is in its nature an executive power." Congress had no right "to draw to itself, or to either branch of it, the power to remove or the right to participate in the exercise of that power." [1] Harold Seidman, a sophisticated student of the federal government, offers a decidedly different view: "Probably more executive branch officials have been fired or reassigned as a result of pressure from the Congress than by the president." [2]

What does Seidman know that Taft declined to tell? Congressional participation in the removal power has been, without question, extensive and ongoing. Members of Congress realize that control over federal programs often means control over federal personnel. For that reason they have been instrumental in driving some officeholders out of government and protecting others who face dismissal, demotion, or reprimand. This chapter identifies the techniques of removal available to Congress, explains the motivations behind their use, and sets general boundaries for legislative involvement.

The Source of the Removal Power

The power to remove executive officials is not mentioned in the Constitution except through the impeachment process. The president, the vice president, and "all civil officers of the United States" shall be removed from office on impeachment for, and conviction of, treason, bribery, or "other high Crimes and Misdemeanors." The House of Representatives, acting by majority vote, has the exclusive power to bring charges of impeachment. The Senate, which has the sole authority to try impeachment charges, needs a two-thirds vote for conviction.

Some members of the First Congress concluded that the Constitution sanctioned one, and only one, means of removal: impeachment. This position was rejected in part because it assumed that every official held office during good behavior—a tenure guaranteed under the Constitution only to judges. Moreover, impeachment was a cumbersome, highly formalized process that could scarcely be directed against every ineffective officer whose conduct fell short of treason, bribery, and "other high crimes and misdemeanors."

Other members of the First Congress believed that since the Senate participates in the appointment of an officer it should consent also to a removal. Most of the debate, however, focused on two alternatives: (1) the president, in order to carry out his constitutional duties, may remove administrators at will, and (2) Congress, since it creates an office, may attach to it any conditions it decides appropriate, including tenure and grounds for removal.

James Madison wanted the removal power vested in the president. He argued that the power to remove was implied in the Constitution as a necessary means of preserving the responsibility and unity of the executive office. To fulfill the president's constitutional duty to "take care that the laws be faithfully executed," Madison said it was essential that the president be allowed to dismiss incompetent, corrupt, or unreliable administrators.[3]

Madison's concern for the integrity of executive power is echoed in Chief Justice Taft's opinion in *Myers v. United States* (1926). Taft reasoned that the delegates at the Philadelphia Convention could not have meant to thwart the president in the exercise of his constitutional duties by "fastening upon him, as subordinate executive officers, men who by their inefficient service under him, by their lack of loyalty to the service, or by their different views of policy, might make his taking care that the laws be faithfully executed most difficult or impossible."[4]

Taft considered only one scenario: presidents unable to execute the laws because of ineffective or disloyal subordinates. He did not admit that presidents might be *unwilling* to execute the laws. What could members of Congress do if political appointees, with the blessing of the White House, flouted the laws? Could Congress act only through the laborious impeachment process? And if career members of the civil service tried faithfully to carry out laws that the president opposed, could he fire them at will?

In their trenchant dissents in *Myers*, Justices Oliver Wendell Holmes, Jr., James McReynolds, and Louis Brandeis sketched out a broader framework for congressional and presidential responsibility. They pointed out that Congress creates offices, abolishes them, and may set conditions on the duration of an office. McReynolds reviewed previous actions by Congress in protecting officeholders: civil service reform, provisions that restricted removals to specified causes (usually inefficiency, neglect of duty, or malfeasance in office), and statutory requirements for notice and hearing prior to removal.

Brandeis, in his dissent, distinguished between high political officers and inferior administrative officers appointed for fixed terms. The removal or suspension of the former "might be deemed indispensable to democratic government and, hence, inherent in the President," but Brandeis refused to extend that argument to lower officials. Their status depended on the statutory conditions attached to the office they occupied.

The broadness of Taft's opinion could not survive. Eventually the Court recognized that Congress, acting through the necessary and proper clause, could limit the president's power to remove. Under Article I, section 8, Congress is empowered to make all laws "which shall be necessary and proper for carrying into Execution the foregoing Powers, and all other Powers vested by this Constitution in the Government of the United States, or in any Department or Officer thereof." In 1935 the Court acknowledged that Congress, in creating agencies to carry out legislative and judicial duties, could restrict the president's removal power to specified causes.[5]

Congressional prerogatives are especially potent in matters pertaining to the District of Columbia. Article I of the Constitution empowers Congress to exercise "exclusive Legislation in all Cases whatsoever, over such District...." When President Ronald Reagan removed a member of the D.C. Judicial Nomination Commission, a federal court in 1981 overturned the removal as a violation of statutory procedures. The court denied that it was an inherent or necessary executive function to remove commissioners whose duties are confined exclusively to local District matters. Because of the unique jurisdiction of Congress, the Constitution "appears to contemplate a larger role for the Congress in managing the District than is the case with the more equal sharing the Constitution speaks of for managing federal matters and the federal government."[6]

Congressional Efforts to Remove Officials

Congress has the power to determine how long a federal employee remains in office. It can define, by statute, the tenure of an office. In 1820 Congress passed legislation that limited a large number of federal officers to a term of four years (3 Stat. 582). Although the legislative debate on this bill fails to explain the legislative motivation, correspondence from contemporaries suggests that the purpose was to institute a regular system of accountability. By reviewing the work of employees after a set period, government could retain the most competent civil servants.[7]

Madison objected to the statute, calling it an encroachment upon the president's removal power. If a law could displace an officer every four years, "it can do so at the end of every year, or at every session of the Senate, and the tenure will then be the pleasure of the Senate, as much as of the President, & not of the P. alone." [8] As it turned out, the statute benefited the president by automatically making available a pool of patronage. President Andrew Jackson removed more officers than all the presidents before him: 252 for Jackson and 193 for his predecessors.[9] Although the numbers are large, they are less impressive as a percentage of a growing bureaucracy. They do not constitute anything near the "clean sweep" often suggested by historians and political scientists.[10]

Abolishing and Recreating Positions

Madison acknowledged that Congress had the power to abolish an office, "by which the officer indirectly looses [sic] his place. . . ." But he worried that if the office were abolished "merely to get rid of the tenant, and with a view, by its reestablishment, to let in a new one, on whom the Senate would have a negative, it would be a virtual infringement of the constitutional distribution of the powers of Government." [11]

Sen. Robert Griffin, R-Mich., suggested this approach in 1973 as a way of dislodging Roy Ash from his position as director of the Office of Management and Budget.[12] The Nixon administration objected that Ash's removal by abolishing his office would amount to a bill of attainder and violate the president's removal power.[13] The bill that reached President Nixon required Senate confirmation of the director and deputy director of OMB at that time (Ash and Frederick Malek). Nixon vetoed the bill because it "would require the forced removal by an unconstitutional procedure of two officers now serving in the executive branch. This step would be a grave violation of the fundamental doctrine of separation of powers." The bill would have abolished the two positions thirty days after the bill's enactment and provided for their immediate reestablishment, subject to Senate confirmation. The veto message continued:

> I do not dispute Congressional authority to abolish an office or to specify appropriate standards by which the officers may serve. When an office is abolished, the tenure of the incumbent in that office ends. But the power of the Congress to terminate an office

cannot be used as a back-door method of circumventing the President's power to remove. With its abolition and immediate re-creation of two offices, S. 518 is a device—in effect and perhaps in intent—to accomplish Congressional removal of the incumbents who lawfully hold those offices.[14]

After failing to override the veto, Congress passed new legislation that applied the confirmation process only to future OMB directors and deputy directors (88 Stat. 11). Nixon's veto message, however, under-scores the ability of Congress to remove an individual by abolishing the office: "When an office is abolished, the tenure of the incumbent in that office ends." One Congress may not bind another. A term of office created by one statute can be reduced or eliminated by another, requiring an employee's discharge.[15]

Instead of abolishing an office, Congress can try to change the qualifications and indirectly remove incumbents. A bill presented to President Carter in 1978 provided that "no person who is serving in an elected Federal, State, or local public office shall be eligible to serve or continue to serve" as a member of the Navajo and Hopi Indian Relocation Commission. Carter vetoed the bill, objecting that it "would oust incumbent members" of the commission "if they happened to be Federal, State or local elected officials." The provision raised constitu-tional concerns, he said, "since it would allow for Congressional removal of officers in the Executive Branch." Interruption of the tenure of appointed officials by imposing new qualifications "should not be lightly undertaken." [16] Congress could have avoided the constitutional issue by applying the new qualifications only to future members of the commission. When Congress rewrote the bill it deleted the section on qualifications (94 Stat. 929).

Concurrent Resolutions

In 1920 Congress sent President Woodrow Wilson a bill to create a national budget system. Although sympathetic to the purposes behind the legislation, the president objected to a provision that restricted the removal of the comptroller general and the assistant comptroller general to impeachment or concurrent resolution, "and in no other manner." A concurrent resolution, which requires only the consent of the House and Senate, is not sent to the president for his signature or veto. Wilson believed that this provision trespassed on the president's implied power to remove executive officials:

> It has, I think, always been the accepted construction of the Constitution that the power to appoint officers of this kind carries with it, as an incident, the power to remove. I am convinced that

the Congress is without constitutional powers to limit the appointing power and its incident, the power of removal derived from the Constitution.

... Regarding as I do the power of removal from office as an essential incident to the appointing power, I cannot escape the conclusion that the vesting of this power of removal in the Congress is unconstitutional and therefore I am unable to approve the bill.[17]

Congress rewrote the bill to provide for removal of the two officers by joint resolution, a form of legislation submitted to the president for his signature or veto. In 1921 President Warren Harding signed this bill, the Budget and Accounting Act, into law. The joint resolution includes the president in the removal process, but the procedure allows Congress to *initiate* a removal. The reliance on a joint resolution to remove the comptroller general remains part of current law (31 U.S.C. 703). Although the comptroller general is generally considered part of the legislative branch, under certain circumstances the courts regard him as an executive officer.[18]

The question of using a concurrent resolution for removal arose again in 1933 when Congress created the Tennessee Valley Authority (TVA). The statute allowed Congress to remove any member of the board by concurrent resolution. Acting attorney general Robert H. Jackson advised President Roosevelt in 1938 that the statutory procedure for removals by concurrent resolution "could not have been intended" to provide an exclusive means of removal. Jackson pointed out that section 6 of the statute provided an alternative means of removal by the president. He interpreted the provision for a concurrent resolution as an effort on the part of Congress "to provide a method of removal by the legislative branch in addition to the more cumbersome method of removal by impeachment." [19] Federal courts agreed that there was not a clear enough intent by Congress in the TVA act to eliminate the president's power to remove TVA board members.[20] Although the removal by concurrent resolution remains part of current law, as section 831c(f) of Title 16 of the U.S. Code, this procedure has never been used. Only one board member has ever been removed: A. E. Morgan by President Franklin D. Roosevelt.

Sense-of-Congress Resolutions

Either house of Congress may pass a simple resolution, or both houses may pass a concurrent resolution, expressing their sentiment that the president should remove an executive official. Unlike the concurrent resolution for TVA, these resolutions are purely hortatory and have no legal effect. Still, they can create a climate that precipitates a removal or resignation.

In 1924, as a result of its investigation into the Teapot Dome scandal, the Senate passed a resolution stating that "it is the sense of the United States Senate that the President of the United States immediately request the resignation of Edwin Denby as Secretary of the Navy." Some senators objected that there was only one method of removal available to Congress: impeachment. To place the "brand of shame" upon an individual, said Sen. Selden Spencer, R-Mo., lacked the essentials of fair play accorded to the accused in legal proceedings. Sen. James Couzens, R-Mich., believed that the Senate had no more right to recommend the removal of a cabinet member than the cabinet could pass a resolution demanding the expulsion of a senator.[21]

In rebuttal, Sen. Robert LaFollette, R-Wis., denied that the Senate was violating the president's prerogatives. Practically every senator agreed that Denby, by transferring to the secretary of the interior the responsibility for the naval oil reserves, had surrendered duties that Congress had placed exclusively with him. Moreover, the Senate had already "invaded" the president's prerogative to enforce the laws. On January 29, 1924, the Senate passed a resolution directing the president to cancel the leases entered into by Secretary of the Interior Albert Fall. LaFollette reasoned that the pending resolution was consistent with the action of January 29.

Sen. Claude Swanson, D-W.Va., reminded his colleagues that Article IV of the Constitution gave Congress exclusive control over all property of the United States: "We are the constitutional guardians of that property. If we designated the President to sell it or otherwise dispose of it, he is our agent. If he designates the Secretary of the Navy to dispose of it, he is our agent." Since the president had the power of removal, it was appropriate for the Senate to ask him to remove an agent "constituted to do our business—because the business of administering the public lands and the public property belongs primarily to Congress."

Sen. Frank Brandegee, R-Conn., opposed the resolution for Denby's resignation. He argued that it was impertinent of the Senate to involve itself in the removal power. What would the Senate think, he asked, if the president sent a messenger with a communication that in his opinion the Senate should eject the president pro tempore of the Senate from his office? This analogy does not hold, however. The president and cabinet members carry out congressional policy. Senators do not execute presidential policy. Brandegee also asked what would be said of a senator who advocated the passage of a resolution stating that a certain judge should resign his office. Again, the analogy is misplaced. Judges do not function as agents of Congress, or certainly not in the manner of Secretary Denby and naval oil reserves.

The resolution passed, 47-34. On that same day President Calvin Coolidge announced that no official recognition could be given to the Senate resolution. The dismissal of an officer, "other than by impeachment, is exclusively an Executive function." [22] Nevertheless, Denby offered his resignation within a matter of days.

The House of Representatives has also adopted resolutions calling for an official's dismissal. In 1867, on the basis of investigative hearings conducted by the Committee on Public Expenditures, the House passed a resolution stating that "[i]t is the sense of this House that Henry A. Smythe should be removed from the office of collector of the port of New York, and that a copy of this resolution and the testimony be transmitted to the President of the United States." Although there were objections that the proper course was the impeachment procedure and that the removal of officers was an executive function, the resolution was agreed to, 68-37.[23]

Party Pressures

In 1862 a caucus of Republican senators passed a resolution calling for the dismissal of William H. Seward as secretary of state. A committee of senators met with President Abraham Lincoln to discuss the matter, and met again with him in the presence of cabinet members. Upon hearing of the caucus action, Seward at once sent his resignation to Lincoln. After further negotiation he remained with the cabinet.[24]

President Reagan's secretary of the interior, James Watt, came under repeated fire from Democrats who wanted him removed from office. Toward the end of 1981, the Sierra Club and other environmentalists presented Congress with petitions bearing more than a million signatures demanding Watt's ouster. Sen. Alan Cranston, D-Calif., called for Watt to step down.[25] In the summer of 1982, after Watt had sent a controversial letter to Israeli ambassador Moshe Arens, implying that U.S. support for Israel might be jeopardized if "liberals of the Jewish community" in America failed to support Reagan's energy policies, several members of Congress, including Sen. Daniel Patrick Moynihan and Rep. Benjamin S. Rosenthal, both New York Democrats, pressed for Watt's removal.[26]

More concerted action was taken against Reagan's secretary of labor, Raymond J. Donovan. After allegations had linked Donovan to organized crime and union corruption, the Senate Democratic Conference unanimously approved a letter asking Reagan to have Donovan step aside until the issues had been satisfactorily resolved.[27] The issue subsided when a lengthy report by a special prosecutor concluded that there was insufficient evidence to sustain the allegations.

Isolated cases of individual members of Congress demanding someone's removal are fairly common. Rep. Allen Ertel, D-Pa., in 1982, along with sixteen other representatives, sent a letter to President Reagan criticizing the expenditure of funds by Robert P. Nimmo, chief of the Veterans Administration, and calling for his dismissal. Responding to congressional criticism, Nimmo had previously reimbursed the government $6,441 for a chauffeur who had driven him between his home and office and announced that he would terminate a $708 per month government lease on a car with gas mileage in excess of government standards. He was awaiting further congressional action against the $54,183 he had spent remodeling his office. In October 1982, shortly before the release of a report on his expenditures from the General Accounting Office, Nimmo resigned.[28] Also in 1982 Sen. Paul Sarbanes and Reps. Michael Barnes and Steny Hoyer called for the resignation of Donald Devine, director of the Office of Personnel Management. The three Maryland Democrats were critical of Devine's announcements on budget reductions and layoffs of federal employees.[29]

Reconsidering a Nomination

In 1930 the Senate confirmed five members of the newly created Federal Power Commission. After some of the commission actions offended a group of senators, the Senate voted to reconsider its confirmation of three of the commissioners and requested President Herbert Hoover to return their nominations. Hoover replied that the appointments had been constitutionally made and that he could not "admit the power in the Senate to encroach upon the Executive functions by removal of a duly appointed executive officer under the guise of reconsideration of his nomination." He said that if the House of Representatives believed that the commissioners had been derelict in the performance of their duties, the "orderly and constitutional manner" of proceeding would be by impeachment.[30]

The Senate voted again on the three commissioners, confirming two but rejecting George Otis Smith.[31] It then instituted a court action to test Smith's right to hold office. In a unanimous decision the Supreme Court held that after the Senate confirms a nomination and the appointee takes the oath and enters into the duties of office, the Senate may not reconsider and possibly reject a nomination.[32]

Withholding Funds

After President Hoover refused to return the nominations of the three commissioners of the Federal Power Commission to the Senate, efforts were made in each house to invoke the power of the purse. Sen.

Burton K. Wheeler, D-Mont., placed in the *Congressional Record* an editorial from the *Washington Herald* that urged Congress to withhold appropriations from the commission "while these three dummies or dupes of the Power Trust continue to discredit its membership." [33] Rep. Fiorello LaGuardia, R-N.Y., offered an amendment to the appropriations bill for independent offices to provide that "none of the money herein appropriated shall be used to pay the salary of a commissioner whose confirmation has been or is being reconsidered by the Senate or against whom ouster or removal proceedings have been instituted or authorized." The House defeated LaGuardia's amendment, 102-37.[34]

The technique of penalizing executive employees by withholding their salaries was revived by the House of Representatives in 1943. It voted 318-62 to accept a rider, attached to the Urgent Deficiency Appropriation Bill, denying payment to three named agency employees suspected of subversive activities.[35] The Senate repeatedly rejected the rider but yielded after a succession of conference reports, continued deadlock on the emergency funding measure, and some modification of the House language.

The three employees, continuing to work without pay, initiated action in the Court of Claims to recover their salaries. The counsel for Congress maintained that congressional powers over appropriations were plenary and not subject to judicial review. The Court of Claims, however, decided that the employees were entitled to back pay. The Supreme Court, affirming that judgment, declared: "Were this case to be not justiciable, congressional action, aimed at three named individuals, which stigmatized their reputation and seriously impaired their chance to earn a living, could never be challenged in any court. Our Constitution did not contemplate such a result." The Court held that the section in the appropriation bill fell precisely within the category of congressional actions that the Constitution proscribes by stating that "[n]o Bill of Attainder or ex post facto Law shall be passed." As the Court noted, those "who wrote our Constitution well knew the danger inherent in special legislative acts which take away the life, liberty, or property of particular named persons because the legislature thinks them guilty of conduct which deserves punishment." [36]

A more recent incident involves a statute in 1981 that withheld funds from CETA (Comprehensive Employment Training Act) employees who advocated the violent overthrow of the federal government. The language, included in a continuing appropriations bill, stated that

[n]one of the funds appropriated or otherwise made available by this Act may be used, pursuant to the Comprehensive Employment

Training Act, for the participation of individuals who publicly advocate the violent overthrow of the Federal Government, or who have within the past five years, publicly advocated the violent overthrow of the Federal Government.

From the legislative history it is evident that this language was meant to exclude Dorothy Blitz of Martinsville, Virginia, from the CETA program. Blitz, a member of the Communist Workers party, challenged the language as a violation of her right of free speech under the First Amendment and a violation of the bill of attainder clause. A federal court in 1982 agreed that the "Blitz amendment" failed to draw a line between mere advocacy (protected by the Constitution) and advocacy that incites and is likely to produce violent action. Having found the statutory language in violation of the First Amendment, the court did not address the question of bill of attainder.[37]

Committee Investigations

Through the pressure of the investigative power, congressional committees can precipitate resignation or removal. In 1924 a special committee under Senator Wheeler investigated the failure of Attorney General Harry Daugherty to prosecute people implicated in the Teapot Dome scandal. Daugherty resigned within a matter of weeks.[38] In 1958, after hearings by a House oversight subcommittee had publicized the financial operations of the Federal Communications Commission, Richard A. Mack, commissioner of the FCC, resigned.[39]

Sensational hearings of this nature are infrequent, and yet hostile questioning by congressional panels can cause any official to review the wisdom of remaining in office. In 1978 a subcommittee of the House Interstate and Foreign Commerce Committee questioned the fitness of William S. Heffelfinger, director of administration within the Department of Energy, to hold office. The subcommittee criticized Heffelfinger for falsifying his resume, claiming to have won the prestigious William A. Jump Award for outstanding public administration when he had merely been nominated for the award. His resume incorrectly claimed an education from the University of Kansas. At an earlier hearing, Heffelfinger stated that he had been business manager for the state of Kansas. In fact, he served as business manager for a state-operated orphanage. The hearings reviewed other charges made against Heffelfinger while he occupied posts in the Department of Transportation. A memo by the subcommittee staff concluded that while any one of the charges "may not be enough to call for his dismissal, these incidents taken as a whole raise serious questions about his fitness as Administrator and Personnel Chief." [40] Heffelfinger survived this attack and later served with the Reagan administration as assistant secretary for management and administration in the Department of Energy. In November 1982 he lost this post to a manager with fewer than two years of federal service.[41]

Congressional Efforts to Protect Incumbents

Congress often intervenes to ensure the tenure and continuity of federal employees. Madison admitted, during the debate of 1789, that the president's removal power need not extend to every administrative official. Some positions, such as the comptroller in the Treasury Department, seemed to him to discharge legislative or judicial duties and therefore required independence from the president. He questioned whether the president "can or ought to have any interference in the settling and adjusting of the legal claims of individuals against the United States." [42] This reasoning would later be used to protect agency employees who carried out a broad range of adjudicatory duties.

Requiring the Senate's Approval

Through its power to advise and consent to presidential nominees, the Senate can try to dictate other personnel decisions, including removals and suspensions. In 1863 Congress began to pass legislation making the removal of certain officials subject to joint presidential-Senate action. Legislation that year created a comptroller of the currency to hold office for the term of five years "unless sooner removed by the President, by and with the advice and consent of the Senate" (12 Stat. 666).

A major assault on the president's removal power occurred in 1867 with passage of the Tenure of Office Act. This statute provided that every person holding civil office, with the advice and consent of the Senate, should be entitled to hold office until the president appointed a successor, with the advice and consent of the Senate. The bill further provided that the secretaries of state, treasury, war, navy, and interior; the postmaster general; and the attorney general should hold office during the term of the president who appointed them, and for one month thereafter, "subject to removal by and with the advice and consent of the Senate." The president was allowed to suspend an officer during a Senate recess. He would, however, have to report to the Senate, upon its return, the evidence and the reasons for the suspension. If the Senate did not concur, the suspended officer would resume office. President Andrew Johnson vetoed the bill, claiming that it violated his powers under the Constitution. Both houses promptly overrode his veto, and the bill became law (14 Stat. 430).

President Ulysses S. Grant, in his first annual message in 1869, urged Congress to repeal the Tenure of Office Act. He criticized the statute as inconsistent with efficient administration: "What faith can an Executive put in officials forced upon him, and those, too, whom he has suspended for reason?"[43] Congress revised the act that year, softening the suspension section but retaining the Senate's involvement in the removal process (16 Stat. 6).

In 1877, after a thorough investigation of the New York customhouse, President Rutherford B. Hayes asked for the resignation of Chester A. Arthur, collector (later president), and Alonzo B. Cornell, naval officer. Both men, under the patronage wing of Sen. Roscoe Conkling, R-N.Y., refused to resign. Hayes then sent the names of their successors to the Senate for confirmation. The nominations were "greeted with derisive laughter" and referred to the Committee of Commerce, chaired by Conkling. The committee rejected the nominations, as did the Senate.[44]

Public opinion turned against the Senate because it appeared to be obstructing reform of the customhouse. A number of Democratic senators indicated that they would not support Conkling if Hayes returned the names to the Senate.[45] After the Senate adjourned in 1878, Hayes dismissed Arthur and Cornell and made recess appointments. Upon the Senate's return he resubmitted his nominations. Conkling was able to delay action for several months, but the Senate voted to confirm early in 1879.

The Senate tried the same tactic against President Grover Cleveland. In his first ten months in office, Cleveland submitted a list of 643 suspensions. The Senate, controlled by Republicans, refused to act on the nominations to replace the suspended officers unless the attorney general delivered to the Senate all papers and information relating to the suspensions. Cleveland rejected the request, saying the Senate had no right, statutory or constitutional, to explore the reasons behind a suspension.[46] The Senate then retaliated by passing four resolutions that rebuked the administration. The third resolution, narrowly passed by a vote of 30-29, stated that it was the duty of the Senate, under the circumstances, to refuse its advice and consent to Cleveland's proposed removal of officers.[47] Passage of these resolutions had the effect of breaking the stalemate. The Senate acted on the nominations and also voted to repeal the Tenure of Office Act. The bill found easy acceptance in the House of Representatives, and it was enacted into law on March 3, 1887.[48]

Legislation on the Post Office continued to give the Senate a role in the removal of executive officers. A statute in 1872 required the postmaster general and three assistant postmasters general to be appointed by the president, by and with the advice and consent of the Senate. They would be removed "in the same manner." In 1876

Congress required the Senate's advice and consent for the removal of all first-, second-, and third-class postmasters. President Wilson challenged the legality of this procedure by removing, without the Senate's consent, a postmaster in Portland, Oregon. His action was upheld by the Supreme Court in the *Myers* case.[49]

Although the Senate's direct participation in removals and suspensions has been eliminated by congressional and judicial action, there are other ways of retaining control. If the president removes career officials for partisan reasons, Congress can respond by making those positions subject to the confirmation process. In 1982, after Secretary of Agriculture John Block fired Norman Berg as chief of the Soil Conservation Service, Sen. Roger Jepsen, R-Iowa, urged Block to reverse his decision. Jepsen, chairman of the Soil Conservation Subcommittee, then drafted legislation to give the Senate confirmation power over future chiefs of the Soil Conservation Service.[50]

Independent Agencies

In cases decided several decades before *Myers,* the Supreme Court recognized that Congress could limit the president's removal power by specifying the grounds for dismissal (inefficiency, neglect of duty, and so forth).[51] This principle is followed most frequently with regard to the independent regulatory commissions, as upheld by the Supreme Court in *Humphrey's Executor v. United States.*[52] It also serves, however, as a precedent for offices located within executive departments. In 1978 Congress established a special prosecutor in the Department of Justice, permitting his removal from office (other than by impeachment and conviction) only for extraordinary impropriety, physical disability, mental incapacity, "or any other condition that substantially impairs the performance of such special prosecutor's duties" (92 Stat. 1872). The officer was later designated an "independent counsel," removable "only for good cause, physical disability, mental incapacity, or any other condition that substantially impairs the performance of such independent counsel's duties." The "good cause" removal restriction was upheld by the Supreme Court in 1988 in *Morrison v. Olson.*[53]

The issue of independence within an executive department arose when President Reagan tried to remove Democratic members of the U.S. Parole Commission, an independent agency within the Department of Justice. Commissioner Oliver J. Keller, with two and a half years remaining in his six-year term, was given the choice either of resigning by January 15, 1982, with the option of serving as a consultant until March 15, or being transferred to Kansas City and removed from office within an even shorter time. Similar notices were scheduled to go to the other Democratic commissioners.

Acting on the advice of attorneys at the commission, Keller refused to resign. Instead, he filed a lawsuit against Reagan and the Justice Department. The chairman and five subcommittee chairmen of the House Judiciary Committee wrote to Attorney General William French Smith, protesting the president's intention to subject the commission to "partisan whim." Rep. Robert W. Kastenmeier, D-Wis., chairman of one of the subcommittees, held oversight hearings and denounced the administration's plan. The Senate Judiciary Committee, partly on the basis of a legal analysis prepared by Morton Rosenberg of the Congressional Research Service, criticized the administration's move and threatened to postpone action on nominations submitted by the president. Caught between this cross-fire, the administration reconsidered its decision and left the Democrats in office.[54]

Procedural Safeguards and Whistleblower Protection

Congress, over the years, has established procedural safeguards for federal employees facing dismissal or disciplinary action. The civil service merit system rests on an elaborate set of procedures that govern the suspension and removal of federal employees. The Lloyd-LaFollette Act of 1912 permitted removal of employees in the classified civil service "for such cause as will promote the efficiency of the service." However, an employee was entitled to reasons given in writing; notice of the action and of any charges preferred against him or her; a copy of the charges and reasonable time to file a written rebuttal, with affidavits; and a written decision on the answer at the earliest practicable date. Those procedures were refined most recently by the Civil Service Reform Act of 1978.

Lloyd-LaFollette, responding to "gag rules" imposed by Presidents Theodore Roosevelt and William Howard Taft, also encouraged agency personnel to inform members of Congress about their operations. Congress declared that the right of federal employees, "individually or collectively, to petition Congress or a Member of Congress, or to furnish information to either House of Congress, or to a committee or Member thereof, may not be interfered with or denied." This provision, an early protection for "whistleblowers," is reiterated in the Civil Service Reform Act of 1978. The Merit Systems Protection Board, established by that statute to investigate and adjudicate federal employee grievances, has within it a special counsel responsible for protecting the rights of whistleblowers.

It is in the interest of Congress to prevent the top layer of the bureaucracy from penalizing federal employees who disclose agency wrongdoing or ineptitude. Congress depends on these employees to call attention to waste, corruption, and other practices that agencies, fearing embarrassment, like to conceal. Civil service employees who are fired for circulating a petition to Congress can be reinstated by resorting to court action.[55] When their communications to Congress contain false or irresponsible information, protection through the courts may not be available.[56]

James Pope, a whistleblower in the Federal Aviation Administration, was fired in 1981 after publicly criticizing the FAA's program to avoid midair collisions. While Pope was appealing to the Merit Systems Protection Board, Sen. Jim Exon, D-Neb., and Reps. Patricia Schroeder, D-Colo., Guy Vander Jagt, R-Mich., and Robert K. Dornan, R-Calif., wrote to Drew Lewis, secretary of transportation, and asked for an immediate halt to all efforts to fire Pope. Their concern was based on "the inescapable conclusion that the personnel action was taken because of Mr. Pope's whistleblowing activity." [57] Ralph Sharer, an auditor assigned to the National Aeronautics and Space Administration, faced dismissal in 1982 after charging corruption and mismanagement in the office of the inspector general. Sen. Orrin G. Hatch, R-Utah, wrote to NASA administrator James Beggs to request a stay in the proposed firing.[58]

Members of Congress resort to hearings, letters to agency heads, and other tactics to prevent someone's removal. Once a removal has taken place, they can decide to press for reinstatement. Members intervene in part for reasons of justice but also to keep open the channels of communication between agencies and Congress.

The cases of Otto Otepka and A. Ernest Fitzgerald offer interesting contrasts. In each case an agency employee offended departmental superiors by supplying a congressional committee with information. Otepka was notified that he was being dismissed; Fitzgerald lost his job in an "economy move." Both men turned to Congress in an effort to retain their positions. There the similarity ends. Otepka became a martyr of the right wing; Fitzgerald was a hero to liberals.

In 1963 the State Department informed Otepka, a security officer, that he was being dismissed for giving classified information to the Senate Internal Security Subcommittee. Otepka found himself caught between conflicting loyalties. Departmental procedures governed the disclosure of information; statutory provisions encouraged civil service employees to furnish information to Congress and its committees. After the subcommittee held hearings on the dismissal and issued a lengthy report critical of the State Department, many of the initial charges against Otepka were dropped. Instead of dismissal he was demoted and reprimanded.[59]

In 1968 Fitzgerald lost his job with the Defense Department after telling the Joint Economic Committee the truth about a massive cost overrun on the C-5A aircraft. Sen. William Proxmire, D-Wis., chairman of the committee, came to Fitzgerald's defense. He conducted hearings to investigate and publicize the dismissal, hired Fitzgerald as a committee consultant, and appeared before the Civil Service Commission as a character witness for Fitzgerald. After more than a decade of arduous litigation, Fitzgerald won back his old job. Former president Nixon, who in a taped White House conversation said of Fitzgerald "get rid of that son of a bitch," later agreed to pay Fitzgerald $142,000 to avoid a public trial.[60]

Frances Knight, longtime director of the Passport Office, retained her position over the years by forging strong ties with Capitol Hill. Providing overnight passport service for senators, representatives, and their constituents was one way to nurture congressional support. When Abba Schwartz, chief of the State Department's Bureau of Security and Consular Affairs from 1962 to 1966, tried to reorganize her out of the Passport Office, congressional defenders helped defeat the proposal. Within a few years Schwartz lost his own job through a reorganization plan. Knight remained head of the Passport Office until 1977.[61] The Senate Internal Security Subcommittee, a vigorous critic of Schwartz, remained a steady supporter of Knight.

Conclusion

Because of a fundamental interest in program implementation, the operation of the civil service, and access to information about agencies, members of Congress will always have an interest in the suspension and removal of federal employees. Federal workers remain in a twilight zone, pulled between the conflicting desires of the president and Congress.

Some of the congressional techniques for participating in removals are off-limits today: these include allowing the Senate to act jointly with the president; using the power of the purse to remove named employees; abolishing a position to put someone else on board; and requiring the president to return to the Senate for reconsideration the name of an official already confirmed and appointed. But Congress can still abolish offices through reorganization and program cutbacks, provided that it does not violate the bill of attainder clause or First Amendment freedoms. And it can still apply irresistible pressure through its investigative power, passage of resolutions, and caucus actions.

On the positive side, Congress has an intrinsic interest in protecting incumbents threatened by presidential or departmental head removal. In creating an office, Congress may establish criteria for removal and require procedural protections. It can design an office as nonpartisan and adjudicatory, placing it outside the control of the president or executive assistants. There will always be circumstances requiring the active intervention of Congress in questions of suspension, removal, demotion, and reassignment. Given the responsibilities of Congress in legislation and program oversight, those matters can never remain the monopoly or exclusive preserve of the president.

Notes

This chapter was originally published in *Congress and the Presidency* 10 (Spring 1983): 63-77. The journal is a joint publication of the Center for Congressional and Presidential Studies and the U.S. Capitol Historical Society.

1. *Myers v. United States,* 272 U.S. 52, 161 (1926).
2. Harold Seidman, *Politics, Position, and Power* (New York: Oxford University Press, 1980), 54.
3. For details on the debate of 1789, see Louis Fisher, *Constitutional Conflicts Between Congress and the President* (Princeton, N.J.: Princeton University Press, 1985), 61-66.
4. *Myers v. United States,* 272 U.S. 52, 131 (1926)
5. *Humphrey's Executor v. United States,* 295 U.S. 602 (1935). See also *Wiener v. United States,* 357 U.S. 349 (1958).
6. *Borders v. Reagan,* 518 F. Supp. 250, 265 (D.D.C. 1981).
7. Frederick W. Whitridge, "Rotation in Office," *Political Science Quarterly* 4 (June 1889): 279-295.
8. Gaillard Hunt, ed., *The Writings of James Madison,* vol. 9 (New York: Putnam's, 1910), 44.
9. George H. Haynes, *The Senate of the United States,* vol. 2 (Boston: Houghton Mifflin, 1938), 793; Leonard D. White, *The Jacksonians* (New York: Free Press, 1954), 317-321.
10. For a careful study, see Erik McKinley Eriksson, "The Federal Civil Service Under President Jackson," *Mississippi Valley Historical Review* 13 (1927): 517ff.
11. Hunt, *Writings of James Madison,* vol. 9, 43-44.
12. *Congressional Record* 119 (1973): 3192.
13. U.S. House of Representatives, *Confirmation of the Director and Deputy Director of the Office of Management and Budget,* hearings before the House Committee on Government Operations, 93d Cong., 1st sess., 1973, 163-166.
14. *Public Papers of the Presidents of the United States, Richard Nixon, 1973* (Washington, D.C.: U.S. Government Printing Office, 1975), 539.
15. *Crenshaw v. United States,* 134 U.S. 99 (1890).

16. *Public Papers of the Presidents of the United States, Jimmy Carter, 1978,* II (Washington, D.C.: U.S. Government Printing Office, 1979), 1925.

17. James D. Richardson, ed., *A Compilation of the Messages and Papers of the Presidents,* vol. 17 (New York: Bureau of National Literature, 1925), 8851-8852.

18. *United States ex rel. Brookfield Const. Co., Inc. v. Stewart,* 234 F. Supp. 94, 99-100 (D.D.C. 1964), affirmed, 339 F. 2d 754 (D.C. Cir. 1964).

19. 39 Op. Att'y Gen. 145-148 (1938).

20. *Morgan v. Tennessee Valley Authority,* 28 F. Supp. 732 (E. D. Tenn. 1939); *Morgan v. Tennessee Valley Authority,* 115 F. 2d 990 (6th Cir. 1940), cert. denied, 312 U.S. 701 (1941).

21. Debate on this resolution appears in the *Congressional Record* 65 (1924): 2223-2245.

22. Ibid., 2335.

23. *Congressional Globe,* 40th Cong., 1st sess., 1867, 255-256, 394-395.

24. Haynes, *Senate of the United States,* vol. 2, 812-815.

25. "Congress Gets Petitions Demanding Ouster of Watt," *Washington Post,* October 20, 1981, A3.

26. "Watt Says He Did Not Intend to Threaten Israeli in Letter," *Washington Post,* July 25, 1982, A1.

27. *Congressional Record* 128 (1982): 13690.

28. "Critics Still Want VA Chief Ousted," *Washington Post,* July 2, 1982, A4; "Embattled VA Chief Steps Down," *Washington Post,* October 4, 1982, A1.

29. "Insensitive Don Devine Asked to Quit OPM Post," *Federal Times,* June 7, 1982, 3.

30. *Public Papers of the Presidents of the United States, Herbert Hoover, 1931* (Washington, D.C.: U.S. Government Printing Office, 1976), 12, 15. Hoover's position had been supported by the attorney general: 36 Op. Att'y Gen. 383 (1931).

31. *Congressional Record* 74 (1931): 3939-3940.

32. *United States v. Smith,* 286 U.S. 6 (1932).

33. *Congressional Record* 74 (1931): 2140.

34. Ibid., 3320-3323.

35. *Congressional Record* 89 (1943): 4605.

36. *United States v. Lovett,* 328 U.S. 303, 306-307, 314, 317 (1946).

37. *Blitz v. Donovan,* 538 F. Supp. 1119 (D.D.C. 1982).

38. Hasia Diner, "Teapot Dome, 1924," in *Congress Investigates, 1792-1974,* ed. A. M. Schlesinger, Jr., and R. Burns (New York: Chelsea House, 1975), 210-211.

39. "Regulatory Agencies Probe," *Congressional Quarterly Almanac, 1958* (Washington, D.C.: Congressional Quarterly, 1958), 687-690.

40. U.S. House of Representatives, *Department of Energy Authorization: Fiscal Year 1979,* vol. 4, hearings before the Committee on Interstate and Foreign Commerce, 95th Cong., 2d sess. (Washington, D.C.: U.S. Government Printing Office, 1978), 117-154, 242-246.

41. "DOE Turns Thumbs on Bill Heffelfinger," *Federal Times,* November 22, 1982, 5.
42. *Annals of Congress,* 1st Cong., 1789, 614.
43. Richardson, *Compilation of the Messages and Papers of the Presidents,* vol. 9, 3992.
44. Leonard D. White, *The Republican Era* (New York: Free Press, 1958), 33.
45. *New York Times,* December 31, 1877, 1.
46. Richardson, *Compilation of the Messages and Papers of the Presidents,* vol. 10, 4960-4968.
47. *Congressional Record* 17 (1886): 2810-2814.
48. Louis Fisher, "Grover Cleveland Against the Senate," *Congressional Studies* 7 (Spring 1979): 11-25.
49. *Myers v. United States,* 272 U.S. 52 (1926).
50. *Washington Post,* April 7, 1982, A1, A14. Eight senators (John Melcher, D-Mont.; David Durenberger, R-Minn.; Wendell Ford, D-Ky.; Dennis DeConcini, D-Ariz.; Edward Zorinsky, D-Neb.; Thomas Eagleton, D-Mo.; Lloyd Bentsen, D-Texas; and Jim Sasser, D-Tenn.) cosponsored Jepsen's bill; *Congressional Record* 128 (1982): 6962.
51. *Reagan v. United States,* 182 U.S. 419 (1901); *Shurtleff v. United States,* 189 U.S. 311 (1903).
52. 295 U.S. 602 (1935).
53. 487 U.S. 654 (1988).
54. Stephen Gettinger, "The Power Struggle Over Federal Parole," *Corrections* 8 (April 1982): 41-43.
55. *Steck v. Connally,* 199 F. Supp. 104 (D.D.C. 1961).
56. *Turner v. Kennedy,* 332 F. 2d 304 (D.C. Cir. 1964).
57. "FAA Fires Official Who Blew Whistle," *Federal Times,* January 11, 1982, 5.
58. "Whistleblower Fights Back," *Federal Times,* February 1, 1982, 1, 22.
59. Part of Otepka's support came from "State Department Security—1963-1965," a report of the Senate Committee on the Judiciary (committee print, December 15, 1967). Congressional support is also described by William J. Gill, *The Ordeal of Otto Otepka* (New Rochelle, N.Y.: Arlington House, 1969).
60. *Washington Post,* August 14, 1981, A1, A11; and June 16, 1982, A3.
61. Sanford J. Ungar, "J. Edgar Hoover Leaves the State Department," *Foreign Policy* 28 (1977): 110-116; and "Frances Knight Ouster Tarnishes Carter Image," *Human Events,* July 16, 1977, 1, 9-10.

13. CONGRESS, THE PRESIDENCY, AND THE AMERICAN EXPERIENCE: A TRANSFORMATIONAL PERSPECTIVE

Lawrence C. Dodd

I approach the study of American politics in the midst of an intellectual crisis of faith. The crisis centers on a sense of intellectual powerlessness, a powerlessness to explain and predict politics in the manner that I was taught to expect and with the theories and frameworks that I had come to believe were appropriate. Much of the literature of political science teaches that repetitive and empirically comparable patterns exist in politics, particularly within a stable democracy such as ours. The key to political explanation is to identify these recurring empirical constants and account for them in terms of a general and perhaps universal theory. The goal of political science is to predict future political behavior from historical patterns and explanatory theories.[1]

The patterns to be explained are the recurring empirical manifestations of American politics, particularly the electoral behavior of voters and parties and the policy behavior of presidents and Congress. To explain the behavior of citizens and politicians, one could choose among or blend a variety of theoretical approaches: a realignment perspective, a value consensus perspective, a pluralist perspective, a class struggle perspective, or an institutional conflict perspective.[2] But whatever approach was adopted, it suggested that the future looked roughly like the past in its empirical particulars. We thus should expect realignment approximately every thirty years, say, with innovative policies coming only with strong party government and presidential leadership in the wake of realignment. Likewise, we should expect the constitutionally prescribed relationships among the three governing branches—Congress, the presidency, and the courts—to break apart under the impact of power struggles within and among these institutions. We then should see the return of equilibrium as institutional actors recognize the overriding systemic importance of constitutional roles and creedal values.

The problem was that the closer I looked at the applications of each theoretical approach, the more disappointed I became with its predictive results. Scholars might be able to adjust theoretical approaches and adapt them after the fact to fit particular empirical circumstances, but the theories seemed unable to predict political developments in any precise way. Realignments, for example, do not come when and as expected, though we may develop new concepts of realignment in order to adapt theory to new facts. Policy innovation, as seen in the years of Ronald Reagan's presidency, does not really require party government, though we can suddenly discover the virtues of divided government for certain kinds of innovation, creating the conditions of shared party responsibility for difficult policy decisions. And the power struggles within and among institutions do not end in a return to a predicted and foreseeable constitutional balance but invariably generate new and unforeseen resolutions. Our governing institutions, then, take on new roles, abandon old ones, develop innovative interinstitutional relationships, and establish new power distributions—all in ways that the nomological theories do not foresee.

Such observations create doubts about traditional approaches to the study of American politics. More important, they generate doubts about whether political scientists can ever find general theoretical explanations that will predict the particulars of politics. Decades of empirical research suggest that politics is not a constant and recurring game with simple and recurring patterns that can be discovered and used to predict future occurrences. It is more nearly a process of cyclical transformation in which political actors create, dissolve, and recreate the structure and logic of an evolving game. As they recreate the political game, the future looks different from the past in critical and unpredictable ways.

These conclusions suggest that the reliance on general nomological theories of behavior—based on expectations of a relatively constant recurring order in the empirical substance of political life—is suspect and probably wrongheaded. If wrongheaded, a nomological approach is dangerous. It suggests to actors in the world—to presidents, members of Congress, journalists, political activists, and ordinary citizens—that they should base their expectations and strategic choices about the future on theories that produce vastly inadequate predictions and that scholars keep alive only by post hoc adjustments. Believing in the truth of these empirical theories, presidents, legislators, and public-spirited citizens may make political choices and pursue political actions that have disastrous consequences, all in the name of political science.

Thus the crisis of faith: does one pursue an intellectual strategy that seems suspect, fraught with potentially disastrous consequences if taken seriously by the world at large? No. Far better to give up the preoccupation with nomological theory; acknowledge the variability, evanescence, and openness of the political world; and find a new way to understand that variability if not to predict its empirical content.[3] Far better to acknowledge the creative and evolving character of politics and focus on clarifying its processes, dilemmas, and opportunities. This is the challenge posed by my crisis of faith, a challenge whose elusiveness has preoccupied me for a decade.

In grappling with this challenge, I have come finally to a transformational perspective of American politics. The goal for political science, I believe, is not to discover and predict a recurring constancy in the structure, substance, and logic of political behavior but to clarify the processes whereby political actors create, operate within, dissolve, and recreate new and unforeseeable political worlds. The goal of the political scientist, in essence, is to understand the form, variability, and contingencies of political change, not to predict a content that is unforeseeable and a constancy that is nonexistent in any long-term and substantive sense.

A comparison with other fields of inquiry may help to clarify this goal. Evolutionary theorists in biology give a systematic accounting of how evolution occurs, with its heavy dose of randomness and chance, but they are unable to predict the species that will emerge through evolution.[4] Psychologists identify the processes whereby individuation and personal growth occur and outline the attendant struggles, choices, and constraints, though they cannot predict how each individual will resolve life crises and create a new life structure.[5] Political scientists likewise may be able to identify the processes of choice, experimentation, and struggle through which societies transform and conduct their politics over time, while being unable to predict specific political structures, policies, and behavior patterns that will emerge. By clarifying and theorizing about such processes, scholars bring to the political world not a prediction of its long-term future course but an awareness of its creative processes, dilemmas, and possibilities.[6]

In order to develop a theory of transformation, students of American politics must address a particular puzzle: how and why does American politics experience extended periods of creation, maintenance, dissolution, and recreation in the structure and logic of political behavior? A solution to this puzzle lies in developing a more accurate understanding of individual and group motivations than exists in political science today. It requires that theorists move beyond a rational-choice approach to politics, in which individuals are seen as purposive, self-interested actors pursuing fixed goals and preferences, to a metarational orientation, in which political actors, while often entranced by fixed goals and maximization of short-term interests, ultimately are seen as reflective and responsive individuals capable of shaping their world through experimental and experiential learning. Such metarational reflection and learning come to the fore in periods of crisis produced by a rigid adherence to, and "rational" pursuit of, fixed beliefs and goals that once had been appropriate but that have become outmoded as the world changed. It is the capacity for reflection and learning that enables political actors, who share a collective understanding of political life and operate within it for a sustained period of time, to dissolve existing political structures in the midst of crisis and evolve new governing arrangements appropriate to the emerging world.

A transformational perspective puts American history and contemporary politics in a different light. It requires that we forgo the desire for predictive certainty. In its stead we may come to see more clearly beyond the historical constraints and cyclical catastrophes predicted by nomological theories.[7] We may see instead both the potential for political empowerment and the promise of enlightened and regenerative self-governance.

My goal here is to outline this transformational perspective and demonstrate its applicability to American politics and congressional-presidential relations. It is appropriate that I introduce the theory in a book on Congress and the presidency, not only because they are my areas of primary specialty but because the institutions are critical agents in the American experience. The heart of the chapter is an interpretation of American political history intended to illustrate the transformative nature of political life and to inform our understanding of contemporary politics. In this interpretation, I underscore the role of Congress and the presidency in our political system. I begin, however, by presenting a general theory of transformation based on a metarational approach to the motivational dynamics of politics.

Transformational Politics:
A Metarational Approach

Much of the problem with American political studies stems from inappropriate assumptions about human motivational dynamics. Like many others, I brought to the study of American politics, particularly Congress and the presidency, a rational-choice perspective.[8] This perspective entails the belief that the most useful analytic strategy is to assume that presidents, members of Congress, and other political actors share a set of fixed goals and preferences, which they seek to maximize through political action. This is an assumption of substantive rationality in politics, a belief that political actors calculate their self-interest in terms of specific, ordered, and constant preferences about the desired outcomes of politics.[9] Concurrent with this assumption is the expectation that the core structures, procedures, and rules of the political game remain stable over time, with the resources and payoffs being known and limited.

I suspect that essentially every theorist about American politics has been to some extent a closet rational choicer. Whether we explicitly say so or not, we assume that political actors pursue specified goals within an identifiable political game that is, in its most basic form, constant across history. We argue that the efforts of individuals, groups, parties, and institutions to maximize their interests within the context of a constant game set in motion recurring cycles, crises, realignments, and periods of institutional restoration. Since it is assumed that the goals, preferences, and structure of the game remain constant, we predict that change occurs within the parameters of the game itself. Transformation of the game is not possible. Thus the future will look much like the past, even the distant past.

In fact, when the future arrives, it does not look like the past. The substance of politics—the character of the policy agenda, the values of voters and politicians, the system of partisan and group conflict, the power of presidents and members of Congress, and the structure of the state—all change in significant ways unforeseen by our substantive theories.[10] To account for unexpected developments, we modify theories in ad hoc and post hoc ways. We do so from a belief that such theorizing is the best analytic tool we have available and from a desire to bring clarity, however inadequate, to the political world. We believe that we must either choose general predictive theory or become political journalists, content to describe political life void of system. This is the first and perhaps gravest mistake in our effort to understand political change.

The mistake lies in our failure to recognize that we could use other models of microdynamics to understand political change in more accurate and useful ways than the traditional ones.[11] What might such models look like, and what might their implications be? To explore these questions, we can move outside the domain of political science and its expectation of substantive rationality. In the next section I develop an alternative model, building on the approach to human behavior outlined by anthropologist Gregory Bateson, into which I incorporate several related approaches, from Carl Jung to Michael Lerner to Thomas Kuhn.[12]

A Batesonian Perspective

In *Steps to an Ecology of Mind,* Bateson argues that each individual develops a personal epistemology—a conception of how the world operates, including moral and empirical dimensions, collective responsibilities, and individual interests—through early experiences and socialization in the world.[13] These individual epistemologies incorporate fixed goals and preferences in a manner that only approximates the ontology, or reality, of the world. An individual's perception of reality, even at its clearest moment, deviates from reality. The difference between perception and reality forces individuals to become accustomed to some ineffectiveness in their understanding of the world and their action in it. Nevertheless, they hold to their epistemologies for security and order, using them to operate within and exercise power over their world.

Within the confines of their world view, and operating through structures and procedures they have created in pursuit of that world view, individuals take for granted the existence of a collective well-being and stress actions that provide them with or maximize short-term personal gratification. So preoccupied, they overlook behavior necessary to promote longer term and familial, group, or collective well-being. Their focus on short-term interests leads them to epistemological crises in which short-term behavior generates unpredicted and counterproductive results. The resultant breakdown in social order occurs in part as individuals sabotage those collective structures and processes necessary to sustain interdependent cooperation in ways that blend self-interested pursuits into a common and mutually enhancing enterprise. Epistemological crises generate anxiety as individuals experience growing powerlessness and disorder. They act to reduce this anxiety by renewing their attention to the full range of appropriate epistemological behavior. Their response can be referred to as epistemological rationality, the pursuit of interests in the world in a manner consistent with maintaining their existing world view.

If the ontology of the political world remained constant, substantive theories based on epistemological rationality, as a modified version of substantive rationality, probably would work. Political actors would pursue behavior maximizing their interests, produce crises and anxiety, and then return to political orthodoxy in efforts to reduce anxiety.[14] But because the ontology of the world is not constant, we are led to a more complicated conception of human change.

The great dilemma of human behavior is that the ontology of the world—the way it really is and really operates—can change extensively over time, while the epistemology that dominates human action—beliefs about the way the world is and operates—remains relatively constant, with fixed goals, preferences, values, and moral visions. This is true in part because of the power of habit and because humans value the appearance of order and security. It is true in part because intense focus on short-term maximization within an existing epistemology and corrections in that maximizing behavior are so all-consuming that individuals overlook ontological change. They simply assume that difficulties in manipulating the world are a product of inappropriate behavior within existing world views. Finally, it is true because of the great difficulty and pain involved in reconstructing epistemologies. An individual must be willing to give up the sense of security and order inherent in traditional beliefs. Rather than holding onto traditional beliefs, the individual must try new behavior patterns and beliefs and, through painful, threatening trial and error, seek forms of action and belief that reduce the sense of powerlessness and thereby seem to fit more clearly with the ontology of the world.

According to Bateson, the insecurity and pain involved in changing epistemologies is so great, and the commitment to and preoccupation with existing world views so extensive, that individuals will allow great gaps to develop between their epistemologies and the ontology of the world.[15] In fact, individuals will not reexamine the accuracy of epistemologies until crises are so great (and the ineffectiveness of epistemological restoration so clear) that they can significantly reduce their pain and powerlessness only by discarding the old world view and developing a new one. I refer to such circumstances as *metacrises,* deep and seemingly intractable dilemmas unresponsive to resolution through the operation of existing epistemological principles, structures, and procedures. When the recognition of metacrises comes—when the individual "hits bottom" so completely that he or she will let go of old assumptions, take responsibility for the self-deception and consequent powerlessness involved in holding to an inappropriate epistemology, and seek to experience the world more directly and experimentally— the process of constructing a new epistemology can begin. I call this act *epistemological reconstruction.*

Epistemological reconstruction occurs through the application of a process I call *experiential rationality*—an individual's experimentation with beliefs, goals, preferences, structures, and procedures until an epistemology of action is found that reduces the experience of powerlessness. Because the gap between an old epistemology and a new ontology can be great, epistemological reconstruction may be long and difficult. The individual may experience feelings of powerlessness and insecurity that arouse irrational fears and unconscious behaviors. Such psychopathological developments, in extreme form, can obstruct the experimentation and reconstruction process, perhaps even sabotaging it so completely that an individual may remain stuck in ineffectual and self-destructive behavior. Alternatively, an individual may create a revised epistemology with significant pathological elements so that, although short-term reempowerment occurs, self-destructive tendencies persist that will subvert long-term empowerment and well-being.[16]

Epistemological reconstruction thus is not assured. It involves trial-and-error experimentation with no guarantee of successful solution. And it may require personal and cathartic confrontation with fears and insecurities that inhibit experimentation. As individuals experience catharsis and experiment with new epistemologies, structures, and procedures, they have the opportunity to construct an epistemology more appropriate to the world than the former one. The new epistemology can empower them to operate in the world as it more truly is.

This, in brief, is a modified and expanded view of Bateson's conception of individual motives and behavior. Central to his thinking is a process I call *metarationality*—the recognition by an individual that adherence to an inappropriate epistemological system engenders a powerlessness and insecurity that is greater in cost than the pain, insecurity, and difficulties involved in creating a new epistemology. Metarational behavior requires an individual to move from epistemological rationality to experiential rationality in order to adjust to ontological change and then to move back to epistemological rationality as a way of regularizing his or her behavior in the world. Ultimately, Bateson suggests, this process occurs in collectivities as well as in individuals and provides us with a way to understand political and social action. Let us turn, then, to the metarational processes as they operate in collectivities.

Metarationality in a Collective World

Like substantive rationality, metarationality posits a world in which political actors relate to one another in terms of a shared understanding of goals, preferences, structures, procedures, and political logic. These shared understandings constitute a collective epistemology of the political world, in a sense a shared imagining of the world.[17] A collective epistemology includes a common understanding of the long-term collective responsibilities of individuals, groups, and institutions (including constitutional roles, moral prescriptions, and social norms) and an understanding of actions appropriate for individual, group, and institutional pursuits of immediate self-interest (whether class and regional interests, electoral success, or political power).

The content of collective epistemologies varies dramatically across historical eras in response to economic, technological, social, and moral possibilities. Before a collective epistemology can be viable, however, social and political actors must recognize that they live in an interdependent world. Because of this interdependence, political actors must act in mutually responsible ways if they are to ensure collective survival and individual enhancement. A viable epistemology thus will entail precepts, structures, and procedures that foster interdependent cooperation and mutuality appropriate to and possible in a historical time and place. At the heart of a viable collective epistemology lies an ecological vision of political and social life, a sense of the way in which political actors, groups, institutions, and processes fit together in a particular time and place to ensure mutual enhancement and survival.[18] A collectivity may also create a pathological epistemology, one that generates a sense of immediate reempowerment through distorted beliefs that ultimately inhibit political renewal, generate deeper crises, and require more catharsis and experimentation before collective renewal can occur.[19]

Collective epistemologies emerge from deep collective metacrises, which are often evident in revolution; in civil war; in social, moral, and economic dislocations; and in military defeat. Once an appropriate collective epistemology is in place and the crisis wanes (if a viable epistemology is found), the success of the epistemological beliefs and structures lead political actors to accept them as a political orthodoxy that defines their goals, preferences, and political possibilities. Political actors lose their concern for epistemological reassessment. Taking for granted the processes that allow collective well-being, they pursue personal interests within the existing world view. In the process, they lose their sense of the importance of mutuality and interdependence and focus on short-term self-interests.

The pursuit of short-term interests by individuals, groups, and institutions initiates a move from political cooperation to competition in ways that erode the structures, norms, and processes that provide for interdependent and mutual interests. The breakdown eventually produces social and political crises, efforts to strengthen cooperative structures to solve the crises, and reassertions of epistemological orthodoxy. This ongoing process of breakdown and restoration within an era involves shifts in power arrangements and policy concerns because of the various skills of political leaders and activists and because of the shifting policy alignments within the collectivity. Such cyclical political phases occur continually during an epistemological era and constitute the substance of daily politics that journalists and political scientists study. The longer political actors hold to the existing epistemology and allow it to constrain their political responses, the more anachronistic their governing structures and processes become. Holding to the extant world view and pursuing reforms and policy objectives within its constraints thus sets the stage for deep collective metacrises that can be resolved only by epistemological reconstruction.

This perspective suggests that we can think of political life in terms of long-term cycles of epistemological transformation and short-term cycles of political adjustment and reform within a reigning world view. The long cycles consist of the creation, maintenance, dissolution, and reconstruction of a collective epistemology.

The short cycles are the recurring processes of breakdown and restoration that occur within an epistemological era. They are characterized by a variety of cyclical dynamics, including ideological mood swings between collective cooperation and competition, organizational shifts between centralization and decentralization, realignments in the groups and parties that win policy struggles within an era, leadership shifts from creative policy assertiveness to managing and salvaging policy agendas, and the like.[20] As long as cyclical oscillations focus on reforms and adjustments within existing world views, societal change will outpace the ability of governments to respond to national problems effectively. Problems will mount and crises will fester to the point that extensive political restructuring will be necessary for crisis resolution and system survival.

Political restructuring requires extensive experimentation and improvisation. These processes occur throughout society, often coming at local and state levels long before they are evident in national governance.[21] They are generally initiated by dissident groups and individuals, often intellectuals, artists, and social activists outside formal political roles, whose creativity is critical to assessing the nation's problems and "reimagining"—to some real extent, "remythologizing"—its future. Ultimately, however, the collective success of such processes requires an authoritative collective leadership, dialogue, and implementation best found in formal institutions such as Congress, the presidency, and the courts.

A key to successful collective restructuring lies in the ability of the members of the governing institutions to engage in experimentation and improvisation. This ability depends on widespread recognition of the severity of the problems and the failure of existing approaches to solve the problems. It probably also depends on the existence of leaders who are personally grappling with epistemological reassessment and transformation.[22] Successful reimagining—a reshaping of the dominant myths, symbols, and stories through which we understand ourselves and guide our actions[23]—sets in motion a new epistemological era, including new political arrangements and a new set of fluctuations and short-term reform cycles. This pattern of short-term reform cycles nested within longer term transformational cycles is strongly evident in American political history. Four examples are outlined in the next section.

The Cycles of American Politics

I outlined a metarational approach in some detail to provide an analytic sense of how one might envision politics from a transformational perspective. The result is a vision of politics characterized by the cyclical creation and recreation of political reality. These transformative cycles are fueled as much by epistemological rigidification, psychopathological conflict, system-threatening crisis, and experimental improvisation as they are by rational choice of alternative futures based on fixed and shared preferences. It is the long-term preoccupation with rational calculation based on fixed and shared preferences within an epistemological orthodoxy that gives rise to a growing unresponsiveness of government, the eventual development of metacrises, and the struggle to restructure dominant epistemologies and governing arrangements.

This perspective provides a useful framework within which to study American politics. We can think of American history, in simplified terms, as separated into four eras, with each era holding distinct shared epistemologies of politics.[24] We can likewise identify four periods of deep crisis and reconstruction from which arose new epistemologies of action. The four eras of shared epistemologies of politics are the agrarian period of the first half of the nineteenth century, the postagrarian transition of the late nineteenth century, the industrial era of the early to midtwentieth century, and the current postindustrial transition. The four reconstructive periods are the Revolutionary War and founding period, which gave rise to the agrarian-era politics; the Civil War and Reconstruction, from which arose the postagrarian era; the Progressive upheavals of the early twentieth century, which set in motion industrial-era politics; and the activist politics of the 1960s and 1970s, which shaped the current postindustrial politics.

In each historical era political actors and citizens held a widely shared and seemingly immutable core understanding of politics that gave order to the politics of the day. In the long run, however, the persistence of a collective epistemology and pursuit of immediate interests within it precipitated the crises that sabotaged the political equilibrium of each era. In the following section, I briefly sketch each era, giving a general sense of the way the dominant world view provoked metacrisis and reconstructive struggle. In these sketches, I highlight the role of Congress and the presidency, beginning with the agrarian period, which can be dated roughly from the late eighteenth century to the late 1850s.[25]

The Agrarian Era

The political logic of the agrarian era centered on a limited and constrained government dominated by regional and state elites, a mixed economy balancing the interests of slavery and free labor, and an isolated nationalism. This shared understanding emerged from the

Revolutionary War and the postwar effort to find a workable form of governance. It fit conditions of the late eighteenth century and the first decade or so of the nineteenth century rather well. By the 1810s, and certainly by the 1820s, the conditions that had made such epistemological solutions possible were shifting. Agrarianism was yielding to the early stages of industrialization, interstate commerce, and a national transportation network.

The development of a truly national economic system, with its differential effect on states and regions and its impetus toward a growing nationalism and international trade, challenged the nation's compromise on slavery, position on states' rights, and inclination toward isolation. But for another forty years political actors adhered to the old epistemology, seeking to maximize what they thought to be their sectional, economic, and partisan interests. The preoccupation with states' rights and sectionalism is particularly evident in the South, of course, where the politics of slavery intensified in the face of societal change and reinforced the antebellum world view. The South was not alone in the politics of sectionalism and state sovereignty, however, a fact witnessed, for example, in the secessionist sentiments in New England and rabid state loyalties from New York to Ohio to Illinois.

Throughout the agrarian era the political actors thought they were behaving rationally, pursuing sectional interests, partisan advantage, and personal career advancement. And in terms of maximizing short-term interests, they were acting rationally. Their short-term rational pursuits produced the cyclical oscillations to be expected from substantive rationality. Among them were two distinct governing cycles: the Jeffersonian regime from 1800 to the late 1820s and the Jacksonian regime from the 1830s to the late 1850s. Within the broader agrarian mind-set, each cycle had its own distinctive policy and power orientations, its own electoral shifts, organizational struggles, and leadership patterns—all of which political scientists can explain to some extent in substantively rational terms.[26] Ultimately, however, understanding agrarian era politics lies not in accounting for these overt actions in "rational" pursuit of an epistemological orthodoxy but in recognizing and understanding the nondecisions, nonactions, and growing sense of collective disempowerment that evolved in the face of mounting societal crisis. Understanding lies in explaining what seems in retrospect to be the country's irrational refusal to let go of an antebellum vision of society, North and South, and to grapple directly with societal and political transformation.

In the verdict of history it was precisely the adherence to an antiquated understanding of politics and society—particularly the pursuit of state and sectional interests through short-term partisan calculations—that was the defining characteristic of the agrarian era. In terms of ultimate consequences it was a characteristic seemingly irrational. After the late 1810s the nation's efforts to salvage the agrarian epistemology and political processes (the Missouri Compromise, the Jacksonian expansion of electoral participation, the nullification doctrine of John C. Calhoun, the Kansas-Nebraska Act, and the Dred Scott decision) merely delayed its confrontation with a new reality. Delay allowed fears and malevolent projections to intensify across the regions and made the confrontation with reality and political restructuring immeasurably more difficult and painful when it came.

During all of this, Congress and the presidency were vital arenas of both decision and nondecision. Their importance lay in their roles in the institutionalization of a founding epistemology in the late eighteenth and early nineteenth centuries, their inventive salvaging of that epistemology throughout the first sixty years of the nineteenth century, and their dramatic efforts in the 1860s and 1870s to save the nation by reinventing the structure of American politics. The great tragedy of the legislative and executive branches was that they were more adept at peaceful adjustments within an existing and increasingly anachronistic world view than at peaceful reassessments of that world view and construction of new structures of policy and governance.

The saving grace of the presidency and Congress came in their providing institutional mechanisms through which the meaning and resolution of civil strife could be addressed in the depth of national self-destruction. Abraham Lincoln, the great imaginer of the new American nation, thus found in the presidency a forum (for example, in the Second Inaugural Address) from which he could articulate the mutual responsibility for and collective costs of civil strife. He could speak to a sense of shared meaning and interdependent destiny and suggest a vision of a people committed to liberty, equality, and compassion. In so doing, Lincoln could address his own transformative struggles between personal ambition and moral purpose. During both the Civil War and Reconstruction, Congress provided the nation with an arena for retribution and catharsis (in the impeachment and conviction trial of Andrew Johnson), for dialogue and negotiation (in the struggle over the shape of Reconstruction), and for experimentation with and eventual restructuring of the constitutional creed and governing arrangements (in the Thirteenth, Fourteenth, and Fifteenth amendments and the implementation of the Compromise of 1876).

The Postagrarian Transition

In the 1870s the nation was freed to pursue a full-fledged transition to industrialization after the slavery issue and the most

destructive elements of sectional rivalry were resolved. With this
transition evolved a new political logic, an almost unbridled alliance
between business and an expansionary government devoted to funding
and fueling laissez faire capitalism. Like the agrarian world view, this
postagrarian image of politics and society took hold in a deep and
ultimately destructive manner. Whereas the business-government alliance (for example, between railroad barons and legislators) may have
energized society in the aftermath of the Civil War and Reconstruction,
the unregulated pursuit of money and power propelled the nation into
some of the worst consequences of capitalist democracy. These ranged
from an electoral corruption that left democracy a mockery in much of
the country to workplace corruption in which exploitation of child labor
and the contamination of food and beverages became the order of the
day. Again, political actors seeking to maximize short-term gain in
ways justified by an extant epistemology—in this case the world view of
social Darwinism—were single-minded in their pursuits, oblivious to
the consequences of the action and to changes in societal conditions that
had given rise to that world view. Thus they failed to understand that a
growing middle class would not support greed and corruption indefi-
nitely. The politicians and business leaders were able to sustain their
orgy at the public trough for almost forty years. During the years of the
Progressive movement, however, rebellious citizens were so angered by
their government that they not only threw the rascals out, but, through
electoral, legislative, and bureaucratic reforms, virtually crippled the
nation's capacity for deliberative government.

In the Progressive Era a new vision arose of how government
might serve the common good. Among the Progressives' ideas were
such reforms as conserving the nation's environment, securing clean
elections, and regulating industry to ensure safe industrial products
and to protect women and children (and men) from the worst abuses
of capitalism. Unfortunately, graft and corruption were so rampant
and political leaders opposed to Progressive ideas so entrenched in
party machines and Congress that the Progressives attacked the very
foundations of party and congressional governance in order to
implement their policy visions. In the Progressives' view, party
organizations and congressional leadership were major culprits hin-
dering democracy. In contrast, the presidency under Theodore Roosevelt and Woodrow Wilson was democracy's salvation, particularly
when the executive controlled a powerful administrative state that
could regulate business and society. With the consequent upheavals of
the 1900s and 1910s and the struggle to break the trusts and oust
corrupt politicians, a new epistemological shift occurred in American
politics.

The shift was away from a strong Congress based on cohesive party government and toward a strong, potentially imperial executive supported by presidential rhetoric, bureaucratic regulation, and interest group politics. Reforms to implement this vision eventually produced a fragmented Congress, oriented to seniority, committee government, special interests, and presidential leadership. The presidency was increasingly predominant, judged by its boldness, service to business and labor interests, and social activism and international assertiveness. The price of epistemological rigidification in the late nineteenth century and the deep crisis of confidence that it produced in the early twentieth century thus was a restructuring of the United States' conception of democratic government. The country moved away from deliberative politics toward the politics of rhetoric and personal charisma.

Like the Civil War, the Progressive crisis and the restructuring it provoked were not rational choices by clearheaded actors, nor was the flourishing of creedal passion resolved by the restoration of a preexisting creedal structure. Rather, they were the irrational and ultimately destructive long-term consequences of "rational" short-term calculations by individuals and groups seeking to maximize immediate self-interests while holding to an outdated and counterproductive world view. The result was as destructive institutionally, if not in terms of lives, as the Civil War. Congressional government was left in shambles, and the foundations were laid for an expansionary executive. In essence, a new balance was created that allowed the government to ensure democratic elections and respond to the demands for industry regulation. But, as with the agrarian era, the long-term adherence to a dominant political orthodoxy and the pursuit of interests within that orthodoxy did damage that had critical long-term consequences. The nation found new epistemological structures that resolved the immediate crisis and provided means for government action. Yet the severity of the crisis left its mark on the political landscape in a way that might have been moderated or prevented with clearer foresight and earlier response than the political actors were able to display.

With the institutional restructuring came a new agenda and a new politics. The new agenda included a socially and internationally activist government committed to a capitalist democracy sustained by domestic government regulation and international interventionism in behalf of American economic interests. The politics centered on universal suffrage and mass democracy, the flourishing of interest group politics, a handmaiden role for Congress in major policy deliberations, and a powerful executive responsible for leading a capitalist democracy.

The Industrial Era

The new structure of politics and policy that arose from Progressive reforms constituted a third American epistemology, a vision of how an interdependent society would work in an era of industrialization. This world view came to dominate the nation just as it entered the "American century," the period in which the country's affluence, domestic resources, and secure and strategic location (together with dynastic reversals in Europe and Asia) helped to ensure its pivotal and even dominant position in the world order.[27] The great architects of this vision were Theodore Roosevelt and Woodrow Wilson, leaders who spoke to issues of mutuality such as conservation, social responsibility, international interdependence, and democratic responsiveness. Hand in hand with their vision, however, came big government, labor and business obsession with controlling government policy, U.S. expansionary intervention abroad, a growing alliance between industry and the military, and the public's disposition to trust presidents as benign protectors of democracy while disparaging Congress in ways that had serious potential consequences for civil liberties and representative government.[28]

During the fifty to sixty years of the industrial era (roughly from the late 1910s into the early 1970s), the nation experienced two broad partisan reform cycles. The first, Warren G. Harding's "age of normalcy," saw Republican dominance, an expansive economy, and economic disaster during a worldwide depression.[29] The second, the New Deal regime that stretched from the presidency of Franklin D. Roosevelt to that of Richard Nixon, saw capitalist democracy saved by the expansion of a bureaucratic state, greater regulation of business, closer attentiveness to the social responsibility of government, and the solidification of an extraordinary military-industrial alliance. The industrial era experienced mood swings, organizational reform cycles, partisan realignments, alterations in leadership patterns, and a sustained period of national economic growth.[30] Yet as the industrial era lengthened, the nation experienced a sense of frustration and powerlessness in the face of problems that seemed unresponsive to the existing political logic.

However appropriate executive government in behalf of capitalist democracy may have been to the policy problems of the early twentieth century, this political epistemology was inappropriate in the second half of the twentieth century. Thus the conflict between labor and business continued to dominate the political parties and the halls of Congress even as the nation moved into a postindustrial service society, leaving unaddressed the issues of social welfare, civil rights, and quality of life endemic to a postindustrial and postmaterialist society. The presidency continued to be seen as relatively benign and relatively unconstrained, particularly in foreign policy, even as the growth of a bureaucratic state and the telecommunications revolution made the executive a threat to civil liberties and democratic government.[31] Congress became fragmented and unresponsive even as the need for a balance to executive power became clear. An interventionist foreign policy continued to dominate American thinking even as the coming of Third World nationalism made interventionism dangerous and counterproductive as a means of ensuring U.S. economic interests. And the country prolonged its economic growth by relying on military and defense spending, even as serious threats to its security decreased and its allies became capable of sharing defense responsibilities. The United States was able to avoid confronting political realities for a remarkably long time—but not forever. The problems seemed to explode almost simultaneously in the 1960s and early 1970s, leaving the nation's self-confidence shaken.

The story of the social breakdown of the 1960s and early 1970s, resulting in the destruction of two presidents, is well known and need not be repeated here. The great tragedy of both Lyndon B. Johnson and Richard Nixon lay in the extent to which they were pursuing, in a classically rational and short-term maximizing sense, the understanding of American politics that they had learned as young politicians. Johnson and Nixon were not aberrations at the end of the American century but its culmination. Their obsession with bold presidential interventionism, at home and abroad, was in the best tradition of Theodore Roosevelt, Woodrow Wilson, Franklin D. Roosevelt, and Harry S. Truman, as were their aggressive partisan politics. Yet approaches to politics and governance that may have worked decades earlier, including military intervention abroad and disingenuous presentation of self and policy actions at home, would not work in a society composed of an increasingly media-oriented and politically sophisticated public.

In essence, by the 1960s there were deep incompatibilities and contradictions between the United States' understanding of itself and the ontological reality of the emerging world, gaps that were leading to metacrisis and disaster, regardless of the individuals in the White House and the partisan control of Congress. The personalities of Johnson and Nixon may have exacerbated matters,[32] and certainly they must be judged as responsible participants in the politics of their time. But the root of the problem was not in Johnson and Nixon but in a broadly shared collective understanding of the world that, for example, expected presidents to act boldly in defense of democracy abroad (and certainly not to lose Southeast Asia to communism) while maintaining order, prosperity, and expanding opportunity at home.[33] In a world of televised war, diminishing resources, and expanding postmaterial expectations, such a world view necessarily led to failure, to a sense of growing powerlessness, and eventually to deep and shattering psychopathological crises in which the nation had to face its limits and recognize the need for new policy objectives and governing strategies.

The struggle to visualize a new America was foreshadowed and addressed in an outpouring of social commentaries.[34] The vision of the new character and interdependence of economic, social, political, and international factors emerged most clearly in the late 1960s, however, as leaders such as Martin Luther King, Jr., and Robert Kennedy sought to link concerns for economic and social issues with the United States' approach to world affairs. They created new political strategies that combined collective nonviolence, televised mobilization of mass outrage, and electoral challenge to the status quo (an overall strategy I call movement politics). The message was that the source of America's crises lay not in communist conspiracies and radical protests but in the nation's own failure to assess realistically its domestic problems and foreign commitments.

For a nation addicted after decades of remarkable achievement to believing in its own specialness, righteousness, and ennobled position in the world, the reversals of the 1960s and the suggestion that the nation itself was responsible for its sudden sense of inefficacy and powerlessness were disturbing and threatening. The resulting sense of rage and frustration evoked psychopathological forces that afflicted far more of the country than Presidents Johnson and Nixon and led to a season of attempted and successful assassinations. Among the assassins' targets were John F. Kennedy, Medgar Evers, Malcolm X, Martin Luther King, Jr., Robert Kennedy, George Wallace, Gerald Ford, and Ronald Reagan. The period from 1963 to 1981 was a time of unrest unlike any other two decades in American history. The crisis evoked far more turmoil than the political assassinations. Civil disobedience was widespread, cities were engulfed in race wars and firestorms of destruction, and freedom of speech and free elections were threatened (for example, in the rhetoric of Vice President Spiro T. Agnew and the Watergate actions of President Nixon). In a way not often recognized, however, the assassinations may have been the greatest tragedy of the period, robbing the nation of individuals who might have served, like Lincoln (and to a lesser extent Theodore Roosevelt and Woodrow Wilson), as transformative leaders who could articulate a vision of interdependence and mutuality and reenergize the public spirit.

The Postindustrial Transformation

A new world view emerged in the 1970s. It was the constrained and confused self-image of a nation adrift, robbed of its historic bearings and sense of limitless possibilities. In their place came a deep sense of malaise, as Jimmy Carter phrased it. The domestic turmoil of the 1960s, the defeat in Vietnam, and the political corruption symbolized by Watergate left the nation bereft of faith in its moral purpose and unsure of its ability to provide its citizens with a viable and rewarding future. During the 1970s and 1980s these doubts were deepened. The oil embargo and the consequent energy crisis demonstrated the nation's growing dependence on increasingly powerful Third World nations. The hostage crisis drove Carter from office and ultimately generated the Iran-contra scandal, which tarnished Reagan's reassertion of American toughness. Inflationary pressures swelled the numbers of American families dependent on two incomes. International borrowing and trade practices left the country one of the world's great debtor nations.

The move to what we can call an epistemology of limits, based on a growing sense of constraints, self-doubt, and retrenchment, constituted in many ways a necessary corrective to the aggressive expansiveness of the American century.[35] This corrective included elements of true collective learning, ranging from a greater understanding of the disadvantages of presidential imperialism and the value of deliberative decision making to a growing appreciation of the complexity and interdependence of environmental, social, economic, and political forces on a global as well as a domestic scale. With this knowledge came some sense of the United States' responsibility for its weakened condition.

These concerns came to be reflected in structural alterations in the nation's participatory processes and governing procedures during the 1970s.[36] The nation witnessed the rise of a new kind of interest group. This new movement included groups such as Common Cause and "Nader's Raiders" that were committed to the pursuit of collective interests and quality of life across many facets of society. These groups expanded the character of democratic participation, not only by involving minorities and eighteen-year-olds in electoral politics and working for the advancement of women in public office but through a broadened conception of legitimate democratic participation encapsulated in movement politics. In 1973 the nation adopted a war powers act to constrain executive imperialism abroad, and it instituted impoundment procedures whereby Congress could limit executive usurpation of domestic spending powers. And it reformed its Congress. It did so by weakening legislative seniority and spreading power more widely among members, by improving congressional policy-making coordination through a new budgetary process, by creating a stronger leadership structure, and by televising congressional debate.

The new epistemology and governing processes allowed the nation to loosen somewhat its grip on the expectations of the preceding decades and to focus energies on immediate national concerns. The presidencies of Ford and Carter witnessed elements of national renewal: Ford pardoned Nixon, moving the nation beyond its preoccupation with retribution, and Carter rekindled, if only momentarily, a sense of national decency, trust, and mutual respect. By the early 1980s, with Reagan's first term, the nation was able to move on to a "politics of normalcy." It was, of course, a divided politics, with a nation still so unsure of direction that it would set in motion divided party control of Congress and the presidency for the longest time span of modern history.

Under Reagan an ideology of limits dominated the public dialogue. The government's role ideally was limited to defense against "evil empires" and to taxation and expenditures focused on defense-related matters designed simultaneously to secure national defense and to fuel economic growth. It was, as one would expect, a period of epistemological orthodoxy and rigidification in which the pursuit of self-interest generated a disintegration of governing norms and procedures.[37]

The disintegrative impulse can be seen across a variety of dimensions. In Congress, budgetary procedures designed to allow for collective judgment have been subverted by automatic decision processes (such as Gramm-Rudman-Hollings procedures and backdoor spending strategies) that allow politicians to avoid judgment and responsibility. War powers provisions designed to expand legislative control over foreign policy have instead come to be seen as processes legitimizing short-term presidential war making, from Grenada to Panama. The politics of public interest—with a broad vision of the range, complexity, and interdependence of the policy issues confronting the nation—have shattered into a single-interest politics in which special interest groups stress the primacy of individual interest at the expense of a collective policy vision.

Nonviolent collective action, a strategy designed to unite and mobilize a disparate and otherwise powerless citizenry in moral outrage over fundamental issues of national governance, has dissolved into a pressure group tactic employed by often well-funded single-interest advocates (as in the abortion conflict) to immobilize government. Television to some extent became in the 1960s a medium of public dialogue through which disenfranchised, disadvantaged, and disempowered citizens could speak to one another and to the nation's conscience (a role seen recently in the political revolution of Eastern Europe). In recent years, however, it has become a vehicle of mass manipulation through negative campaigning. The politics of negativity and manipulation, fueled by massive corporate and PAC funding of election campaigns, are driving voters away from democratic participation, raising the costs of electoral politics to new heights, and addicting politicians to large corporate clients (such as the savings and loan industry) in a way that blinds them to public interest concerns.[38]

There are, of course, positive signs amidst such disintegrative dynamics. Congress continues to reassess budgetary procedures and is even discussing methods of revenue enhancement. Executive officials, such as Lt. Col. Oliver L. North and Adm. John M. Poindexter, have been convicted for their roles in the Iran-contra affair. And legislators, such as the "Keating Five," have been investigated for alleged unethical pursuit of corporate funding.[39] Unfortunately, such developments are the exception rather than the rule. The nation appears trapped in self-interested pursuits that erode the mechanisms and processes which evolved in the 1970s as a means of collective empowerment. Even more troubling, it is trapped in an epistemological vision of American politics that may be inappropriate to international and domestic circumstances.

An epistemology of limits may well have been a necessary corrective to the hubris of the American century, but it is questionable whether a limited vision of the role of government is appropriate as the nation approaches the twenty-first century. Internationally, the world has seen dramatic changes since the early 1970s, most notably the breakdown of Soviet dominance in Eastern Europe, the disturbances in the Middle East, the emergence of Japan as an economic world power, the reunification of Germany, and the possibility of a united Europe. Perhaps the greatest issue facing the nation is whether it can embrace a responsible, interdependent, and cooperative role in the world, or whether it will allow the wounds of Vietnam and the setbacks of the 1980s to fester and push it deeper into a chauvinist mentality in which the world is seen in terms of enemies to conquer and friends to save.

The country faces similar domestic concerns. Americans have learned that government cannot solve all of its citizens' problems, that both tax dollars and planning sagacity are limited. Yet the nation's economic structure and society continue to change in ways that create an interdependent and mobile citizenry in need of mechanisms for collective cooperation and mutual support. The great challenge for domestic politics is to create a model of activism in which the government facilitates collective well-being for its citizens without overreaching its capacities, depriving its citizens of responsibility for their own lives, or creating new foreign enemies to justify defense spending. Discovering such a model will take considerable experimentation, at state and local as well as national levels. It may prove particularly difficult if international developments lead the United States to reduce domestic reliance on a military-industrial complex as the engine of its national economy. Ultimately, it may require an American perestroika that we cannot yet envision.

My concern, in raising these issues, is that the nation not remain so fixated on the politics of limits, so contemptuous of the "vision thing" that once again we let our problems fester until our crises appear unsolvable and psychopathological conflict again engulfs us. However appropriate an epistemology of limits may have been two decades ago, the changes at play in the world today suggest that the United States needs to move beyond a concern with its limits, in which we concentrate on national defense and sustenance of our economy by military and industrial spending, and create a responsible and assertive role both domestically and globally. If we fail to do so, we risk even greater national reversals than we have had in the past. Insofar as we engage in epistemological reassessment and search for a responsible role, we truly sow the seeds of national renewal.

Escaping the Web of History

I have briefly sketched the story of American politics to lend credence to the transformational perspective outlined at the beginning of the chapter. Obviously, my sketch does not prove that such an interpretation is true. I believe, however, that it suggests the plausibility of metarational insights, a plausibility that taken seriously leads one to think differently about American history.

A transformational perspective sensitizes us to the realization that collective disempowerment in the world, and the deep and debilitating crises that come with it, is a product of human choice and political myopia. It is a product of our tendency to embrace as a permanent belief system a collective world view that momentarily empowers us and then to pursue our self-interests within that world view even as ontological reality changes in ways that erode the appropriateness and effectiveness of our beliefs and consequent actions. This is true whether we look at the United States' preoccupation with slavery, sectionalism, and states' rights that led to the Civil War; the social Darwinism that produced the Progressive upheavals; or the fixation on presidential imperialism, U.S. interventionism, and interest group politics that led to the social turmoil and international reversals of the 1960s and 1970s. I suggest that it also is true in the 1990s, insofar as we ignore the changes at play in the world today and hold rigidly to an epistemology of limits.

Within a transformational perspective, the responsibility of each generation is to develop a collective epistemology and governing structures appropriate to the ontological reality of its world. This process is difficult, with reassessment and reconstruction coming only as deep societal crises force us to confront our illusions about the world. My suspicion is that epistemological reassessment and reconstruction is ultimately so difficult that societies will never be able to avoid crises, however reflective and self-aware the citizenry and political leadership may be. Yet a nation attentive to the lessons of history,[40] to the transformational possibilities of political life, and to the message such lessons and possibilities hold for its time and place may become sensitive to the early warning signs of crisis. Such sensitivity can enable its citizens, its Congress, and its president to act responsibly and diligently, even as the shadow of the future descends, to redress its pathologies and disintegrative impulses, even as they threaten to destroy it. This is the challenge of American politics, the challenge to Congress and the presidency, in the 1990s.

Conclusion

These, then, are some thoughts on a transformational interpretation of American politics. I propose that we see American politics as a process in which political actors create, pursue, dissolve, and recreate a collective political epistemology appropriate to a changing world. This process exists because political actors operate in a world of metarationality—a changing world in which the pursuit of fixed goals and preferences leads to long-term powerlessness and metacrises that can be resolved only by reassessing goals, preferences, and values and by reconstructing collective epistemologies in ways appropriate to the emerging world.

The reconstructive and transformational nature of politics works against the long-term existence of recurring substantive patterns in American political life. The structure and procedures of American politics evolve and change so that its logic alters in ways that require a continual deciphering. An understanding of American politics comes thus not through the creation of general theories of party government, congressional reform, realignment, presidential leadership, class conflict, or creedal passions applied as substantive constants across history. It comes through an attentiveness and sensitivity to the ways political actors create and pursue new political epistemologies in new historical eras; in this process, as central agents of authoritative decision making, Congress and the president are critical participants in the transformational struggle.

Scholars can facilitate reconstructive change insofar as they clarify the existence and nature of the reconstructive process. Such awareness empowers political actors to look beyond distortions, orthodoxies, and psychopathological conflicts to experiment with new beliefs and structures and create political world views appropriate to the emergent political world. Conversely, scholars inhibit successful reconstructive politics and disempower political actors insofar as they suggest the existence of general substantive theories and hold to them even as empirical evidence suggests that a changing world operates otherwise. Scholars then become agents of political myopia, the creators of orthodoxies that blind political actors to the changing nature of the world and thus to the necessity of experimentation and epistemological reconstruction.

It is for this reason that I have found it necessary to rethink my approach to American politics. It is not simply that assumptions of substantive rationality and general substantive theories of politics are wrong. It is that they are dangerous. They imply a regularity to history that is not true but that political actors might take seriously. To expect, to believe as a scientific law, that realignments come every thirty years, that political innovation requires realignment, that institutional recentralization is inherent and guaranteed as a cyclical regularity, that the polity always reaffirms its original creedal principles, and so forth, is to hitch one's political and intellectual wagon to a falling star.

What scholars can attempt to do is to decipher the substantive logic of particular eras and thereby understand the political dynamics of a time and place, including, let us hope, our own. We can begin to grasp the ways in which rigid adherence to an existing world view disempowers us and thereby become attentive to ontological change and epistemological reassessment. We can also hope to clarify abstract processes of reconstructive change, realizing that change itself is in no sense assured, that our understanding of the processes of change is approximate at best, and that a degree of experimentation, reflectiveness, and creativity exists in political life that limits our predictive powers. In so doing we can begin to see that the ultimate goal of scholarship is, to paraphrase Marx, not to predict the future but to change it, to so clarify the workings of history that we as a people learn from it in ways that enable us to escape history's relentless machinations.[41]

Such a recognition limits the prospects of a formal science of American politics, if by that we mean a discipline that generates predictive laws subsumed in formalized and transhistorical theory. Yet such a perspective should liberate us to construct a transformational science, a science sensitive to the transformational character of human existence and political life. A transformational vision ultimately is an empowering one, one that helps political actors to recreate and renew politics in ways appropriate to collective self-governance in a changing world.

Notes

This essay is part of a book-length project, *Transformational Politics: The American Experience*. I wish to thank those who provided written critiques of this work, including Leslie Anderson, Douglas Ashford, Ron Brunner, Richard Fenno, Jeff Fishel, Joan Fiore, Ted Robert Gurr, Calvin Jillson, Peter Katzenstein, David Mapal, Sidney Milkis, T. J. Pempel, Steven Smith, and Jim Thurber. I am also grateful to the graduate students in my seminar on scope and methods and in my American politics core seminar at the University of Colorado. This essay is dedicated to the memory of my mother, Louise Pierce Dodd, whose encouragement and example instilled in me a belief in the transformational capacities of the human spirit.

1. Heinz Eulau, *The Behavioral Persuasion in Politics* (New York: Random House, 1963); Carl Hempel, *The Philosophy of Natural Science* (Englewood Cliffs, N.J.: Prentice-Hall, 1966); Robert T. Holt and John M. Richardson, "Competing Paradigms in Comparative Politics," in *The Methodology of Comparative Research,* ed. Robert T. Holt and John E. Turner (New York: Free Press, 1970); William H. Riker, "The Future of a Science of Politics," *American Behavioral Scientist* 21 (September 1977): 11-38; William H. Riker, "The Two-Party System and Duverger's Law," *American Political Science Review* 76 (December 1982): 753-766.

2. Samuel P. Huntington, *American Politics: The Promise of Disharmony* (Cambridge, Mass.: Harvard University Press, 1981); Robert A. Alford and Roger Friedland, *Powers of Theory: Capitalism, the State and Democracy* (Cambridge: Cambridge University Press, 1985); Raymond Seidelman and E. J. Harpham, *Disenchanted Realists* (Albany: State University of New York Press, 1985).

3. Georg Henrik von Wright, *Explanation and Understanding* (Ithaca, N.Y.: Cornell University Press, 1971); Gabriel Almond, *A Discipline Divided* (Beverly Hills, Calif.: Sage, 1990).

4. Ernst Mayr, *The Growth of Biological Thought* (Cambridge, Mass.: Harvard University Press, 1984); Stephen J. Gould, *A Wonderful Life: The Burgess Shale and the Nature of History* (New York: Norton, 1989).

5. Erik H. Erikson, *Childhood and Society* (New York: Norton, 1964).

6. Brian Fay, *Social Theory and Political Practice* (Boston: Allen & Unwin, 1975); Peter Winch, *The Idea of a Social Science* (London: Routledge & Kegan Paul, 1958); Jurgen Habermas, *Legitimation Crisis* (Boston: Beacon Press, 1973).

7. Huntington, *American Politics;* Mancur Olsen, *The Rise and Decline of Nations* (New Haven, Conn.: Yale University Press, 1982).

8. Morris P. Fiorina, *Congress: Keystone of the Washington Establishment* (New Haven, Conn.: Yale University Press, 1977); David Mayhew, *Congress: The Electoral Connection* (New Haven, Conn.: Yale University Press, 1974); Riker, "Future of a Science of Politics"; William H. Riker, *Liberalism Against Populism* (San Francisco: Freeman, 1982). See also Lawrence C. Dodd, "Congress and the Quest for Power," in Lawrence C. Dodd and Bruce I. Oppenheimer, *Congress Reconsidered,* 1st ed. (New York: Praeger, 1977), 269-307.

9. Herbert Simon, "Human Nature in Politics: The Dialogue of Psychology with Political Science," *American Political Science Review* 79 (June 1985): 293-304.

10. Margaret Weir, Ann Shola Orloff, and Theda Skocpol, eds., *The Politics of Social Policy in America* (Princeton, N.J.: Princeton University Press, 1988); Ronald Inglehart, *Culture Shift in Advanced Industrial Societies* (Princeton, N.J.: Princeton University Press, 1989); David Mayhew, *Placing Parties in American Politics* (Princeton, N.J.: Princeton University Press, 1986); James Sundquist, *The Decline and Resurgence of Congress* (Washington, D.C.: Brookings Institution, 1982); Stephen Skowronek, *Building a New American State* (Cambridge: Cambridge University Press, 1982).

11. H. D. Lasswell, "The Developing Science of Democracy," in *The Analysis of Political Behavior,* ed. H. D. Lasswell (Hamden, Conn.: Archon Press, 1970); Ronald D. Brunner, *The Policy Movement as a Policy Problem* (Discussion paper 48, Center for Public Policy Research, University of Colorado, Boulder, 1989).

12. Carl Jung, *Memories, Dreams, Reflections,* recorded and edited by Aniela Jaffe (New York: Pantheon, 1963); Michael Lerner, *Surplus Powerlessness* (Oakland, Calif.: Institute for Labor and Mental Health, 1986); Thomas Kuhn, *The Structure of Scientific Revolutions* (Chicago: University of Chicago Press, 1970).

13. Gregory Bateson, *Steps to an Ecology of Mind: A Revolutionary Approach to Man's Understanding of Himself* (New York: Ballantine, 1972).

14. Leon Festinger, *A Theory of Cognitive Dissonance* (Evanston, Ill.: Row, Peterson, 1957); Huntington, *American Politics.*

15. Bateson, *Steps to an Ecology of Mind,* esp. 309-337.

16. Ibid., 469-487.

17. Benedict Anderson, *Imagined Communities* (London: Routledge, Chapman & Hall, 1983); Jung, *Memories, Dreams, Reflections.*

18. Bateson, *Steps to an Ecology of Mind,* 469-505; Leslie Anderson, "The Political Ecology of the Modern Peasant" (Unpublished manuscript, Comparative Politics Research Center, University of Colorado, Boulder, 1990).

19. Thus, for example, Bateson argues that the Versailles treaty at the end of World War I, while momentarily empowering France and Britain, was

unnecessarily vindictive toward Germany. It engendered pathological conflict within Germany and between Germany and the Western allies that gave rise to Hitler and World War II. In many ways the European world is still involved in experimentation and reconstruction efforts designed to redress the pathologies of the epistemological world view that dominated Versailles.

20. Arthur Schlesinger, Jr., *The Cycles of American History* (Boston: Houghton Mifflin, 1986); Lawrence C. Dodd, "A Theory of Congressional Cycles," in *Congress and Policy Change*, ed. Gerald Wright et al. (New York: Agathon, 1986); Bert Rockman, *The Leadership Question: The Presidency and the American System* (New York: Praeger, 1984); Terry M. Moe, "The Politicized Presidency," in *The New Direction in American Politics*, ed. John E. Chubb and Paul E. Peterson (Washington, D.C.: Brookings Institution, 1985), 235-272; V. O. Key, "A Theory of Critical Elections," *Journal of Politics* 17 (February 1955): 3-18; Walter Dean Burnham, *Critical Elections and the Mainsprings of American Politics* (New York: Norton, 1970); James Sundquist, *Dynamics of the Party System* (Washington, D.C.: Brookings Institution, 1973); Jerome Clubb, William Flanigan, and Nancy Zingale, *Partisan Realignment* (Boulder, Colo.: Westview Press, forthcoming); James D. Barber, *The Pulse of Politics: The Rhythm of Presidential Elections in the Twentieth Century* (New York: Norton, 1980); Skowronek, *Building a New American State*.

21. David Osborne, *Laboratories of Democracy* (Cambridge, Mass.: Harvard Business School Press, 1988).

22. Erik H. Erikson, *Gandhi's Truth* (New York: Norton, 1970).

23. Jung, *Memories, Dreams, Reflections;* Murray Edelman, *The Symbolic Uses of Politics* (Urbana: University of Illinois Press, 1985); Robert Coles, *The Call of Stories: Stories and the Moral Imagination* (Boston: Houghton Mifflin, 1989); Robert Reich, *Tales of a New America* (New York: Random House, 1990); Max Weber, *The Protestant Ethic and the Spirit of Capitalism* (New York: Scribner's, 1976).

24. Samuel P. Huntington, "Postindustrial Politics: How Benign Will It Be?" *Comparative Politics* 6 (January 1974): 163-192. See also Lawrence C. Dodd, "Congress, the Constitution, and the Crisis of Legitimation," in *Congress Reconsidered*, 2d ed., ed. Lawrence C. Dodd and Bruce I. Oppenheimer (Washington, D.C.: CQ Press, 1981).

25. See also James MacGregor Burns, *The Deadlock of Democracy* (Englewood Cliffs, N.J.: Prentice-Hall, 1963); Robert A. Dahl, *Democracy in the United States*, 4th ed. (Boston: Houghton Mifflin, 1981); Edward S. Greenberg, *Capitalism and the American Political Ideal* (New York: M. E. Sharpe, 1985); Huntington, *American Politics;* Theodore Lowi, *The End of Liberalism* (New York: Norton, 1979); Walter J. Stone, *Republic at Risk* (Pacific Grove, Calif.: Brooks/Cole, 1990).

26. Riker, *Liberalism Against Populism*.

27. Paul Kennedy, *The Rise and Fall of the Great Powers: Economic Change*

and Military Conflict from 1500 to 2000 (New York: Random House, 1987).

28. H. D. Lasswell, *National Security and Individual Freedom* (New York: McGraw-Hill, 1950).

29. Kim Q. Hill, *Democracies in Crisis: Public Policy Responses to the Great Depression* (Boulder, Colo.: Westview Press, 1988).

30. James Stimson, *Public Mood* (Boulder, Colo.: Westview Press, forthcoming); Sundquist, *Decline and Resurgence of Congress;* Edward Carmines and James Stimson, *Issue Evolution: Race and the Transformation of American Politics* (Princeton, N.J.: Princeton University Press, 1989); Stephen Skowronek, "Presidential Leadership in Political Time," in *The Presidency and the Political System,* ed. Michael Nelson (Washington, D.C.: CQ Press, 1984).

31. Richard E. Neustadt, *Presidential Power* (New York: Wiley, 1960).

32. James David Barber, *Presidential Character* (Englewood Cliffs, N.J.: Prentice-Hall, 1985).

33. Daniel Ellsberg, "The Quagmire Myth and the Stalemate Machine," *Public Policy* 19 (Spring 1971): 217-274.

34. Among the most influential were Gunnar Myrdal, *An American Dilemma* (New York: Harper & Row, 1944, 1962); Rachel Carson, *Silent Spring* (Boston: Houghton Mifflin, 1962); Michael Harrington, *The Other America* (New York: Macmillan, 1962); and Barbara Ward, *Spaceship Earth* (New York: Columbia University Press, 1966).

35. Lester Thurow, *The Zero-Sum Society* (New York: Basic Books, 1980).

36. Nelson Polsby, "Contemporary Transformation of American Politics," *Political Science Quarterly* 96 (Winter 1982): 551-570; Richard Harris and Sidney Milkis, eds., *Remaking American Politics* (Boulder, Colo.: Westview Press, 1987); Steven S. Smith, "New Patterns of Decisionmaking in Congress," in *New Direction in American Politics.*

37. Charles O. Jones, ed., *The Reagan Legacy* (Chatham, N.J.: Chatham House, 1988).

38. Gary Jacobson, "Parties and PACs in Congressional Elections," in *Congress Reconsidered,* 4th ed., ed. Lawrence C. Dodd and Bruce I. Oppenheimer (Washington, D.C.: CQ Press, 1989); Frank J. Sorauf, *Money in American Elections* (Glenview, Ill.: Scott, Foresman, 1988).

39. The Keating Five are Republican senator John McCain of Arizona and Democratic senators Alan Cranston of California, Dennis DeConcini of Arizona, John Glenn of Ohio, and Donald W. Riegle, Jr., of Michigan, who reportedly intervened with regulators on behalf of the Lincoln Savings and Loan in early 1987. The five senators received $1.3 million from Charles H. Keating, Jr., and his associates for their reelection campaigns or political organizations with which they were affiliated.

40. Richard E. Neustadt and Ernest R. May, *Thinking in Time: The Uses of History for Decision-Makers* (New York: Free Press, 1986).

41. Max Weber, "Science as a Vocation," in *From Max Weber,* ed. H. H. Gerth and C. Wright Mills (New York: Oxford University Press, 1958).

CONTRIBUTORS

Philip Brenner is associate professor of international relations at American University. He is the author of *The Limits and Possibilities of Congress* (1983) and *From Confrontation to Negotiation: U.S. Relations with Cuba* (1988) and is the coeditor of *The Cuba Reader* (1988). He is working on a major study of the Cuban missile crisis.

Roger H. Davidson is professor of government and politics at the University of Maryland, College Park. He is the author or coauthor of more than one hundred articles or books dealing with national policy making, including *The Role of the Congressman* (1969) and *Congress and Its Members* (third edition, 1990). He serves as coeditor of the forthcoming *Encyclopedia of the United States Congress*.

Christopher J. Deering is associate professor of political science at George Washington University and director of academic planning and development for the APSA Congressional Fellowship Program. He is the editor of *Congressional Politics* (1989) and coauthor of *Committees in Congress* (second edition, 1990) and has written numerous articles on legislative politics and Congress's role in foreign and defense policy.

Lawrence C. Dodd is professor of political science and director of the Center for the Study of American Politics at the University of Colorado, Boulder. He is the author of *Coalitions in Parliamentary Government* (1976), coeditor of *Congress and Policy Change* (1986), and coauthor of *Congress and the Administrative State* (1979) and *Congress Reconsidered* (fourth edition, 1989).

Louis Fisher is senior specialist in separation of powers at the Congressional Research Service, Library of Congress. His books include *The Politics of Shared Power* (1987), *Constitutional Dialogues* (1988), *American Constitutional Law* (1990), and *Constitutional Conflicts Between Congress and the President* (forthcoming).

Christopher H. Foreman, Jr., is research associate in the Governmental Studies Program at the Brookings Institution and assistant professor in the School of Public Affairs at American University. He is the author of *Signals from the Hill: Congressional Oversight and the Challenge of Social Regulations* (1988) and is currently working on a book about bureaucratic responses to public health hazards.

William M. LeoGrande, professor of political science at American University, has written widely in the field of Latin American politics and U.S. foreign policy. He is the author of *Cuba's Policy in Africa* (1980), coauthor of *Confronting Revolution: Security Through Diplomacy in Central America* (1986), and coeditor of *The Cuba Reader: The Making of a Revolutionary Society* (1988).

Michael L. Mezey, professor of political science and associate dean of the College of Liberal Arts and Sciences at DePaul University, is the author of *Comparative Legislatures* (1979) and *Congress, the President, and Public Policy* (1989). He was written widely in the areas of American politics and comparative legislative behavior.

Walter J. Oleszek is senior specialist in American national government at the Congressional Research Service and an adjunct professor of political science at American University. Among his books on Congress are *Congress Against Itself* (1977), *Congressional Procedures and the Policy Process* (third edition, 1989), and *Congress and Its Members* (third edition, 1990).

James P. Pfiffner, professor of government and politics at George Mason University, is the author or editor of several books on the presidency, including *The Strategic Presidency* (1988) and *The Managerial Presidency* (1990). He was senior associate on the presidential appointee project of the National Academy of Public Administration and project director for the National Commission on the Public Service.

James A. Thurber is professor of government and director of the Center for Congressional and Presidential Studies at American University. He is coauthor of *Setting Course: A Congressional Management Guide* (third edition, 1988) and has published numerous articles on Congress, interest groups, and congressional budgeting.

INDEX